FUNDAMENTALS OF OPERATIONS RESEARCH FOR MANAGEMENT

an introduction to quantitative methods

Shiv K. Gupta
and
John M. Cozzolino

Wharton School
University of Pennsylvania

Holden-Day, Inc.

San Francisco
Düsseldorf   Johannesburg   London   Mexico
São Paulo   Panama   Singapore   Sydney

To my parents and my son Rana

S. K. G.

To Carol, Billy, Stephen, and my parents

J. M. C.

FUNDAMENTALS OF OPERATIONS RESEARCH
FOR MANAGEMENT

Copyright © 1975 by Holden-Day, Inc.
500 Sansome Street, San Francisco, California 94111

Library of Congress Catalog Card Number: 73-94384
ISBN: 0-8162-3476-0

34567890   HA   80798765

Printed in the United States of America

PREFACE

This book is the product of actual teaching experience over several years and many introductory courses. The authors believe that introductory courses are the most challenging ones because they require a high degree of both teaching and research experience. Such courses reach the most people and help create the public image of the subject.

Operations research has passed through a period of explosive growth; there was a time when the newness itself seemed to represent evidence for its potential value. At this time the novelty is wearing off, and yet there remains as much or more opportunity than ever. For the growth to continue and the potential to be realized, we teachers must now do a better job of communication. The concepts must be made more clear to both the potential executives and the potential analysts. We must reorganize, streamline, and clarify our subject. We must reveal that it is not just a collection of mathematical techniques but rather a coherent set of useful concepts which have great potential value to society.

The goal of this book is to present a concept orientation of the subject. The approach that is followed to achieve this goal is to develop concepts through the use of realistic examples. We hope this approach will motivate the students to learn because they find the subject fascinating and recognize the importance of the ideas behind these concepts.

This concept approach does not imply neglect of the mathematical methods of solution. Methods of solution are always given, but with the purpose of increasing the understanding of the ideas involved. Therefore every procedure is explained and motivated in great detail. It is this explanation that will clarify the ideas being presented and lead to greater long-run retention because the ideas will be remembered longer than the mathematical procedures.

This concept approach puts the mathematics in perspective as a tool rather than as a primary goal. For example, the second-order conditions for optimality are not presented because that would divert the student's attention from the significance of the first-order conditions. Similarly, matrix algebra is not used in this book. It is a wonderful notational tool for those who know it already but an impediment to understanding the ideas for those students who have not yet learned it.

One benefit of a concept orientation is that it increases the flexibility of the book to respond to the needs of students possessing different levels of mathematics proficiency. The emphasis upon concepts both supplements the mathematical understanding and motivates it. There is an intentional unevenness in the level of mathematics used; it enables instructors to use selection in adapting the text to the level of mathematics appropriate for each class.

One final but very important general characteristic of this book is that it emphasizes applications through a large number of examples and homework problems. They are taken from many functional areas and levels of decision making, from our direct experience and our knowledge of the literature. This is highly appropriate for business school students and students of operations research because both are interested in the broad range of executive decision making.

The essential background for this book is one course in differential and integral calculus. The book is not self-sufficient in this respect. However, this is a common prerequisite level for courses of this type. It has been our experience over several years of teaching introductory courses that although many students have studied calculus, most have forgotten much of it. Their working knowledge of even the simple manipulative skills of algebra has grown rusty with time. Thus the typical course at which this book is aimed is composed of students with a wide diversity of working mathematical skills. They do not need review chapters, which typically have little motivational value, to induce them to relearn something they have already studied and found to be of little use. That approach is counterproductive. They need a review of algebra and calculus, which is embedded in the early chapters and is motivated by the concepts being presented.

Chapters 2 and 3 use the skills of algebra and differential and integral calculus immediately, with only a clear explanation of why those operations are useful. The appendixes contain some formulas for review, and the instructor can supplement these as he perceives the needs of his particular class. Chapter 4 represents a sudden change of pace because none of these prerequisite mathematical skills are required there. This gives students a chance to catch up with their colleagues. The mathematics level builds up again from there.

The organization of this book is based upon the belief that good concepts and good applications go together, as opposed to the view that theory and practice are poles apart. We have found that students strongly prefer to learn ideas rather than techniques. We feel that the examples and homework problems amply demonstrate that the concepts presented are applicable in many fields.

The book is organized according to the complexity of the ideas presented. The concepts, in order of presentation, are Decision, Model, Optimization (Chapters

1 and 2), Constraints and Their Cost (Chapters 3 to 8), Uncertainty and Decision (Chapters 9 and 10), Risk Aversion (Chapter 11), Conflict and Decision (Chapter 12), and Stochastic Processes (Chapters 13 and 14), and Simulation (Chapter 15).

One innovative thrust is to emphasize very early the concept of a constraint and its cost. This is one of the most fundamental and practical ideas developed by the subject of operations research. It is introduced in Chapter 3 with a problem having just one decision variable. This sets the stage for two decision variables, the Lagrange multiplier and both equality and inequality constraints. The ideas of this key chapter are referred to from subsequent chapters on allocation problems. This enables the discussion of the "shadow prices" or cost of constraints in linear programming without teaching duality theory.

A second innovative thrust is to link operations research and statistical decision theory by presenting probability in a decision-making context in Chapter 9, using decision trees. Continuous distributions are introduced in Chapter 10, along with the newsboy inventory problem. Chapter 11 presents utility theory, with an emphasis upon practical problems from finance, insurance, oil exploration, and other areas.

The use of an analytic utility function (the exponential) simplifies the calculation of the certainty equivalent (risk-adjusted value) to the point where many interesting problems can be solved. We believe this topic is at least as important to students of both business and operations research as more traditional topics such as queuing theory.

Game theory is presented in terms of a more intuitive language. For example, the rationale of a random strategy is explained in terms of protecting the information about the player's decision. Furthermore, the notion of "best nonsecret strategy" is used throughout, and this becomes the best nonsecret random strategy in the case where a saddle-point (deterministic) solution is not present.

The chapter on stochastic processes introduces the Markov process, explaining the meaning of both the transient and steady-state probabilities. The chapter on queuing is developed as an application of the Markov process. We have found that this Markovian approach to queuing is pedagogically efficient. The limitations of the Markov assumptions are explained at the end of the chapter.

This book is designed for a one-term course, with about four extra chapters for flexibility of topic selection. However, the amount of material covered in one term depends strongly upon the mathematical skill of the particular class. In many schools where a one-term course is required the balance of the book can be used as an elective follow-on course.

For students with the minimum mathematical level, the following adaptations are suggested: (1) Spend extra time on Chapter 2; (2) skip the derivation of Lagrange multiplier in Chapter 3; (3) do Chapter 4 completely; (4) skip the algorithm for solution improvement and test for optimality in Chapter 5 (transportation); (5) skip the tabular simplex in Chapter 6; (6) skip Chapter 7; (7) skip Chapter 8; (8) do Chapter 9 completely; (9) skip continuous probability in Chapter 10, emphasizing the tabular solution of the newsboy problem; (10) skip Chapter 11; (11) do Chapter 12, but skip the section on linear programming; (12) do Chapter 13; and (13) skip Chapters 14 and 15.

An intermediate-level course would do all of Chapters 5 to 7. However, Chapter 8 and the continuous probability distribution parts of Chapters 10 and 11 could well be skipped. Time limitations would still require deletion of one or two of the last four chapters.

For classes with a strong mathematics background, the book could be covered completely in one term, with little or no supplementary material. Alternatively it could be assigned just as outside supplementary reading for a course taught at a higher mathematical level. In the first case the book could be covered at the rate of two ($1\frac{1}{2}$-hour) lectures per chapter, except for Chapters 1 and 4, which would take one lecture each. This would give 28 classes of $1\frac{1}{2}$ hours length and would rely heavily upon the students to read much by themselves.

No text will ever replace the teacher. The teacher must always adapt a text to the needs of the individual class, contributing both insight and enthusiasm. We can only hope that the teachers who use this book will find it to be a flexible tool which will repay them for the effort they have invested in using it.

We wish to acknowledge the indispensable experience of the education we received from our teachers. Their enthusiasm, their belief in the importance of this subject, and their insightful explanations have strongly influenced our views, and therefore this book. We are indebted to Professors Russell Ackoff; the late Glen Camp; Ronald Howard, John Little, and Philip Morse for these inspirational qualities. We are indebted also to our many students who honestly questioned the relevance of our subject. Their alert questions and good sense forced us to always try our best to explain the ideas behind the techniques. Finally, the many teaching fellows who worked with us wrote many of the homework problems. We acknowledge the assistance given by Toshi Taga, who wrote the computer programs for simulation, and Bill Wright, who provided the appendix tables.

Shiv K. Gupta
John M. Cozzolino

CONTENTS

Chapter 1

INTRODUCTION

1.1 OPERATIONS RESEARCH

Operations research is the application of scientific method to the decision problems of business and other units of social organization, including government and military organizations. To understand this definition it is necessary to consider the nature of scientific method. The purpose of science is the efficient prediction of the consequences of actions. To this end, science seeks to discover rules describing the behavior of phenomena. These rules, or models of behavior, form an efficient way to predict future behavior, to store man's accumulated experience, and to communicate and teach it efficiently. Scientific method is a continuing process of observation, development of rules to describe both past and future observations, prediction of future observations, and finally observation again. As this cycle is repeated, better rules for prediction are evolved.

These rules for prediction of future behavior are represented by a *model*. The concept of a model plays a central role in operations research, as in other sciences. A model is a representation of reality. It is a tool whose purpose is the prediction of future events. A common property of all tools is the gain of usefulness at the sacrifice of scope or generality. A model is designed to answer *specific questions*. It achieves this ability through the simplicity of representing the most relevant properties while ignoring other properties judged irrelevant to the task of interest.

A road map is a useful example of a model. Its purpose is to predict, for any origin and destination of interest, what roads are available and their lengths. Without road maps, each individual would need years of driving experience upon which to base his future travel plans. It is, without question, a useful model. Yet there is an infinity of detail in your driving experience that the road map does not represent. It is not meant to predict the weather conditions at the time of your arrival, for example, although this may be an important input to your travel decisions. Nor does it predict the congestion on the roads. The important point is that this model achieves its usefulness by restricting its purpose to specific questions.

The road map is an interesting example also in terms of its composition. It is made of paper marked with ink. The most convenient medium for composition of models in operations research is mathematics. There are a few cases where other media could be more useful, such as maps, clay models, electrical circuits, and the like. However, mathematics does seem to be the natural language of the subject.

The understanding of what operations research is can be augmented by consideration of the alternative method of making business decisions and the reasons why this new method has become useful recently. The alternative method of making decisions is that of intuition or insight *based upon personal experience.* The need for insight and intuition will always be present. They are just as important in the scientific method as they are in business. What has changed in the recent history of human organizations is the scope of personal experience. The size and pace of business, government, and military organizations have grown tremendously in the past few decades. As the population and the economy grow, and as natural economies of scale and trade and new technology are exploited, the executive's degree of specialization grows and the scope of an individual's experience diminishes. Specialization of managerial functions has its direct benefits, but it also creates a need for the augmentation of individual experience by formal scientific methods.

The growth of operations research can be seen as a natural consequence of the growth of the economy and the exploitation of economies of scale in economic activities. This understanding can be derived directly from the earliest activity of operations research. The first operational research group was a group of scientists and engineers formed early in the second world war in England. A new device called radar was being introduced into military operations. The problem was that no single person had the years of experience to know how to make efficient use of it. Help was sought from the people who at least understood how it worked: the scientists and engineers. After many successes during that war, operations research began to be transplanted to the industrial environment. This period was one of rapid growth in the economy, rapid growth of technology, and great increases in the size of business operations. Just as the new opportunity inherent in radar had transcended the scope of personal experience of the operational managers, so also the new business opportunities set the stage for scientific methods to augment the personal experience of the business managers.

Of course operations research did not spring up from nothingness into a homogeneous entity. The seeds of its development and much of the theoretical content were already present in the fields of economics, statistics, industrial engineering, electrical engineering, actuarial science, and other fields. What the wartime stress did achieve was a new central organizing concept into which these pieces of the puzzle all fit. This central theme is that of *decision making;* the problems that the new field, whether called operations research, management science, or decision analysis, would study would be the decision problems confronting the managers of any social organization.

1.2   DECISION MAKING

The notion of decision making as a fundamental organizing concept of the field of operations research implies some important direct consequences: that there is a decision maker, or executive or manager, who has the authority and responsibility to make a decision within some specified framework, and that the decision maker does in fact perceive a problem which is worth some effort in investigation. Thus the problems studied are operational, regardless of whether they involve repetitive operations or a high strategic level of decision, because of the fact that a decision must be made.

An operations research study begins with a *problem situation*. This may be a verbal discussion or a written description of a problem perceived by the decision maker or by his delegated representatives. It is inherently an imprecise and incomplete, but insightful, description of a problem situation as perceived by the manager. From this initial starting point the operations research process seeks to develop a model of the problem situation. This process, called "structuring the problem," relies upon the knowledge and experience of the decision maker, the knowledge and experience of the operations research analyst, and the richness of experience encoded into the fabric of the operations research subject.

The result of the structuring process is a complete model of the problem situation. It must contain the following elements of a problem situation:

x *The decision variable.* This is one or more variable quantities. The decision variable represents the decision, and any set of specified values corresponds to a specific decision.

E *The objective function.* This is one single variable quantity. It changes value as the decision variable is changed and measures the desirability or "utility" of the consequences of a decision. Just as there can be no decision problem unless there is a decision variable, there can be no decision problem in the absence of a measure of the relative desirability of the consequences of decisions.

X *The set of possible decisions.* This is, in concept, just a list of values of the decision variables that correspond to acceptable or "feasible" decisions. Limitations upon this set of feasible decisions are called *constraints*.

y *The uncontrollable parameters.* This is any number of variables that are *not* under the control of the decision maker but still may vary. The usefulness of the problem description is greatly enhanced by foreseeing the possibility of differing values of these parameters.

$E = f(x,y)$ *The model.* The model of a problem situation is a relationship that yields the E value associated with any set of x and y values. Thus it predicts the level of desirability that will result from any of the feasible decisions.

$E^* = f(x^*, y)$ *The best attainable objective level (E*) and the best decision (x*).* Once the problem has been formulated and all elements are precisely defined, there remains the mathematical step of *optimization,* or searching for the best decision x^*. This operation can be represented symbolically by the expression

$$E^* = \max_{x \in X} \{f(x, y)\} \tag{1.1}$$

if the objective is to be maximized. Here E^* and x^* are both functions of y although the notation does not show it explicitly.

It has long been recognized that science consists not only of deductive reasoning, a precise, logical process, but also of inductive reasoning, a process not so easily described. In operations research the deductive side begins after the completion of the structuring process and deduces the optimal solution and its properties from the structure given. The inductive side is the structuring process. It requires judgments about which questions should be answered, which effects are of greatest importance, and, finally, which structures adequately represent reality. This process does not rely upon proof but upon skill of communication with those who perceive the problem and upon judgment, insight, and creativity. This part of the subject is the most difficult and useful one. However, it can not be taught directly in an introductory course. The most useful subject matter for an introductory course is the description of structures already known from problems that have been useful in the past and are likely to be useful in the future. The study of elements of these structures and the results of these models is the basis for understanding this subject.

1.3   EXAMPLE OF A PROBLEM STRUCTURE

The following example illustrates a recurring problem structure in the context of a plausible content situation. An airline operates a training program for stewardesses. The cost of the training program consists of two parts: a fixed cost of $1500 regardless of the number trained plus a variable cost of $200 per student including the student's salary. The training program lasts 2 weeks. The demand for stewardesses throughout the airline is 24 per month from existing jobs vacated. This demand is quite predictable and is constant over the year. The training is performed in advance of the demand so that vacant positions are effectively avoided; however, this results in an "inventory" of trained stewardesses waiting for job openings. The airline has experimented with differing class sizes. They find that if they train frequently with small classes, the training cost per stewardess is relatively high although fewer trained stewardesses are waiting for job openings. With larger, less frequent classes, the training cost per person is lower but more trained stewardesses are waiting for useful positions to open. The company initiates a study to find the best class size and frequency. They find that the cost of waiting, after subtracting the value of duties performed while waiting for a job opening, is \$300/month per stewardess. How many should be trained to minimize the average cost per stewardess of training plus waiting?

The first step of analysis is to identify the elements of the problem. The process is a periodic one: each cycle begins with a training program and is followed by a waiting period. The first element to identify is the decision variable. Let x represent the number of stewardesses to be trained in one cycle. The length of the waiting period $T(x)$ is related to x by the rate of job openings: $T(x) = x/24$ because in $T(x)$ months the trained stewardesses will all be assigned to jobs. The decision to train class size x will also determine the frequency of training programs: there will be $1/T(x) = 24/x$ training programs per month. The next problem element to consider is the objective: the airline wishes to minimize the cost per stewardess trained. Call this $E(x)$. Next consider the set of possible values of the decision variable. If it is assumed that training programs must not overlap in time, the smallest value of x is such that $x/24 = 1/2$ month; therefore the smallest x allowed is $x = 12$. This *constraint* represents the consideration that a duplication of training facilities required to run parallel sessions would raise the cost of training considerably and is not considered feasible at the outset. The set of possible x values is $x = 12, 13, 14, \ldots$. The next problem element to consider is the model that relates E and x. This can be derived by finding the total cost of one cycle and then dividing by the number trained in that cycle. This is possible because the process is cyclic. The cost per stewardess averaged over any sufficiently large number of stewardesses is the same as the average over the group size of one cycle. The resulting model, to be explained in more detail in the next chapter, relates the cost per stewardess trained to the size of the class:

$$E(x) = \frac{1500}{x} + 200 + 300 \times \frac{1}{2} \times \frac{x}{24} \tag{1.2}$$

This function of one variable can be graphed or simply tabulated as in Table 1.1.

TABLE 1.1 Tabulating the Function of One Variable

Decision (x)	$1500/x$	200	$(6.25)x$	$E(x)$
12	125.0	200	75.0	400.0
13	115.3	200	81.3	396.6
14	107.1	200	87.5	394.6
15	100.0	200	93.7	393.7
16	93.7	200	100.0	393.7
17	88.2	200	106.3	394.5

The next step of analysis is the optimization. The best x can be read off from the graph or table. The best solutions are 15 and 16 students per class. However, the outline objective function is not very sensitive to the decision variable; it would cost only \$6.30 per stewardess (400 − 393.7) to use the class size of 12 instead of 16. This is true even though the variable training cost per stewardess increases by 33 percent with such a change. Such information can be a useful by-product of the analysis.

This simple example illustrates all the elements of an operations research problem with minimum use of advanced mathematics. However, one can readily imagine that calculus is a useful tool of analysis in more complex problems.

1.4 EFFICIENCY OF OPERATIONS RESEARCH

Human experience is the essential resource for good decision making. It is the resource whose supply has become limited during the past decades of economic growth. The operations research approach is an efficient way to collect, distill, store, and then "reconstitute" this limited resource and apply it where needed.

There are two aspects of a problem situation: the aspect viewed by the decision maker is the *content* of the problem; the aspect of the operations research analyst is the *structure* of the problem. The difference in viewpoint is caused by the different training and knowledge of these two individuals. The decision maker may be, for example, a personnel manager whose expertise is organized around his tasks of determining and staffing the airline's job requirements, administering salary and fringe benefits, and other functions. Administering the stewardess training program is just one of his many tasks. He sees the problem in concrete terms and may be able to guess a good answer based upon his experience. Both the manager and the beginning student of operations research will wonder how the operations research analyst, who may know nothing about either airline operations or personnel management, is of use in this decision problem.

The operations research analyst sees that aspect of the problem called structure. He sees the problem as an inventory process. His knowledge of this structure is based upon similar inventory structures that have arisen in many problem situations from different contexts. This crucial understanding can be illustrated by considering several different content areas that may give rise to inventory problems of similar structure.

An inventory structure is one in which resources—men, machines, materials, and so forth—are held idle in anticipation of future demands. The store of idle resources is depleted by a demand process and increased periodically by a replenishment process. Some examples are given in Table 1.2. These problems all have something in common: their inventory structure, or the relationships between their elements. They may not all have the same structures, but they are close enough that the knowledge of their similarities is useful for making decisions about any one of them. The problems may face the personnel manager, retail store manager, corpo-

TABLE 1.2   Examples of Inventory Content Areas

Idle Resource	Demand Process	Replenishment Process	Economic Considerations
Trained personnel	Job openings	Training program	Cost of training, waiting, unfilled jobs
Retail goods	Customers	Wholesale distributor	Costs of setup, storage, out of stock
Cash for operating expenses	Corporation's operating expenses	Sale of treasury bills or other short-term assets	Cost of borrowing to pay bills, opportunity cost of forgone investments
Highway capacity (lanes)	Growing traffic demand	Road construction	Cost of congestion, cost of capital tied up
Water in hydroelectric dam	Generation of electricity	Riverflows and rainfall	Cost of alternative generation, value of electricity produced

rate treasury officer, highway department planner, and hydroelectric agency manager. It is not efficient to train all these individual managers in the quantitative techniques that are useful to solve all these problems by themselves. Since these problems are usually small parts of their own responsibilities, they often lack the experience to recognize these general structures and to guess good solutions intuitively.

The experience of these and other problems has built the fabric of *inventory theory* in operations research. The analyst, possibly not even aware of the depth of experience built into inventory theory, has been trained to recognize this structure, retrieve the understanding common to all these problems, and apply it efficiently to the problem at hand.

The question of why operations research is useful has thus been answered. It is simply an efficient way to collect, distill, and retrieve experience. The expertise of the analyst is his ability to recognize problem structures, distill experience into abstract terms, study it, record it, and later retrieve from these theories the understanding to solve new decision problems arising in new content areas.

Another example of problem structure is that of search theory—a process of acquisition of information about the location of targets. Some examples of search content areas are given in Table 1.3.

The ability of abstraction is the basis of insight and understanding. The operations research analyst is a specialist in abstract structures. His task is to apply the power of abstractions to the specific operational problems of managers. Managers often find it difficult to understand how "all those books, symbols, and computers can help me find oil." The communications between the two groups is a problem because their knowledge and experience are organized so differently. This communications problem is a serious bottleneck frequently delaying the benefits that are

TABLE 1.3 Examples of Search Content Areas

Object of Search	Method of Search	Economic Considerations
Submarines	Airplane patrol	Cost of patrolling, loss caused by hostile submarines
Mineral and hydrocarbon deposits	Drill test holes to depth of deposit	Cost of drilling, value of targets
Accounting errors	Audit process	Cost of audit vs. cost of undetected errors
Production errors	Quality inspection	Cost of inspection, cost of errors
Forest fires	Photo reconnaissance	Cost of destruction, cost of search

possible. The purpose of an introductory course such as this is to educate both groups, the future analysts and the future managers, to realize the potential.

1.5 TEACHING STRATEGY AND ORGANIZATION

The teaching of operations research is organized around problem structures that are illustrated by problem situations which have been useful in the past. Although the real goal is to equip the reader with knowledge that will be useful for tomorrow's problems, it is not possible to predict what problem situations will arise then. But problem *structures,* because of their commonality, have a long useful life.

Illustrations and problems play a crucial role in this subject. One of their functions is to illustrate the wide variety of problem situations where operations research has been useful or is likely to become useful. Thus they help to define the subject itself. A second function is to define the problem structures. Nothing defines a problem structure as quickly as a few interesting examples; these form a basis for intuition and for reasoning by analogy. A third function is to develop the ability to formulate the structure of problem situations. This skill comes partly from solving problems that differ in some important respect from the fundamental structures presented in the text.

Students will find that the best way to study the material in this text is to solve many individual problems. The subject cannot be reduced to a set of formulas that can be memorized without understanding and will then enable the solution of all problems. That approach will not even solve all the problems in the text, let alone the problems the student will encounter in his future career. However, the repeated solution of many individual problems will develop a set of analogies and a way of thought that will outlive memorized formulas. This set of analogies and concepts may be useful in the far future even to a person who will not actually perform the quantitative analysis upon which the insights and understanding were based.

The study of operations research is a series of problem structures of increasing complexity. Within each structure it is important to begin with the simplest formulation that has most of the common features of that structure. After the simplest structure is understood, modifications of the initial structure can be considered in an order dictated both by mathematical complexity and by potential usefulness. Further modifications are left for exercises and homework problems.

Those who practice operations research usually agree that only a small fraction of problem situations can be formulated within the framework of the simplest structures. However, the simplest structures, when augmented by a few modifications, are powerful enough to encompass a much larger fraction of the problem situations that arise.

The set of operations research structures in this book form most of the subject. One component of teaching strategy embodied here is that it is better to teach the initial portion of almost all the useful structures than to delete some in order to invest more effort in a few. This is based upon the idea that the purpose of this book is to convey concepts, insights, and the ability of abstraction rather than calculational skills. Such insight is gained more rapidly from the simplest structures than from the modifications that follow. If insight is the objective, there appears to be a decreasing marginal gain with time spent on a single structure. The deep analysis of individual structures is the appropriate goal of advanced courses.

The operations research structures to be studied are listed here in order of presentation. They correspond roughly to chapter titles:

Inventory structures
Present value
Decision subject to constraints
The assignment problem
The transportation problem
Linear programming
Dynamic programming
Decision under uncertainty
Expected-value decision making
Aversion toward risk
Problems of conflict
Stochastic processes
Stochastic service systems

Most of these terms will become meaningful only after the chapters have been studied. The ordering of the structures is by complexity of concept and mathematical skill requirements.

1.6 DESCRIPTIONS OF OPERATIONS RESEARCH

The definition of operations research is not uniformly agreed upon by all participants in the activity. Even the term itself is not uniformly accepted. As used here it includes management science, decision science, and decision analysis. The distinctions between these have some historical importance and represent some differences in emphasis and direction. This is actually a healthy state of affairs for an active discipline. Older disciplines also change their emphasis and direction gradually, in an evolutionary way. The only difference is that the outsiders think they know what the older disciplines are, whereas they are more aware of their ignorance about the newer disciplines. It is not common for a person to inquire about the definition of physics, for example, yet most people actually know very little about the areas of current research and concern within that field.

Although this chapter already contains a definition of operations research, more can be learned from the definitions and comments of other authors. The student should seek many opinions. An interesting description of operations research was given by R. Nichols Hazelwood in his article Operations Research, published in *International Science and Technology,* January 1966, pp. 36–49 (excerpt reprinted by permission):

> OR defies easy definition because it is a way of using some of the tools of scientific research to study things that often are not conventionally the province of the scientists. As its techniques become accepted they become part of everyone's way of research. Then there is a tendency to dismiss OR as simply plain "horse sense." True. But such fancy horses!
>
> An engineer or scientist may see relations between variables in an operation that are directly analogous to things he knows in the physical or biological world. This first struck me when I read a brief discussion of an operations research study on the effect of advertising on sales. The mathematical model used in this study was the same set of equations I knew also applied to the growth of radioactivity and attainment of secular equilibrium in cyclotron bombardment of a target. The same equations, with different coefficients, also apply to the growth and limitation of numbers of a bacterial colony on an agar plate.
>
> Thus, it suddenly became beautifully clear to me that when an advertising campaign starts, sales respond by first showing an exponential growth. As time goes on, fewer new customers are attracted, and finally sales reach a plateau, higher than before the campaign started. As long as advertising continues, the sales hold at this new level. When the advertising effort is cut off, sales decay and show a typical half-life.
>
> When I first saw this analogy, I felt a new world had just been revealed! I decided that if people would pay good money to have old equations applied to new problems, I should get in on the gravy train. Time and experience have taught me now that it takes more than just a few handy equations and a glib tongue, but I have never forgotten the unbounded joy of that initial insight.
>
> I still believe the most important thing both customer and analyst get from an

operations research study is a better understanding of the way an operation (or system) behaves—though one must not stop at theorizing.

Robert H. Hayes published a paper in the *Harvard Business Review* (July–August 1969, pp. 108–117) (excerpt reprinted by permission) titled Qualitative Insights from Quantitative Methods. He emphasizes the contribution of quantitative methods to the perception and communication of management problems:

> Many people are aware that quantitative methods can be immediately useful in improving our communication, even about traditional problems.
>
> It is also well known that quantitative methods are useful in dealing with problems of unusual scale. To help management come to grips with problems that are so large and complicated that many people must work on them simultaneously, quantitative people have developed entirely new structures for describing and talking about them. PERT networks and decision trees, for example, are two ingenious frameworks for thinking and talking about certain types of large, complex problems and for gathering information needed to resolve them. Such structures represent valuable progress, but they are by no means the end of the story.
>
> On a higher and more conceptual level, quantitative analysis is facilitating communication where it never existed before. When a problem has been stated quantitatively, one can often see that it is structurally similar to other problems (perhaps problems in completely different areas) which on the surface appear to be quite different. And once a common structure has been identified, insights and predictions can be transferred from one situation to another, and the quantitative approach can actually increase communication.

Russell L. Ackoff and Patrick Rivett wrote "A Manager's Guide to Operations Research" (John Wiley & Sons, Inc., New York, © 1967) (excerpts reprinted by permission of John Wiley & Sons, Inc.), which gives an excellent description of the history, nature, and promise of this field. In describing the historical situation prior to the development of operations research they wrote

> As industrial enterprises expanded, it was no longer possible for one man to perform all the necessary managerial functions. Consequently mechanization, which led to a division of manual labor, also led to a division of managerial labor. Functional managers were created, usually responsible for production, marketing, finance, personnel, and engineering or research and development.
>
> In this parallel development of management and applied science, however, there was one conspicuous gap. Except for a few abortive efforts, science did not come to the aid of the executive function created by the segmentation of management.

After describing the historical development and the nature of operations research they explained the distinction between form (structure) and content:

> By now some managers will have asked themselves, "How can a group of scientists and engineers, however ingenious they are, come into my organization and learn enough

about it to help me solve problems that give me difficulty? It took me years to learn what I know of my company, and I don't know enough to solve such problems." In effect, each executive feels his problems are different (and usually more difficult) than those confronting any other executive. Familiarity breeds complexity. Even if OR can help others how can it help him?

The executive is right in thinking that his problems are different from anyone else's, but he is wrong in thinking they are different in *every* respect. There are two different ways of looking at problems and, as usual, the Greeks had words for them. They differentiated the *form* and the *content* of problems. Two problems seldom if ever arise which have the same content, but there are relatively few forms which problems can assume. *About eight different forms account for almost all the problems that ever confront a manager.* An understanding of this distinction, then, is essential for an understanding of how OR can help an executive.

Most managers will know that the equation

$$y = a + bx$$

represents a straight line. The remarkable thing about this recognition is that the person involved does not know what y, a, b, or x represents. Therefore, the equation is an expression of pure form; it has no content. It gains content only when the symbols are defined and hence given meaning.

Now, when OR men work on an executive problem the necessary knowledge of its content is provided primarily by management and operating personnel. This is supplemented by study of the operations themselves. From the information obtained in these ways the researchers can *abstract* the form of the problem and describe it in a mathematical model. Once this is done, the form can be classified and the appropriate body of mathematical techniques can be brought to bear on its solution. It is in the design of the implementation procedures that the form of the solution is given meaning and is brought back into the real world.

Hence managers, operating personnel, and OR men must work together if meaningful solutions to real problems are to be obtained. Such research must be a joint venture in which management plays a very active role.

Stafford Beer also wrote a book to explain this subject: "Management Science" (Doubleday Science Series, Doubleday & Company, Garden City, N.Y., 1968. © 1967 Aldus Books, London. Excerpts reprinted by permission). He first describes the executive function of management:

As I was saying, then, managers manage to manage by knowledge and experience. This means to say that they rely on their knowledge of the business, and of businesses in general, to tell them what policies to formulate and what decisions to contemplate. It is experience, above all, that teaches them how to control. No wonder people say that management is an art. It is.

Next he describes the nature of science:

By building up a codified knowledge of what experience teaches, man has acquired a body of knowledge that can be communicated. That is the whole point about the codification. Instead of passing on information from generation to generation, and from one craftsman to another, by a process of imitated action and by a mystique of unexplained hints and wrinkles, science distills all that wisdom into something more pithy. Codification incorporates the notions of *coherence* and of *rigor* and of *pattern*. Essentially, it is all aimed at better communication, both as to how knowledge may be transmitted and as to what insight there is to transmit.

He defines management science as the science of management:

When it comes to the business of management, however, there is a strange silence. It is not generally agreed that there *is* such a subject as management science, nor is there unanimous support for the idea that management can at all be taught. The most obvious reason for this would be that no one has managed to codify the experience mankind has had of managing things. But surely that stage ought to be reached? This book will try to persuade you that it has been reached.

About the relationship between science and practice he says

Let us get the claim right from the outset. To say that there can be a science of management is not to deny that management is an art. The man with the genius for designing buildings is not less of an artist because he is a competent architect. It is a very good thing for us all that he is.

D. V. Lindley puts his emphasis upon the concept of decision. His book "Making Decisions" (John Wiley & Sons, Inc.-Interscience Publishers, New York, 1971; excerpt reprinted by permission) states, in the first chapter,

Decision-making is, therefore, something which concerns all of us, both as makers of the choice and as sufferers from the consequences, and there can be no doubt about the importance of the subject. It is, therefore, somewhat surprising that so little has been written about it from a scientific viewpoint. Historians and politicians have discussed in detail how particular decisions were made; lawyers have studied certain types of decision-making in great detail; but until recently the scientific eye had not looked at the field. The process had not been dissected in the laboratory; and literacy, rather than numeracy, had been the major talent of the investigator. Recently, however, some results have been obtained by statisticians which seem to be of importance to all concerned with decision-making (and therefore to everyone). The aim of this book is to inform a wider audience of these results, in the hope that they will find them of value in their work.

Although there are many more excellent descriptions available in books and journals, perhaps the best way to proceed is to study the following chapters—which the authors hope constitute a readable, balanced introduction to the application of scientific method to executive decision problems.

Chapter 2 EXAMPLES OF PROBLEM STRUCTURES

This chapter uses simple recurring problem structures to illustrate the basic elements of the problem structure. Each section of the chapter contains one example that has a decision variable, objective function, parameters, and a model relating them. The presentation of several simple models from different content areas serves an important purpose for an introductory chapter: It allows the student to compare these different situations and observe that they possess a commonality. This is the essential nature of operations research. Ultimately the goal is development of the skill of recognizing problem structures by making analogies with structures previously studied. A further function of the chapter is to refresh the reader's mathematics, including algebraic operations and calculus, in the context of interesting problems.

2.1 THE INVENTORY MODEL

The simplest type of inventory process is one in which the future demand is very predictable. Consequently there is no reason to be unable to supply the demands. However, there are costs of operating the inventory. The magnitude and frequency of these costs depend upon the way in which the inventory is operated.

The inventory process involves storage of idle resources until they are demanded. The inventory level is continually depleted by demands. It is increased by a replenishment operation. The usual costs involved are of two types: a cost of replenishment and a cost of storage. The decision variable is usually taken to be the order quantity or number of units in one replenishment order. The decision variable and the parameters are

x = order quantity (number of units per order)
c_s = cost of one replenishment order regardless of size ($ per order)
c_h = holding or storage cost ($ per unit per unit time)
D = demand rate (units per unit time)

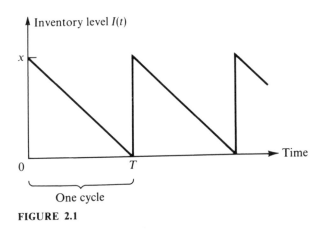

Inventory level $I(t)$

x

0

T

Time

One cycle

FIGURE 2.1

The first step of the analysis is to think of the inventory level as a function of time. This is illustrated by the graph in Fig. 2.1. First observe that this curve has been drawn as a smooth curve rather than as a descending staircase. It is as if the inventory were a liquid decreasing at a constant rate. This is not entirely accurate, but it can be justified as an approximation that is useful enough for many applications.

The graph starts at x, indicating that time zero is the start of one period. Let t represent time, measured from the start. The inventory then decreases linearly with time until it reaches zero. The equation of this function is $I(t) = x - Dt$ during this first cycle. A new supply of x units has been scheduled to arrive when $I(t) = 0$ and it brings the level back up to its initial point. This completes the cycle. As this process goes on in time, it generates an indefinitely long stream of costs. An objective of minimizing total cost would be incomplete without a specification of what period of time generated those costs. However, this process repeats itself indefinitely with all inventory cycles identical. Therefore the cost averaged over a large number of cycles will be the same as the average cost over one cycle. The model that relates this objective function to the decision variable x, the cost parameters c_s and c_h, and the demand rate D will now be developed.

Let $T(x)$ be the length of one cycle of the inventory process. This is simply related to the decision variable x because it is the time required for x units to be demanded; therefore $T(x) = x/D$, as can be found by solving $I(T) = 0$. The total cost of one complete cycle will be denoted by $E_T(x)$. It is the sum of one order cost plus the total cost of holding the inventory over the cycle. During the small interval of time from t to $t + dt$ the inventory level is $I(t)$, approximately constant over a small interval. This interval contributes an amount $c_h I(t)\, dt$ to the total cost of one cycle. Thus the total cost of one cycle can be expressed as an integral:

$$E_T(x) = c_s + \int_0^{T(x)} c_h I(t)\, dt \tag{2.1}$$

This expression holds true even when the demand rate D is time dependent. However, when it is a constant, as in this case, the total holding cost can be found simply as the product of the holding cost per unit per unit time c_h, times the time T, times the average inventory level, which is simply one-half the maximum. Thus

$$E_T(x) = c_s + c_h T \frac{x}{2} \tag{2.2}$$

Replacing T by x/D, the total cost of one cycle is

$$E_T(x) = c_s + c_h \frac{x^2}{2D} \tag{2.3}$$

The objective of the model is to find the cost per unit time of one cycle. Let $E_A(x)$ represent the cost per unit time averaged over one cycle. It is a function different from $E_T(x)$, as the subscript indicates. It is found by dividing the total cost by $T(x) = x/D$. The result is

$$E_A(x) = \frac{E_T(x)}{T(x)} = \frac{c_s D}{x} + c_h \frac{x}{2} \tag{2.4}$$

This completes the development of the model. The final expression contains one decision variable, x, and three parameters, c_s, c_h, and D. Considered as a function of x for fixed values of the parameters, it expresses the fact that the inventory cost per unit time is a sum of two types of costs: the order cost plus the holding cost. As x increases, the order cost per unit time decreases. However, the holding cost per unit time increases with x. This is shown in the graph in Fig. 2.2. This situation implies that there is an order size such that the two types of costs are in balance: that an increase or decrease from that x can only increase the total cost. This optimum value, denoted by x^*, can be found from a carefully drawn graph or by some other

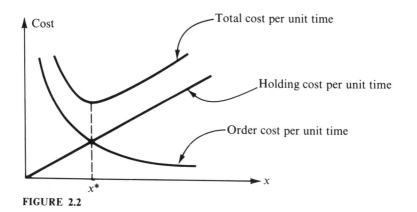

FIGURE 2.2

search method. The easiest method is calculus because x^* is characterized by the fact that the rate of change of the function is zero only at x^*. The derivative as a function of x is

$$\frac{dE_A(x)}{dx} = -\frac{c_s D}{x^2} + \frac{c_h}{2} \tag{2.5}$$

The search for the point where the derivation is zero is conducted by solving the equation

$$\frac{dE_A(x)}{dx} = 0$$

The only positive solution of the equation $- c_s D/x^2 + c_h/2 = 0$ is

$$x^* = \left(\frac{2c_s D}{c_h}\right)^{\frac{1}{2}} \tag{2.6}$$

It can be verified that this solution does indeed minimize the objective function.[1]

Thus the model has been constructed and utilized to find the decision that minimizes the inventory cost per unit time. One remaining operation is to find the value of the objective function under the optimum decision. It is found by substitution of x^* into $E_A(x)$. The result is

$$E_A(x^*) = (2D \, c_s c_h)^{\frac{1}{2}} \tag{2.7}$$

This set of results has been of great value in the past. The optimum decision x^* is known as the *economic order quantity*. It is likely to be of similar value in the future.

EXERCISES

1. Show that the integral of $I(t)$ over the first cycle is $x^2/2D$ after elimination of T by substitution.

2. Show that and explain why minimization of the total cost of one cycle, $E_T(x)$, leads to a meaningless result.

3. Based upon the expressions for x^* and $E_A(x^*)$, explain what will happen when either c_h, c_s, or D is very small.

4. A company is attempting to minimize its cost of inventory storage and production setup for a particular product. It has two alternative methods of production that are equally efficient. One has a setup cost of $25,000 but a maximum of

---

[1] Instructors may wish to discuss the "second-order" conditions for maxima and minima here as a digression.

25 units can be produced on one run. The other has a setup cost of $35,000 and no limit on production per run. There is a uniform demand of 100 units/month for the product. The cost of storing 1 unit for a month is $5,000. Which method of production minimizes inventory holding and setup cost, and which production run size produces this minimum?

Possible Modifications

Understanding the simplest model gives the capability of making modifications. The simple model together with several useful modifications is a far more powerful tool than the simple model alone. Consider the following modifications:

1. Let the inventory level be a discrete function of time instead of the continuous $I(t) = x - Dt$. The total inventory holding cost can be found by summing the area of the rectangles. The formula for the sum of the integers is useful for finding this area and is given in the next section.

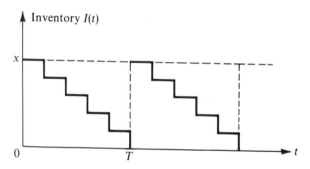

2. Let the demand rate be a function of time within the inventory cycle. This may occur if the demand rate is larger when the inventory is larger.

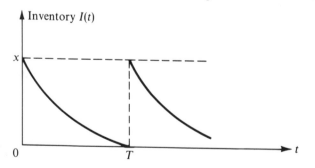

3. Suppose that the inventory is replenished by a process which produces new units at a finite rate P, where P is greater than D. Now $I(t)$ looks like

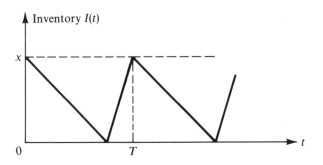

4. Suppose that the inventory can become negative. This may have the interpretation that the customers cannot have their demands satisfied elsewhere. Their demands, after inventory has been exhausted, are recorded and will be filled from the new stock when it arrives. The inventory cycle looks like

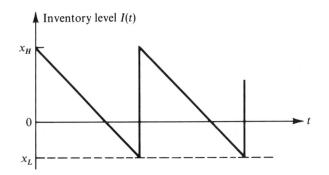

5. Suppose that the cost of replenishing x units depends upon the size of the order. This may occur with price "breaks" or a continuous function for price. Let $p(x)$ be the unit price as a function of quantity x purchased. Now the total setup cost of one cycle is $c_s + xp(x)$ and the objective function now includes the cost per unit time of the units in addition to the cost per unit time of inventory operation. This new term will be $Dp(x)$.

2.2 THE REPLACEMENT MODEL

A replacement problem is one in which a machine, or capital asset, is performing a job. Furthermore its capacity to perform the job decreases with time, and so it has to be replaced periodically by a new machine. The simplest replacement structure is when the deterioration process is predictable and is represented by an increasing operating cost and possibly a decreasing salvage value of the machine. The work

TABLE 2.1 The Replacement Model

| | Problem Description | | | | Analysis | | |
| (1) | (2) | (3) | (1) | (2) | (3) | (4) | (5) |
Year	Operating Cost	Salvage Value	Depre- ciation	Total Depreciation	Total Operating Cost	Total Cost	Average Cost
1	1800	6000	3000	3000	1800	4800	4800
2	2100	4000	2000	5000	3900	8900	4450
3	2400	3000	1000	6000	6300	12,300	4100
4	2700	2250	750	6750	9000	15,750	3937
5	3000	1500	750	7500	12,000	19,500	3900
6	3600	900	600	8100	15,600	23,700	3950
7	4500	500	400	8500	20,100	28,600	4086

capacity of the machine may hold constant or actually decrease with time. This process is similar to the inventory process in that a new capital asset is a stock, or inventory, of job capacity. The deterioration is a demand against that capacity. The cost of the new machine is like a cost of replenishment; the cost of deterioration, usually expressed by the operating cost, is really a holding cost.

Consider the following example. One truck is required for an indefinitely long period. The deterioration of the truck is reflected in an increasing operating cost and decreasing salvage value. Its job capacity remains constant. Suppose that a new truck will always cost $9000. Table 2.1 gives the operating cost for each successive full year and the resale value of the truck at the end of each year. Thus the first three columns describe the problem.

The purpose of the analysis is to determine how long to hold the truck before replacing it by a new one. Since the data are given for full years, the decision variable can only take on integer values: 1, 2, 3, ..., and so on. The objective often used for problems of this type is to minimize the average cost per year of the process. Again the process consists of a repetition of identical cycles, and consequently the average cost per year averaged over one complete cycle is representative of the whole process. In this example the analysis is done completely within the table. The first analysis column gives the depreciation cost of each individual year. The next column gives the total depreciation cost of the first n years. The third column gives the sum of the first n operating costs. The fourth column gives the total cost of the first n years. The last column is obtained by dividing the total cost of the first n years by the number of years n to obtain the average cost over the first n years. This column shows that the average cost per year is $4800 for 1-year cycles and $4450 for 2-year cycles. The minimum cost per year is obtained from 5-year cycles: $3900. This apparently is the optimum replacement cycle length. Notice, however, that 4-year cycles cost only $37/year more. It is characteristic of problems of this type that the objective function is not highly sensitive to the decision for decision values near the optimum.

EXERCISES

1. Suppose that it is possible to buy 1-year-old trucks for $6000. How long should they be kept, and how do they compare to new trucks?

2. Suppose that a one-truck capacity will be needed for exactly 7 years and no more. What objective should be used now? What is the optimum policy when starting with a new truck?

Replacement problems can also be solved efficiently by analytic methods if the input is given by analytic functions. A fact that is often useful in solving such problems, and also discrete inventory problems, is that the sum of the first n integers, $1 + 2 + 3 + \cdots + n$, is given by

$$\sum_{i=1}^{n} i = \frac{n(n + 1)}{2} \tag{2.8}$$

The following problem illustrates the analytic method. A fleet owner finds from his past records that the costs are $1000 for the first year of running a truck whose purchase price is $4500. The operating costs during a year are $360 more than the previous year. Assuming that the objective is to minimize the average cost per year, how many years should a truck be kept? Assume that there is no salvage value.

The operating cost in year i can be expressed analytically by

$$C_0(i) = 1000 + 360(i - 1) \qquad \text{for } i = 1, 2, 3, \ldots \tag{2.9}$$

Let $E_T(n)$ be the total cost of an n-year cycle. It is the sum of the initial cost plus the sum of the first n years of operating costs:

$$E_T(n) = 4500 + \sum_{i=1}^{n} C_0(i) \tag{2.10}$$

This summation can be expressed as

$$\sum_{i=1}^{n} [1000 + 360(i - 1)] = 1000n + 360 \sum_{i=1}^{n} (i - 1)$$

Thus utilizing the expression the sum of the first $(n - 1)$ integers, the result is

$$E_T(n) = 4500 + 1000n + 360 \frac{(n - 1)(n)}{2} \tag{2.11}$$

The objective is to minimize the average cost over the complete cycle. Therefore define $E_A(n)$ to be the average cost over the first n years. It is obtained from $E_T(n)$ by division by n:

$$E_A(n) = \frac{4500}{n} + 1000 + \frac{360(n - 1)}{2} \tag{2.12}$$

Although an integer answer may be desired for the optimum cycle length n^*, it is efficient first to use the derivative to locate the point where the rate of change of the objective function is zero:

$$\frac{dE_A(n)}{dn} = -\frac{4500}{n^2} + 180 = 0 \qquad (2.13)$$

The solution is $n^* = 5$ years. Since the "stationary" point is an integer it is also the optimum integer solution. The average cost per year over the 5-year cycle is easily found to be $2620.

EXERCISE

Suppose that the cost of truck engine overhaul is A and the operating costs are at the rate $a + bn$ per mile when the engine has run n miles since the last overhaul. Find the total cost of one overhaul cycle of M miles. Find the value of M that minimizes the total cost per mile over the overhaul cycle. Evaluate this for $A = 1000, $a = .03$, and $b = .00002$.

2.3 PRESENT VALUE

The problems studied so far have involved operations that generate indefinitely long streams of costs. The objective functions considered were based upon cost per unit time. Another approach to evaluating streams of transactions is known as *present value*. It is superior to cost per unit time, when the costs are large and unevenly spread out in time, because it takes account of the "time value" of money. As an illustration, consider an oil well that will produce oil at a constant rate per unit time for 10 years. Suppose that the oil produced is worth $30,000/year. Thus the cash stream, treated as continuous in time, can be represented by the graph in Fig. 2.3. The total cash produced by the 10-year oil production of the well is the area under the rate curve. This can generally be found by integration. Here, however, the area

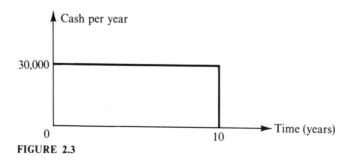

FIGURE 2.3

is that of a rectangle. The result is

$$\text{Value} = 10 \times 30{,}000 = 300{,}000$$

However, this total value will be realized only over a 10-year period. What is it worth today? Consider another oil well that produces oil at half the rate, \$15,000/ year, but will last for more than twice as long, 21 years. The total value it will produce is \$315,000 over its lifetime. Compare this with the first well: which is more valuable? On a total cash value basis the second well is more valuable. However, this basis does not take into account the time value of money.

Suppose that a bank will pay interest at rate 5 percent compounded yearly. Therefore \$1 deposited at the start of 1 year will be worth \$1.05 at the end of the year. More generally, for interest rate r compounded yearly it will be worth $(1 + r)^n$ at a time n years after it was deposited.

If it were held for just 1 year but were compounded m times per year, the dollar would be worth

$$\left(1 + \frac{r}{m}\right)^m \tag{2.14}$$

at the end of the year. Would you expect there to be much difference between compounding yearly, weekly, monthly, and daily? Table 2.2 gives the answer for the case $r = .05$. It becomes clear that the value is not very sensitive to the number of compounding periods as that number gets large. In fact it approaches a limit:

$$\lim_{m \to \infty} \left(1 + \frac{r}{m}\right)^m = e^r \qquad e^{.05} = 1.0513 \tag{2.15}$$

where $e = 2.71828\ldots$ is the base of the natural log system. This limit is a useful fact in the following sense: A function of two arguments r and m has been replaced by a function of one argument only and is therefore easier to work with. The function e^r is so useful in the mathematics of business that a table is given in Appendix D.

Let the symbol A represent future dollar value and let P represent present dollar value. Let these two values be separated by a time period of length t years, where the present value enters the bank at the start and the future value is the value at the

TABLE 2.2   Value of \$1 at End of Year

Yearly	Monthly	Weekly	Daily
1.05	$\left(1 + \dfrac{.05}{12}\right)^{12}$	$\left(1 + \dfrac{.05}{52}\right)^{52}$	$\left(1 + \dfrac{.05}{365}\right)^{365}$
= 1.05000	= 1.05117	= 1.05124	= 1.05127

end of the period. Then

$$A = P(1 + r)^t \quad \text{and} \quad P = A\left(\frac{1}{1 + r}\right)^t \qquad \begin{array}{l}\text{for interest rate } r \\ \text{compounded once} \\ \text{per year}\end{array} \qquad (2.16)$$

$$A = P\left(1 + \frac{r}{m}\right)^{tm} \quad \text{and} \quad P = A\left(1 + \frac{r}{m}\right)^{-tm} \qquad \begin{array}{l}\text{for interest rate } r \\ \text{compounded } m \\ \text{times per year}\end{array} \qquad (2.17)$$

$$A = Pe^{rt} \quad \text{and} \quad P = Ae^{-rt} \qquad \begin{array}{l}\text{for interest rate } r \\ \text{compounded continuously}\end{array} \qquad (2.18)$$

The operation of greatest use here is that of finding the present value of a stream of transactions. Such a stream can be represented by a diagram. For example, the following set of four transactions:

Transaction	Time
Receive $5	0 (now)
Pay $2	1 year away
Pay $1	2 years away
Receive $6	3 years away

can be represented by the diagram in Fig. 2.4.

With interest rate r compounded once yearly, this stream has present value

$$P = 5 - \frac{2}{1 + r} - \frac{1}{(1 + r)^2} + \frac{6}{(1 + r)^3} = 7.371 \qquad \text{for } r = .05 \qquad (2.19)$$

The simple rule being followed here is that the present value of a stream of transactions is the sum of the present values of each transaction. When using continuous compounding the corresponding present value is

$$P = 5 - 2e^{-r} - e^{-2r} + 6e^{-3r} = 7.357 \qquad \text{for } r = .05 \qquad (2.20)$$

The present values of a stream represent its value at the current time based upon the fact that that amount could be invested at interest rate r to produce the same amount of money at the end of the time. The appropriate interest rate and compounding

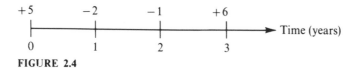

FIGURE 2.4

rate are the best riskless rate available to the decision maker. Thus a decision maker who has the opportunity to invest his money in a riskless investment having interest rate r compounded continuously is indifferent between owning the stream of transactions shown above or owning the present value at the present time.

Present value represents the time value of money and enables the comparison of whole streams of transactions on a one-number basis. Consider a constant stream to infinity consisting of \$1/year for every year without end. This has present value when compounded once per year at interest rate r:

$$P = \sum_{n=0}^{\infty} \left(\frac{1}{1+r}\right)^n \tag{2.21}$$

This sum is finite if $r > 0$. Recall that the sum of the complete geometric series $1 + a^1 + a^2 + \cdots$† is simply $(1 - a)^{-1}$. In the present case a is replaced by $(1 + r)^{-1}$. Therefore

$$\sum_{n=0}^{\infty} \left(\frac{1}{1+r}\right)^n = \frac{1}{1 - (1/1+r)} = \frac{1+r}{1+r-1} = \frac{1+r}{r} \tag{2.22}$$

At 5 percent interest rate the stream is worth \$21. With continuous compounding, the present value is

$$P = \sum_{n=0}^{\infty} e^{-rn} = \frac{1}{1 - e^{-r}} \tag{2.23}$$

At 5 percent interest rate this stream is worth \$20.51. A finite geometric series can be evaluated as the difference between two infinite series. Thus

$$\sum_{n=0}^{N} a^n = \sum_{n=0}^{\infty} a^n - \sum_{n=N+1}^{\infty} a^n$$

$$= \sum_{n=0}^{\infty} a^n - a^{N+1} \sum_{n=0}^{\infty} a^n = \frac{1 - a^{N+1}}{1 - a} \tag{2.24}$$

This is a useful formula to remember because it appears later in this text.

A continuous stream of transactions is evaluated according to the same additivity principle as a discrete stream. Naturally money cannot "flow continuously" as a liquid any more than "continuous compounding" can be performed by successive multiplications. The justification of these abstractions is that they are useful; in fact they are easier in some cases than the discrete operations from which they came. Consider a continuous flow of cash with rate $v(t)$ at time t from zero to time T. The total cash value can be found by an integral. The interval $(t, t + dt)$ contributes

---

†This sum is a finite number if $0 < a < 1$.

$v(t) dt$ to the sum. Hence the total cash value is

$$V = \int_0^T v(t)\, dt \tag{2.25}$$

With continuous compounding at rate r, the interval $(t, t + dt)$ contributes amount

$$v(t)e^{-rt}\, dt$$

to the present value summation. The total present value is

$$P = \int_0^T v(t)e^{-rt}\, dt \tag{2.26}$$

This can be used to evaluate the two oil wells with constant flow rates. Their characteristics are

Well	Flow Rate $v(t)$	Time Period $(0, T)$
A	\$30,000/year	(0,10)
B	\$15,000/year	(0,21)

$$P_A = \int_0^{10} (30{,}000)e^{-rt}\, dt\dagger$$

$$= 30{,}000 \left(-\frac{1}{r}\, e^{-rt}\right)\bigg|_0^{10}$$

$$= 30{,}000 \left(\frac{1}{r}\right)(1 - e^{-10r}) \tag{2.27}$$

For $r = .05$ the result for well A is \$236,081. Well B has present value

$$P_B = 15{,}000 \left(\frac{1}{r}\right)(1 - e^{-21r}) \tag{2.28}$$

For the same r this present value is \$195,019. Recall that well B was more desirable on a total cash basis. This is clearly reversed on a present-value basis of comparison.

EXERCISES

1.   Find the present value of the continuous cash flow from an oil well that produces at a constant rate \$20,000/year for the first 20 years and then declines linearly to zero in the next 5 years. Use $r = 5$ percent.

---

†Students can refer to the appendixes for integration and differentiation rules.

2. Suppose that a cask full of whiskey costs $15,000 initially and that it will be worth

$$W(t) = 10,000 (1 + t)^{1/2}$$

when sold at a time t years later. The decision variable is t. Suppose that your best alternative investment has rate of return r compounded continuously. Solve for the optimum t as a function of r. Is the investment desirable when $r = .05$? (*Hint:* Find the present value of the stream of two transactions—buy and sell. Find the t that maximizes this objective function.)

2.4 MARKETING UNDER COMPETITION

An important class of problems are those involving competition. Competition occurs when two or more decision makers have a decision to make and each of their decisions affects the objective function of the other decision makers. This means that each decision maker must consider in his reasoning what the opponents will do. A decision maker who utilizes formal analysis must include in his model the actions of others. This can be very difficult. The simplest model of the opposition often is that they are equally intelligent and well informed and that therefore they too will be attempting to optimize their objective functions. This assumption may not always be realistic. However, it does illustrate the simplest model of competition.

Suppose for illustration that two firms produce competing products. They split a total market of fixed size: 10,000 units/year. The price range of these products usually is $15 to $25. Suppose that the annual sales of each firm depend upon the price difference between their products. Let p_i be the price charged by firm i for $i = 1, 2$. The firm with the lower price will have 5 percent more of the total market per dollar of price difference. If both charge the same price they will split the market evenly. This situation is represented by the following equations for the annual sales of each firm:

$$q_1 = 10,000 \left[\frac{1}{2} + .05(p_2 - p_1) \right] \tag{2.29}$$

$$q_2 = 10,000 \left[\frac{1}{2} + .05(p_1 - p_2) \right] \tag{2.30}$$

Suppose that firm 1 is trying to maximize its profit given that its cost of production is $8/unit. Firm 1 believes that firm 2 is trying to achieve the same objective but has a higher unit cost of production: $10. The decision variable for firm 1 is price p_1 to be set for the coming year. Let $\pi_i(p_i)$ represent the annual profit of firm i if it sets price p_i. For firm 1 it is

$$\pi_1(p_1) = (p_1 - 8)q_1 = 10,000 \left[\frac{1}{2} + .05(p_2 - p_1) \right](p_1 - 8) \tag{2.31}$$

Similarly for firm 2,

$$\pi_2(p_2) = (p_2 - 10)q_2 = 10,000 \left[\frac{1}{2} + .05(p_1 - p_2)\right](p_2 - 10) \qquad (2.32)$$

Firm 1 will seek to maximize $\pi_1(p_1)$ for a fixed level of p_2. The derivative with respect to p_1 is

$$\frac{d\pi_1(p_1)}{dp_1} = \left[\frac{1}{2} + .05(p_2 - p_1) - .05(p_1 - 8)\right] 10,000 \qquad (2.33)$$

This is equated to zero and the equation is solved for p_1 as a function of p_2:

$$p_1 = 9 + .5p_2 \qquad (2.34)$$

Now firm 1 has solved its problem as a function of the decision of firm 2. However, the model is not complete until it gives the solution also for p_2. By the assumption that firm 2 also seeks to maximize its profit, the derivative of $\pi_2(p_2)$ is also equated to zero and the solution for the optimum p_2 as a function of p_1 is found:

$$\frac{d\pi_2(p_2)}{dp_2} = \left[\frac{1}{2} + .05(p_1 - p_2) - .05(p_2 - 10)\right] 10,000 \qquad (2.35)$$

$$p_2 = 10 + .5p_1 \qquad (2.36)$$

Since both firms are maximizing their profits, both of these equations must simultaneously be satisfied. The solution of these two equations in two unknowns is

$$p_1 = 18.66$$

$$p_2 = 19.33$$

The solution of these equations can be represented by the graph shown in Fig. 2.5.

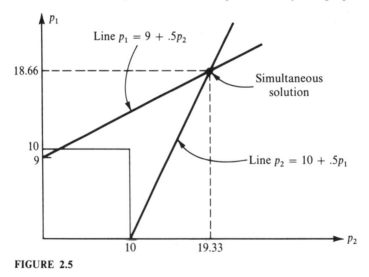

FIGURE 2.5

Only one point satisfies both equations. At these prices firm 1 has share 53.33 percent of the market and firm 2 has 46.66 percent. Firm 1 has annual profit $56,888 and firm 2 has profit $43,550.

EXERCISES

1.   If firm 1 believes that firm 2 will charge a price of $16 regardless of firm 1's price, what price will firm 1 charge?

2.   If firm 2 believes that firm 1 will charge a price of $17 regardless of firm 2's price, what price will firm 2 charge?

3.   Show that the prices $p_1 = 18.66$ and $p_2 = 19.33$ are the only ones such that the prior knowledge of the opponent's decision does not change a firm's decision.

2.5   SUMMARY AND EXAMPLE

This chapter presented four problem structures: inventory, replacement, present value, and competition. One aspect common to all these topics is the review of algebra and calculus. Students who experience difficulty with this chapter often find that it is due to their lack of mechanical mathematical skills. Mathematics is the language of this subject, but it is not the subject itself. Nevertheless one cannot learn the subject without knowing the language with which it is being taught. Therefore extra practice with mechanical operations of algebra and calculus can indirectly contribute to the comprehension of the subject by removing this language barrier.

In addition to their review function, the topics of this chapter have higher-level purposes:

Inventory illustrates one of the simplest models having many applications and many possible modifications. Moreover it illustrates an objective function (cost per unit time) for an ongoing periodic process that repeats itself indefinitely.

Replacement is another simple but widely applicable model. It illustrates similarity of models by its similarity to the inventory model.

Present value shows how to evaluate cash flows that are spread out in time. It also constitutes an alternative objective function for inventory and replacement problems and is the most reasonable objective function for many problems.

Marketing competition shows the simplest model of competition: The competitors are regarded as equally intelligent and seeking to optimize their objective functions.

This chapter contains more than one model because it is important to build a set of experiences upon which to base the activity of model formulation. It is this activity that has the highest level of usefulness and requires the highest level of skill within this subject. The mental process of model formulation depends highly upon

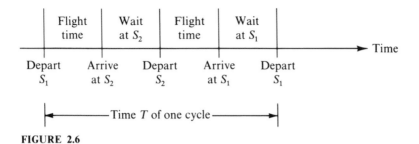

FIGURE 2.6

the use of analogies. Therefore it is important to build up a set of examples, from both the text and the homework problems, that will serve as the basis for future model formulation. Students naturally observe first the dissimilarities between problems and thus may question the cohesiveness of this chapter. Only with hindsight will the similarities begin to outweigh the dissimilarities. The remainder of this chapter presents an example of a problem situation with an inventory structure. It serves as an illustration of problem formulation by analogy to a known structure.

A feasibility study is being conducted for a proposed helicopter transportation route. The helicopter will transport passengers from the top of a tall building (station 1) in the center of a large city to the airport (station 2). It will also carry passengers on the return trip, periodically repeating the schedule shown in Fig. 2.6.

It is estimated that passengers will arrive at S_1 at a constant rate of 40 passengers/hour and at S_2 at a constant rate of 30 passengers/hour. The feasibility study must determine the frequency of operation. This will be expressed in terms of the cycle time T, which is also the time between any two successive departures from either station. The decision variable T has the following effects. As T is made shorter, fewer passengers per trip will be carried. However, on the average the passengers will have a shorter waiting time for service. Thus the setting of T involves a tradeoff between the ticket cost and the waiting cost of the typical passenger.

Suppose that one helicopter round trip costs the company \$90 in operating costs. The ticket cost to the passenger will be set by multiplying \$90 by a markup factor of 1.4 and then dividing by the number of passengers carried in one typical round trip. Furthermore it is believed that passengers for this type of service will act as though their time is worth about \$10/hour while waiting for service. The feasibility study can now determine the optimum T that minimizes the total ticket cost plus waiting cost of the typical passenger. Proceeding by analogy with the inventory structure, it can be seen that the round-trip charge of $90 \times 1.4 = 126$ is like a setup or order cost because it is incurred once per cycle regardless of the number of passengers carried. The waiting time cost is exactly similar to a holding or storage cost. Passengers are "stored" in the stations until carried away by the helicopter.

During one cycle of length T minutes the number of passengers accumulating at S_1 is $(40/60)T$. The number accumulating at S_2 is $(30/60)T$. The total number to be carried in one round trip, as a function of T, is

$$\frac{2}{3} T + \frac{1}{2} T = \frac{7}{6} T$$

The time average of the number of passengers waiting is one-half the maximum number present. Thus the accumulated waiting time cost of one cycle is

$$\frac{1}{2} \times \left(\frac{2}{3} T + \frac{1}{2} T \right) \times T \times \frac{10}{60}$$

This is the product of the average number of passengers, times the cycle length in minutes, times the waiting cost per passenger per minute. The total cost of one cycle is the sum of setup plus waiting costs:

$$126 + \frac{1}{2} \left(\frac{2}{3} T + \frac{1}{2} T \right) T \frac{10}{60}$$

This is then divided by the number of passengers carried in one round trip. The result is the objective function $E_A(T)$:

$$E_A(T) = \frac{126}{(2/3) T + (1/2) T} + \frac{1}{2} T \frac{10}{60}$$

This is simplified to

$$E_A(T) = \frac{108}{T} + \frac{T}{12}$$

This function is optimized by finding the T at which the derivative is zero:

$$T = \sqrt{1296} = 36 \text{ minutes}$$

Using this T will result in a ticket cost of $3 and an average waiting time of 18 minutes.

EXERCISE

Show that the solution given above also minimizes the total cost per unit time.

PROBLEMS

1. The Smith Steel Company requires raw iron at a constant rate of 10,000 tons/year. Each time they place an order they are charged $60. It costs $0.40/year to store a ton of raw iron. Shortages will not be allowed.

    (a) How large should each order be, and what should be the time interval between orders?

- (b)   Illustrate part (a) by using a simple diagram.
- (c)   It is learned that the costs given in part (a) are incorrect. The true order cost is merely $30 and the inventory storage cost is really $0.50. Compute the size of each order using the correct costs.
- (d)   How much was the company losing due to imperfect cost information?

2.   Railroad cars arrive at a classification yard and are sorted by destination. When enough cars have accumulated, a train leaves for that destination. The cost of waiting, due in part to a rental charge, is A dollars per car per day. The cost of moving the train to its destination depends upon its size; a train consisting of N cars has a transportation cost of $(B + CN)$ dollars. Suppose that cars arrive uniformly with rate R cars per day for one particular destination. What value of N minimizes the total cost per car?

3.   Beta Corporation uses 25,000 units/year of component A, which it purchases from Alpha Corporation at $1 each if it buys 5000 or more per order and $1.05 each if it buys less per order. Ordering costs are estimated at $32/order independent of the quantity ordered. The cost of holding inventory in stock has been assigned a value of $0.10/unit/year. How many should be ordered per lot?

4.   An investor buys a piece of real estate for appreciation. He pays $100,000 and believes that the market value at time t in the future will be $v(t) = 100,000 + 100,000 (1 - .5^t)$. For the purpose of planning other investments he wants to do an analysis that will tell him how long he ought to hold this investment before selling it at the marketplace, if this value curve is true. His objective is to maximize the present value of the transactions using interest rate .05 and continuous compounding. Find the optimum t.

5.   Deserted automobiles accumulate on the city streets at a constant rate of R cars per week within the city. The city police department removes them but does so periodically because of the economy of scale that makes it cheaper per car to find them when more are present. The total cost (in $1000) of removing N cars is given by the function $AN + BN^2$. There is a setup cost of C (in $1000) to initiate the removal operation. Also there is a social disutility cost of S (in $1000) per car per week while the abandoned cars are present.

- (a)   Find the time period T^* between the removal operations that minimizes the total cost per unit time.
- (b)   Find the time period T^* between the removal operations that minimizes the total cost per car.

6.   The Retractable Pen Corporation has two divisions: division 1 and division 2. Division 1 produces ballpoint pen cartridges with the following cost function: $cx + dx^2 + f$ (where x = number of cartridges produced). These cartridges are "sold" to division 2 at a transfer price of g per cartridge. Division 2 manufactures holders that when assembled with the cartridges are marketed as ball-

point pens at a price s. Division 2 has the following cost function for producing the holders and assembling the pens: $ay + by^2 + e$ [the cost of the cartridge to division 2 (g) is not included in this cost function; further, y = number of holders produced and pens marketed by division 2]. Assume that no other costs are involved and that the Retractable Pen Corporation produces only one product. Assume further that division 1 is the sole supplier of cartridges and that division 2 purchases all the cartridges that division 1 produces.

With division 1 pursuing a policy of profit maximization and with division 2 pursuing a policy of profit maximization, is there a unique value for the transfer price g such that $x^* = y^*$ and the profits of the corporation as a whole will be maximized?

(a) Solve symbolically.

(b) If a = \$30, b = \$1, c = \$50, d = \$2, e = \$10, f = \$10, and s = \$200, find the values for x^*, y^*, and g and the maximum profit of the corporation.

7. A company knows that a certain machine will produce gross revenue of \$1000 each year and that the maintenance cost in the ith year is \$100i. The initial cost of the machine is \$10,000 and the interest rate is 10 percent. Assuming that the company wants to maximize the present value of the machine's lifetime, how long should they keep it? How much longer should the machine be kept if it is now 2 years old? Assume no salvage value. *Hint:* Find the present value if held k years, $P(k)$. Then find $P(k + 1) - P(k)$, the gain of increasing from k to $k + 1$.

8. A state wishes to construct a new highway. Present traffic requires a two-lane highway, but it is anticipated that in 5 years a three-lane highway will be needed and in 10 years a four-lane highway. The state has to decide whether to construct four lanes now or to build only two or three now and, in the latter cases, when to add the extra lanes. The relevant costs of building n lanes (in \$ million) are as follows:

Value of n	Initially	As Addition to Existing Road
1	. . .	4
2	5	7
3	7	. . .
4	9	. . .

What building policy will minimize present discounted cost if the internal opportunity rate (discount factor) is 10 percent?

9. An oil company is planning a pipeline to carry oil a distance D miles from the producing wells to the refinery. They want to limit the risk of oil spills resulting from breaks in the pipeline. They plan to place automatic shutoff valves in the pipeline every α miles, but we must decide what value to use for α. These valves can sense a pressure drop from a break and automatically stop the flow. The loss due to spilled oil is then proportional to just the distance between valves; the cost per mile of spillage is C_s (in $1000) per mile. Therefore the spillage cost of one break is $C_s\alpha$. The cost of the valves is C_v (in $1000) per valve. The total number of pipeline breaks over the projected life of the pipeline is B. Find the total cost of the valves plus spillage over the life of the pipeline. It should be a function of the decision variable α, the parameter D, the costs, and the quantity B. Find the optimum value of α using the estimates

$$C_v = 10 \qquad C_s = 6 \qquad D = 10,000 \qquad B = 1$$

10. Machine A costs $9000. Annual operating costs are $200 for the first year, and they increase by $2000 every year (in the fourth year, for example, operating costs are $6200).

   (a) Determine the best age at which to replace the machine. If the optimum replacement policy is followed, what will be the average yearly cost of owning and operating the machine? (Assume that the machine has no resale value when replaced and that future costs are not discounted.)

   (b) Machine B costs $10,000. Annual operating costs are $400 for the first year, and they increase by $800 every year. You now have a machine of type A that is 1 year old. Should you replace it with B? If so, when?

Chapter 3 DECISIONS SUBJECT TO CONSTRAINTS

Operations research obtains its importance as a subject because it is a new organizing principle that emphasizes identification of elements, model construction, and optimization from the viewpoint of identifiable decision makers. Most of the mathematical and theoretical content is not new but adapted from other disciplines. One relatively new concept is identified with operations research: the inequality constraint. This has led to the formulation of particularly new and useful problem structures and the development of new and efficient methods for their solution. Much of the impetus for the growth and identification of operations research has come from the tremendous achievements of *linear programming*, a structure that was unknown only a few decades ago. This has led to the further extension and generalization now called *mathematical programming*. Linear programming and its special cases of *assignment* and *transportation* problems are covered in later chapters. This chapter introduces the idea of an inequality constraint and relates it to the older, simpler equality constraints and the method of the *Lagrange multiplier*.

A constraint is simply a restriction upon the set of values of the decision variables. Values that are acceptable solutions are called *feasible* solutions; all others are called *infeasible*. The constraint set determines the acceptability of a solution and is therefore a vital element of the problem structure. Constraints represent the idea of acceptability as a binary classification: Every solution is either feasible or infeasible. Alternatively it may be possible to represent degrees of feasibility by including the extra costs required to make a given solution entirely feasible. This choice involves a tradeoff between realism and the resulting power of the model. The power of the concept of constraint is that it allows the model builder to represent complicated situations in a way that is simple to understand and communicate and enables him to utilize the power of analytic methods of solution.

It is often useful to compare problems having constraints with corresponding problems without the constraints. By this comparison it is possible to identify the cost of the constraints. A constraint either affects the optimal solution or it does not. If it does affect the solution it can only make it worse compared to the solution of the unconstrained problem. The cost of the constraint is this difference in the value of the objective function.

3.1 EXAMPLE OF ONE CONSTRAINT

A wholesale distribution company buys large lots of products and sells to many small retail outlets. One of their products is a beverage they sell at a predictable constant rate of 600 cases/month. They hold an inventory based upon costs of $60/order and a $0.20/case/month holding cost for this product. The unconstrained problem is to find the distributor's optimum order quantity, the associated inventory cost per month for the product, and the time between orders. The manufacturer, concerned with product age, sets a new condition that the distributor must not hold the product in inventory for more than 3 weeks. Find the distributor's inventory policy subject to this new constraint. What is the distributor's additional cost per month due to this constraint?

The unconstrained problem is clearly an inventory problem with the parameters

Demand: D = 600 cases/month (constant)
Order cost: c_s = $60/order
Holding cost: c_h = $0.20/case/month

The order quantity that minimizes the inventory cost rate is

$$x^* = \sqrt{\frac{2c_sD}{c_h}} = \sqrt{\frac{2 \times 60 \times 600}{.2}} = 600 \text{ cases}$$

The total inventory cost per month is

$$E_A(x) = \frac{c_sD}{x} + \frac{c_hx}{2}$$

$$E_A(600) = 60 + 60 = \$120/\text{month}$$

The cycle length is

$$T(x^*) = \frac{x^*}{D} = \frac{600}{600} = 1 \text{ month}$$

The graph in Fig. 3.1 shows the objective function as a function of the decision variable. It also shows the point that exactly satisfies $T(x)$ = .75 month. It is the point satisfying $x/600$ = .75 or x = ¾ (600) = 450. The constrained problem requires that the solution have the property that $T \leq$ .75 month. This implies the restriction $x \leq 450$ upon the decision variable. The points to the left of the line x =

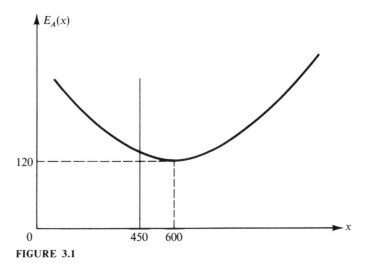

FIGURE 3.1

450 obey this constraint and are feasible; those to the right are infeasible.   The reader may wonder what kind of beverage deteriorates so suddenly and completely at age $T = .75$ month.   The answer of course is that the sharpness of the constraint is a property not of the beverage but of the model.   It is more useful here to represent the situation with a constraint than to investigate and model the complicated processes of deterioration of the beverage and the reaction of the consumers to the deterioration as a function of beverage age.

The solution to the constrained problem in this case is easily seen from the graph. The x within (0,450) that gives the minimum value of the objective function is $x = 450$ because the function $E_A(x)$ is decreasing in that interval.   The best value of the objective function is

$$E_A(450) = 80 + 45 = \$125/\text{month}$$

The constraint has the effect of reducing the cycle length and increasing the total cost.   The distributor's additional cost due to the constraint is $125 - 120 = \$5/$ month. This is $\$5/600 = \$5/6 \times .01 = {}^5\!/_6$ cent/case.

A few observations are worth making from the vantage point of having solved this problem.   The "feasible region" given this constraint is the set of points in the interval (0,450).   This is a subset of a one-dimensioned space.   In a two-decision-variable problem the feasible region is usually a subset of a two-dimensional space. The solution in this case was "on the constraint"; it was determined by the constraint *as an equality*, $x = 450$.   It is said that the constraint is "binding" in this solution.   If this fact had been known at the outset of the analysis, the analysis would have required only the solution of the equality-constrained problem, which is an easier problem: $x/D = .75$. The determination of whether the constraint is binding is an essential part of the analysis.

EXERCISES

1.   Suppose the constraint had been that the distributor must not hold the beverage for more than 1.25 months. What is the feasible region? What is the optimal constrained solution and what is the cost of the constraint? What is the efficient way to analyze problems of this type?

2.   Let a second constraint be added: each case requires a volume of 1 cubic foot. The distributor's warehouse has only 400 cubic feet of space reserved for this product. Solve the problem with this constraint together with the original constraint.

3.   The distributor is planning the construction of a new warehouse. What is the value of having a larger space available to this product?

3.2   PROBLEMS WITH TWO DECISION VARIABLES

Problems involving two decision variables play an important role in the development of our intuition; they illustrate the properties of many-variable problems but still allow useful graphic presentation that serves as a basis for developing intuition. This section introduces an example that illustrates later sections. However, the only principle used in this section is that when there are two continuous-valued decision variables and no constraints, the optimum solution is one where both partial derivatives are simultaneously equal to zero. This is an easy generalization of the one-variable case and generalizes further to n decision variables.

Consider an investor who has two risky stock investment opportunities, both for the same 1-year period. His decision variables are x_1 (the dollar amount to invest in stock 1) and x_2 (the dollar amount to invest in stock 2). His complete decision is represented by the pair of values x_1 and x_2 that specify his investment portfolio. The investor seeks to maximize an objective function that represents a risk-adjusted net value to him of the portfolio:

$$E(x_1, x_2) = .028x_1 + .016x_2 - \frac{1}{2} \times 10^{-6}(9x_1^2 + 12\rho x_1 x_2 + 4x_2^2)$$

The first two terms represent the amount by which the expected returns exceed the return from a riskless investment. The third term represents a discount due to the investor's risk aversion. It contains measures of the volatility (variance) of each stock and a parameter ρ called the *correlation* of the two stocks. This can go from the lowest value $\rho = -1$, which represents perfect negative correlation, to the highest value $\rho = +1$, which m .ns that the two stocks are perfectly correlated and move in the same direction. A correlation of zero means that the two stocks move completely independently.

A necessary condition for optimality of a solution (x_1, x_2) is that both partial derivatives are zero for that solution. The partial derivatives, as a function of the decision variables, are

$$\frac{\partial E}{\partial x_1} = .028 - \frac{1}{2} 10^{-6}(18x_1 + 12\rho x_2)$$

$$\frac{\partial E}{\partial x_2} = .016 - \frac{1}{2} 10^{-6}(12\rho x_1 + 8x_2)$$

The first two terms of E have contributed positive constant amounts to both derivatives. It is the risk adjustment term that contributes negative amounts, representing the fact that as x_1 and x_2 get very large the risk of the portfolio must grow and eventually make it undesirable. These two derivatives are equated to zero. Usually ρ is a known constant; however, it is treated as a parameter of the problem in this section and the solution will be sought for all possible ρ values. The resulting derivative equations are

$$x_1 = 3111 - \frac{2}{3} \rho x_2$$

$$x_2 = 4000 - \frac{3}{2} \rho x_1$$

Now it is possible to observe that if ρ were zero the optimal portfolio for this investor would be $x_1 = \$3111$ and $x_2 = \$4000$. Furthermore a positive correlation results in smaller investments whereas a negative correlation is apparently desirable because it results in larger investments.

The simultaneous solution is

$$x_1 = \frac{3111 - 2666.6\rho}{1 - \rho^2}$$

$$x_2 = \frac{4000 - 4666.6\rho}{1 - \rho^2}$$

This is satisfied by exactly one point for any given ρ value (see Table 3.1 for *specific* ρ values). That this solution does indeed maximize the objective function can be proved by evaluating E for any nearby point and showing that it yields a smaller E value. The optimum solution as a function of ρ can be illustrated in the graph in Fig. 3.2. The solution can be summarized as follows:

Region 1: $\rho < 0$ A large investment is optimum because of the favorable negative correlation, which reduces the portfolio's risk.

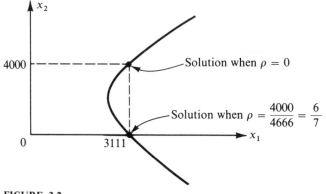

FIGURE 3.2

TABLE 3.1   Solutions for Specific ρ Values

ρ	x_1	x_2	Total Investment
$-\dfrac{5}{6}$	17,451	25,813	43,264
0	3111	4000	7111
$\dfrac{1}{5}$	2685	3194	5879
$\dfrac{5}{6}$	2905	368	3273
$\dfrac{6}{7}$	3111	0	3111

Region 2: $0 < \rho < \dfrac{6}{7}$ A positive investment in both stocks but increasing ρ drives stock 2 to zero investment.

Region 3: $\dfrac{6}{7} < \rho$ The high positive correlation implies the opportunity to "sell short" stock 2, thus utilizing the high correlation of the inferior stock to reduce the portfolio's risk.[1]

3.3   EQUALITY CONSTRAINTS SOLVED BY SUBSTITUTION

Suppose in the investment problem of Sec. 3.2 that the investor has a budget of $5000 to invest and desires to invest exactly that amount. This constraint is rep-

---

[1] To "sell short" means to sell stock you do not yet own. You owe the stock to the purchaser until you purchase stock to repay your stock debt.

resented by the equality

$$x_1 + x_2 = 5000$$

Suppose further that the correlation parameter of the previous section is known to have value $\rho = .2$. Then the unconstrained optimum portfolio is $x_1 = \$2685$, $x_2 = \$3194$. This is a total investment of \$5879. The value of the objective function for this unconstrained optimum is

$$E(2685,3194) = 63.14$$

The constrained optimization problem is to find the (x_1,x_2) pair that maximizes $E(x_1,x_2)$ while satisfying the constraint $x_1 + x_2 = 5000$.

Consider the general problem first. The objective function $E(x_1,x_2)$ is to be maximized or minimized subject to the equality constraint

$$g(x_1,x_2) = b$$

The method of substitution is important because it is often the most practical method. Also it is the basis of the method of the next section. To use substitution one must first "solve the constraint" for one variable as a function of the other. Let us represent this solution by

$$x_2 = f(x_1)$$

This relationship tells what the value of x_2 must be for a given x_1 value such that the constraint is satisfied as an equality. Therefore

$$g[x_1,f(x_1)] = b \qquad \text{for all possible } x_1$$

Now the substitution step is done: x_2 in $E(x_1,x_2)$ is replaced by $f(x_1)$ to obtain the objective function as a function of x_1 only. Call this

$$E_s(x_1) = E[x_1,f(x_1)]$$

It is now clear that the remaining problem is easier; substitution of an equality constraint reduces the dimensionality of the problem. This holds true for higher-dimensional problems also. A problem with m decision variables and n equality constraints is equivalent to an unconstrained problem with $m - n$ decision variables (if $m \geq n$). Substitution is not always practical. The difficulty of solving the n constraint equations for n variables as functions of the other $m - n$ variables constitutes a practical limitation of this method. If this can be done, the next step is to optimize the function of the remaining variables. Differentiation gives

$$\frac{dE_s(x_1)}{dx_1} = \frac{\partial E[x_1,f(x_1)]}{\partial x_1} + \frac{\partial E[x_1,f(x_1)]}{\partial x_2} \frac{df(x_1)}{dx_1}$$

by the rule for the total derivative and the chain rule. If $E_s(x_1)$ has been found, then the left-hand side can be used; otherwise the right-hand side is needed.

Returning to the example problem, the objective function is

$$E(x_1, x_2) = .028x_1 + .016x_2 - \frac{1}{2} \times 10^{-6}(9x_1^2 + 2.4x_1x_2 + 4x_2^2)$$

The constraint is

$$x_1 + x_2 = 5000$$

There are no other restrictions upon the values of x_1 and x_2; negative values are considered feasible here. The solution for the x_2 coordinates corresponding to x_1 values of points obeying this equality constraint is

$$x_2 = 5000 - x_1$$

The substitution step gives

$$E_s(x_1) = .028x_1 + .016(5000 - x_1) - \frac{1}{2} \times 10^{-6}[9x_1^2 + 2.4(5000 - x_1)x_1$$

$$+ 4(5000 - x_1)^2]$$

The total derivative with respect to x_1 is found directly:

$$\frac{dE_s(x_1)}{dx_1} = .028 - .016 - \frac{1}{2} \times 10^{-6}[18x_1 + 2.4(5000 - x_1 - x_1)$$

$$+ 8(5000 - x_1)(-1)]$$

$$= .012 - \frac{1}{2} \times 10^{-6}(21.2x_1 - 28{,}000)$$

This derivative is equated to zero, and the solution for x_1 is

$$x_1 = 2453$$

The corresponding x_2 value is next found from the constraint equation

$$x_2 = 5000 - x_1 = 2547$$

Thus the optimum solution to the constrained problem is found. The value of the objective function for this solution is

$$E(x_1, x_2) = E(2453, 2547) = 61.89$$

The amount by which this solution is inferior to the optimum unconstrained solution is called the *cost of the budget constraint*. This difference is the gain that would result from removing the budget constraint entirely. An interesting quantity to evaluate is the rate of gain in the objective function as the constraint is moved *marginally* in the favorable direction. This information is a useful by-product of the method of the next section.

3.4   EQUALITY CONSTRAINTS SOLVED BY THE LAGRANGE MULTIPLIER[1]

The method of the Lagrange multiplier works when substitution is impractical because of the difficulty of solving the constraint equations. However, it is often used even when substitution is practical, because the extra work required is usually more than offset by the additional information obtained by this method.

The derivation of the Lagrange multiplier method is also based upon substitution. Resuming from the general discussion of the preceding section, the necessary condition for an optimum is

$$\frac{dE_s(x_1)}{dx_1} = 0$$

This implies that

$$\frac{\partial E[x_1, f(x_1)]}{\partial x_1} + \frac{\partial E[x_1, f(x_1)]}{\partial x_2}\frac{df(x_1)}{dx_1} = 0 \tag{3.1}$$

Furthermore, it is known that $f(x_1)$ has the property that $g(x_1, f(x_1)) = b$ for all possible x_1, and differentiation of this gives

$$\frac{dg}{dx_1} = \frac{\partial g[x_1, f(x_1)]}{\partial x_1} + \frac{\partial g[x_1, f(x_1)]}{\partial x_2}\frac{df(x_1)}{dx_1} = 0 \tag{3.2}$$

Solve Eq. (3.2) for

$$\frac{df(x_1)}{dx_1} = -\frac{\partial g/\partial x_1}{\partial g/\partial x_2}$$

and substitute this into Eq. (3.1) to obtain

$$\frac{\partial E}{\partial x_1} - \frac{\partial E}{\partial x_2}\frac{\partial g/\partial x_1}{\partial g/\partial x_2} = 0 \tag{3.3}$$

The reasoning is that the derivative of f may be difficult to compute because of the difficulty in solving the constraint equations. Perhaps the determination of its value can be postponed. This motivates the following definition:

$$\lambda \equiv \frac{\partial E/\partial x_2}{\partial g/\partial x_2}$$

Then Eq. (3.3) can be written

$$\frac{\partial E}{\partial x_1} - \lambda \frac{\partial g}{\partial x_1} = 0 \tag{3.4}$$

---

[1] The following derivation of the Lagrange multiplier method is not essential for the understanding of its use.

The defining equation for λ can be written

$$\frac{\partial E}{dx_2} - \lambda \frac{\partial g}{\partial x_2} = 0 \tag{3.5}$$

The partial derivatives in Eqs. (3.3) and (3.4) are easily obtained. Equation (3.3) has come from the original Eq. (3.1) and represents the necessary condition for optimality. Equation (3.5) represents the definition of λ. These two equations determine x_1 and x_2 as functions of λ. The final step is to use the constraint equation to determine the value of λ. Thus the Lagrange multiplier method eliminates the necessity of solving the constraint equations. It shows that only the ratio of the partial derivatives is required and that the determination of this ratio can be postponed to the last step. The variable λ is called *Lagrange's undetermined multiplier*. Its value is determined in the last step and represents a valuable by-product of this method.

The complete statement of the Lagrange multiplier method can be restated as follows. The optimization problem

$$\max\{E(x_1,x_2)\}$$

subject to the equality constraint

$$g(x_1,x_2) = b$$

can be reformulated as an unconstrained maximization of the Lagrangian function of three variables:

$$F(x_1,x_2,\lambda) = E(x_1,x_2) - \lambda[g(x_1,x_2) - b]$$

Optimization of this unconstrained function is performed by equating its three partial derivatives to zero:

$$\frac{\partial F}{\partial x_1} = \frac{\partial E}{\partial x_1} - \lambda\frac{\partial g}{\partial x_1} = 0$$

$$\frac{\partial F}{\partial x_2} = \frac{\partial E}{\partial x_2} - \lambda\frac{\partial g}{\partial x_2} = 0$$

$$\frac{\partial F}{\partial \lambda} = -[g(x_1,x_2) - b] = 0$$

It is easily observed that these three equations in three unknowns are (3.4), (3.5), and the constraint equality. They determine the values of three unknowns x_1, x_2, and λ that obey the necessary conditions for optimality.

This method can now be illustrated with the problem of the previous section. The Lagrangian function is

$$F(x_1,x_2,\lambda) = .028x_1 + .016x_2 - \frac{1}{2}\ 10^{-6}(9x_1^2 + 2.4x_1x_2 + 4x_2^2)$$

$$- \lambda(x_1 + x_2 - 5000)$$

The partial derivative equations are

$$\frac{\partial F}{\partial x_1} = .028 - \frac{1}{2} 10^{-6}(18x_1 + 2.4x_2) - \lambda = 0$$

$$\frac{\partial F}{\partial x_2} = .016 - \frac{1}{2} 10^{-6}(2.4x_1 + 8x_2) - \lambda = 0$$

$$\frac{\partial F}{\partial \lambda} = - (x_1 + x_2 - 5000)$$

The first two equations can be solved simultaneously for x_1 and x_2 as if λ were a constant. Their solutions are

$$x_1 = 2685 - 81,017\lambda$$
$$x_2 = 3194 - 225,694\lambda$$

The final determination of λ can be made by substitution of these into the third equation:

$$(2685 - 81,017\lambda) + (3194 - 225,694\lambda) = 5000$$
$$306,711\lambda = 879$$
$$\lambda = .002866$$

Finally, returning to x_1 and x_2 the following results are obtained:

$$x_1 = 2685 - 232 = 2453$$
$$x_2 = 3194 - 647 = 2547$$

A simple interpretation of the Lagrange multiplier method can be made by utilizing the graph in Fig. 3.3, which shows the decision space (x_1,x_2) and the constraint curve $x_1 + x_2 = 5000$ and some iso-E curves. An iso-E curve has the property that every point on the curve yields the same E value. All iso-E curves enclose the unconstrained optimum solution. As one moves away from that point in any direction, the E value decreases. The Lagrange multiplier method expresses the condition that the best iso-E curve attainable is the one which is just tangent to the constraint curve. No iso-E curve having higher E value can obey the constraint. All iso-E curves of lower E value give solutions that satisfy the constraint but have inferior values of E.

This condition of tangency and the Lagrange method can be extended to higher-dimensional problems and more than one constraint. For m decision variables and n constraints $(m > n)$ the problem is

$$\max E(x_1, x_2, \ldots, x_m)$$

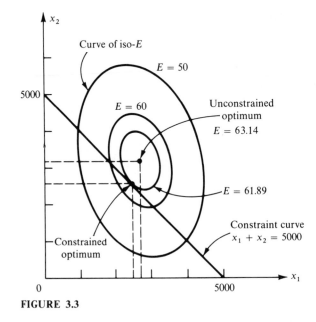

FIGURE 3.3

subject to

$$g_1(x_1, x_2, \ldots, x_m) = b_1$$
$$g_2(x_1, x_2, \ldots, x_m) = b_2$$
$$\vdots$$
$$g_n(x_1, x_2, \ldots, x_m) = b_n$$

This problem can be replaced by the unconstrained problem having $m + n$ variables $x_1, x_2, \ldots, x_m, \lambda_1, \lambda_2, \ldots, \lambda_n$:

$$\max E - \sum_{i=1}^{n} \lambda_i (g_i - b_i)$$

Interpretation of the Lagrange Multiplier

Returning to the two-dimensional general problem of maximizing $E(x_1, x_2)$ subject to the equality constraint $g(x_1, x_2) = b$, the optimum solution is denoted by $x_1^*(b)$, $x_2^*(b)$ to show that it is a function of the constraint level b. The optimum solution can be written $E^*(b) = E[x_1^*(b), x_2^*(b)]$ to emphasize that it too is a function of b. Consider the rate of change of $E^*(b)$ with respect to b:

$$\frac{dE^*(b)}{db} = \frac{\partial E}{\partial x_1} \frac{dx_1^*}{db} + \frac{\partial E}{\partial x_2} \frac{dx_2^*}{db} \qquad (3.6)$$

This equation would be difficult to work with, but some help is available. The optimum solution must satisfy the constraint. Therefore

$$g(x_1^*, x_2^*) = b$$

and differentiation with respect to b gives

$$\frac{\partial g}{\partial x_1}\frac{dx_1^*}{db} + \frac{\partial g}{\partial x_2}\frac{dx_2^*}{db} = 1$$

This equation can be multiplied by λ and the terms transposed to obtain

$$\lambda - \lambda\frac{\partial g}{\partial x_1}\frac{dx_1^*}{db} - \lambda\frac{\partial g}{\partial x_2}\frac{dx_2^*}{db} = 0$$

The zero quantity can be added to Eq. (3.6) and rearranged to obtain

$$\frac{dE^*(b)}{db} = \frac{dx_1^*}{db}\left(\frac{\partial E}{\partial x_1} - \lambda\frac{\partial g}{\partial x_1}\right) + \frac{dx_2^*}{db}\left(\frac{\partial E}{\partial x_2} - \lambda\frac{\partial g}{\partial x_2}\right) + \lambda$$

The terms inside the two sets of parentheses are zero for an optimum solution because they are the derivatives of the Langrangian function. Therefore the simple result remains

$$\frac{dE^*(b)}{db} = \lambda$$

Thus the λ value tells the marginal rate of change of the objective function with respect to the constraint quantity. It is a derivative evaluated at one point, the current b value. As b changes, so will λ. This is useful for evaluating small changes in b. It is extremely useful even when used only to tell in what direction b should be changed. In the example of this section the constraint was $x_1 + x_2 = 5000.$ Thus b represents the investment budget level $b = 5000$. The positive value of λ implies that the objective function would increase if b were increased from 5000. In fact the rate of change of E is $0.002866 per dollar of b. In more meaningful units, it is $2.866 per thousand-dollar increase in budget as the budget starts to increase from 5000.

3.5 EXTENSION TO INEQUALITY CONSTRAINTS

Inequality constraints can be more difficult than equality constraints, as indicated in Sec. 3.1, because one does not know at the outset of analysis whether the constraint will be "binding" in the optimum solution. With knowledge that it will be binding, one can proceed to solve the equality-constrained problem. With knowledge that it will not be binding, one can ignore the constraint and proceed to solve the unconstrained problem. Without knowledge of which case is true, one can proceed to the simpler problem first.

Consider the problem of Sec. 3.2 with $\rho = \frac{5}{6}$ instead of $\frac{1}{5}$, and the inequality constraint $x_1 + x_2 \leq 5000$, which places an upper limit upon the amount to be invested. The solution of the unconstrained problem is $x_1 = 2905$, $x_2 = 368$. This is a total investment of only \$3273. It clearly obeys the inequality constraint, and thus the analysis is complete without solving an equality-constrained problem.

This method extends in principle to the case of several constraints. A guess of which inequality constraints can be ignored can be tested by determining whether the resulting solution obeys the inequality constraints that were ignored. However, when there are many constraints there are many combinations to consider and the method is not very practical. With n inequality constraints there are 2^n possible cases to consider because each constraint is either binding or not binding. A similar approach that is appropriate when the constraint appears likely to be binding in the optimum solution is to solve the equality-constrained problem first and then utilize the λ value to determine whether the constraint is binding or not.

Consider the example again but with $\rho = \frac{1}{5}$. Let the budget constraint be the inequality constraint $x_1 + x_2 \leq 5000$. Solve the equality-constrained problem to obtain $\lambda = +.00286$. This solution implies that E would increase as b increases from \$5000 and would decrease if b were decreased from \$5000. This implies that the constraint is binding. In other words there is no better solution such that $x_1 + x_2 < 5000$; the best solution has $x_1 + x_2 = 5000$.

The opposite outcome can be illustrated by the same problem having $\rho = \frac{1}{5}$ but with the inequality constraint

$$x_1 + x_2 \leq 10,000$$

The Lagrange multiplier method for the equality-constrained problem gives

$$x_1 = 2685 - 81,017\lambda$$
$$x_2 = 3194 - 225,694\lambda$$

The λ value is determined from the constraint equation

$$(2685 - 81,017\lambda) + (3194 - 225,694\lambda) = 10,000$$
$$306,711\lambda = -4121$$
$$\lambda = -.0134$$

The negative value of λ implies that the E value can be increased as b is decreased from 10,000. Therefore there is a solution having $x_1 + x_2 < 10,000$, which is a better solution. At this point it is known that the unconstrained solution is desired. It is quickly obtained from the equations for x_1 and x_2 by setting $\lambda = 0$. Thus the optimum solution obeying $x_1 + x_2 \leq 10,000$ is $x_1 = 2685$, $x_2 = 3194$. This method is also useful for up to a few inequality constraints but suffers from combinational problems when there are many constraints.

3.6 EXAMPLE OF TWO INEQUALITY CONSTRAINTS

Again consider the original investment problem with $\rho = \frac{1}{5}$. Suppose that there are two inequality constraints:

$$x_1 + x_2 \leq 5000$$

$$x_1 \leq 2400$$

The set of feasible solutions is the two-dimensional space of points that satisfy both constraints simultaneously. This is illustrated in Fig. 3.4. The Lagrangian function is

$$F(x_1, x_2, \lambda_1, \lambda_2) = .028x_1 + .016x_2 - \frac{1}{2} \times 10^{-6}(9x_1^2 + 2.4x_1 x_2 + 4x_2^2)$$

$$- \lambda_1(x_1 + x_2 - 5000) - \lambda_2(x_1 - 2400)$$

The necessary conditions in terms of derivatives are

$$\frac{\partial F}{\partial x_1} = .028 - \frac{1}{2} \times 10^{-6}(18x_1 + 2.4x_2) - \lambda_1 - \lambda_2 = 0$$

$$\frac{\partial F}{\partial x_2} = .016 - \frac{1}{2} \times 10^{-6}(2.4x_1 + 8x_2) - \lambda_1 = 0$$

$$\frac{\partial F}{\partial \lambda_1} = -(x_1 + x_2 - 5000) = 0$$

$$\frac{\partial F}{\partial \lambda_2} = -(x_1 - 2400) = 0$$

The solutions of the first two equations for x_1 and x_2 are

$$x_1 = 2685 - 81,017\lambda_1 - 115,741\lambda_2$$

$$x_2 = 3194 - 225,694\lambda_1 - 34722\lambda_2$$

From the graph of the feasible region it is easily seen that the solution must be one of the following:

1. On the constraint $x_1 + x_2 = 5000$
2. On the constraint $x_1 = 2400$
3. On the intersection of the two constraints
4. No constraints binding (inside the feasible region)

In case 1 the best solution, subject to the first equality constraint but ignoring the second constraint, has been found previously: it is $x_1 = 2453$, $x_2 = 2547$, $\lambda_1 = .002866$. However, this solution breaks the second constraint. It is not a feasible solution.

In case 2 the best solution, subject to the second equality constraint $x_1 = 2400$

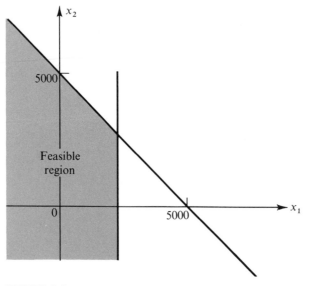

FIGURE 3.4

but ignoring the first constraint, is found by setting $\lambda_1 = 0$ and solving for x_1, x_2, and λ_2. Substitution into the constraint

$$2685 - 115{,}741\lambda = 2400$$

gives the result $\lambda_2 = +.00246$. Then

$$x_1 = 2685 - 285 = 2400$$
$$x_2 = 3194 - 9 = 3185$$

This solution is not feasible with respect to the first constraint because $2400 + 3185 = 5585$.

For case 4 the unconstrained solution is sought. This solution is already known to be $x_1 = 2685$, $x_2 = 3194$. It is infeasible with respect to both constraints.

Finally case 3 is considered. Only one point can solve both constraints as equalities simultaneously. That point is the simultaneous solution of the two equations

$$x_1 + x_2 = 5000$$
$$x_1 = 2400$$

The result is $x_1 = 2400$, $x_2 = 2600$. By elimination of all other possibilities it is clear that this is the optimum solution subject to the two inequality constraints.

It is interesting to observe that the solution to this problem was at the intersection of two constraints, the "corner" of the feasible region. Had this fact been known at the outset, the analysis would have been very simple: Just find that point.

No calculus would have been required. The problem studied in this section had a nonlinear objective function. Consequently the analysis shown was necessary. However, it will be shown later that when the objective function is linear and the constraints are linear inequalities the optimum solution will *always* be at a corner point of this feasible region. This fact leads to an efficient way to search for the optimum solution.

PROBLEMS

1. In the helicopter transportation problem of Sec. 2.5, Chap. 2, the characteristics of the helicopter were not considered. Suppose that the helicopter being considered has a maximum capacity of 20 passengers and a flight time of 10 minutes for a one-way trip between the two stations. Write the three constraints upon T that are implied by these facts. Test and show whether the solution that minimizes $E(T)$ is feasible with respect to each of these constraints. What value of T is optimum in the presence of these constraints? What is the increased cost to the average customer caused by these constraints?

2. The earnings function for a certain store is given by

    $$E(x,y) = 4x + 5y + xy - x^2 - y^2 + 5$$

    where E = earnings (in $\$10^5$)

    $\quad\quad x$ = investment in inventory (in $\$10^5$)

    $\quad\quad y$ = floor space used for displays (in 10^4 square feet)

    Working capital is required to run the store. Each dollar invested in inventory requires half a dollar in working capital. Each square foot of floor space requires $10 in working capital.

    (a) Let $W(x,y)$ = working capital required as a function of x and y (in units of $\$10^5$). Write the function W. Write the constraint $W \leq {}^{41}\!/_{6}$ (that is, $683,333).
    (b) Solve the problem of maximizing the earnings with no constraints. Find the working capital required for this solution.
    (c) Solve the problem with the equality constraint $W = {}^{41}\!/_{6}$.
    (d) Solve the problem subject to $W \geq 7$.

3. The East Coast Power and Light Corporation is currently building two new power facilities. The company wishes to determine the optimal allocation of capital funds to the two projects. Management has estimated that funds invested in plant A, a fossil fuel facility, will yield a 10 percent return. Plant B, using nuclear power, yields 15 percent. Because of strong pressure from conservation groups, the company feels it must consider the impact of various investment alternatives upon society. Let x = investment in plant A (in $\$10^6$) and

let y = investment in plant B (in $\$10^6$). The social utility of combination (x,y) is shown below:

$$u(x,y) = 1 - \frac{x^2}{100} - \frac{y^2}{200}$$

East Coast Power and Light has agreed to choose the combination (x^*,y^*) that maximizes $u(x,y)$ subject to the condition that their return is at least $2 million.

(a) Let $R(x,y)$ = return from investing x million dollars in plant A and y million dollars in plant B. Write $R(x,y) \geq 2$.

(b) Find the optimal values (x^*,y^*) for $u(x,y)$ subject to the constraint $R(x,y) \geq 2$. Is $R(x,y) \geq 2$ a binding constraint?

4. A student's expenses for a school year generally consist of

$$T = \text{tuition and fees (in } \$10^3)$$
$$x = \text{room and board (in } \$10^3)$$
$$y = \text{other living expenses (in } \$10^3)$$

Suppose the comfort of a student can be expressed in terms of his expenditures as follows:

$$E(x,y) = \frac{5}{2}(xy + x)$$

(a) Given a budget of $5000 for the school year and fixed $3000 for tuition and fees, how should he appropriate his budget to maximize his comfort?

(b) If in addition he does not want to spend more than 25 percent of his total budget for room and board (x), how will his expenditures differ?

(c) Are the constraints binding in parts (a) and (b)? Explain in terms of λ's obtained.

5. The management of ABC Enterprises has found that annual sales S in millions of dollars may be expressed by the function

$$S(x,y) = \frac{160x}{10 + x} + \frac{320y}{5 + y}$$

where x = research and development (in $\$10^6$)

y = plant improvement expense (in $\$10^6$)

Financial and other considerations have convinced the management of the company that approximately $15 million should be spent on research and development (R & D) and plant improvements. How could such a sum be allocated between R & D and plant improvement so that net profit is maximized? (Management has projected a profit of 25 percent of sales.) Use the Lagrange multiplier method and show the marginal value of relaxing the budget constraint.

6. A company carries an inventory composed of two products A and B for which there is a uniform yearly demand of 10,000 and 20,000 units, respectively. Product A costs the company $2/unit to purchase, $1/unit/year to store, and $100 in administrative costs every time it is reordered. Product B costs the company $4/unit to purchase, $2/unit/year to store, and $200 in administrative costs for each reorder.

   (a) Set up the total cost equations for each product separately and solve for their optimum order quantities.

   (b) Because of a liquidity problem the company requires that the average yearly investment in inventory for the two products taken together be less than or equal to $6000. Is the answer found in part (a) consistent with this added constraint?

   (c) Use both substitution and the Lagrange multiplier method to find the optimum solution when the average yearly investment in inventory must be less than or equal to $5000. Average yearly investment is the dollar value of the average amount of inventory present.

7. A shop sells two products that it orders periodically from one supplier. The demand rates for both products are predictable and constant. Demand rates and inventory costs are given by the following table:

Product	Demand Rate, units/month	Order Cost, $/order	Holding Cost, $/unit/month
A	$D_A = 100$	$C_{SA} = 50$	$C_{HA} = 25$
B	$D_B = 300$	$C_{SB} = 50$	$C_{HB} = 3$

   (a) Find the optimum values of the inventory cost per month and the length of both inventory cycles under the assumption that both inventory processes are managed separately.

   (b) The shop finds that they could save the order cost of product B if both products were ordered together. This course of action can be evaluated by finding the minimum total inventory cost per month subject to the constraint that the two inventory periods be equal. Write the objective (function) and the constraint. Show how to solve this by substitution and by Lagrange multiplier.

8. A company sells a product that cannot be easily obtained elsewhere. They have a constant demand rate $D = 100$ units/month, an order cost of $C_s = $50/order$, and a holding cost of $C_h = $10/unit/month$. Because of the high order cost and the captive nature of their market they do not order immediately when inventory reaches zero but continue to take orders until orders for y units are accumulated. They compensate their customers who had to wait by reducing the

cost by $C_p = \$5$ per unit per month waited for delivery. At the end of the cycle they order $x + y$ units to bring the inventory level up to x at the start of the new cycle. The total cost per month of this inventory process as a function of x and y is

$$E_A(x,y) = \frac{C_sD}{x + y} + \frac{C_hx^2}{2(x + y)} + \frac{C_py^2}{2(x + y)}$$

(a) Sketch the graph of the inventory level as a function of time. Solve the derivative equations for the optimum value of the two decision variables.

(b) Suppose there is a constraint that the order quantity be less than or equal to 40 units. Solve the equality-constrained problem by substitution and by Lagrange multiplier.

Chapter 4

THE ASSIGNMENT PROBLEM

The assignment problem is a simple yet useful problem structure. It is perhaps the simplest example of a class of linear optimization problems called *linear programming problems*. A characteristic of this whole class of problems is that the method of solution looks quite different from the methods used in the previous chapters. Problems of this type are solved by a repetitive series of steps called an *algorithm* or *program*. It is a process of searching for the optimum solution. The efficiency with which this search is performed is important because larger problems can be economically solved using more efficient algorithms. Consequently each special case of linear programming problems has its own efficient algorithm. The assignment problem of this chapter has its own algorithm; the transportation problem of the next chapter has a different algorithm suited to its special features. Finally the general linear programming problem has its own algorithm called the *simplex method*.

It is important for the student to realize that these problems are all closely related even though they will appear to be unrelated. Their common properties cannot be appreciated until each problem has first been studied intensively. Consequently the order of presentation follows the rule of study in order of increasing complexity. A secondary theme is the observation of the fundamental unity that extends through this series of problems and to the methods of the previous chapter.

One advantage of beginning this class of problems with the assignment problem is that it is a simple enough problem that the student can see the reasoning behind the algorithm for its solution. Although the purpose of this book is not to teach the design of algorithms, the student should strive to obtain some understanding of why an algorithm works.

TABLE 4.1   Applications of the Assignment Problem

Job	Facility
Sales districts	Salesmen
Scheduled trains	Railroad locomotives
Tasks	Employees
New products	Production plants

4.1   PROBLEM STATEMENT

The assignment problem consists of the following elements:

1. A set of jobs; let n be the number.
2. A set of facilities such that the number of facilities is also n.
3. A set of costs, one for each job-facility pair. Let C_{ij} represent the cost of assigning job i to facility j. The number of possible pairs is n^2.

The objective for the assignment problem is to assign one job to each facility in such a way as to achieve the minimum possible total cost. This problem arises in many different content areas; some of the possibilities of this problem are shown in Table 4.1.

4.2   SOLUTION BY ENUMERATION

Consider an assignment problem having three jobs and three facilities. The costs of all possible assignments are given by the following cost matrix:

		Job		
		J1	J2	J3
	F1	5	4	6
Facility	F2	9	3	7
	F3	3	2	1

The word "solution" is conventionally used here to denote a complete assignment of every job, one to each facility (and therefore one facility to each job). The simplest approach to finding the optimum solution is to list and evaluate all possible solutions and then select the one having the lowest cost. This is done in Table 4.2. After all possible solutions have been listed and compared, it is possible to draw the conclusion that the first assignment (J1,J2,J3) is the best. This method has an advantageous feature: It shows the second-best solution also; here the best solution is superior to the next contender by 3 units of cost.

TABLE 4.2   Solution by Enumeration

Assignment of Jobs to Facilities F1, F2, F3	Costs	Total Cost
J1, J2, J3	5, 3, 1	9 (optimum)
J2, J1, J3	4, 9, 1	14
J3, J1, J2	6, 9, 2	17
J1, J3, J2	5, 7, 2	14
J2, J3, J1	4, 7, 3	14
J3, J2, J1	6, 3, 3	12

However, this "brute force" method has a strong disadvantage: The number of possible solutions can be very large. The current example has $n = 3$ jobs. There are exactly six possible solutions. Counting the number of possible solutions is not difficult; if there are n jobs, the first assignment of one job to one facility can be made in n different ways. After making the first assignment, the number of jobs remaining is $(n - 1)$. Therefore the next assignment of one job to one facility can be made in $(n - 1)$ different ways. Successive assignments can be made in $(n - 2)$, $(n - 3)$, ... different ways. The last assignment can be made in only one way. The total number of possible assignments is the product of the numbers in each step: $(n)(n - 1)$ $(n - 2) \cdots (1) \equiv n!$ Thus for $n = 3$, $n! = 6$; and for $n = 5$, $n! = 120$. Six solutions are easily handled. However, for 120 solutions even a novice could learn the efficient method of solution faster than he could solve one problem. The amount of work involved in enumeration grows rapidly with n and becomes prohibitive even for a computer. For example, $12! = 4.79 \times 10^8$, $15! = 1.31 \times 10^{12}$, and $20! = 2.43 \times 10^{18}$. It is important to realize that if you considered only 119 possible solutions to a problem of size $n = 5$, simply forgetting the last one of them could make your solution entirely wrong because the one forgotten solution could have been the best. From this viewpoint it is clear that a method of recognizing the optimality of a given solution *without relying upon direct comparison with all its competitors* is a virtual necessity.

4.3   PROPERTIES OF THE ASSIGNMENT PROBLEM

The efficient method of solution is based upon the two following properties of the problem that are easily seen to be true (the use of each property is also discussed):

Property 1

If a constant quantity is subtracted from all elements in any row or column of the cost matrix, the costs of all the $n!$ possible solutions are reduced by that same constant quantity.

REASON WHY 1 IS TRUE Every possible assignment utilizes exactly one element in every row and one element in every column. Thus every solution utilizes the modified row or column exactly once. Since the total cost of a solution is the sum of individual assignment costs, the sum will be reduced by the constant quantity subtracted.

USE OF 1 This property shows how it is possible to modify the original problem in a way that leaves the solutions modified in a known way. Reducing the costs of all solutions by the same quantity leaves their ranking unchanged. The best solution to the original problem is also the best solution to the modified problem. Thus it is possible to modify the problem repeatedly until one is found that is easy to solve. The solution to the last problem in the series of modifications is known to be the solution to the original problem.

Property 2

For an assignment problem having all nonnegative costs, a solution having zero total cost is an optimum solution.

REASON WHY 2 IS TRUE Sums of nonnegative numbers are nonnegative numbers. The cost of a solution is a sum of individual assignment costs. Therefore a solution having zero total cost may not be the only optimum solution, but it cannot be inferior to any other solution; it is optimal.

USE OF 2 This property is used to recognize the optimality of a solution. A modified problem having a solution whose assignments all have zero cost is indeed an easy problem to solve.

4.4   METHOD OF SOLUTION

The efficient method can now be stated as an algorithm, or series of repeatable steps. The statement of the algorithm, like a computer program, is designed to be precise and *not* self-explanatory. Some explanatory comments are included for guidance, but they are not meant to be a derivation or proof of the efficient algorithm. The method begins with an $n \times n$ square matrix of nonnegative numbers. Each step generates a new matrix. At each step only the current matrix is used. Each step is illustrated here with the example problem.

5	4	6
9	3	7
3	2	1

$(M1)$

Step 1

For each row select the smallest number in that row and then subtract it from every element in that row. Repeat this step for all rows, entering the results in a new matrix.

EXAMPLE The resulting new matrix is

1	0	2
6	0	4
2	1	0

$(M2)$

Step 2

For each column select the smallest number in that column and subtract it from every element in that column. Repeat for all columns, entering the results in a new matrix.

0	0	2
5	0	4
1	1	0

$(M3)$

COMMENT Steps 1 and 2 could have been interchanged in order. The results may not be the same but both are equally acceptable. In this example the reverse order of row and column operations would have resulted in the following matrix:

0	0	3
5	0	5
0	0	0

$(M3')$

Step 3a

Search for a solution having all zero-cost assignments. If one is found, it is the optimum solution. The next part of step 3 is a procedure to determine that the current matrix does *not* have a solution with all zero-cost assignments.

Step 3*b*

Draw a set of lines through the rows or columns (each line covering one row or one column) such that all zero elements are covered using as few lines as possible. Let m represent the minimum number of lines that cover all zero elements at least once. If $m < n$ then a solution with all zero-cost assignments is *not* present.

COMMENT   The number of lines used in step 3 must be the smallest number possible. An error in this step can easily go undetected and lead to an erroneous solution.

EXAMPLE   It is easy to find a zero cost in matrix $M3$. The solution is marked by circles around the elements used in the assignment:

⓪	0	2
5	⓪	4
1	1	⓪

This is an optimal solution. A quick search for other zero-cost solutions indicates that it is the unique optimum, as was already known from the solution by enumeration. The real total cost of this solution can be obtained most efficiently from the original cost matrix: $5 + 3 + 1 = 9$. Notice that an alternative way to obtain it is by summation of all the subtractions performed up to this point: $4 + 3 + 1 + 1 + 0 + 0 = 9$. Now that this example is complete another example will be used to illustrate the further steps of the algorithm:

3	5	7	1
9	8	12	10
13	8	14	2
5	7	10	6

After doing the first two steps, row and column subtractions, the cost matrix then becomes the following:

2	4	2	0̶
1̶	0̶	0̶	2̶
11	6	8	0̶
0̶	2̶	1̶	1̶

The zero elements of this matrix can be covered by three lines but not by two. Hence $m = 3$ while $n = 4$. Step $3b$ thus concludes with the knowledge that a zero-cost solution is not yet present.

Step 4

Select the smallest uncovered element. Subtract it from all uncovered elements. Add it to all twice-covered elements. Do not change the singly covered elements. Return to step 3.

COMMENT   This step is equivalent to a series of row and column subtractions and additions whose purpose is to make zero-cost cells in new places. It is important to realize that step 4 may have to be repeated many times before a subsequent step 3 arrives at a zero-cost solution.

EXAMPLE   The smallest uncovered element in this matrix is a 2. Step 4 yields

0	2	⓪	0
1	⓪	0	4
9	4	6	⓪
⓪	2	1	3

Now, returning to step 3, a zero-cost solution is found. Examination for alternative assignments shows that this solution is the unique optimum. Its total cost, by reference to the original matrix, is $5 + 8 + 7 + 2 = 22$.

EXERCISE

Rework this problem doing column operations (step 2) before row operations (step 1) and show that it results in the same solution on the first use of step 3. No use of step 4 is required. It is a characteristic of most algorithms that some arbitrary choices must be made. The alternatives usually generate different intermediate steps and involve different amounts of work, but they always arrive at the same or equivalent results.

4.5   USEFUL PROBLEM MODIFICATIONS

The assignment structure can be broadened by a few simple modifications.

Maximization Problems

Given a profit matrix or some other measure to be maximized, a conversion is performed:

1. Select the largest element in the profit matrix.
2. Form a new cost matrix whose elements are each the largest element of step 1 minus the corresponding profit element.
3. Find the solution with minimum cost. It has maximum profit in the original problem.

EXAMPLE   The profit matrix

2	8
5	3

is transformed to a cost matrix

6	0
3	5

Unbalanced Problems

If the number of jobs is not equal to the number of facilities, the problem is called *unbalanced*. This condition is removed by adding dummy jobs or facilities, whichever had the deficiency, until the numbers are equal. The costs or profits to be put into the new rows or columns are determined from the context of the problem.

Impossible Assignments

If some assignment is infeasible—for example, job 1 cannot be performed by facility 3—then that assignment can be effectively avoided by putting a large cost in that cell. This high cost prevents that assignment from appearing in the optimal solution.

Negative Costs

If the cost matrix has mostly positive or zero cells but has a few negative cells also, it is necessary to add to rows or columns a quantity sufficient to make all cells nonnegative. Property 1 shows that the modified problem will have the same ranking of solutions as the original problem.

4.6   EXAMPLE OF REAL ESTATE ASSIGNMENT

A realtor has five purchasers for six sites. The ith purchaser is willing to pay price P_{ij} (or less) for the jth site. The values of P_{ij} are given in the following matrix. The realtor wishes to know which site to offer to each purchaser at what price so as to maximize his total receipts. Find the answer for him, and find his total revenue.

Site

		1	2	3	4	5	6
	1	6	7	6	2	9	4
Purchaser	2	0	5	8	1	1	10
	3	5	10	6	5	10	3
	4	2	7	12	4	10	7
	5	6	9	9	5	7	9

The first step in solving this problem is to balance it by adding a dummy purchaser. The site assigned to this fictitious purchaser will, in reality, go unsold. Therefore a profit of zero is generated. The dummy row will contain all zeros. The next step is to observe that the matrix represents profits, not costs, and the objective function is to be maximized. Therefore the conversion must be performed to reverse the magnitude. The largest entry is 12. The new cost matrix has entries obtained from the original matrix by subtraction from 12:

	1	2	3	4	5	6
1	6	5	6	10	3	8
2	12	7	4	11	11	2
3	7	2	6	7	2	9
4	10	5	0	8	2	5
5	6	3	3	7	5	3
6	12	12	12	12	12	12

Next the row and column subtractions are performed. The result is

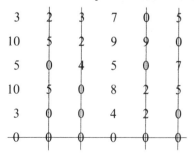

The minimum number of lines to cover all zero entries is 5, as shown. Therefore there is no solution present among the zero entries. The smallest uncovered entry is a 3. Step 4 is performed and the result is

$$
\begin{array}{cccccc}
\boxed{0} & 2 & 3 & 4 & \textcircled{0} & 5 \\
7 & 5 & 2 & 6 & 9 & \boxed{\textcircled{0}} \\
2 & \textcircled{0} & 4 & 2 & \boxed{0} & 7 \\
7 & 5 & \boxed{\textcircled{0}} & 5 & 2 & 5 \\
\textcircled{0} & \boxed{0} & 0 & 1 & 2 & 0 \\
0 & 3 & 3 & \boxed{\textcircled{0}} & 3 & 3 \\
\end{array}
$$

Two optimal solutions are now present: One is marked by circles and the other by squares. Both give a total revenue of 47.

PROBLEMS

1. A firm plans to begin production of three new products. They own three plants and wish to assign one new product to each of the three plants. The unit cost of producing i at plant j is C_{ij}, as given by the following table:

Plant

		1	2	3
	1	10	8	12
Product	2	18	6	14
	3	6	4	2

(a) Find the assignment that minimizes total unit cost.
(b) Suppose that the production quantities are not identical for all three products:

Product	Quantity
1	10,000
2	1000
3	1000

Find the assignment that minimizes total production cost.

(c) Find the total production cost of the solution found in part (a), using the production quantities of part (b). Does it differ from that found in part (b)? If so, which is better?

2. A computing center has four keypunchers: Ann, Beth, Claire, Diane. The director receives five jobs that must be punched. All jobs take one full day. The setup cost of having two women work on one job is high; therefore he wishes to assign one job to each woman and reject one job. The profit of each job depends upon which woman is assigned to it, as is shown in the following table. The director wishes to assign the jobs so as the maximize profit under the added conditions that Ann cannot do job 1 and that there would be an additional penalty of 3 if job 2 is the one which goes undone.

Job Profits

Keypuncher	Job				
	1	2	3	4	5
Ann	1	5	2	0	4
Beth	4	7	5	6	3
Claire	5	8	4	3	5
Diane	3	6	6	2	6

3. A college department chairman has the problem of providing teachers for all courses offered by his department at the highest possible level of educational quality. He has available two professors, two associate professors, one assistant professor, and one teaching assistant (TA). Six courses must be offered, and, after appropriate introspection and evaluation, he has arrived at the following relative ratings (100 = best rating) regarding the ability of each instructor to teach each of the six courses, respectively.

Professor	Course 1	Course 2	Course 3	Course 4	Course 5	Course 6
1	40	40	90	30	20	90
2	60	40	60	70	30	70
3	20	60	50	70	50	60
4	20	30	40	60	40	60
5	90	80	70	40	50	40
TA	30	10	30	40	20	10

How should he assign his staff to the courses to maximize educational quality in his department?

4. A firm that markets one product has four salesmen, A, B, C, and D, and three customers, 1, 2, and 3. The firm's profit for selling 1 unit of its product to

customer 1 is $10, to customer 2 it is $20, and to customer 3 it is $30. Sales of the firm's product to each customer depend upon the salesman's customer rapport. The probability matrix for the sale of 1 unit of the product to each customer by each salesman is as follows:

Salesman	1	2	3
A	.6	.6	.6
B	.5	.8	.7
C	.3	.6	.4
D	.7	.8	.5

For example, the probability that salesman B can sell 1 unit of product to customer 3 is .7. The firm would have an expected profit of .7 × 30 = 21 from that assignment. If only one salesman can be assigned to each customer, what is the optimum assignment? What is the total expected profit?

5. Robert Roark is an independent agent for life insurance. At the present time he has four prospective customers who desire the following coverage:

Customer	Age	Type of Insurance Desired	Amount Requested ($)
1	25	20-year term	70,000
2	35	Whole life (WL)	40,000
3	40	Life paid up at 85 (LP = 85)	10,000
4	50	Endowment at 75 (E = 75)	5000

Mr. Roark has approached five insurance companies, who have expressed interest in these four customers. However, although each could easily insure more than one risk, each has requested Mr. Roark to send them only one client. The companies show the following *total* commissions for the size of policy desired:

Insurer	20-year Term	WL	LP = 85	E = 75
A	140	480	240	100
B	105	480	220	140
C	110	360	210	95
D	120	390	225	115
E	125	420	225	125

If Mr. Roark wishes to maximize his total commission earnings, how should he place the policies?

6. A company plans to start manufacturing three new products. It owns five plants, three of which are to be selected to produce the three new products. The following tables give the estimated production costs and distribution costs per unit of each product if it were manufactured at each plant:

Unit Production Costs ($)

Product	Plant				
	1	2	3	4	5
1	10	15	20	7	20
2	4	20	3	20	20
3	2	4	1	1	5

Unit Distribution Costs ($)

Product	Plant				
	1	2	3	4	5
1	10	30	10	3	5
2	3	50	3	15	30
3	2	2	2	7	3

Plans call for the following annual production of each product to be sold at the following prices:

Product	Planned Production	Planned Price ($)
1	3,000	13
2	15,000	10
3	2,000	4

Formulate this problem as an assignment problem to maximize total profit. Find the solution and the profit associated with it.

7. A distiller has five equally sized lots of whiskey being aged. The present ages of the different lots are

Lot	Age (in years)
A	0
B	1.5
C	2
D	4.5
E	5

Suppose the market is such that single lots have to be taken from storage according to the following schedule: 0, 1, 1.5, 2.5, 3, meaning that one lot is required at the present time, one lot is required for issue 1 year from now, another lot is required 1.5 years from now, and so on. Further assume that the expected-profit function of the distiller is such that the following values can be calculated:

Age of Lot at Issue	Expected Profit ($1000)
0	2
0.5	1
1	2
1.5	4
2	7
2.5	11
3	16
3.5	21
4	29
4.5	41
5	48
5.5	52
6	55
6.5	59
7	63
7.5	65
8 or older	69

(a)   Give the issuing schedule that maximizes the total expected profit for the five lots of whiskey.

(b)   Give the total expected profit associated with this schedule.

Chapter 5

THE TRANSPORTATION PROBLEM

The transportation problem is another problem structure that is often useful. Like the assignment problem, it is another special case of the general class of problems known as linear programming problems. It also has a special-purpose algorithm that exploits its special characteristics to obtain the optimum solution efficiently. It is a more complex problem, however, and the algorithm is less intuitively clear.

5.1 PROBLEM STATEMENT

The elements of the problem are

1. A set of m origins: $O_1, O_2, \ldots, O_m$.

2. A set of n destinations: $D_1, D_2, \ldots, D_n$.

3. A set of supplies of identical units: a_1 units at O_1, a_2 units at $O_2, \ldots, a_m$ units at O_m.

4. A set of requirements: b_1 units required at D_1, b_2 units required at $D_2 \ldots$, b_n units required at D_n.

5. A set of unit shipment costs: c_{ij} is the cost of shipping 1 unit from O_i to D_j. There are $m \times n$ such costs as input to the problem.

The objective is to find a shipment plan that satisfies all the requirements with minimum total shipment cost. The decision variables of the problem are x_{ij} = number of units to ship from O_i to D_j. There are $m \times n$ such variables. The total cost of the shipment schedule, as a function of the decision variables, is

$$
\begin{aligned}
E = \; & x_{11}c_{11} + x_{12}c_{12} + \cdots + x_{1n}c_{1n} \\
& + x_{21}c_{21} + x_{22}c_{22} + \cdots + x_{2n}c_{2n} \\
& \quad \vdots \\
& + x_{m1}c_{m1} + x_{m2}c_{m2} + \cdots + x_{mn}c_{mn}
\end{aligned}
$$

This is conveniently expressed as a double summation:

$$E = \sum_{i=1}^{m} \sum_{j=1}^{n} c_{ij} x_{ij}$$

A "balanced" transportation problem is one in which the total supply exactly equals the total requirement. There is no loss in generality to assume that this is true because all unbalanced problems can be easily converted to balanced problems, as is shown later. In symbols, the total supply is

$$a_1 + a_2 + \cdots + a_m = \sum_{i=1}^{m} a_1$$

The total requirement is

$$b_1 + b_2 + \cdots + b_n = \sum_{j=1}^{n} b_j$$

A balanced problem is one where

$$\sum_{i=1}^{m} a_i = \sum_{j=1}^{n} b_j$$

With the assumption that the problem is balanced, there are no excess units of supply nor will any requirements go unsatisfied. A *feasible* solution is a complete set of shipments meeting these conditions.

The constraints of the problem are equality constraints. The supply constraints express the fact that the total shipment from O_i must exactly equal the supply there, a_i. Thus

$$\sum_{j=1}^{n} x_{ij} = a_i \qquad \text{for } i = 1, 2, \ldots, m$$

There is one such constraint for each origin. The requirement constraints express the fact that the total shipment into D_j must exactly equal the total requirement at that destination. Thus

$$\sum_{i=1}^{m} x_{ij} = b_j \qquad \text{for } j = 1, 2, \ldots, n$$

There is one such constraint for each destination. In terms of these constraints, a feasible solution is a set of values x_{ij} of the decision variables such that all $n + m$ constraints are satisfied. In a balanced problem, one of these $m + n$ constraints is redundant. The algorithm for this problem has the structure shown in Fig. 5.1. Thus it is necessary always to start with a feasible solution. Section 5.2 shows methods of finding a feasible solution.

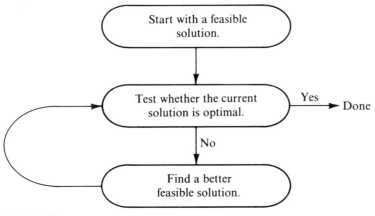

FIGURE 5.1

EXERCISES

1. Show that a transportation problem with $m = n$ and $a_1 = a_2 = \cdots = a_n = b_1 = b_2 = \cdots = b_n = 1$ is an assignment problem and can therefore be solved by the method of Chap. 4.

2. When $m = n = 2$ and $a_1 = a_2 = b_1 = b_2 = 2$, can this also be solved as an assignment problem?

5.2   THE INITIAL FEASIBLE SOLUTION

There are at least a few reasonable methods for finding a first feasible solution.   It is worthwhile to study more than one method because they illustrate a tradeoff between the sophistication and difficulty of the method and the quality of the results. The methods are all explained here with examples; the formal notation of Sec. 5.1 will be of little use in succeeding sections.

The following example has $m = 3$ origins and $n = 4$ destinations.   The supplies at the origins are 18, 5, and 7 units, respectively.   The requirements at the destina-

TABLE 5.1   Transportation Example

	D_1	D_2	D_3	D_4	Supply
O_1	21	36	43	20	18
O_2	60	30	50	43	5
O_3	18	10	48	72	7
Requirements	4	18	6	2	30

tions are 4, 18, 6, and 2 units, respectively. The problem is balanced because the total supply and total requirements are both 30 units. All this information and the unit shipment costs can be represented on one table, shown in Table 5.1.

Table 5.1 completely represents the whole transportation problem. For example, the unit shipment cost from origin 2 to destination 3 is $c_{23} = 50$. The problem of this section is to find a feasible solution: a set of shipments x_{ij} such that all supplies are used and all requirements are satisfied exactly.

Northwest Corner Rule

The first method to be considered is the easiest to use but the least likely to give a good solution. In fact this method does not even utilize the cost information, but only the supplies and requirements. The rule is

Step 1   Select the northwest (upper left-hand) corner cell for a shipment.

Step 2   Make as large a shipment as possible. This will completely exhaust either the supply at one origin or the requirement at one destination.

Step 3   Adjust the supply and requirement numbers to reflect the remaining supplies and requirements. If any remain, return to step 1.

This procedure can be carried out in one table if certain handy bookkeeping rules are adopted. Shipments can be indicated in a box within each cell. Supplies and requirements remaining can be entered to the right of the original numbers. Rows corresponding to origins can be lined out after their supply is exhausted. Columns corresponding to destinations can be lined out after their requirements are completely filled.

A transportation problem of size $m \times n$ requires $m + n - 1$ or fewer iterations of these three steps. For the first illustration it is best to show intermediate stages of the six iterations in separate tables. The first iteration of three steps produces the result

2⎺⎺⎺⎺⎺⎺⎹4	36	43	20	18,14
6⎸0	30	50	43	5
1⎸8	10	48	72	7
4⎸0	18	6	2	

The shipment of 4 units is indicated from O_1 to D_1. The supply remaining at O_1 is 14 units. The requirement at D_1 is filled and so column 1 is lined out. After the next iteration the table looks like

21 [4]	36 [14]	43	20	18,14,0
60	30	50	43	5
18	10	48	72	7
4,0	18,4	6	2	

The northwest corner at the start of this iteration was cell $(1,2)$. The largest shipment possible was 14 units. Now O_1's supply is exhausted and so row 1 is lined out. The new northwest cell in the next iteration is $(2,2)$. Four units is the largest shipment possible. This iteration plus the remaining iterations finally result in the following table:

21 [4]	36 [14]	43	20	18,14,0
60	30 [4]	50 [1]	43	5,1,0
18	10	48 [5]	72 [2]	7,2,0
4,0	18,4,0	6,5,0	2,0	

The sixth iteration results in the exhaustion of the supply at O_3 and the simultaneous satisfaction of the requirement at D_4. The six iterations have resulted in six shipments that as a whole constitute a feasible solution. The total cost of this solution is

$$4(21) + 14(36) + 4(30) + 50 + 5(48) + 2(72) = 1142$$

It would be quite surprising if this were the lowest possible cost because the method used to construct this feasible solution did not make use of the cost information.

Low-cost Cell Method

The low-cost cell method differs from the northwest corner rule in the way in which a cell is selected for a shipment. The new step 1 is

Step 1   Consider all cells that have not yet been lined out. Select the cell with the lowest unit cost.

The initial cell selected in this example is cell $(3,2)$, whose unit cost is 10. The successive selections have unit costs 20, 21, 30, 36, and 43. The final table shows

21 ⌐4	36 ⌐6	43 ⌐6	20 ⌐2	18,16,12,6,0
~~60~~	~~30~~ ⌐5	~~50~~	~~43~~	~~5,0~~
~~18~~	~~10~~ ⌐7	~~48~~	~~72~~	~~7,0~~
4,0	18,11,6,0	6,0	2,0	

This method also takes six iterations and gives a feasible solution with six shipments. Its total cost is

$$4(21) + 6(36) + 5(30) + 7(10) + 6(43) + 2(20) = 818$$

This solution has a much lower total cost. In fact it will be shown later that this particular solution is optimal. However, these methods of generating feasible solutions usually do not give optimal solutions nor are they able to recognize optimality when, by chance, it is present. Therefore the presence of an optimal solution goes undetected at this stage.

Penalty Method

The previous method can be improved by basing the cell selection not upon the cost but upon the difference in cost between the best cell and the next best. This measure often gives superior results because it looks farther ahead to the consequences of current selections. Again only step 1 is modified:

Step 1 Consider all rows and columns that have not yet been lined out. For each such row compute a row penalty as the difference between the lowest cost and next-lowest cost that are not lined out. Enter this at the right. Repeat for each column not yet lined out and enter the column penalty at the bottom. Select for a shipment the cell that avoids the largest penalty. Ties are to be broken arbitrarily.

21	36	43	20 ⌐2	18,16	1
60	30	50	43	5	13
18	10	48	72	7	8
4	18	6	2,0		
3	20	5	⟨23⟩		

The row penalties are 1, 13, 8; the column penalties are 3, 20, 5, 23. The largest penalty, 23, is avoided by selecting cell (1,4) for a shipment. The largest shipment possible is 2 units, and this eliminates D_4 from the problem. Its removal may alter the row penalties of the next iteration. The next iteration, performed on the same table, gives the following results:

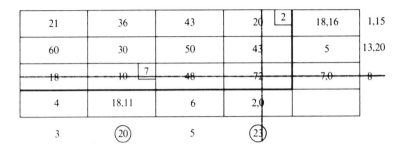

Step 1 has resulted in the calculated penalties of 15, 20, and 8 for rows 1, 2, and 3. Column penalties are 3, 20, 5 for columns 1, 2, 3. Column 4 is out. Of these penalties either one of the 20s could be selected. For this illustration the column penalty has been selected. A later exercise requests the alternative selection. The penalty selected is avoided by a shipment of 7 units from O_3 to D_2. Now O_3's supply is exhausted and row 3 is lined out.

After completion of all remaining iterations the resulting table is

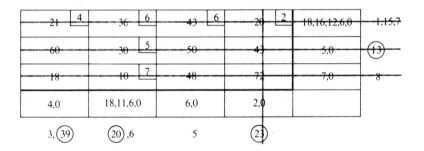

This solution is the same feasible solution previously obtained by the method of low-cost cells. The penalty method frequently produces the optimal solution. However, the important point is that it does not always do so and that it gives no way of knowing whether its result is optimal or not.

EXERCISES

1. Show that the penalty method does not always give the best solution by returning to the example at the point where either the row penalty of 20 or the col-

umn penalty of 20 could be selected. Select the row penalty this time and complete the iterations. Compare the resulting solution with the alternative one found in the text.

2. Given a transportation problem having unit profits (profit matrix) instead of unit costs:

Destination

		D_1	D_2	Supply
	O_1	10	30	25
Origins	O_2	12	15	5
	Requirements	12	18	30

Show how to find a feasible solution by each of the three methods shown.

5.3 CONCEPT OF A BASIC FEASIBLE SOLUTION (BFS)

A basic feasible solution for a transportation problem of size $m \times n$ is a feasible solution having $n + m - 1$ or fewer nonzero shipment cells. A basic feasible solution having fewer than $n + m - 1$ nonzero shipments is called a *degenerate basic feasible solution.* It is easily seen that the methods studied in Sec. 5.2 produce only basic feasible solutions. Step 2, the same in all three methods, requires each shipment to be as large as possible. Therefore every iteration resulted in the elimination of at least one origin or one destination until the last iteration, which always eliminated one of each kind. Therefore n destinations and m origins would be eliminated in at most $n + m - 1$ steps. Each step produced one shipment and therefore the number of shipments resulting would always be $n + m - 1$ or fewer.

The reason why the concept of a basic feasible solution is important is not easily explained at this stage. However, linear programming theory proves that there is an optimum solution among the set of all basic feasible solutions. Therefore, although the set of all feasible solutions is much larger than the set of all basic feasible solutions, it is necessary to search for an optimum only within this smaller (finite) set of basic feasible solutions. This powerful fact has been built into the algorithm of the following sections. An intuitive reason for the superiority of basic feasible solutions can be seen from the low-cost cell method. Low-cost cells are a scarce resource. Each step uses one and leaves a set of unused cells having higher unit costs. Therefore each step should use its low-cost cell as intensively as possible, and this implies making as large a shipment as possible.

5.4   TEST FOR OPTIMALITY OF A BFS

The test for optimality must begin with a basic feasible solution. It will compare the BFS with a subset of all other basic feasible solutions. That subset has the property that if it does not contain a better solution then the current BFS is the optimum BFS. The method determines a set of relative costs, denoted Δ_{ij}, having two properties:

1. The current BFS has zero relative cost because the cost system is to be relative to the current BFS.

2. Any other BFS that differs from the current BFS by having a shipment in cell (i,j) has a positive relative cost if it is a higher-cost solution and a negative relative cost if it is a lower-cost solution. (A zero relative cost indicates the existence of an equally costly solution.)

A more exact definition of Δ_{ij} is that it is the relative cost of that BFS obtained from modifying the current BFS to include a shipment in cell (i,j) and making all balancing adjustments required such that the new solution is also a BFS. It is not easy to characterize more sharply the set of BFSs being compared to the current solution or to see why the failure of this set to contain a better solution implies optimality of the current solution. For the purpose of this text it suffices to know that the test for optimality yields

1. A condition by which to recognize optimality when it is present: All Δ_{ij} are positive or zero in a cost-minimization problem or all negative or zero in a profit-maximization problem.

2. A method to generate a better BFS when the current BFS is not optimal.

It is also known from the Lagrange multiplier method that the relative costs have the analytic form

$$\Delta_{ij} = c_{ij} - u_i - v_j$$

where c_{ij} is the unit cost of cell (i,j) and the u_i's are undetermined quantities associated with rows of the table and the v_j's are undetermined quantities associated with columns of the table.

The method determines the Δ_{ij} values by determining first the u_i and v_j values. There are m origins and thus m u_i values to be determined. There are n destinations and thus n v_j values to be determined. Hence there is a total of $n + m$ unknowns. The conditions that determine these unknowns are based upon the requirement that $\Delta_{ij} = 0$ for all cells of the current solution. Assuming that the current solution is not degenerate, there are $n + m - 1$ nonzero shipment cells whose $\Delta_{ij} = 0$. For those cells the $n + m - 1$ equations

$$c_{ij} = u_i + v_j$$

must hold. These conditions are almost enough, but not quite; $n + m - 1$ equations cannot fully determine the values of $n + m$ unknowns. Fortunately, however, it turns out that any one of the $n + m$ unknowns can be set arbitrarily without changing the Δ_{ij} that will result. This is because one of the $n + m$ constraints in a balanced problem is redundant. This fact will be demonstrated as an exercise. A convenient convention to be used here is to set $u_1 = 0$ at the outset. This leaves $n + m - 1$ unknowns to be determined by the same number of equations.

The method of determining the relative costs will now be illustrated by using the BFS already found by the low-cost cell method in Sec. 5.3. The organization of the calculations shown first in Table 5.2 is *not* the most efficient one but is useful at first to explain the process. It begins by listing the cells with nonzero shipments and their unit costs. The equation follows. In the next column the order of steps is given; the last column gives the results of the step. The reader can reconstruct the solution process by following the step numbers. The order of steps is somewhat arbitrary, but the outcome is not.

TABLE 5.2   Organization of Calculations

Cell	c_{ij}	$c_{ij} = u_i + v_j$	Step	Result
(1, 1)	21	$21 = u_1 + v_1$	1	Set $u_1 = 0$, then $v_1 = 21$
(1,2)	36	$36 = u_1 + v_2$	2	$v_2 = 36$
(2,2)	30	$30 = u_2 + v_2$	3	$u_2 = -6$
(3,2)	10	$10 = u_3 + v_2$	4	$u_3 = -26$
(1,3)	43	$43 = u_1 + v_3$	5	$v_3 = 43$
(1,4)	20	$20 = u_1 + v_4$	6	$v_4 = 20$

Next construct a table to display the results in terms of Δ_{ij} (Table 5.3). The

TABLE 5.3   Table of Equations: $c_{ij} - u_i - v_j = \Delta_{ij}$

$21 - 0 - 21 = 0$	$36 - 0 - 36 = 0$	$43 - 0 - 43 = 0$	$20 - 0 - 20 = 0$	$u_1 = 0$
$60 + 6 - 21 = 45$	$30 + 6 - 36 = 0$	$50 + 6 - 43 = 13$	$43 + 6 - 20 = 29$	$u_2 = -6$
$18 + 26 - 21 = 23$	$10 + 26 - 36 = 0$	$48 + 26 - 43 = 31$	$72 + 26 - 20 = 78$	$u_3 = -26$
$v_1 = 21$	$v_2 = 36$	$v_3 = 43$	$v_4 = 20$	

results show that all Δ_{ij} are zero for the nonzero cells of the current solution, as required, and furthermore that all other Δ_{ij} values are positive. Therefore all other solutions have higher total costs. The additional fact that no zero shipment cell has a zero value of Δ_{ij} implies that this solution is the *unique* optimum; no other solution is as good.

The work involved in this test of optimality of a BFS can be reduced somewhat by efficient organization of the steps. In fact it can all fit into one table. This is accomplished by making each cell large enough to fit three numbers. The first is the original c_{ij}. To its right is placed the result of the first subtraction: $c_{ij} - u_i$ or $c_{ij} - v_j$, whichever happens to be performed first. A cell having only one subtraction performed can be conveniently termed a "half-done" cell. After the second subtraction the cell will contain $c_{ij} - u_i - v_j$, which is the completed relative cost of that cell. The u_i's and the v_j's will be placed in the outside row and column.

The method begins with a BFS in a table showing the shipments in boxes as before. The first step is to set $u_1 = 0$. Then $u_1 = 0$ is subtracted from the c_{ij}'s in each cell of that row. Subtraction by zero gives the c_{ij}'s again but they are written anyway because showing the result has place-keeping value. The table at this stage looks like

21,21 ⌐4	36,36 ⌐6	43,43 ⌐6	20,20 ⌐2	$u_1 = 0$
60	30 ⌐5	50	43	
18	10 ⌐7	48	72	

Observe that at least one nonzero shipment cell is half-done. The process continues from one of these. The fact that there are four of them means that it could continue from any one of the four. Select cell (1,1) for continuation. The important reasoning is this: The third entry in cell (1,1) results from subtraction of v_1 from the second entry. Since (1,1) is a shipment cell in the current solution, its third entry must be zero. Therefore $v_1 = 21$ is determined. This entry is made and 21 is subtracted from all cells in this column. The result is

21,21,0 ⌐4	36,36 ⌐6	43,43 ⌐6	20,20 ⌐2	$u_1 = 0$
60,39	30 ⌐5	50	43	
18,−3	10 ⌐7	48	72	
$v_1 = 21$				

Now three half-done shipment cells remain. The next step could utilize any one of them. If cell (1,2) is selected, it results in the determination that $v_2 = 36$:

21,21,0 [4]	36,36,0 [6]	43,43 [6]	20,20 [2]	$u_1 = 0$
60,39	30, -6 [5]	50	43	
18, -3	10, -26 [7]	48	72	
$v_1 = 21$	$v_2 = 36$			

Now four half-done shipment cells remain: (1,3), (1,4), (2,2), and (3,2). Any one of them can be selected and eventually all will be used. Cell (1,3) determines that $v_3 = 43$. Similarly cell (2,2) determines that $u_2 = -6$. Cell (3,2) determines that $u_3 = -26$. Cell (1,4) determines that $v_4 = 20$.

The final resulting table is now shown. It is the only table that is needed because it contains all the work and results. The ones previously shown served only to illustrate intermediate stages of work.

21,21,0 [4]	36,36,0 [6]	43,43,0 [6]	20,20,0 [2]	$u_1 = 0$
60,39,45	30, -6,0 [5]	50,7,13	43,49,29	$u_2 = -6$
18, -3,23	10, -26,0 [7]	48,5,31	72,98,78	$u_3 = -26$
$v_1 = 21$	$v_2 = 36$	$v_3 = 43$	$v_4 = 20$	

The method has determined a Δ_{ij} value for every cell. It is easily seen that this method of organizing the work is more efficient and gives the same results. The method shown here arrives at a complete determination of relative costs unless the current BFS is degenerate. When the current BFS is degenerate, the method gets stuck prematurely, with no half-done cells available from which to continue. A later section shows how this condition is easily surmounted.

One more illustration of the test for optimality will be given. The evaluation of the BFS obtained by the northwest corner method results in the following table:

21,21,0 [4]	36,36,0 [14]	43,43, -13	20,20, -60	$u_1 = 0$
60,39,45	30, -6,0 [4]	50,56,0 [1]	43,49, -31	$u_2 = -6$
18, -3,5	10, -26, -18	48, -8,0 [5]	72,80,0 [2]	$u_3 = -8$
$v_1 = 21$	$v_2 = 36$	$v_3 = 56$	$v_4 = 80$	

In this case the current BFS is clearly not optimal. It could be improved by \$60/unit from O_1 to D_4, by \$31/unit from O_2 to D_4, by \$18/unit from O_3 to D_2, or by \$13/unit from O_1 to D_3, after all balancing adjustments are made. Thus when the test for optimality confirms the existence of a solution superior to the current BFS, it also shows how to find one.

EXERCISE

Pick the first illustration of the test method and select $u_1 = 2$ instead of $u_1 = 0$. Show that the method generates the same values of all Δ_{ij}.

5.5 CONSTRUCTION OF A BETTER SOLUTION

Continuing with the last illustration, it is clear that the current BFS could be modified in several different ways. It seems reasonable to follow the rule that the one to select is the one indicating the highest unit gain. In this case a shipment of 1 unit from O_1 to D_4 would result in a net gain of \$60. This is the highest unit gain. The total gain (unit gain times number of units), although it is more relevant, is not known in time to be useful.

The difficulty in construction of the new BFS lies ahead. Given that cell (1,4) will be used, it is necessary to find those balancing adjustments that will make the new solution both basic and feasible. Consider the following table:

21 [4]	36 $-\theta$ [14]	43	20 θ
60	30 $+\theta$ [4]	50 $-\theta$ [1]	43
18	10	48 $+\theta$ [5]	72 $-\theta$ [2]

Let θ stand for a positive undetermined increase in the shipment. Cell (1,4) is to be increased by this amount. Therefore some shipment in column 4 must be reduced by the same amount so that D_4 total receipt remains constant. It must be cell (3,4). Once that is done, the last row is now unbalanced. Therefore cell (3,3) must have an increase. Then column 3 becomes unbalanced. Cell (2,3) must have a decrease. Then row 2 becomes unbalanced. This is corrected by an increase in cell (2,2). This in turn requires a decrease in cell (1,2). Finally this last adjustment balances both column 2 and row 1 simultaneously. Thus a set of balancing adjustments has been found, as shown in the table.

In general the set of balancing adjustments forms a closed path with at least four corners but often more. The important rule implicitly followed in the example is that all changes after the first should be made on cells already having a nonzero shipment. Certainly this is obvious for changes that are decreases. A zero shipment cannot be further reduced. However, for changes that are increases in shipment size one might be tempted to increase a zero shipment. But this is not allowed because the method must yield a *basic* feasible solution. Arbitrarily increasing the number of nonzero shipments usually results in a nonbasic solution.

The path can now be tested. The unit cost of the path is found from the individual cost changes. These are read off following along the path:

$$+20 - 72 + 48 - 50 + 30 - 36 = -60$$

This check indicates that the path found is correct and shows more fundamentally how the savings in cost are obtained.

Finally the size of θ can be determined. The rule is simply to make it as large as possible because every unit saves \$60. An examination of the current shipments along the path shows that this value is $\theta = 1$. Any larger shipment would imply a negative net shipment in cell (2,3) and this is not possible. This work can be done on the table of the last test for optimality rather than drawing the preceding table.

Finally a new table is constructed showing this new solution. The total cost of the new solution can be found directly from the total cost of the old solution, which was 1142. The new solution has total cost $1142 - 60 = 1082$.

21 ⌐4	36 ⌐13	43	20 ⌐1
60	30 ⌐5	50	43
18	10	48 ⌐6	72 ⌐1

The method for generating a new BFS does in fact always generate a basic solution because although it starts by creating one new nonzero shipment cell, the fact that θ is made as large as possible implies that at least one old nonzero shipment cell will become a zero shipment cell in the new solution. Therefore there cannot be an increase in the number of nonzero shipment cells.

The next table shows the test for optimality of the new solution:

21,21,0 ⌐4	36,36,0 ⌐13	43,43,47	20,20,0 ⌐1	$u_1 = 0$
60,39,45	30, −6,0 ⌐5	50,56,60	43,49,29	$u_2 = -6$
18, −3, −55	10, −26, −78	48, −4,0 ⌐6	72,52,0 ⌐1	$u_3 = 52$
$v_1 = 21$	$v_2 = 36$	$v_3 = -4$	$v_4 = 20$	

This table implies that the new solution was not optimal either. A net savings of $78/unit can still be made by using cell (3,2) and making all balancing adjustments.

EXERCISE

Starting with the results of the last table, show that the path of balancing adjustments is increase (3,2), decrease (1,2), increase (1,4), and finally decrease (3,4). Show that this has a cost of 1004. Test the optimality of this new solution. Show that it is not optimal but that the next one is optimal.

5.6 DEGENERACY

A degenerate BFS is one with fewer than $n + m - 1$ nonzero shipment cells. It may be deficient by one or by more than one nonzero shipment cell. A degenerate problem is one with one or more degenerate solutions. It is important to realize that a degenerate problem may not appear immediately to be degenerate, if a degenerate solution happens not to be discovered immediately.

The following problem is degenerate. A degenerate solution has been found immediately by the northwest corner method:

23 $\boxed{2}$	42	33	2
17 $\boxed{2}$	25 $\boxed{1}$	45	3
3	12	8 $\boxed{5}$	5
4	1	5	10

The problem has $n + m - 1 = 3 + 3 - 1 = 5$. However, this BFS has only four nonzero shipment cells. It is degenerate. If, instead of the northwest corner method, the low-cost cell method had been used to find the initial BFS, the result would not have been degenerate:

23	42	33 $\boxed{2}$	2
17	25 $\boxed{1}$	45 $\boxed{2}$	3
3 $\boxed{4}$	12	8 $\boxed{1}$	5
4	1	5	10

Although this solution has five nonzero shipment cells and so is not degenerate, future solutions generated on the way to optimality may be degenerate.

The important point about degeneracy is that the test for optimality always gets stuck when trying to test a degenerate solution. It runs out of half-done cells prematurely. The following table illustrates the point at which it gets stuck for the degenerate BFS found by the northwest corner method:

23,23,0 ⌐2	42,42,11	33,33	$u_1 = 0$
17,−6,0 ⌐2	25,31,0 ⌐1	45,51	$u_2 = -6$
3,−20	12,−19	8 ⌐5	
$v_1 = 23$	$v_2 = 31$		

The method is stuck because there are no half-done shipment cells present. There are four half-done cells but they have no shipments. The solution to this dilemma is almost obvious: Treat one of these half-done cells as if it had a shipment. First place an ϵ in the cell temporarily to mark the cell selected. The notation ϵ conventionally represents a number small enough to be considered zero for some purposes.

There is one more important rule to observe: Because not all choices among the half-done cells are equally desirable, select the one whose second number ($c_{ij} - u_i$ or $c_{ij} - v_j$, whichever it is) is smallest. Here the choice is among cells having second numbers of -20, -19, $+33$, and $+51$. The cell with second number -20 is selected. The method then resumes and gives the final table:

23,23,0 ⌐2	42,42,11	33,33,5	$u_1 = 0$
17,−6,0 ⌐2	25,31,0 ⌐1	45,51,23	$u_2 = -6$
3,−20,0 ⌐6	12,−19,1	8,28,0 ⌐5	$u_3 = -20$
$v_1 = 23$	$v_2 = 31$	$v_3 = 28$	

All relative costs are nonnegative, and consequently this solution is optimal. (There is no reason why a degenerate solution cannot be the optimal solution.)

The rules for coping with degeneracy, no matter how large the deficiency, are as follows:

1. Proceed normally until the method gets stuck for lack of a half-done shipment cell.

2. Select among the half-done zero shipment cells that which has the lowest second number.

3. Enter an ϵ and then resume the normal procedure until it terminates or until it again gets stuck.

EXERCISES

1. Referring to the point in the example where the normal procedure got stuck, select cell (2,3), whose second cost is 51, for placement of the ϵ. Show that the next complete iteration results only in shifting the ϵ from cell (2,3) to cell (1,3).

2. Solve the assignment problem of Chap. 4:

5	4	6
9	3	7
3	2	1

Use the method for the transportation problem. How many deficiencies does it have?

5.7 MODIFICATIONS

Profit Maximization

A transportation problem formulated in terms of unit profits instead of unit costs can be solved similarly. Only one rule need be reversed: A relative cost is now interpreted as a relative profit. Therefore positive Δ_{ij}'s indicate that there remains opportunity for profit. The current solution is optimal only if all relative profits are negative or zero. The rules for finding an initial BFS can also be modified easily. The low-cost cell rule is replaced by the high-profit cell rule. The penalty in the penalty method becomes the difference between the highest unit profit and the next highest.

Unbalanced Problem

The problem is unbalanced if the total supply is not equal to the total requirement. An unbalanced problem is easily balanced by addition of a "slack" or "dummy" row or column having just enough supply or requirement to balance the problem. The unit costs or profits to be entered in the matrix are determined by the context of the problem.

5.8   SHIPMENT THROUGH TIME

Although the term "transportation problem" encourages the image of physical movement, the problem structure is often useful for production scheduling problems. Origins may be production periods and destinations may be sales periods. Thus shipment from O_i to D_{i+1} may represent production one period ahead of time being stored in inventory for sales in the next period. Storage can be viewed as a shipment through time. The following example illustrates this use of the transportation structure.

A subcontractor has made arrangements to supply another company with 13 assemblies in January, 15 assemblies in February, and 27 assemblies in March. They start in January with no inventory. Using an 8-hour shift the contractor can produce only 16 assemblies each month. By working the regular shift for 2 hours overtime, an additional four assemblies can be made, each with an overtime penalty of $20. Assemblies can be stored at a cost of $8/unit/month. The subcontractor wishes to determine the amount to be produced in each of the three months so as to minimize total cost.

The origins here are the January, February, and March regular shifts and the corresponding overtime shifts: six origins with a total capacity (supply) of 60 units. The destinations are the delivery commitments of January, February, and March: a total requirement of 55 units. Thus there is an excess capacity of 5 units. To balance the problem it is necessary to include a dummy column called "unused capacity." The costs of interest are of two types: the cost of overtime and the cost of storage. The objective is to find a production schedule that minimizes the total of these costs. Certain shipments are not possible. For example, February production cannot be used toward January's requirement because it will not be ready on time (unless there were some way to borrow against future production). Such shipments are assigned a high cost (100) to prevent their appearance in the solution. The complete formulation as a balanced transportation problem is given in Table 5.4.

TABLE 5.4   Formulation of the Scheduling Problem

Shift	Jan. Delivery	Feb. Delivery	Mar. Delivery	Unused Capacity	Supply Capacity
Jan. regular	0	8	16	0	16
Jan. overtime	20	28	36	0	4
Feb. regular	100	0	8	0	16
Feb. overtime	100	20	28	0	4
Mar. regular	100	100	0	0	16
Mar. overtime	100	100	20	0	4
Commitment	13	15	27	5	60

An optimal solution (not unique) and its test for optimality are given next in Table 5.5. The total cost of overtime plus storage is $220.

TABLE 5.5   Optimal Solution of the Scheduling Problem

0, 0, 0 $\quad$ 13	8, 8, 0	16, 16, 0 $\quad$ 3	0, 0, 12	$u_1 = 0$
20, 20, 8	28, 20, 8	36, 20, 8	0, 12, 0 $\quad$ 4	$u_2 = 12$
100, 100, 108	0, 8, 0 $\quad$ 15	8, −8, 0 $\quad$ 1	0, 8, 20	$u_3 = -8$
100, 100, 88	20, 8, 0	28, 12, 0 $\quad$ 3	0, −12, 0 $\quad$ 1	$u_4 = 12$
100, 100, 116	100, 116, 108	0, −16, 0 $\quad$ 16	0, 16, 28	$u_5 = -16$
100, 100, 96	100, 96, 88	20, 4, 0 $\quad$ 4	0, −4, 8	$u_6 = 4$
$v_1 = 0$	$v_2 = 8$	$v_3 = 16$	$v_4 = 12$	

5.9   THE TRANSPORTATION PROBLEM BY LAGRANGE MULTIPLIER

The Lagrange multiplier method can be used to explain the method of solution of the transportation problem. The general transportation problem is

Subject to
$$\text{Minimize} \quad \sum_{j=1}^{n} \sum_{i=1}^{m} c_{ij} x_{ij}$$

$$\sum_{j=1}^{n} x_{ij} = a_i \qquad i = 1, 2, \ldots, m$$

$$\sum_{i=1}^{m} x_{ij} = b_j \qquad j = 1, 2, \ldots, n$$

and
$$\text{all } x_{ij} \geq 0$$

This problem has $n + m$ equality constraints and $n \times m$ inequality (nonnegativity) constraints. The Lagrangian formulation must have one Lagrange multiplier for each of these constraints. These will now be defined.

Let the Lagrange multiplier u_i be associated with the equality constraint upon the amount a_i of supply at origin O_i. The Lagrangian will have m such terms, one for each i.

$$u_i \left[\sum_{j=1}^{n} x_{ij} - a_i \right] \qquad \text{for } i = 1, 2, \ldots, m$$

Let the Lagrange multiplier v_j be associated with the equality constraint upon the requirement b_j at destination D_j. The Lagrangian will have n such terms, one for each j.

$$v_j \left[\sum_{i=1}^{m} x_{ij} - b_j \right] \qquad \text{for } j = 1, 2, \ldots, n$$

Let the Lagrange multiplier Δ_{ij} be associated with the inequality constraint $x_{ij} \geq 0$. The Lagrangian will have $n \times m$ such terms.

$$\Delta_{ij}(x_{ij} - 0) \qquad \text{one for each } i, j$$

The Lagrangian function, if all constraints are required to hold as equalities, is

$$F = \sum_{j=1}^{n} \sum_{i=1}^{m} c_{ij} x_{ij} - \sum_{i=1}^{m} u_i \left[\sum_{j=1}^{n} x_{ij} - a_i \right] - \sum_{j=1}^{n} v_j \left[\sum_{i=1}^{m} x_{ij} - b_j \right] - \sum_{j=1}^{n} \sum_{i=1}^{m} \Delta_{ij} x_{ij}$$

The derivative of F with respect to x_{ij} is

$$\frac{\partial F}{\partial x_{ij}} = c_{ij} - u_i - v_j - \Delta_{ij} = 0$$

This gives $n \times m$ derivative equations that explain the relationship stated earlier between u_i, v_j, and Δ_{ij}.

$$\Delta_{ij} = c_{ij} - u_i - v_j$$

It is clear that not all nonnegativity constraints can hold as equalities; not all shipments can be zero. For each x_{ij} allowed to be positive, the corresponding Δ_{ij} will be set to zero. Therefore

$$c_{ij} - u_i - v_j = 0 \qquad \text{for each } i, j \text{ pair such that } x_{ij} \geq 0$$

Furthermore, for each zero shipment cell $\Delta_{ij} > 0$.

The Lagrange multiplier method does not tell directly how many nonzero shipment cells there will be in the optimal solution, nor does it tell how to search out all possibilities efficiently. The theory of linear programming, which is presented in the next chapter, shows that an optimal solution can be found among the set of solutions having $n + m - 1$ or fewer nonzero shipment cells.

A practical implication of this section follows from the known interpretation of the Lagrange multipliers. If the supply at origin O_i is increased and simultaneously the demand at destination D_j is increased by the same amount, the rate of increase of E^* is given by

$$u_i + v_j$$

This can give useful information about the value of relocating the supplies and requirements, when such changes are possible.

Notice that in a cost-minimization problem the optimal solution has all $\Delta_{ij} \geq 0$. Therefore all

$$c_{ij} - [u_i + v_j] \geq 0$$

or

$$u_i + v_j \leq c_{ij} \qquad \text{for all } i, j \text{ pairs}$$

An increase of 1 unit in both a_i and b_j usually increases the total cost E. However, the smallest increase is obtained from the i, j pair having the smallest value of

$$u_i + v_j = c_{ij} - \Delta_{ij}$$

Recall the problem of Sec. 5.2. The optimal solution and the test for optimality were shown in Sec. 5.4. Table 5.6 shows the values of $c_{ij} - \Delta_{ij}$ obtained from Sec. 5.4. It can be seen that most of these values are positive, indicating that an increased total cost would result from a simultaneous increase of a_i and b_j. However, two are negative. For example, an increase of 1 unit of supply at origin 3 and an increase of 1 unit of requirement at destination 4 would actually reduce the total cost of the optimal solution by 6 units of cost.

TABLE 5.6   Values of $c_{ij} - \Delta_{ij}$

Origin	Destination			
	1	2	3	4
1	21	36	43	20
2	15	30	37	14
3	−5	10	17	−6

EXERCISE

Modify the problem of Sec. 5.2 by changing a_3 from 7 to 8 and b_4 from 2 to 3. Solve the new problem and show that the total cost of the optimal solution is 812. Compare this with the optimal solution to the original problem and explain why shipping more units can actually cost less.

PROBLEMS

1. A certain company has three plants, P1, P2, P3; five warehouses, W1, W2, W3, W4, W5; and the following table of per unit transportation costs in dollars. The requirements and capacity figures represent thousands of product units.

Plant	W1	W2	W3	W4	W5	Maximum Capacity at Plant
P1	.05	.07	.10	.15	.15	5
P2	.08	.06	.09	.12	.14	10
P3	.10	.09	.08	.10	.15	12.5
Requirements	3	3	10	5	4	

The company decides to make the shipments

Plant	W1	W2	W3	W4	W5
P1	2.5	0	0	0	0
P2	.5	3	2.5	0	4
P3	0	0	7.5	5	0

(a) Formulate this problem as a balanced transportation problem. Evaluate this shipment policy to determine whether it is optimal. Show your formulation.

(b) The production costs at each of the three plants are linear; that is, production at the plant, plus a variable cost per unit produced. If x_1, x_2, and x_3 represent total production in units at plants P1, P2, and P3, respectively, the total costs are

$$\text{Total cost at P1} = \$5000 + (1.00)x_1$$
$$\text{Total cost at P2} = \$10,000 + (.90)x_2$$
$$\text{Total cost at P3} = \$12,000 + (.80)x_3$$

How do these production costs alter the problem? Formulate the problem to minimize the sum of the production plus shipment costs. Is the current shipment policy optimal given this additional information?

2. The Airline Product Corporation has a plant made up of five separate buildings scattered around the outskirts of a city. They ship from these buildings to the one railroad freight dock in the center of the city. Normally the company's own trucks carry all the material needed. However, because of a recent strike next month's shipments will be very heavy. They have collected bids from three trucking firms for shipments to the railroad dock. The prices per hundred parts from the various buildings are as follows:

Building	Own Trucks	Firm 1	Firm 2	Firm 3	Building Hauling Requirements
A	10	8	2	7	500
B	6	9	5	1	700
C	4	3	7	5	200
D	7	2	4	6	900
E	5	9	8	4	700
Hauling Capacity	800	1000	700	500	

Find a feasible schedule of shipments to the railroad dock. Evaluate the total cost of this solution and determine whether it is an optimum solution. If it is not optimum, find a better solution and its total cost.

3. A corporation has decided to produce three new products. Five branch plants now have excess production capacity. The unit manufacturing cost of the first product would be $26, $28, $24, $30, and $27 in plants 1, 2, 3, 4, and 5, respectively. The unit manufacturing cost of the second product would be $29, $33, $28, $32, and $31 in plants 1, 2, 3, 4, and 5, respectively. The unit manufacturing cost of the third product would be $40, $43, and $39 in plants 1, 2, and 3, respectively; plants 4 and 5 do not have the capability for producing this product. Sales forecasts indicate that 300, 200, and 400 units of products 1, 2, and 3, respectively, should be produced per day. Plants 1, 2, 3, 4, and 5 have the capacity to produce 200, 400, 200, 500, and 300 units daily, respectively, regardless of the product or combination of products involved. Assume that any plant having the capability and capacity can produce any combination of the products in any quantity. Formulate and solve the problem of determining how management should allocate the new products to the plants in order to minimize total manufacturing cost.

4. A company has signed contracts to deliver 27 units of their product in June, 15 units in July, and 13 units in August. They begin June with no inventory. They can produce 15 units/month on regular time shifts at a unit cost of $100 and 5 additional units per month on an optional overtime shift at a unit cost of $120. They can store units at $8/unit/month. They also have the option to "borrow" units from a similar producer at a cost of $10/unit/month until they can repay him in units from their own production. This allows them to deliver units ahead of the time they produce them. They wish to minimize total cost.

   (a) Formulate this problem and give a feasible solution and also its cost.
   (b) Test for optimality of your first solution. If it is not optimal, use the algorithm to find a better solution. Compute the improvement in total cost.

5. Walter Roth is a broker for five prospective insureds. The following table summarizes the information available about each client:

Insureds	Age	Policy Desired	Amount of Coverage ($1000)
1	40	Whole life (WL)	10
2	55	20-year endowment (20 end)	5
3	30	20-year term (20-T)	40
4	35	Life paid up at 65 (LP-65)	25
5	40	Whole life	5

Mr. Roth desires to place the insureds in such a manner as to minimize the total premiums paid. He can place the insurance for each client in any of three companies, who quote the following premiums on the various contracts (at the relevant ages). Premiums are stated in dollars per thousand.

Insurer	WL	20 End	20-T	LP-65
A	20	65	8	18
B	25	60	10	14
C	24	73	12	15

Additionally each company has stated its total insuring capacity:

Insurer	Total Insurance Capacity (All Lines Combined)
A	$25,000
B	32,000
C	28,000

Mr. Roth is allowed to place the business of any insured in more than one company.

(a) Formulate and find a feasible solution to his problem. What is his total premium?

(b) Test the optimality of your first solution. If it is not optimal, find a better solution and show how much better it is.

6. A manufacturer has a fixed cycle of demand with a period of 1 week. The demand pattern (in units) is

M	T	W	Th	F
9	17	2	0	19

The company is set up to produce 10 units/day but does not work on Wednesday or on the weekend. Production is available on the same day and stored at most three more days at a cost of $4/unit/day (including Saturday and Sunday). Production cost is $5/unit. Unsatisfied demands result in a penalty of $3/unit on Monday only. Formulate this problem to minimize production and storage costs and penalty. Find an initial basic feasible solution and test its optimality. Find a better solution if possible.

7. The Number 2 Rent-a-Car Agency has eight outlets in a large metropolitan area. They have found from experience that it is best to begin each day with all their cars evenly distributed among the eight outlets, assuming that all 80 cars are present. Suppose that at the end of a particular day the number of cars at the outlets is as follows:

A	B	C	D	E	F	G	H
1	11	3	15	20	5	7	18

They wish to transport the cars from the "surplus" outlets to the "deficit" outlets to attain an even distribution. The best set of movements is that which has the smallest total distance traveled. The distances (in miles) between the outlets are given by the following table:

	A	B	C	D	E	F	G	H
A	$\cdots$	13	3	11	12	5	8	7
B		$\cdots$	11	11	25	16	23	9
C			$\cdots$	19	11	16	7	15
D				$\cdots$	31	26	16	3
E					$\cdots$	4	9	12
F						$\cdots$	8	9
G							$\cdots$	14

(a) Formulate this problem and find a feasible solution and its total distance.
(b) Test whether your current feasible solution is the best. If it is not, find a better solution and the amount by which it is better.

8. The planned sales of Alpha Manufacturing Company during the coming year are less than the company's capacity. The bulk of the excess capacity is assigned to

plant 1, leaving plants 2 and 3 to operate at nearly full capacity. As a result the cost of production at plant 1 exceeds that at the other two plants. The plant manager of plant 1 reasons that a more equitable distribution of excess capacity would reduce the total cost and hence increase the profit. Alpha produces a small component for an industrial product and distributes it to five wholesalers at a fixed delivered price of $3/unit. Sales forecasts indicate that monthly deliveries to the five wholesalers during the next year will be as follows:

Wholesaler	Monthly Deliveries
1	4000
2	4000
3	7000
4	12,000
5	8000
	Total 35,000

The three plant characteristics are as follows (the fixed costs of production shown below are incurred in any month for which the level of production is greater than zero):

Plant	Production Capacity	Fixed Monthly Cost of Production, $	Direct Cost of Production per Unit, $
1	10,000	10,000	1.40
2	15,000	14,000	1.20
3	18,000	15,000	1.00

Transportation costs per unit from the plant to the wholesaler are as shown below:

Plant/Wholesaler	1	2	3	4	5
1	.20	.15	.18	.17	.05
2	.15	.10	.07	.15	.25
3	.10	.25	.20	.05	.07

(a) Find a feasible solution having all excess capacity assigned to plant 1. Evaluate it.

(b) Find a solution by the penalty method and evaluate it.

(c) Test its optimality and improve it if possible.

Chapter 6

LINEAR PROGRAMMING

Considering all analytic methods that have ever been applied to business problems, linear programming is probably the most economically valuable method. Its widespread use was certainly stimulated by the parallel development of the digital computer, which made the solution of large-scale linear programming problems possible. The simplex method, an efficient algorithm for solving linear programming problems, was developed by Dantzig in 1947. This development, recent from the perspective of mathematics, has contributed much to the general belief in the practicality of analytic methods for business and operational problems.

The essential feature of linear programming problems is that of linear inequality constraints. The concept of a constraint has been found to be extremely useful in representing complex problems. In addition to linear inequality constraints, the other characteristic of linear programming problems is the linearity of the objective function as a function of the decision variables. This implies that the derivatives of the objective function are of limited use in the characterization of the optimal solution. The student will observe that calculus is not used in solving these problems. The nature of the solution process is again an algorithm, similar in concept to those of Chaps. 4 and 5. The relationship between the two linear programming chapters and Chap. 3, where constraints were first introduced, is important on a conceptual level. There both the iso-E lines and the constraint lines could be curves (nonlinear) in the decision-variable space. The question to be answered in this chapter is "What useful implications can be drawn when all those curves must be straight lines?" It is the efficient exploitation of these implications that has made linear programming the powerful tool it is today.

6.1 PROBLEM STATEMENT

The general mathematical structure of linear programming problems is as follows:

$$\text{Max } E = c_1 x_1 + c_2 x_2 + \cdots + c_n x_n$$

where $x_1, x_2, \ldots, x_n$ are n decision variables and $c_1, c_2, \ldots, c_n$ are n parameters of the problem. The objective function E is a linear function of each variable. The space of possible solutions is limited by the following constraints:

$$a_{11}x_1 + a_{12}x_2 + \cdots + a_{1n}x_n \leq b_1$$
$$a_{21}x_1 + a_{22}x_2 + \cdots + a_{2n}x_n \leq b_2$$
$$\vdots$$
$$a_{m1}x_1 + a_{m2}x_2 + \cdots + a_{mn}x_n \leq b_m$$

The coefficients a_{ij} and the constraint quantities b_i are parameters of the problem. These m constraints are linear functions of all decision variables. In addition the decision variables are constrained to be nonnegative: $x_j \geq 0$ for $j = 1, 2, \ldots, n$.

A more compact representation, utilizing summation signs, is

$$\text{Max} \sum_{j=1}^{n} c_j x_j$$

subject to

$$\sum_{j=1}^{n} a_{ij}x_j \leq b_i \qquad \text{for } i = 1, 2, \ldots, m$$

and

$$x_j \geq 0 \qquad \text{for } j = 1, 2, \ldots, n$$

This general problem statement is useful in conveying the formal statement of the problem. However, the goal for this text is not general proof but rather useful understanding. The following sections use a two-variable example to demonstrate the features of the problem.

6.2   EXAMPLE OF THE LINEAR PROGRAMMING PROBLEM

Business management is both an undergraduate and a graduate-level subject. Consider a hypothetical business school with a large M.B.A. program as well as a large undergraduate program in business. The M.B.A. program officials wish to study the size of the class that should be admitted, considering a medium-range time horizon and the relevant policies of the university.

Let x_1 represent the number of first-year students to be admitted every year. These students have degrees from other fields and will take the whole 2-year program. Let x_2 represent the number of students to be admitted every year who already have a bachelor's degree in business. They will not need to take the first-year courses but will take only the second year of the M.B.A. program. The size of the first-year class is x_1. The university has a policy constraint based upon present facilities and the size of other programs: x_1 may not exceed 500 students.

There is a 20 percent attrition rate during the first year of the program and a negligible attrition during the second year. The number of second-year students every year is composed of those who took the first year and wish to continue, $.8x_1$, plus those admitted into the second year directly, x_2. The university also has a policy constraint upon the size of the second-year class: it may not exceed 600.

The third constraint in the medium-range time horizon is due to the size of the faculty. Suppose that the faculty size is such that the maximum number of courses they can give in 1 year is 487.5. First-year courses all have 32 students per course and all students take 10 courses per year. The number of courses per year required by first-year students is

$$\frac{10x_1}{32}$$

However, the second-year courses all have 16 students per course. The number of courses required by second-year students is

$$10 \frac{.8x_1 + x_2}{16}$$

The sum of the numbers required by each year gives the constraint upon x_1 and x_2 implied by the limited faculty size:

$$10 \frac{x_1}{32} + 10 \frac{.8x_1 + x_2}{16} \leq 487.5$$

This simplifies to

$$2.6x_1 + 2x_2 \leq 1560$$

No constraints are included to represent the limitations due to building size or number of classrooms because those are constraints only in the relatively short run.

The objective of the problem is to maximize the "direct" profit, defined as tuition revenue minus faculty cost per course minus other costs that vary with class size. Suppose that the tuition revenue per course is $400 per student and average faculty salary per course is $3200. First-year courses, having 32 students per course, cost $100 per student. Second-year courses, having only 16 students per course, cost $200 per student. Other marginal costs of operating the school total $100 per student of either class. Thus the direct profit per first-year student is $(400 − 200) × 10 courses per year = $2000/year. Similarly, for a second-year student the direct profit per student per year is

$$(400 - 300) \times 10 \text{ courses/year} = \$1000/\text{year}$$

This "profit" is really a contribution to the overhead expenses of the university. The objective function, scaled to $1000 units per year, is

$$E(x_1, x_2) = 2x_1 + (.8x_1 + x_2)$$

The complete statement of the problem is

$$\text{Max } E(x_1, x_2) = 2.8x_1 + x_2$$

subject to

1.	$x_1 \leq 500$	first-year class size constraint
2.	$.8x_1 + x_2 \leq 600$	second-year class size constraint
3.	$2.6x_1 + 2x_2 \leq 1560$	faculty size constraint
4.	$x_1 \geq 0$	nonnegativity constraint
5.	$x_2 \geq 0$	nonnegativity constraint

6.3 GRAPHIC ANALYSIS

Two-variable linear programming problems can be solved easily by a graphic method of analysis. The important purpose of this section is to extract and understand those properties of the linear programming problem that are true also for higher-dimensional problems and will lead to an efficient algorithm for any dimension.

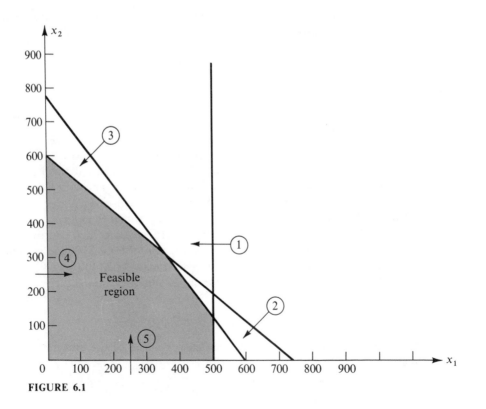

FIGURE 6.1

The first step is to construct the feasible region in the space of the decision variables. Every point in this space corresponds to a decision or solution. The subset of points corresponding to solutions that obey all constraints simultaneously is called the *feasible region*. The graph in Fig. 6.1 shows one line for each constraint. The line represents the *constraint boundary:* that set of points which obey the constraint as an equality. For example, the boundary of constraint 2 is the line $.8x_1 + x_2 = 600$. Recall that straight lines are easily plotted by finding the two points where the line intersects the two axes. For example, the line $.8x_1 + x_2 = 600$ intersects the x_1 axis at $x_2 = 0$, $x_1 = 600/.8 = 750$. It intersects the x_2 axis at $x_1 = 0$, $x_2 = 600$. The graph shows the constraint boundary line for each constraint. Each constraint is labeled with its number for easy reference and has an arrow indicating its direction of feasibility. There are five lines including the lines $x_1 = 0$ and $x_2 = 0$, which coincide with the x_2 axis and x_1 axis, respectively.

Any point in this feasible region is a decision that satisfies all constraints simultaneously. For example, $x_1 = 0$, $x_2 = 600$ might be an unusual way to run an M.B.A. program but it is apparently considered feasible. The underlying reason why it might be considered unusual may be contained in the objective function. The point $x_1 = 300$, $x_2 = 200$ is an interior point in the feasible region. It, like all others, is a candidate for optimality. Is it possible that this point is superior to all its neighbors? Examination of the objective function will answer this. This examination begins with the partial derivatives. Since the objective function is linear, its derivatives are constant. For example,

$$\frac{\partial E(x_1, x_2)}{\partial x_1} = 2.8$$

$$\frac{\partial E(x_1, x_2)}{\partial x_2} = 1$$

Thus a gain of 2.8 units per first-year student admitted can be made regardless of the current number of first-year students. Similarly a gain of 1 unit per second-year student admitted is always possible. Thus the derivatives tell only which way to go but not when to stop. For any interior solution, such as $x_1 = 300$, $x_2 = 200$, the derivatives imply that the best direction is along a line with slope $1/2.8 = .357$. This direction gives the greatest possible rate of increase of E. The important conclusion from this reasoning holds for a linear programming problem of any dimension: The linearity of the objective function implies that an interior point cannot be a unique optimum solution as was possible in the problems of Chap. 3.

This point can be further developed by use of iso-E lines in the decision space. For example, consider the iso-E lines corresponding to the E values 700, 1000, 1400, and 2100. For each one, the points of intersection with the axes are found and the line is drawn. The iso-E line

$$2.8x_1 + x_2 = 700$$

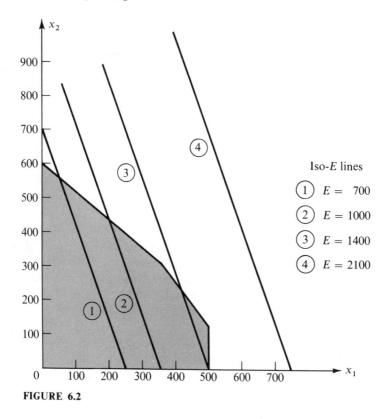

FIGURE 6.2

intersects the x_1 axis at $x_2 = 0$, $x_1 = 700/2.8 = 250$ and the x_2 axis at $x_1 = 0$, $x_2 = 700$. All other iso-E lines are parallel to each other and to this line because of the linearity of the objective function. Even in higher dimensions the family of iso-E "hypersurfaces" is a set of parallel "hyperplanes." The graph in Fig. 6.2 shows several iso-E lines and their relationship to the feasible region.

The object of the problem is to be on the highest attainable iso-E line. Clearly the optimal solution cannot be in the interior of the feasible region. For any such candidate for optimality there is another iso-E line close by that has higher E value. Therefore the optimal solution must be at a corner point. Corner points are the only ones with the property that they do not always have a superior neighbor point. This property also generalizes to many dimensions. In this example it is clear that the highest attainable E value is that of the iso-E line which passes through the corner point formed by the intersection of the boundaries of constraints 1 and 3. The value of E, now bounded by 1400 and 2100, can be further refined by drawing lines. However, there is a simpler way, using algebra.

Consider changing the coefficients in the E function. This will have the effect of changing the slope of all iso-E lines. However, the property will still remain that an optimal solution is at a corner point.

Consider changing the constraints. If they still remain linear inequality constraints, the constraint boundaries will still be unbroken straight lines and the property will still remain true that there is an optimum solution among the set of corner-point solutions.

This property holds true for any linear programming problem regardless of the number of dimensions or the number of constraints. Its importance is due to the fact that it narrows the set of candidates from an infinity of points in the feasible region and on its boundaries to the *finite* set of corner points. This property still needs to be exploited efficiently. Consider first a simple method, now known to be correct, of simply evaluating *all* corner-point solutions and comparing them to find the best.

6.4   ENUMERATION OF INTERSECTIONS

Since the goal is a method that does not depend upon graphic information, this method of enumeration is conducted as if the graphic solution were not known. However, if you cannot see the feasible region you cannot see its corners. All that is known about the corners is that they are formed by intersections of two constraint boundaries. Therefore the method of enumeration begins with a complete listing of all pairs of constraints. There are 10 in this example. However, many of these intersections of constraint boundaries are not corner points. This is determined by testing the feasibility of each intersection. A flowchart of this method for this problem is presented in Fig. 6.3. The results of this method are presented in Table 6.1.

TABLE 6.1   Results of the Enumeration of Intersections

Constraint Pair	Equations of Constraint Boundaries	x_1	x_2	Feasibility	E
1 and 2	$x_1 = 500, .8x_1 + x_2 = 600$	500	200	No	. . . . . .
1 and 3	$x_1 = 500, 2.6x_1 + 2x_2 = 1560$	500	130	Yes	1530
1 and 4	$x_1 = 500, x_1 = 0$	Parallels		. . .	. . . . . .
		No solution			
1 and 5	$x_1 = 500, x_2 = 0$	500	0	Yes	1400
2 and 3	$.8x_1 + x_2 = 600, 2.6x_1 + 2x_2 = 1560$	360	312	Yes	1118.4
2 and 4	$.8x_1 + x_2 = 600, x_1 = 0$	0	600	Yes	600
2 and 5	$.8x_1 + x_2 = 600, x_2 = 0$	750	0	No	. . . . . .
3 and 4	$2.6x_1 + 2x_2 = 1560, x_1 = 0$	0	780	No	. . . . . .
3 and 5	$2.6x_1 + 2x_2 = 1560, x_2 = 0$	600	0	No	. . . . . .
4 and 5	$x_1 = 0, x_2 = 0$	0	0	Yes	0

This method is not efficient but it does lead to an understanding of the difficulties involved. Consider how it would apply to a problem having

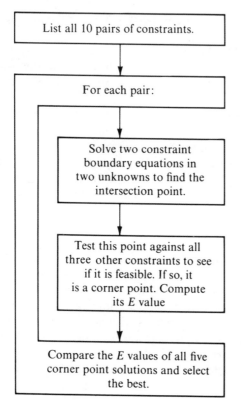

FIGURE 6.3

n decision variables (instead of two)
m inequality constraints (instead of three)
n nonnegativity constraints (one on each decision variable)

Now there are a total of $(n + m)$ constraint boundaries in an n-dimensional space. Every corner point in an n-dimensional space is an intersection of n constraint hyperplanes. (Recall that it takes three planes intersecting in a three-dimensional space to produce a single point.) The number of intersections to be tested is the number of ways in which n items can be selected from $(n + m)$ items, where order of selection is irrelevant. This is

$$\frac{(n + m)!}{n! \, m!}$$

In our example this number is

$$\frac{(2 + 3)!}{2! \, 3!} = 10$$

However, this number becomes prohibitively large for large n and m.   Furthermore the work required in each step grows with n; it requires the simultaneous solution of n linear equations in n unknowns to determine each intersection point.   Finally each point must be tested against the other m constraints to determine whether or not the intersection point is a corner point.

The deficiencies of this "brute force" method of solution motivate the desire for a better method that can

1. Distinguish between infeasible intersection points and corner points so that no time is wasted on the infeasible intersection points

2. Evaluate the optimality of a given corner-point solution without the need to compare it with all others

3. Find a better corner-point solution after determining that the current one is not optimal

All these abilities are found in the *simplex method*.   Section 6.5 shows how the use of slack variables facilitates the ability to recognize corner points in many dimensions.

EXERCISES

1. Find the corner points of the following feasible sets:

    (a) $3x_1 + x_2 \leq 10$ (b) $x_1 - x_2 \leq 2$

        $x_1 + 2x_2 \leq 12$ $3x_1 + 4x_2 \leq 8$

        $x_1, \quad x_2 \geq 0$ $x_1 + 2x_2 \leq 6$

                          $x_1 \geq 0$ x_2 unconstrained

2. In the problem of Sec. 3.6, Chap. 3, the constraints were

$$x_1 + x_2 \leq 5000$$
$$x_1 \leq 2400$$

What does the form of the objective function imply about the possible location of the optimum?   If it is known that the unconstrained optimal solution lies outside the feasible region, where can the optimum solution be?   If the objective function were changed to

$$E(x_1, x_2) = x_1 + x_2$$

what is implied about the possible location of the optimum solution?

3. A mining company has two mines with different production capacities that produce the same type of ore. After crushing, the ore is graded into three classes: high, medium, and low. There is some demand for each ore grade. The company has contracted to provide a smelter with 12 tons of high-grade, 8 tons of

medium-grade, and 24 tons of low-grade ore per week. It costs \$200/day to run the first mine and \$160/day to run the other. In a day's operation the first mine produces 6 tons of high-grade, 2 tons of medium-grade, and 4 tons of low-grade ore. The second mine produces 2, 2, and 12 tons per day of each grade, respectively. How many days a week should each mine be operated to fulfill the company's orders most economically? Which grade is overproduced at the optimum? Use a graphic method to obtain these answers.

6.5 SLACK VARIABLES

The purpose of slack variables is to convey feasibility information in a usable way. Slack variables are supplementary variables, one for each inequality constraint, that "take up the slack" in the inequality and thereby convert it from an inequality to an equality.

In the current example, there are three inequality constraints (excluding the non-negativity constraints). Therefore there will be three slack variables. The first is defined by

$$x_1 + s_1 = 500$$

Thus s_1 has the interpretation of an unused or excess class size capacity. If the slack variable s_1 is required to be nonnegative, the original constraint

$$x_1 \leq 500$$

is necessarily obeyed. Similarly the slack variable s_2 is defined by the second constraint:

$$.8x_1 + x_2 + s_2 = 600$$

and

$$s_2 \geq 0$$

The third is defined by

$$2.6x_1 + 2x_2 + s_3 = 1560$$

and

$$s_3 \geq 0$$

The problem has apparently been expanded from two variables to five:

$$x_1, x_2, s_1, s_2, s_3$$

There are three equality constraints and five nonnegativity constraints, one for each variable.

The question now is "How can these slack variables be put to use?" The basic idea is that the boundary of the constraint $x_1 \leq 500$ can now be described as the

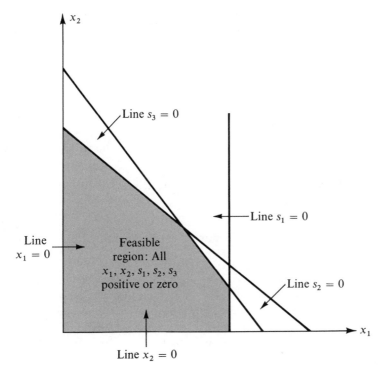

FIGURE 6.4

line such that $s_1 = 0$ at all points on that line. Similarly the boundary of the constraint

$$.8x_1 + x_2 \leq 600$$

can now be described as the line

$$s_2 = 0$$

This idea is shown in Fig. 6.4.

An *interior solution* has all five variables positive because it is not on any constraint line. A *solution on one constraint boundary* has one variable equal to zero and the other four positive. A *corner-point solution* is on two constraints at once and therefore has two variables out of five equal to zero; the other three are positive.

Thus given a list of the values of x_1, x_2, s_1, s_2, and s_3 corresponding to a particular solution, a count of the number of positive, zero, and negative variables is sufficient to determine what type of solution it is. This can be generalized to n nonnegative decision variables and m inequality constraints. The number of slack variables to be added is m. The total number of nonnegative variables becomes $n + m$. Given a list of the values of the $(n + m)$ variables corresponding to a particular solution, a count of the number of positive, zero, and negative-valued variables determines the nature of the solution. The summary rules are

1. If any variable is negative, the solution is not feasible.
2. If all $(n + m)$ variables are positive or zero, the solution is feasible.
3. If all variables are strictly positive, the solution is in the interior of the feasible region and no constraints are active.
4. If $k < n$ variables are zero and the others are positive, the solution is on the boundary but not at a corner point of the boundary.
5. If $k = n$ variables are zero and the others are positive, the solution is a corner point and is a candidate for optimality.
6. If $k > n$ variables are zero and the others are positive, the problem is degenerate. This can happen only if more than n constraints intersect at one corner point.

It is conventional to term the corner-point solution a *basic feasible solution:* a solution having n or more zero-valued variables while the other m or fewer variables are positive. Furthermore n of the zero-valued variables are called *zero variables* and the other m variables are called *basic variables.* In a nondegenerate BFS there are exactly m positive basic variables and n zero variables. In a degenerate BFS some of the m basic variables have value zero but are still called basic.

6.6 ALGEBRAIC SIMPLEX METHOD

The *simplex method* is an algorithm for searching among corner-point solutions. It is described as follows:

Start with an initial BFS.

Step 1 Solve m constraint equations for the m basic variables as functions of the n zero variables.

Step 2 Express E as a function of the n zero variables only.

Step 3 Test for optimality of current BFS by testing whether E can be increased by increasing any one of the zero variables from zero.

Step 4 If the current BFS is not optimal, select the zero variable that gives greatest rate of increase of E. Let it become basic and increase it as much as possible until one of the current basic variables becomes zero. This is an improved BFS. Return to step 1.

The use of this method will now be illustrated with the example problem. The best initial BFS is the origin, where n of the decision variables are zero. This choice is not a necessity but is most reasonable in terms of the total work required. The alternative choice to be made when the origin is not feasible is shown in Chap. 7.

The first iteration begins with the initial BFS, in which x_1, x_2 are zero variables and s_1, s_2, s_3 are basic. Step 1 requires the solution of the three equations

$$x_1 + s_1 = 500$$
$$.8x_1 + x_2 + s_2 = 600$$
$$2.6x_1 + 2x_2 + s_3 = 1560$$

for the basic variables s_1, s_2, s_3 in terms of the zero variables x_1, x_2. However, these equations are already in this form because, by the nature of slack variables, there is at most one in each equation. Of course this is why the origin is a good choice for the initial solution. The E expression also is already in terms of the zero variables only. The results of steps 1 and 2 are

$$s_1 = 500 - x_1 \tag{6.1}$$
$$s_2 = 600 - .8x_1 - x_2 \tag{6.2}$$
$$s_3 = 1560 - 2.6x_1 - 2x_2 \tag{6.3}$$
$$E = 2.8x_1 + x_2 \tag{6.4}$$

Since x_1 and x_2 are zero, these equations simply say that $s_1 = 500$, $s_2 = 600$, $s_3 = 1560$, and the E value of this solution is $E = 0$. Clearly this is a basic feasible solution. If the origin were not feasible the discovery would be made at this stage that one or more of s_1, s_2, s_3 were negative.

In steps 3 and 4 the coefficients in the E expression are examined. (Since the E expression is linear, these coefficients are actually partial derivatives.) Clearly E can be increased by increasing either x_1 or x_2 from zero. The largest rate of gain, 2.8, is obtained from increasing x_1. Therefore x_1 becomes a basic variable. Now the information in the current set of equations is utilized to determine how much x_1 can be increased. The first equation shows that if x_1 were increased to 500, then s_1 would be driven to zero. The second equation shows that if x_1 were increased to 750, then s_2 would be zero. The third equation shows that if it were increased to 600, then s_3 would be zero. It is desirable to increase x_1 as much as possible; this is $x_1 = 500$. Any larger value would result in s_1 being negative, which implies that a movement to outside the feasible region has occurred.

The conclusion of these four steps is that an improvement of $(2.8)(500) = 1400$ is made by moving to the new BFS, which differs from the old one by the exchange of x_1 becoming basic while s_1 becomes zero.

The second iteration begins with the new solution. s_1, x_2 are zero variables; x_1, s_2, s_3 are basic. Step 1 requires the solution for x_1, s_2, s_3 in terms of s_1 and x_2. This requires some work. First Eq. (6.1), which relates the new basic variable (x_1) to the new zero variable (s_1), is solved for the new basic variable. This is called the *pivot* equation. The result is

$$x_1 = 500 - s_1 \tag{6.5}$$

This equation is next used to eliminate x_1 from all other equations by substitution. For example,

$$s_2 = 600 - .8(500 - s_1) - x_2 = 200 + .8s_1 - x_2$$

Similar substitutions result in the following equations:

$$x_1 = 500 - s_1 \tag{6.5}$$

$$s_2 = 200 + .8s_1 - x_2 \tag{6.6}$$

$$s_3 = 260 + 2.6s_1 - 2x_2 \tag{6.7}$$

$$E = 1400 - 2.8s_1 + x_2 \tag{6.8}$$

Step 3 leads to the conclusion that this BFS is not optimal because E can still be increased by increasing x_2 from zero. In step 4 it is seen that Eq. (6.6) implies a limit of 200 upon the increase of x_2. Equation (6.7) implies a limit of 130 and Eq. (6.5) implies no limit because x_1 cannot be driven to zero by an increase of x_2. The largest possible increase is $x_2 = 130$. This will result in an improvement of 130 in the E value.

The third iteration begins with the new BFS having x_1, x_2, and s_2 basic while s_1 and s_3 are zero variables. Steps 1 and 2 utilize Eq. (6.7) as the pivot equation. Solving it for x_2 gives

$$x_2 = 130 + 1.3s_1 - .5s_3 \tag{6.7'}$$

After using this for substitution to eliminate x_2 from all equations, the result is

$$x_1 = 500 - s_1 \tag{6.5'}$$

$$s_2 = 70 - .5s_1 + .5s_3 \tag{6.6'}$$

$$x_2 = 130 + 1.3s_1 - .5s_3 \tag{6.7'}$$

$$E = 1530 - 1.5s_1 - .5s_3 \tag{6.8'}$$

Now Eq. (6.8') shows that E can only be decreased if either of the zero variables were increased from zero. Therefore the conclusion of step 3 is that the current BFS is the

TABLE 6.2 Summary of Iterations and Solutions

Iteration	Basic Variables	Zero Variables	E
First	$s_1 = 500$, $s_2 = 600$, $s_3 = 1560$	x_1, x_2	0
Second	$x_1 = 500$, $s_2 = 200$, $s_3 = 260$	s_1, x_2	1400
Third	$x_1 = 500$, $x_2 = 130$, $s_2 = 70$	s_1, s_3	1530

optimal solution. The optimum E value is $E = 1530$, obtained by $x_1 = 500$ and $x_2 = 130$. The fact that s_1 and s_3 are zero in this solution indicates that constraints 1 and 3 are binding or active, that is, holding as equalities. Since s_2 is positive, it is known that constraint 2 is not binding but instead has some slack in it.

Table 6.2 summarizes the iterations and solutions found. Reference to Fig. 6.1 confirms that the simplex method moves the solution along the boundary of the feasible region, from one corner to an adjacent corner point, until the best corner point is found. In this case the movement was counterclockwise because this was the direction of greatest rate of improvement.

EXERCISE

Find the optimal values of x_1 and x_2 by both the graphic and the algebraic simplex methods:

1. Maximize $3x_1 - 2x_2$
    subject to

    $$3x_1 + x_2 \leq 10$$
    $$x_1 + 2x_2 \leq 12$$
    $$x_1, x_2 \geq 0$$

2. Maximize $x_1 + 3x_2$
    subject to

    $$x_1 - x_2 \leq 2$$
    $$3x_1 + 4x_2 \leq 8$$
    $$x_1 + 2x_2 \leq 6$$
    $$x_1 \geq 0 \qquad x_2 \text{ unconstrained}$$

6.7 TABULAR SIMPLEX METHOD

Although the algebraic version of the simplex method is quite efficient, further streamlining can be done by eliminating the need to write algebraic symbols and variables. The whole operation can be performed in a series of tables, one for each iteration, known as the simplex *tableau*. This is just a more efficient way to organize and standardize the work. It is not an improvement in understanding and is actually less intelligible than the algebraic version.

This book uses a convenient form of the tableau method that differs only slightly from the older conventions and looks almost exactly like the equations. In fact, if all nonnumerical symbols were deleted from Eqs. (6.1) to (6.4) and row and column headings were added, the result would be the first tableau:

	Const.	x_1	x_2	Ratio
E	0	2.8	1	
s_1	500	−1	0	
s_2	600	−.8	−1	
s_3	1560	−2.6	−2	

The first steps of the tabular simplex method are the same as in the algebraic method: Slack variables are defined to convert all inequalities to equalities. The initial BFS is taken to be the origin, and the set of equalities is written as solutions for the slack variables as functions of the zero variables. The feasibility of the origin is checked. Finally the coefficients of all equations are entered into the first tableau. The rules for performing the iteration of the simplex method can now be expressed more efficiently in terms of rows and columns. They are the same rules as before, but it is worthwhile to restate them:

Step a If all coefficients in the E row, corresponding to zero variable columns, are negative or zero, then the current BFS is a maximizing solution. Otherwise select the highest positive coefficient. The variable associated with this column is to become a basic variable in the next tableau. This column is called the *pivot column*.

Step b For each row after the E row, compute the ratio of the row constant to the pivot column element in that row. Enter this in the ratio column for that row.

Step c Consider all rows having negative or negative zero ratio. Select from among these the row with the largest ratio (smallest absolute value ratio). This is the *pivot row*. (Ties can be broken arbitrarily.)

Step d Construct a new tableau from the old one by interchanging the variable names associated with the pivot row and column. Other row and column labels remain unchanged.

Step e The *pivot element* of the new tableau, lying at the intersection of the pivot row and column, is denoted P^*; that of the old tableau is P. Compute and enter

$$P^* = \frac{1}{P}$$

Step f The coefficients in the remainder of the pivot row are the corresponding coefficients of the old tableau divided by the absolute value of P.

Step g The coefficients in the remainder of the pivot column are computed from the corresponding values in the old tableau by dividing them by P.

Step h Compute all other elements by the following rule: The new coefficient is obtained from the old coefficient by subtracting from it the amount (obtained from the old tableau):

$$\frac{\text{Pivot row coefficient} \times \text{pivot column coefficient}}{\text{Pivot element}}$$

This completes one iteration.

The results of steps a to g, performed upon the first tableau of the example, are shown in the partially complete second tableau:

	Const.	s_1	x_2	Ratio
E		-2.8		
x_1	500	-1	0	
s_2		$+.8$		
s_3		$+2.6$		

Step h results in the following calculations:

Cell (E, const.): $0 - \dfrac{(2.8)(500)}{-1} = 1400$

Cell (E, x_2): $1 - \dfrac{(2.8)(0)}{-1} = 1$

Cell (s_2, const.): $600 - \dfrac{(500)(-.8)}{-1} = 200$

Cell (s_2, x_2): $-1 - \dfrac{(-.8)(0)}{-1} = -1$

Cell (s_3, const.): $1560 - \dfrac{(500)(-2.6)}{-1} = 260$

Cell (s_3, x_2): $-2 - \dfrac{(-2.6)(0)}{-1} = -2$

The first iteration is completed when these values are entered into the tableau:

	Const.	s_1	x_2	Ratio
E	1400	-2.8	1	
x_1	500	-1	0	
s_2	200	$+.8$	-1	
s_3	260	$+2.6$	-2	

The second iteration begins with the selection of the x_2 column as pivot column. Row x_1 has ratio ∞. Row s_2 has ratio -200 and row 3 has ratio -130. Thus row 3 becomes the pivot row. The new tableau is

	Const.	s_1	s_3	Ratio
E	1530	-1.5	$-.5$	
x_1	500	-1	0	
s_2	70	$-.5$	$+.5$	
x_2	130	1.3	$-.5$	

This tableau can be compared with the equations already found by the algebraic method. Step a of the next iteration shows that this new solution maximizes the objective function.

6.8 MODIFICATIONS

When the objective function is to be minimized, two approaches are possible. One way is to multiply the objective function by -1 and then maximize. The other is to retain the original objective function but reverse the rules. The reversed rules are (a) stop when only positive coefficients are present in the E row and (b) select the pivot column giving the largest decrease in the objective function, that is, the negative coefficient with the largest magnitude.

PROBLEMS

1. The Proteus Company makes two products—X and Y. Each must be processed on a milling machine and on a turret lathe. The total amount of machine time available weekly on each machine is 100 hours; the company's earnings are $4/unit on X and $3/unit on Y. Product X requires 1 hour of machine time on the milling machine and 3 hours on the turret lathe; product Y requires 2 hours on the milling machine and 1 hour on the turret lathe.

    (a) Formulate this production problem as a linear programming model.
    (b) Solve both graphically and by the simplex method to find the quantities of X and Y that should be produced for maximum profitability.
    (c) What is the value of the maximum profitability?

2. Consider a small private college that receives a large number of applications for admission to the undergraduate program. It is the policy of the college to admit two categories of students: good athletes and brilliant students. Some-

times applications are received from good athletes who happen to be scholastically brilliant. But the number of such cases is so small that they can be virtually ignored. The college is interested in admitting not more than 1000 students from both categories. Also, for the sake of athletic competition, at most 900 applicants from the second category should be admitted to make room for athletes. Roughly 25 percent of the students admitted in category 1 are known to drop out of the program without getting a degree; only 10 percent drop out from category 2. The college is anxious to admit only those who have the potential to complete the undergraduate program. The problem then is to admit students from the two categories meeting the given constraints so as to maximize the total number of graduates. Assume that a fixed percentage of students drop out. If x_1 is the number of students admitted from category 1, then $.25x_1$ will drop out and the remaining $.75x_1$ will graduate. Similarly, if x_2 is the number of students admitted from category 2, then $.10x_2$ of them will drop out and $.90x_2$ will graduate. Thus the total number of graduates would be $.75x_1 + .90x_2$. The total number of entrants should not exceed 1000. This constraint is $x_1 + x_2 \le 1000$. Similarly the total number of students admitted from category 2 should not exceed 900. That is, $x_2 \le 900$. Formulate this problem and find the optimum solution.

3. The capacity of a communications system is considered to be the maximum number of call-miles that can be set up simultaneously in the system. The following system connects three locations: A, B, and C. The distance between locations A and B is 50 miles, between A and C 150 miles, and between B and C 125 miles. For example, two calls between A and C use two access lines from A to the switching station plus two from there to C and count as 300 call-miles. Formulate the problem of determining the capacity of this system as a linear pro-

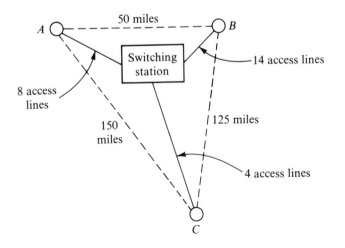

gram that finds the set of calls which yields the largest total number of call-miles. Use the decision variables x_{AB}, x_{AC}, x_{BC} to denote the number of calls simultaneously in progress between the pairs of locations. Give the objective function and the constraints. Assuming that the optimal solution exactly utilizes all the eight-line capacity from A to the switching center, can you find the optimal solution?

4. Two products, A and B, are processed in batches of 100 on three machines. Inspections occur after each process, and the failure rates at these inspections are as follows:

	Machine		
Product	1	2	3
A	25%	50%	20%
B	20%	25%	50%

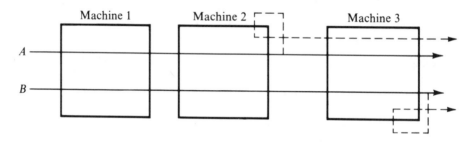

Since there are two processes, A on machine 2 and B on machine 3, with very high failure rates, the items failing these inspections are reworked on these machines (dashed lines in the material flow diagram). The failure of parts after reworking is negligible. The time taken on the machines for each product is as follows, the figures being minutes per batch:

Product	Machine 1	Machine 2	Machine 2 Rework	Machine 3	Machine 3 Rework
A	10	24	48	28	---
B	15	15	---	35	70

The profits per batch are \$10 for A and \$25 for B. The working day can be considered to be 8 hours long, of which machine 1 is down 2 hours for maintenance; machine 2 and machine 3 require 1 hour of maintenance each.

    Management proposes to produce six batches of A per day and three batches of B. With the failure rates as given, this requires that a higher number of batches be started through the processes. Determine these numbers, and determine also whether the policy proposed is feasible. Further, show whether or not this policy is optimal. If it is not, determine the optimal policy.

5. A small machine shop manufactures two models, standard and deluxe, of an unspecified product. Each standard model requires 4 hours of grinding and 2 hours of polishing; each deluxe model requires 2 hours of grinding and 5 hours of polishing. The manufacturer has two grinders and three polishers available in his 40-hour week. He makes a profit of $3 on each standard model and $4 on each deluxe model. He can sell all he can make of both. How many of each model should he make to maximize his profit?

6. A trucking company with $400,000 to spend on new equipment is contemplating three types of vehicles. Vehicle A has a 10-ton payload and is expected to average 35 miles/hour. It costs $8000. Vehicle B has a 20-ton payload and is expected to average 30 miles/hour. It costs $13,000. Vehicle C is a modified form of B; it carries sleeping quarters for one driver, and this reduces its capacity to 18 tons and raises the cost to $15,000.

   Vehicle A requires a crew of one man and, if driven on three shifts per day, could be run for an average of 18 hours/day. Vehicles B and C require a crew of two men each; but whereas B would be driven 18 hours/day with three shifts, C could average 21 hours/day. A driver can work for no more than one shift a day. The company has 150 drivers available each day and would find it difficult to obtain further crews. Maintenance facilities are such that the total number of vehicles must not exceed 30. How many vehicles of each type should be purchased if the company wishes to maximize its capacity in ton-miles per day?

7. A farmer has 1000 acres of land on which he can grow corn, wheat, or soybeans. Each acre of corn costs $100 for preparation, requires 7 man-days of work, and yields a profit of $30. An acre of wheat costs $120 to prepare, requires 10 man-days of work, and yields $40. An acre of soybeans costs $70 to prepare, requires 8 man-days, and yields $20 profit. If the farmer has $100,000 for preparation, and can count on 8000 man-days of work, how many acres should he devote to each crop to maximize profits?

8. Given the nonlinear programming problem

$$\text{Minimize } E = Y - 3X$$

subject to

$$\frac{1}{2} X \geq Y - 3$$

$$4 \geq Y$$

$$X^2 \leq Y$$

and

$$X, Y \geq 0$$

(a)   Graph the problem.

(b)   Approximate the curve $X^2 = Y$ by two lines constructed from the points $(0,0)$, $(1,1)$, $(2,4)$.

(c)   Obtain the solution by using the simplex method. Is this a lower or upper bound to the original problem?

Chapter 7

LINEAR PROGRAMMING EXTENSIONS

The previous chapter presented the linear programming problem and the simplex method of solution. Certain topics were mentioned but their study was postponed in order to maintain emphasis on the properties of the simplex method. The sections of this chapter consider these topics and others about the implied cost of constraints and general types of linear programming problem structures.

7.1 ALGEBRA OF INEQUALITY CONSTRAINTS

Algebraic operations can be performed on inequality constraints. If done correctly, they change the algebraic appearance of the constraint without changing its meaning; the position of the constraint boundary in the decision space remains unchanged. It is possible to add or subtract the same quantity from both sides of a constraint and to transpose terms exactly as if dealing with an equation. It is also possible to multiply or divide an inequality constraint by a *positive* quantity. For example, the constraint

$$.8x_1 + x_2 \leq 600$$

can be divided by .8 to obtain the form

$$x_1 + 1.25x_2 \leq 750$$

Yet it is still the same constraint in essence.

Multiplication or division by a positive quantity preserves the direction of an inequality. However, the same operation with a negative quantity *reverses* the direction of the inequality. For example, the constraint

$$5x_1 - 3x_2 \geq -10$$

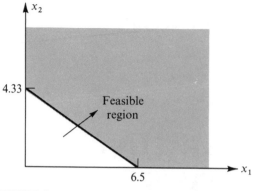

FIGURE 7.1

can be multiplied by -1 to yield

$$-5x_1 + 3x_2 \leq 10$$

The other point of this section is that slack variables must always be put on the slack side (the small side) of an inequality to obtain an equality.[1] For example, the slack variable s for the inequality constraint

$$2x_1 + 3x_2 \geq 13$$

is put on the right:

$$2x_1 + 3x_2 = 13 + s$$

This can then be transposed to obtain

$$2x_1 + 3x_2 - s = 13$$

or written as an equation for s directly:

$$s = -13 + 2x_1 + 3x_2$$

The graph of this constraint is shown in Fig. 7.1. A constraint like this prevents the origin from being a corner point of the feasible region.

EXERCISE

Draw the following linear constraints and mark the feasible area. Determine the corner points of the feasible region.

$$-2x + 5y - 10 \leq 0$$

---

[1]Most texts call s a *surplus* rather than a slack variable when the slackness is on the right-hand side.

$$2x + y - 6 \le 0$$
$$x + 2y - 2 \ge 0$$
$$-x + 3y - 3 \le 0$$

Add slack variables and then describe each corner point by listing which variables are zero at each one.

7.2   INFEASIBLE ORIGIN

Infeasibility of the origin means that the origin can no longer be selected as the first BFS. The simplex method requires *some* initial BFS. The origin is the most efficient choice when it is possible, but it is not always possible. Consider the M.B.A. admissions problem in Chap. 6 with one constraint added. The new constraint reflects the fact that certain fixed costs could not be covered, and the school would be closed, unless the total enrollment meets or exceeds 300. Total enrollment is $x_1 + (.8x_1 + x_2)$ and therefore the constraint is

$$1.8x_1 + x_2 \ge 300$$

With this additional constraint, constraint 6, the feasible region becomes as shown in Fig. 7.2. This is a reasonable constraint, and it is clear that it will not change

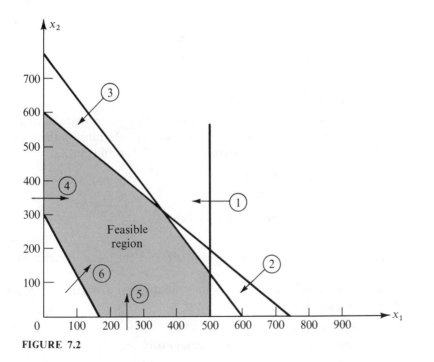

FIGURE 7.2

the optimal solution because added constraints can only reduce the feasible region. The piece of the old feasible region chopped off by this constraint did not contain the optimum solution. Therefore the optimum must remain unchanged. That insight comes from the graph entirely and is not easily observable in a many-variable problem.

In this brief example it is tempting to conclude that one has only to find another corner point for the simplex method to take as the initial BFS. The point $x_1 = 166.66$, $x_2 = 0$ seems reasonable. Now solve the equations for the basic variables x_1, s_1, s_2, s_3 in terms of the zero variables x_2 and s_4 (the new slack variable associated with the new constraint). This approach is possible but is not consistent with the goal of developing methods that are independent of graphic information.

What is desired is a method that does not depend upon the problem at hand but works for any problem regardless of size. The method to be used is called the method of *artificial slack variables*. Although it is illustrated here with the same example, it is a general method. The example, restated in algebraic form with slack variables included, is

$$\max 2.8x_1 + x_2$$

subject to

$$x_1 + s_1 = 500$$
$$.8x_1 + x_2 + s_2 = 600$$
$$2.6x_1 + 2x_2 + s_3 = 1560$$
$$1.8x_1 + x_2 - s_4 = 300$$

and

$$x_1, x_2 \quad \text{nonnegative}$$

Without using graphic information, it may not be known at this point that the origin is infeasible. However, the attempt to use the origin requires solution for the basic variables s_1, s_2, s_3, s_4 in terms of the zero variables x_1, x_2. This results in

$$s_1 = 500 - x_1$$
$$s_2 = 600 - .8x_1 - x_2$$
$$s_3 = 1560 - 2.6x_1 - 2x_2$$
$$s_4 = -300 + 1.8x_1 + x_2$$

The fact that s_4 is negative demonstrates infeasibility and the need for the new method.

The method of artificial slack variables modifies the original problem to obtain a new problem having two properties:

1. It has a simple initial BFS.
2. It has the same optimal solution as the original problem.

Two initial steps are required.

STEP 1   For every constraint whose slack variable is negative at the origin solution, insert an additional nonnegative variable (an artificial slack variable) *with the opposite sign* into the constraint.[1] For example, the constraint

$$1.8x_1 + x_2 - s_4 = 300$$

becomes

$$1.8x_1 + x_2 - s_4 + a_1 = 300$$

and $a_1 \geq 0$ in the *new* problem. The effect of this is to change the constraint purposefully to one that is easy to work with. For example, if $a_1 = 300$ the constraint has been moved to pass *through* the origin instead of above it. In the initial BFS the artificial slack variable a_1 is a basic variable instead of s_4. Thus the initial BFS still has one basic variable in each equation and is therefore easy to work with. Here the basic variables are s_1, s_2, s_3, and a_1.

STEP 2   The problem has been modified to possess a simple initial BFS. Another modification must be made to guarantee that the optimal solution to the new problem is also the optimal solution to the original problem. Observe that any solution to the new problem which has all artificial slack variables equal to zero is also a solution to the original problem because the only way in which the two problems differ is by the presence of the artificial slack variables. Therefore this motivates the following modification to the objective function:

$$\max E = 2.8x_1 + x_2 - La_1$$

The coefficient L stands for a large number. Its purpose is to make any solution having positive a_1 so costly as to be inferior to solutions having $a_1 = 0$. Usually an actual number is chosen; $L = 10$ appears reasonable here. Now the modifications of the problem are complete; the new problem is ready to be solved.

However, one more difficulty remains in setting up the new tableau. The artificial slack variables newly introduced into the objective function are basic variables in the initial BFS. Therefore they must be eliminated by substitution from the E expression for the first tableau. For example, the equations for the basic variables are

$$s_1 = 500 - x_1$$
$$s_2 = 600 - .8x_1 - x_2$$
$$s_3 = 1560 - 2.6x_1 - 2x_2$$
$$a_1 = 300 - 1.8x_1 - x_2 + s_4$$

---

[1] A more descriptive, although unconventional, name for an artificial slack variable would be *temporary variable.*

This last equation must be substituted into the objective function to eliminate a_1. The step is

$$E = 2.8x_1 + x_2 - 10(300 - 1.8x_1 - x_2 + s_4)$$
$$E = -3000 + 20.8x_1 + 11x_2 - 10s_4$$

Now E is expressed in terms of zero variables only. The first tableau is

	Const.	x_1	x_2	s_4	Ratio
E	−3000	+20.8	+11	−10	
s_1	500	−1	0	0	
s_2	600	− .8	−1	0	
s_3	1560	−2.6	−2	0	
a_1	300	−1.8	−1	+1	

The setup of the problem is now complete. All that remains is to apply the simplex method until optimality is reached.

An alternative version of this method sets up two objective functions. The first, "artificial," objective function is minus the sum of the artificial slack variables. The second is the real objective function. In this version the E rows appear as

	Const.	x_1	x_2	s_4	Ratio
E_a	−300	+1.8	+1	−1	
E	0	2.8	1	0	

This results from $E_a = -a_1$, followed by substitution for a_1. The artificial objective E_a is maximized first. During those operations of the simplex method the E row is operated upon but not used in the selection of pivot column. After optimality with respect to the first objective is reached, the artificial slack variables will all be zero. Therefore an initial BFS to the original problem has been found. The columns associated with the zero-valued artificial slack variables can be deleted along with the row for the first objective function. The real objective function is then used.

It is of little importance which version is used. Either the two separate objective functions or the single combined objective function accomplish the same result. The example here uses the single function.

In the first iteration the x_1 column has the largest positive coefficient and is therefore chosen as the pivot column. The ratios are −500, −750, −600, and

-166.66. Therefore the pivot row is the a_1 row. The new basic variable is x_1, and a_1 becomes zero. The resulting tableau is

	Const.	a_1	x_2	s_4	Ratio
E	$466\frac{2}{3}$	$-11\frac{5}{9}$	$-\frac{5}{9}$	$+\frac{14}{9}$	
s_1	$333\frac{1}{3}$	$+\frac{5}{9}$	$+\frac{5}{9}$	$-\frac{5}{9}$	
s_2	$466\frac{2}{3}$	$+\frac{4}{9}$	$-\frac{13}{9}$	$+\frac{4}{9}$	
s_3	$1126\frac{2}{3}$	$+\frac{13}{9}$	$-\frac{5}{9}$	$-\frac{13}{9}$	
x_1	$166\frac{2}{3}$	$-\frac{5}{9}$	$-\frac{5}{9}$	$+\frac{5}{9}$	

This solution is feasible in the original problem because a_1 has become a zero variable. Now the a_1 column can be removed. The column with the highest coefficient is that of s_4 and therefore it is the next pivot column. The ratios are -600, $+1050$, -780, and $+300$. Therefore s_1 becomes basic and its row is now pivot row. The next iteration gives

	Const.	a_1	x_2	s_1	Ratio
E	1400		1	-2.8	
s_4	600		1	$-\frac{9}{5}$	
s_2	200		-1	$-.8$	
s_3	260		-2	$+2.6$	
x_1	500		0	-1	

This is not yet the optimal solution. However, it is the second solution obtained in Chap. 6. From that chapter it is known that the next iteration will obtain the optimal solution.

In a larger problem there may be several artificial slack variables. So long as there is some feasible solution to the original problem, the simplex method eventually results in setting all of them to zero. When this occurs, a solution feasible with respect to the original problem is first present.

EXERCISE

Construct a first simplex tableau for the following linear programming:

$$\min -x_1 + 2x_2$$

subject to

$$-x_1 + x_2 \leq 1$$
$$6x_1 + 4x_2 \leq 24$$
$$x_2 \geq 2$$

and

$$x_1 \geq 0, x_2 \geq 0$$

Perform one iteration and show the results. What variables will be basic in the next iteration? Draw the feasible region and show what corner you are at.

7.3 DEGENERACY

A degenerate linear programming problem is one having one or more degenerate corner points. Degeneracy is really a property of corner points. A degenerate corner point in a two-dimensional problem is one having more than two constraints passing through the same corner point. In an n-dimensional problem, a corner point is an intersection of n constraints. If more than n constraints pass through that point, it is degenerate. Degeneracy is not a practical difficulty. However, it is illustrated here so that its characteristics will be understood.

Suppose that the constraint $x_2 \geq x_1 - 500$ is added to the constraint set of the original problem. The complete problem, with slack variable included, is

$$\max E = 2.8x_1 + x_2$$

subject to

$$x_1 + s_1 = 500$$
$$.8x_1 + x_2 + s_2 = 600$$
$$2.6x_1 + 2x_2 + s_3 = 1560$$
$$x_1 - x_2 + s_4 = 500$$

The graph of the feasible region is shown in Fig. 7.3.

Clearly this added constraint does not change the feasible region and, therefore, does not change the optimal solution. The new feature of this problem is that the point $x_1 = 500$, $x_2 = 0$ has three constraints passing through it. Therefore it can be described in three distinct ways: the point where x_2 and s_1 are zero variables, where x_1 and s_4 are zero variables, or where s_1 and s_4 are zero variables. These three

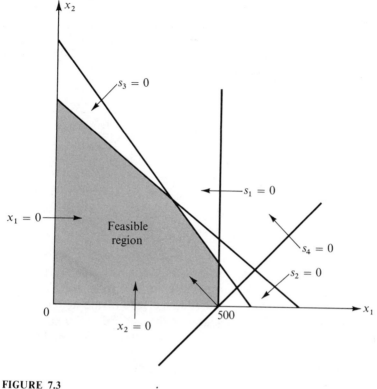

FIGURE 7.3

are the same point. This fact would not be known without the graph. The goal now is to see how this situation appears in the simplex method.

The first tableau uses the origin as the initial BFS:

	Const.	x_1	x_2	Ratio
E	0	2.8	1	
s_1	500	−1	0	−500
s_2	600	− .8	−1	−750
s_3	1560	−2.6	−2	−600
s_4	500	−1	+1	−500

The column associated with x_1 is the pivot column. The ratios are computed. Now the first symptom of degeneracy is observed: There is a tie among the candidates for pivot row. This symptom is always observed when the current BFS is adjacent to a degenerate BFS that is in the direction of movement and will be the next solution. Although the selection between s_1 and s_4 is arbitrary and both lead to the same result, it turns out that one involves fewer iterations than the other. This will be illustrated. If s_1 is selected as the pivot row, the result is

	Const.	s_1	x_2	Ratio
E	1400	-2.8	1.0	
x_1	500	-1.0	0	$+\infty$
s_2	200	$+.8$	-1.0	-200
s_3	260	$+2.6$	-2.0	-130
s_4	0	$+1.0$	$+1.0$	$+0$

The next pivot column is x_2. The ratios include a positive zero. Recall that a positive zero is quite different, for the purpose at hand, from a negative zero. A positive zero implies no limitation upon the possible increase of the new basic variable x_2. Therefore the pivot row is that associated with s_3. The new solution is better by 130. It will have $x_1 = 500$, $x_2 = 130$, and $s_4 = 130$ as basic variables. This is the optimal solution.

If s_4 had been selected as pivot row, the result would have been

	Const.	s_4	x_2	Ratio
E	1400	-2.8	$+3.8$	
s_1	0	$+1.0$	-1.0	-0
s_2	200	$+.8$	-1.8	-111.1
s_3	260	$+2.6$	-4.6	-56.5
x_1	500	-1.0	$+1.0$	$+500$

This tableau represents the same corner point as the previously shown tableau. The variables and the objective function all have the same values. However, s_4 and x_2 are zero variables here instead of s_1 and x_2. The pivot column here is x_2 and the ratios shown include a negative zero. Apparently this description of the degenerate corner point is less favorable than the previous one. The row corresponding to the negative zero must be selected as the pivot row even though it gives a zero gain in the objective function. The result is

	Const.	s_4	s_1	Ratio
E	1400	+1.0	−3.8	
x_2	0	+1.0	−1.0	+0
s_2	200	−1.0	+1.8	−200
s_3	260	−2.0	+4.6	−130
x_1	500	0	−1.0	+∞

It is clear that no gain in E was made. However, given the initial choice of s_4 instead of s_1 at the outset, this extra iteration was necessary. In this solution the same corner point is being represented by the pair s_1 and s_4 being zero variables. (We have now seen the three different ways of representing the same corner point.) The next pivot column is s_4 and the resulting ratios are shown. The pivot row is s_3. (Remember that a positive zero is not a candidate.) It is now known from previous results that the next solution will be the optimum solution; thus the example is complete.

In summary, degeneracy leads to a tie in the choice for pivot row. This tie is to be broken arbitrarily. Although differing amounts of work are involved, the determination of the best choice is not worth the work required. Both lead to the same results. When the degenerate corner happens also to be the optimum corner, one of the possible descriptions of that point may indicate optimality while another indicates the need for another iteration. However, even when extra iterations are required the final results will be the same.

EXERCISE

Solve by simplex method and illustrate graphically each step of the solution:

$$\max E = 2x_1 + x_2$$

subject to

$$x_1 \leq 4$$
$$x_2 \leq 6$$
$$x_1 \leq 10 - x_2$$

and

$$x_1, x_2 \geq 0$$

7.4   EQUALITY CONSTRAINTS

Equality constraints are sometimes found in linear programming problems. Equality constraints are simpler than inequality constraints and can always be used to reduce the dimension of the problem. This is done by using the constraint equation to substitute for one variable and eliminate it from the problem. Substitution in the nonnegativity constraint can guarantee the nonnegativity of the eliminated variable. This is illustrated with the following problem:

$$\max 2.8x_1 + x_2$$

subject to

    ① $x_1 \leq 500$

    ② $.8x_1 + x_2 \leq 600$

    ③ $2.6x_1 + 2x_2 = 1560$

    ④ $x_1 \geq 0$

    ⑤ $x_2 \geq 0$

In the context of the original M.B.A. admissions problem this means that the faculty will be allowed no free time. The feasible region is now just a segment of a line—a one-dimensional space of solutions having just two corner (end) points, as shown in Fig. 7.4. The graph of the feasible region shows that it still includes the

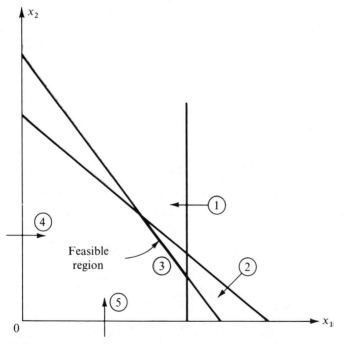

FIGURE 7.4

optimum point of the original problem. Therefore it is known from the graph and from previous sections that the optimum solution is $x_1 = 500$, $x_2 = 130$.

Now consider the algebraic method with substitution. Solve the equality constraint for x_2 to get

$$x_2 = 780 - 1.3x_1$$

This is used for substitution:

$$\max 2.8x_1 + (780 - 1.3x_1)$$

subject to

① $x_1 \leq 500$
② $.8x_1 + (780 - 1.3x_1) \leq 600$
③ gone
④ $x_1 \geq 0$
⑤ $(780 - 1.3x_1) \geq 0$

After collection of terms, it is

$$\max 780 + 1.5x_1$$

subject to

① $x_1 \leq 500$
② $x_1 \geq +360$
④ $x_1 \geq 0$
⑤ $x_1 \leq 600$

These four constraints require x_1 to be in the interval $(360, 500)$. The objective function has a positive coefficient with x_1 and so x_1 should be made as large as possible. Therefore the optimal solution is $x_1 = 500$. This implies that

$$x_2 = 780 - 1.3(500) = 130$$

and

$$E = 780 + 1.5(500) = 1530$$

This method is not always used. It is shown here only to convey the meaning of equality constraints. A method that is easier to set up and then relegates all the work to the simplex method is usually preferred in practice. This is accomplished by using artificial slack variables. The equality constraint is modified to

$$2.6x_1 + 2x_2 + a_1 = 1560 \quad \text{and} \quad a_1 \geq 0$$

In the modified problem, it is feasible to have idle faculty. However, the next step of modification assigns a high cost to their free time (a cost of 10 suffices here):

$$E = 2.8x_1 + x_2 - 10a_1$$

The other constraints, with their slack variables included, are

$$x_1 + s_1 = 500$$
$$.8x_1 + x_2 + s_2 = 600$$

The initial BFS has s_1, s_2, a_1 as basic variables and x_1, x_2 as zero variables. Finally a_1 is eliminated from E to obtain

$$E = 2.8x_1 + x_2 - 10(1560 - 2.6x_1 - 2x_2)$$
$$= -1560 + 28.8x_1 + 21x_2$$

Now the problem is ready for the simplex method. Much work remains but computers thrive on such tasks.

EXERCISE

Given the following linear program:

$$\text{Minimize } 2x_1 + x_2 - x_3 - x_4$$

subject to

$$x_1 - x_2 + 2x_3 + x_4 = 2$$
$$2x_1 + x_2 - 3x_3 \leq 6$$
$$x_1 + x_2 + x_3 \geq 7$$

and

$$x_1, x_2, x_3, x_4 \geq 0$$

Add slack variables and rewrite this problem as a maximization problem.

   Use the method of artificial slack variables as needed to find an initial basic feasible solution. State the basic variables in that solution and the objective function in terms of the nonbasic variables.

   Perform the first complete iteration of the simplex method. State, if you can, how many more iterations are required until the current solution is feasible with respect to the given problem.

7.5   UNUSUAL CONDITIONS

There are a few other unusual conditions that can be encountered in the simplex method. They have simple explanations, which are stated here and left to be illustrated by exercises:

1. Zero coefficients in E row in final tableau: indicates that the optimal solution is not unique. An adjacent corner point and all points between it and the current solution are equally good.

2. One or more artificial slack variables remain in final tableau: indicates that there are no feasible solutions to the original problem or that the coefficient given to the artificial variable in the objective function was not large enough.

3. Ratios all positive at some iteration: indicates that there is no bound upon the possible increase of the zero variable selected to become basic. The solution is at infinity. This implies an unrealistic problem formulation or an error.

EXERCISES

Solve the following three problems by the simplex method and illustrate graphically:

1. $\max E = x_1$

subject to

$$x_1 - x_2 \leq 1$$
$$-x_1 + x_2 \leq 1$$

and both variables nonnegative

2. $\min E = x_1 + 3x_2$

subject to

$$5x_1 + 4x_2 \leq 20$$
$$6x_1 + 8x_2 \geq 48$$

and both variables nonnegative

3. $\max E = 3.5x_1 + 5.25x_2$

subject to

$$x_1 \geq 2$$
$$x_2 \geq 3$$
$$2x_1 \leq 16 - 3x_2$$

Given that all calculations up to the following tableau are correct:

	Const.	s_1	s_2
E	22.75	3.5	5.25
x_1	2	1	0
x_2	3	0	1
s_3	3	-2	-3

7.6 COST OF CONSTRAINTS

The final tableau of a linear programming problem contains valuable information about the cost of the constraints or, equivalently expressed, the value of relaxing constraints. The information is always there and no extra calculations are needed. This section explains what it is and how to use it.

A general statement of the linear programming problem with n decision variables and m inequality constraints is

$$\max E = c_1 x_1 + c_2 x_2 + \cdots + c_n x_n$$

subject to

$$a_{i1} x_1 + a_{i2} x_2 + \cdots + a_{in} x_n \le b_i \qquad \text{for } i = 1, 2, \ldots, m$$

and

$$x_j \ge 0 \qquad \text{for } j = 1, \ldots, n$$

The quantities $b_1, b_2, \ldots, b_m$ can be called *resource levels* or *constraint levels*. Relaxing a constraint naturally means increasing its resource level. The optimal solution E^* is a function of the resource levels: $E^* = E^* (b_1, b_2, \ldots, b_m)$. As any b_i is increased, the optimum value of the objective function, E^*, may change. The natural meaning of "the value of relaxing constraint i" is thus the instantaneous rate of change, or derivative: $\partial E^* / \partial b_i$. The values of these derivatives are in the final tableau; it remains only to recognize them.

In the process of solution, slack variables are used to convert inequality to equality constraints. The ith constraint becomes

$$a_{i1} x_1 + a_{i2} x_2 + \cdots + a_{in} x_n + s_i = b_i$$

Thus there is a one-to-one correspondence between slack variables s_i and constraint levels b_i. The information being sought will be found to be associated with the slack variables. The final tableau contains a description of the optimum corner point (BFS). If this corner point is not degenerate, every slack variable is either a basic variable with positive value or a zero variable.

If slack variable s_i is positive, the resource level is not being completely used in the optimal solution. A marginal increase in b_i would contribute nothing to E^*; the extra resource would also go unused. Therefore, in summary,

$$\text{If } s_i > 0, \text{ then } \frac{\partial E^*}{\partial b_i} = 0$$

If the slack variable s_i is zero, the constraint is active. Since the resource *is* being fully utilized, it is reasonable to expect that more of it would also be utilized and result in an increase in E^*. Recall that if s_i is a zero variable in the final tableau, it has a coefficient in the E row. It turns out that the rate of change being sought is the negative of this coefficient, as shown by the following diagram:

	Const.		s_i
E			$-\dfrac{\partial E^*}{\partial b_i}$

Recall also that in the final tableau all such coefficients are negative or zero in a maximization problem. Therefore the value of relaxing constraint i will be positive or zero because it is found by changing the sign.

The reason why the coefficient of s_i in the E row has the meaning just claimed can now be explained. If resource level b_i is to be increased by a small amount ∂b_i from b_i to $b_i + \partial b_i$, then to maintain feasibility of the current solution the slack variable s_i must also be increased, from 0 to ∂b_i. The current solution is not optimal to the newly modified problem. It can be made optimal by decreasing s_i from its new level ∂b_i to zero. This increases the E value by $-\partial E/\partial s_i$. This is the negative of the coefficient of s_i in the E row. Therefore the result

$$\frac{\partial E^*}{\partial b_i} = -\frac{\partial E}{\partial s_i} \qquad \text{at optimum corner point}$$

Consider the example of the previous chapter, with its three constraints:

$$\max 2.8x_1 + x_2$$

subject to

$$x_1 \leq 500 \qquad \text{first-year class size}$$
$$.8x_1 + x_2 \leq 600 \qquad \text{second-year class size}$$
$$2.6x_1 + 2x_2 \leq 1560 \qquad \text{faculty size}$$

The first two constraints result from policy rules of the university. If it is profitable to operate this program of study, these constraint levels can be thought of as resources, just as faculty time is a resource. The final tableau was previously found to be

	Const.	s_1	s_3
E	1530	-1.5	$-.5$
x_1	500	-1	0
s_2	70	$-.5$	$+.5$
x_2	130	1.3	$-.5$

Recall the units of the problem. The objective function represents $1000 units of "direct profit." Class sizes are numbers of students. The number 1560 is the product of the equivalent faculty size 97.5, times 5 courses per year times 32 students per course, divided by 10 courses per year. This is the first-year class size supported by 97.5 faculty members. One new faculty member could support 1560/97.5 or 16 more first-year students.

The tableau shows that

$s_1 = 0$ and $\partial E^*/\partial b_1 = \$1500$ ($= 1.5 \times 1000$) per student position in the first-year class.

$s_2 = 70$; therefore $\partial E^*/\partial b_2 = 0$. The authorization of more second-year students would not increase E.

$s_3 = 0$ and $\partial E^*/\partial b_3 = \$500 (= .5 \times 1000)$. This is for one unit increase from 1560. A 16-unit increase would give $(16)(500) = \$8000$ per faculty member.

The question of whether these constraint levels should be changed cannot be answered without more information. For example, does direct profit cover the fixed costs involved? What is the cost of the new faculty member? However, the information available can be extremely useful in assessing the importance of the constraints.

A finite, as opposed to infinitesimal, change in a constraint level is often of interest but is somewhat more difficult. As a constraint level is increased, the gain accumulates at a constant rate until the corner point becomes infeasible. At that point, as the BFS changes, the rate of gain will also change. This change of corner point could happen several times or not at all during a finite change in a constraint level.

EXERCISE

A varnish maker has 121 gallons of alcohol and 49 gallons of shellac. He can produce and sell two mixtures of these materials:

1. Cheap mixture: 80 percent alcohol, 20 percent shellac

2. Quality mixture: 30 percent alcohol, 70 percent shellac

He sells the cheap mix at $0.50/gallon and the quality mix at $0.80/gallon.

(*a*) How many gallons of each mixture should he produce to make the highest possible profit?

(*b*) What are the values of an additional gallon of shellac and an additional gallon of alcohol in terms of marginal contributions to the total revenue?

7.7 LINEAR PROGRAMMING AND THE LAGRANGE MULTIPLIER METHOD

In Chap. 3 the concept of constraint was introduced and the method of Lagrange multiplier was used to solve both equality- and inequality-constrained problems. The method of Lagrange multiplier can also be used to solve linear programming problems. The reason why it is not used is based entirely upon efficiency. For example, the linear program having two nonnegative decision variables and three inequality constraints really has a total of five inequality constraints because the nonnegativity conditions must also be considered. The special characteristics of the linear programming problem imply that the solution is at the intersection of two of the five constraints. Thus five Lagrange multipliers would be defined, one for each constraint. All ten possible ways of selecting two out of five Lagrange multipliers to be nonzero must be considered. This search process, just like the method of enumeration of intersections, is not efficient; but it is correct.

To illustrate this fact, consider the example problem. One of the possible solutions will be sought: that having the first and third constraints holding as equalities. Thus the Lagrangian function to be maximized is

$$F = 2.8x_1 + x_2 - \lambda_1(x_1 - 500) - \lambda_3(2.6x_1 + 2x_2 - 1560)$$

Equating the derivatives to zero gives

$$\frac{\partial F}{\partial x_1} = 2.8 - \lambda_1 - 2.6\lambda_3 = 0$$

$$\frac{\partial F}{\partial x_2} = 1 - 2\lambda_3 = 0$$

$$\frac{\partial F}{\partial \lambda_1} = -(x_1 - 500) = 0$$

$$\frac{\partial F}{\partial \lambda_3} = -(2.6x_1 + 2x_2 - 1560) = 0$$

The first two equations involve only λ's. Their simultaneous solution gives

$$\lambda_1 = 1.5 \qquad \lambda_3 = .5$$

The second two equations involve only x's. Their simultaneous solution gives

$$x_1 = 500 \qquad x_2 = 130$$

This is just one candidate for optimality. All nine others would have to be tried before concluding that this is the optimal solution. Actually it can be shown that the fact that this solution has both positive λ values and feasible x values implies its optimality. Even if this fact is utilized, however, the resulting method involves guessing.

Recall that the λ values have the interpretation of

$$\lambda_i = \frac{\partial E^*}{\partial b_i}$$

Therefore the Lagrange multiplier method has just confirmed the values found in the previous section for the value of relaxing the constraints.

EXERCISES

1.   Use the Lagrange method to evaluate the solution having the first and second constraints holding as equalities. Check the feasibility of the result.

2.   Use the Lagrange method to evaluate the solution having the second and third constraints holding as equalities.

7.8   COMMON LINEAR PROGRAMMING STRUCTURES

Two common linear programming structures have already been studied, the assignment and the transportation problems. These have sufficiently special characteristics so that special algorithms are used for them. This section considers two common linear programming structures. The purpose in drawing attention to their special features has nothing to do with special algorithms. Rather the identification of the special features is meant to help develop the skill of problem formulation. It comes naturally at this point in the discussion, after many linear programming problems have been seen, because it can now help consolidate the experience already gained in formulating linear programming problems.

The first common structure is the *allocation of limited resources*. The typical problem is one in which there are n products or production processes. The decision variables are

$$x_i = \text{amount of product } i \text{ to produce} \qquad \text{for } i = 1, 2, \ldots, n$$

The constraints are upon resources that are either inputs or production capacities. Let

$$b_j = \text{amount of limited resource } j \text{ available} \qquad \text{for } j = 1, 2, \ldots, m$$

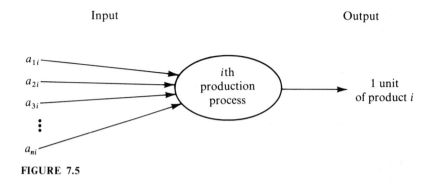

FIGURE 7.5

The objective is to maximize profits:

$$\max E = c_1 x_1 + c_2 x_2 + \cdots + c_n x_n$$

where c_i = profit per unit of product i. The production process is described by technological coefficients:

$$a_{ji} = \text{amount of resource } j \text{ required to produce 1 unit of product } i$$

These represent input lists for each product, as shown by Fig. 7.5, for product i.

The constraints in a problem of this type are upon the total amounts used of each scarce resource. Thus

$$a_{j1} x_1 + a_{j2} x_2 + \cdots + a_{jn} x_n \leq b_j$$

expresses the requirement that the total resource j used in all n production processes cannot exceed the supply b_j.

It may be possible to have by-products produced in a production process. This can be represented by a negative input. Thus a negative value of a_{ji} means that an additional quantity $- a_{ji}$ of resource j is produced by making 1 unit of product i. Other types of constraints may also be involved, but many linear programming problems have this general structure.

EXERCISE

An enterprise produces three products: A, B, and C. It uses four types of raw materials: a, b, c, and d. Producing 1 unit of A requires 3.5 units of a and 2 units of d. In addition, .5 units of b are produced as a by-product of that operation. Producing 1 unit of B requires 2 units of a and c each and 1 unit of d. Producing 1 unit of c requires 2 units of b and produces 1 unit of d as a by-product. A long-term contract has been placed for 4, 3, 3, and 2 units per month of a, b, c, and d, respectively. Their total cost is $100/month even if not entirely used. Products A, B, and C sell for $30, $10, and $20, respectively. Formulate the profit-maximization problem. If the firm has a policy that for every unit of C produced at least 2 units of B must be produced, how can the problem be reformulated to satisfy this condition?

A second common structure is the *blending problem.* Here the production process is not fixed but is the subject of the decision. There are n inputs or ingredients that can be used. The decision variables are

$$x_i = \text{amount of input } i \text{ to use} \qquad \text{for } i = 1, 2, \ldots, n$$

The output is required to meet certain quality characteristics. Let b_j be the minimum acceptable level of the jth characteristic of the product. The characteristics of the output are determined by those of the input. Let

$$a_{ji} = \text{contribution to characteristic } j \text{ of 1 unit of input } i$$

The constraints are upon the quality characteristics of the output. Thus

$$a_{j1}x_1 + a_{j2}x_2 + \cdots + a_{jn}x_n \geq b_j$$

expresses the requirement that the total contribution to the jth quality characteristic be at least b_j. The objective is to minimize the cost of meeting the requirements. Let E represent the total cost:

$$\min E = c_1 x_1 + c_2 x_2 + \cdots + c_n x_n$$

where c_i is the cost per unit of input i.

This structure can be illustrated by the following problem: A poultry farmer needs to supplement the vitamins in the feed he buys. He is considering two products, each of which contains the four vitamins required but in differing amounts. Naturally he wants to meet or exceed the minimum requirements at the least cost. Should he buy one product or the other, or should he mix the two? The facts are summarized in Table 7.1. The farmer must provide, per 100 pounds of feed, at least 50 units of vitamin 1, 100 units of vitamin 2, 60 units of vitamin 3, and 180 units of vitamin 4.

TABLE 7.1   Summary of Vitamin Problem

	Product 1	Product 2
Cost per ounce	3 cents	4 cents
Vitamin 1 per ounce	5 units	25 units
Vitamin 2 per ounce	25 units	10 units
Vitamin 3 per ounce	10 units	10 units
Vitamin 4 per ounce	35 units	20 units

The decision variables are x_i, the number of ounces of product i per 100 pounds of feed. The objective function is the cost, in cents, per 100 pounds of feed of the vitamin supplement:

$$E = 3x_1 + 4x_2$$

There are four constraints, one for each vitamin requirement:

$$5x_1 + 25x_2 \geq 50$$
$$25x_1 + 10x_2 \geq 100$$
$$10x_1 + 10x_2 \geq 60$$
$$35x_1 + 20x_2 \geq 180$$

and

$$x_1, x_2 \geq 0$$

The feasible region for this problem is shown in Fig. 7.6. This feasible region is

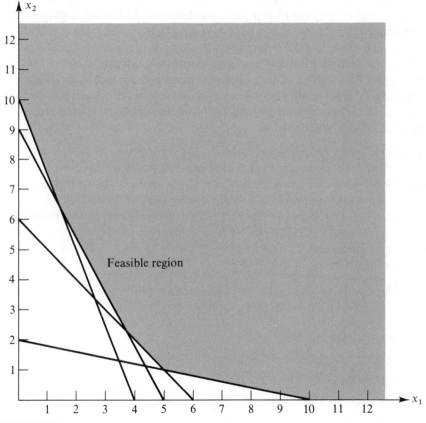

FIGURE 7.6

characteristic of blending problems. It is unbounded from above. However, the objective is to be minimized and so the feasible region is bounded in the direction of improving (decreasing) objective function. When this problem is solved by the simplex method, the infeasibility of the origin requires the method of artificial slack variables.

EXERCISE

Find the minimum-cost product mix that satisfies the vitamin requirement.

PROBLEMS

1. A mining company has two mines with different production capacities that produce the same type of ore. After crushing, the ore is graded into three classes: high, medium, and low. There is some demand for each ore grade. The company has contracted to provide a smelter with 12 tons of high-grade, 8 tons of medium-grade, and 24 tons of low-grade ore per week. It costs $200/day to run the first mine and $160/day to run the other. In a day's operation the first mine produces 6 tons of high-grade, 2 tons of medium-grade, and 4 tons of low-grade ore. The second mine produces 2, 2, and 12 tons per day of each grade, respectively. How many days a week should each mine be operated to fulfill the company's orders most economically? Which grade is overproduced at the optimum? Use the simplex method.

2. A poultry farmer raises chickens, ducks, and turkeys and has room for 500 birds on his farm. He does not want more than 300 ducks on his farm at any given time. Suppose that to raise chickens, ducks, and turkeys to maturity costs $1.50, $1.00, and $4.00, respectively. Assume also that chickens sell for $3 apiece, ducks for $2, and turkeys for $T each. The farmer wants to maximize his profit by raising the best mix of birds. Let x = number of chickens raised and y = number of ducks raised. The number of turkeys is then $500 - x - y$, assuming that the total number of birds is 500.

   (a) Formulate an expression for the farmer's profit function as a function of T.
   (b) If $T = \$6$, what is the farmer's best policy? What is his maximum profit with this policy?
   (c) Repeat with $T = \$5$.
   (d) Repeat with $T = \$5.50$.

3. The following linear program is given with slack variables x_4, x_5:

$$\max z = 3x_1 + 6x_2 + 2x_3$$

   subject to

$$3x_1 + 4x_2 + x_3 + x_4 = 2 - a \qquad \text{resource no. 1 constraint}$$

$$x_1 + 3x_2 + 2x_3 + x_5 = 1 + a \qquad \text{resource no. 2 constraint}$$

and

$$\text{all } x_i \geq 0$$

The parameter a is a constant that is unknown to you. Given a corner solution having basic variables x_1 and x_2 and given that the solutions for x_1 and x_2 are

$$x_1 = \frac{2}{5} - \frac{7}{5}a + x_3 - \frac{3}{5}x_4 + \frac{4}{5}x_5$$

$$x_2 = \frac{1}{5} + \frac{4}{5}a - x_3 + \frac{1}{5}x_4 - \frac{3}{5}x_5$$

(a) What can be said about the possible value of a? State why this is a basic feasible solution.

(b) Given that $a = 0$, what change in profit results from increasing a from 0 to .10?

(c) What further change in profit results from increasing a from .10 to .20?

4. In the M.B.A. admissions problem, the objective function was direct profit in \$1000 units.

$$E = 2x_1 + 1(.8x_1 + x_2) = 2.8x_1 + x_2$$

The coefficients 2 and 1 represent \$2000 per student in the first-year class and \$1000 per student in the second-year class. Now suppose that the alumni association objects to this formulation, claiming that alumni are more valuable than students because of their contributions to the alumni fund. The association believes that many more second-year students should be admitted, in spite of their higher demands upon the faculty, because 100 percent of them will graduate and become alumni. The implication of this argument is that the correct objective function is

$$2x_1 + (1 + I)(.8x_1 + x_2)$$

for some value of the parameter I. How large must the parameter I be before the optimal solution will have a greatly increased admission of second-year students?

5. The army is interested in building storage facilities in three states. The cost per site is \$1 million in state A, \$1.5 million in state B, and \$1.2 million in state C. Inventory and replacement demands for goods necessitate the building of at least 15 facilities. However, the strategic planning board has dictated that the number of sites developed in state A be at least twice the number developed in B. Finally the army is required to limit total employment to less than 4000; each facility in A will employ 200, each in B 750, and each in C 300. Formulate this problem and, using the simplex method with an appropriate linear programming technique, determine the optimal site allocation in A, B, and C.

6. The Turned-On Transistor Radio Company manufactures models A, B, and C, which have profit contributions of 8, 15, and 25, respectively, per unit. The weekly minimum production requirements are 100 for model A, 150 for model B, and 75 for model C. Each type of radio requires a certain amount of time for the manufacturing of component parts, for assembling, and for packaging. Specifically a dozen units of model A require 3 hours for manufacturing, 4 hours for assembling, and 1 hour for packaging. The corresponding figures for a dozen units of model B are 3.5, 5, and 1.5; for a dozen units of model C they are 5, 8, and 3. During the forthcoming week the company has available 150 hours of manufacturing, 200 hours of assembling, and 60 hours of packaging time. Formulate the production scheduling problem as a linear programming model.

7. An oil refinery utilizes two grades of crude oil and produces two grades of gasoline and motor oil as output. From each barrel of grade 1 crude they obtain .5 barrel of high-grade gasoline, .3 barrel of low-grade gasoline, and .1 barrel of motor oil. From each barrel of grade 2 crude they obtain .2 barrel of high-grade gasoline, .3 barrel of low-grade gasoline, and .4 barrel of motor oil. Grade 1 crude costs $5/barrel. Grade 2 crude costs $4/barrel. Each day 1000 barrels of high-grade gasoline, 600 barrels of low-grade gasoline, and 100 barrels of motor oil must be produced. How many barrels of each type of crude should be purchased to minimize total crude costs while fulfilling the production requirements? Interpret all entries in the top row and the constant column of your final simplex table.

8. Set up the following problem. ("Set up" means show the first tableau but do not perform the first pivot. Do indicate the first pivot element.) A wholesaler deals in one product. He stores his items in a warehouse that holds 200 items. Each month he can buy—on the first day of the month—as much as he wishes (and his warehouse can hold) and then he delivers these items throughout the month. Assume that demand is constant so that you do not have to consider probability distributions for demand. He has the following schedule of costs and prices for the next 3 months:

Month	1	2	3
Cost/unit	10	11	10
Sales price/unit	12	12	15

He currently has a stock of 50 units. What should his ordering policy be? *Hint:*

There are six variables here:

$$x_i = \text{number of units purchased in month } i$$
$$y_i = \text{number of units sold in month } i$$

There are several restrictions, which fall under two general headings: restrictions dealing with the fact that he cannot sell what he does not own, and those dealing with the fact that he cannot overstock his warehouse.

9. Two companies, call them A and B, merge. Both have the same product lines consisting of two products: product 1 and product 2. Company A has a production labor force of 28,000 man-hours/month whose productivity enables them to produce 1 unit of product 1 per man-hour or 3 units of product 2 per man-hour. Company B has a labor force of 15,000 man-hours and can produce 2 units of product 1 per man-hour or $\frac{1}{2}$ unit of product 2 per man-hour. Company A pays \$2/hour to workers making product 1 and \$3/hour to workers making product 2. Company B pays its product 1 workers \$5/hour and its product 2 workers \$4/hour. The combined company wants to consider adjusting its work forces at each of the two plants without changing its wage policy or hiring any new workers; however, workers may be laid off or switched from one product to the other. Formulate and solve a linear program that will minimize the labor costs and meet the combined production requirement of 10,000 units of product 1 and 15,000 units of product 2.

Chapter 8

DYNAMIC PROGRAMMING

Dynamic programming is basically about decision problems where decisions must be made not just at one point in time but sequentially at many points in time. For this reason such problems are called *dynamic, multistage,* or *sequential* decision problems. Naturally a decision made at one point in time has consequences that may extend far into the future. It may affect both the range and the value of possible future decisions. It is essential in such problems to consider not only the direct effects of present decisions but also their effects that "propagate" into the future. Sometimes it is also useful to take a problem that involves many decisions at one point in time and view it as if the decisions were made sequentially. Dynamic programming can be useful then as a method of decomposing a many-variable, single-time problem into many single-variable problems at different times.

Most of the problems considered in previous chapters were about decisions at one point in time. Some were about repetitive decisions, but usually with a periodic repetition of identical situations, such as in the inventory and the replacement structures. Dynamic programming is a broad problem structure. Its essential characteristic is a series of decisions, distributed in time, where there is an interrelationship between decisions. Current decisions cannot be made independently of future decisions because of this interrelationship.

8.1 DYNAMIC PROGRAMMING CONCEPTS

The concepts of dynamic programming can best be explained in terms of a simple (but unrealistic) example of a multistage decision problem. A traveler wants to go from a fixed origin to a fixed destination. The trip will proceed in four stages because he must stop each night to rest. Several paths of travel are possible. He will stop each night in a city. Each morning he will decide which of several possible cities he will travel to during the day.

The traveler's origin is city C_{41}. The first subscript indicates that there are four stages of travel remaining as he starts the process; the second indicates that this city is the first with that property. The traveler must decide first whether to proceed to city C_{31}, city C_{32}, or city C_{33} next. These are the only possibilities.

The traveler's objective is to minimize the total cost of the whole trip. He knows the cost of traveling from each city to each other city for each stage of the trip. The problem is to consider the total cost of every possible complete trip from the origin to the destination and to select from these the one having minimum total cost.

The complete problem can be described by the diagram in Fig. 8.1, which shows the possible stop-over cities and the possible travel paths between them. Associated with each path is a travel cost. The stages of travel (days) are numbered backward to indicate the number of future stages remaining. The process begins with stage 4. At the start of stage 4 the traveler must decide his destination for that day, either city C_{31}, C_{32}, or C_{33}. The destination for day 4 is also the starting point for stage 3. Again at the start of stage 3 he must decide whether to travel to city C_{21}, C_{22}, or

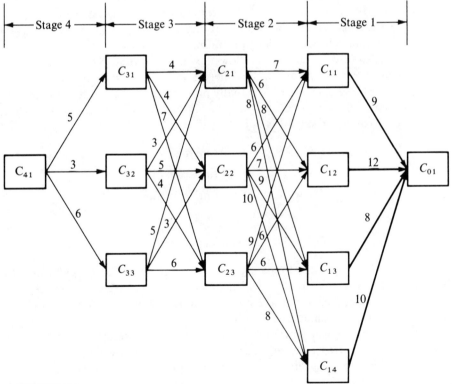

FIGURE 8.1

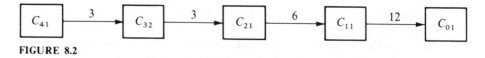

FIGURE 8.2

C_{23}. The destination for stage 3 is the starting point for stage 2 and so on. The final destination is city C_{01}. The traveler will arrive there at the end of the fourth day of travel and the process will then be over.

A shortsighted traveler might make his decisions on the basis of minimizing the cost of each single day of travel. At the start of stage 4 he would select C_{32} to be his destination because the cost of 3 units is less than the cost of traveling to C_{31} or C_{33}. This implies that he would start stage 3 from city C_{32}. His stage 3 destination would be C_{21} because that is the least-cost destination from C_{32}. Continuation of this reasoning leads to the complete path shown in Fig. 8.2. This path has a total cost of 24 units and is not the best possible path. What is wrong with the short-sighted decision rule used? It has ignored the interrelatedness of the decisions. A lower cost in today's stage may lead to a large cost in some future stage. In fact one cannot decide upon today's destination without considering all possible futures it will lead to and their costs. Since all possible futures must be considered in making each stage decision, the stage having the shortest future is easiest to solve. The stage 1 decision is easy to solve because it has no future. On the other extreme the stage 4 decision is harder to solve because it is followed by three more stages.

Consider the stage 1 decision. State 1 begins with the traveler in city C_{11}, C_{12}, C_{13}, or C_{14}. In all these cases there is actually no decision to be made. All that remains of the journey is to proceed to the final destination. The cost of the whole future process starting with stage 1 is

$$F_{11} = 9 \qquad \text{if starting from } C_{11}$$
$$F_{12} = 12 \qquad \text{if starting from } C_{12}$$
$$F_{13} = 8 \qquad \text{if starting from } C_{13}$$

and

$$F_{14} = 10 \qquad \text{if starting from } C_{14}$$

These results can be used in the following way: Replace cities C_{11}, C_{12}, C_{13}, and C_{14} by the symbols F_{11}, F_{12}, F_{13}, and F_{14}, which stand for the entire future process starting from stage 1. Label them with the costs of the future process as just calculated. The new problem is represented by Fig. 8.3.

The stage 2 problem can now be solved. The entire future, beginning from the start of stage 2, is represented in two parts: stage 2 itself plus the future following stage 2. Let F_{21}, F_{22}, and F_{23} represent the total cost of the optimal path from cities C_{21}, C_{22}, and C_{23}, respectively. This can be expressed as the sum of the cost in stage

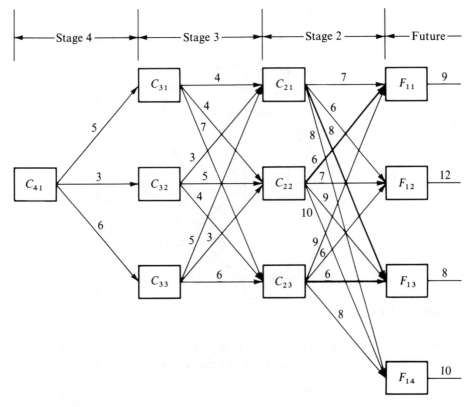

FIGURE 8.3

2 plus the cost of the future following stage 2. For each starting point there are four possible decisions. Their costs, for starting point C_{21}, are

$$7 + F_{11} = 7 + 9 \qquad \text{if } C_{11} \text{ is selected as next destination}$$
$$6 + F_{12} = 6 + 12 \qquad \text{if } C_{12} \text{ is selected}$$
$$8 + F_{13} = 8 + 8 \qquad \text{if } C_{13} \text{ is selected}$$

and

$$8 + F_{14} = 8 + 10 \qquad \text{if } C_{14} \text{ is selected}$$

The calculation and selection of the best destination can be expressed as

$$F_{21} = \min \{7 + F_{11}, \quad 6 + F_{12}, \quad 8 + F_{13}, \quad 8 + F_{14}\}$$
$$= \min \{16, 18, 16, 18\} = 16$$

Thus the cost of the optimum path from city C_{21} is 16 and is obtained by setting

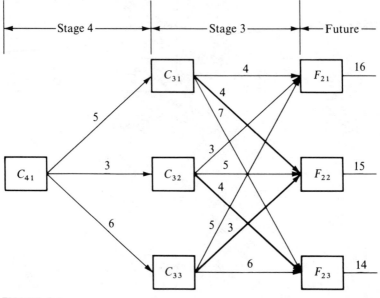

FIGURE 8.4

either C_{11} or C_{13} as the next destination. Similarly, for the starting point C_{22} the optimum cost and decision are found by the following calculations:

$$F_{22} = \min \{6 + F_{11}, \quad 7 + F_{12}, \quad 9 + F_{13}, \quad 10 + F_{14}\}$$
$$= \min \{15, 19, 17, 20\}$$
$$= 15 \quad \text{obtained with destination } C_{11}$$

The last possible starting point is C_{23}. The total cost of the best path from C_{23} is

$$F_{23} = \min \{9 + F_{11}, \quad 6 + F_{12}, \quad 6 + F_{13}, \quad 8 + F_{14}\}$$
$$= \min \{18, 18, 14, 18\}$$
$$= 14 \quad \text{obtained with destination } C_{13}$$

The results of the stage 2 calculations, which can be used in the stage 3 calculations, are represented by the diagram in Fig. 8.4.

The stage 3 calculations proceed as follows:

$$F_{31} = \min \{4 + F_{21}, \quad 4 + F_{22}, \quad 7 + F_{23}\}$$
$$= \min \{20, 19, 21\}$$
$$= 19 \quad \text{obtained with destination } C_{22}$$

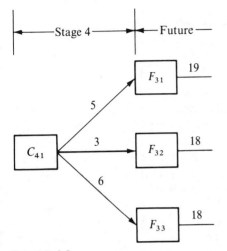

FIGURE 8.5

$$F_{32} = \min \{3 + F_{21}, \quad 5 + F_{22}, \quad 4 + F_{23}\}$$
$$= \min \{19,20,18\}$$
$$= 18 \qquad \text{obtained with destination } C_{23}$$

$$F_{33} = \min \{5 + F_{21}, \quad 3 + F_{22}, \quad 6 + F_{23}\}$$
$$= \min \{21,18,20\}$$
$$= 18 \qquad \text{obtained with destination } C_{22}$$

The results of the stage 3 calculations can be represented as shown in Fig. 8.5.

The stage 4 calculations use the stage 3 results:

$$F_{41} = \min \{5 + F_{31}, \quad 3 + F_{32}, \quad 6 + F_{33}\}$$
$$= \min \{24,21,24\}$$
$$= 21 \qquad \text{obtained with destination } C_{32}$$

The complete solution is now known. The best path, shown in Fig. 8.6, has a total cost of 21 units. Notice that the optimal solution has been obtained for every possible intermediate starting point. Thus even if the traveler made the wrong choice in stage 4 by selecting C_{31} instead of C_{32}, the method of solution has found the optimal path from C_{31} also, as shown in Fig. 8.7. It has a total cost of 19 for the remaining three stages.

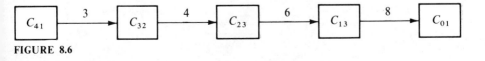

FIGURE 8.6

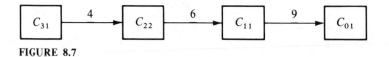

FIGURE 8.7

One way to organize and display all the results of the solution just obtained is by the diagram in Fig. 8.8, which shows only the travel paths that should be used from each possible starting point. Furthermore the box for each city tells the cost of the optimum path from that city for the remainder of the journey. This is a complete decision rule for any possible starting point because it tells the traveler, wherever he is, where to go next and how much it will cost to do so.

The dynamic programming concepts illustrated by this example can now be summarized. An N-stage decision problem can be expressed as a one-stage problem followed by an $N - 1$ stage future. This can be done for any N value. It is natural to begin with $N = 1$ and solve a one-stage problem first. This solution is used to obtain the solution to the two-stage problem. That in turn is used to solve the three-stage problem. This iterative method of solution can be continued to solve any number

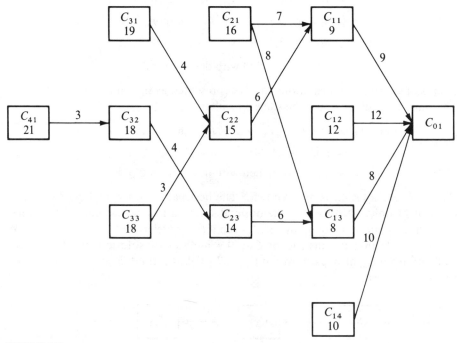

FIGURE 8.8

of stages. The principle of optimality embodied in dynamic programming is that an optimal path has the property that, for any intermediate point along that path, the remaining path is an optimum path from that starting point.

8.2   REPLACEMENT EXAMPLE

A more realistic problem that clarifies the concepts of dynamic programming is the replacement problem studied previously in Chap. 2. Suppose that the work capacity of one truck is required for N years. The work capacity of an individual truck, if properly maintained, remains constant in time. However, its deterioration is reflected in an increasing operating cost and decreasing salvage value. Suppose that a new truck will always cost $9000. Table 8.1 gives the operating cost for each successive full year, $C_0(n)$, and the resale value of the truck at the end of each year, $R_s(n)$.

TABLE 8.1   Operating Cost and Resale Value

Year (n)	Operating Cost [$C_0(n)$]	Resale Value [$R_s(n)$]
1	1800	6000
2	2100	4000
3	2400	3000
4	2700	2250
5	3000	1500
6	3600	900
7	4500	500
8	5500	200

The objective of the problem is to minimize the total cost of the truck capacity over whatever period of time the truck capacity is needed. For simplicity the costs will not be discounted to reflect the time value of money nor will the effects of income tax be considered. The application of dynamic programming to this problem begins with the identification of the stage and the state of the process. The stages are 1-year periods because it is understood that replacement actions are considered only at 1-year intervals. The stage number is the number of future years for which the one-truck capacity will be required. This can be viewed as a *planning horizon*. The state of the process is the age of the current truck at the start of the stage (year). The decision at the start of each stage is whether to retain the current truck for another year or to replace it and start the new year with a new truck. The notation for the objective function is $f_N(n)$ = total cost of future N stages if the current truck is n years old at the start and if optimum decisions are made in all future stages.

Dynamic programming decomposes the N stages into a one-stage problem (Nth)

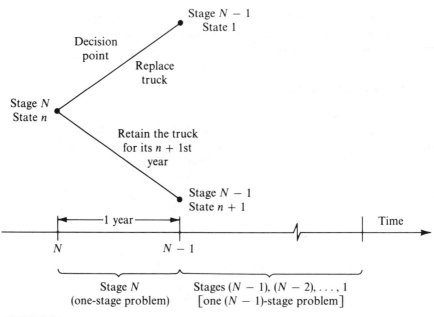

FIGURE 8.9

followed by an $(N - 1)$ stage problem. The state at the start of the $(N - 1)$ stage problem depends upon the decision made at the start of stage N. This is illustrated in the diagram (called a *decision-tree diagram*) in Fig. 8.9. The dynamic programming equation can be derived from this diagram. Suppose that $f_N(n)$ is to be computed and $f_{N-1}(n)$ is already known. The cost of the next year, stage N, depends upon whether or not the n-year-old truck is replaced at the start. If it is not replaced, the operating cost during the coming year will be $C_0(n + 1)$. The cost of the future $N - 1$ stages will be $f_{N-1}(n + 1)$. The total cost if it is not replaced will be

$$C_0(n + 1) + f_{N-1}(n + 1)$$

If the truck is replaced at the start of stage N, there will be a purchase cost of $9000 less the resale value $R_s(n)$ of the current n-year-old truck plus the operating cost $C_0(1)$ of the new truck during its first year. The total cost of the future $N - 1$ stages following this year will be $f_{N-1}(1)$. The total future cost if the truck is replaced is

$$9000 - R_s(n) + C_0(1) + f_{N-1}(1)$$

The best decision at the start of stage N is that having the lower of these two costs. Thus

$$f_N(n) = \min \{C_0(n + 1) + f_{N-1}(n + 1), \quad 9000 - R_s(n) + C_0(1) + f_{N-1}(1)\}$$

If it were possible to purchase used trucks or to rent trucks, there would be more decisions to consider; such possibilities are not considered in this equation.

This equation shows how to compute $f_N(n)$ when you already know $f_{N-1}(n)$. The beginning point for this iterative procedure is $N = 1$. Then the equation relates $f_1(n)$ to $f_0(n)$. This function $f_0(n)$ is the cost of zero future stages when starting with an n-year-old truck. This is the negative of the resale value of the truck because it is no longer needed.

$$f_0(n) = -R_s(n)$$

Then the equation for $f_1(n)$ is

$$f_1(n) = \min\{C_0(n + 1) - R_s(n + 1),\quad 9000 - R_s(n) + C_0(1) - R_s(1)\}$$

This calculation is performed for each n value.

$$
\begin{aligned}
f_1(1) &= \min\{C_0(2) - R_s(2),\quad 9000 - R_s(1) + C_0(1) - R_s(1)\} \\
&= \min\{2100 - 4000,\quad 9000 - 6000 + 1800 - 6000\} \\
&= \min\{-1900, -1200\} \\
&= -1900 \text{ (retain)}
\end{aligned}
$$

Similarly

$$
\begin{aligned}
f_1(2) &= \min\{2400 - 3000,\quad 9000 - 4000 + 1800 - 6000\} \\
&= \min\{-600, 800\} \\
&= -600 \text{ (retain)}
\end{aligned}
$$

The results of the next three calculations are

$$
\begin{aligned}
f_1(3) &= 450 \text{ (retain)} \\
f_1(4) &= 1500 \text{ (retain)} \\
f_1(5) &= 2700 \text{ (retain)}
\end{aligned}
$$

The next calculation shows that a 6-year-old truck should not be kept for its seventh year even when there is just 1 year to go:

$$
\begin{aligned}
f_1(6) &= \min\{4500 - 500,\quad 9000 - 900 + 1800 - 6000\} \\
&= \min\{4000, 3900\} \\
&= 3900 \text{ (replace)}
\end{aligned}
$$

A truck 6 years old or more would always be replaced because the operating costs continue to increase. The calculations are carried up to $n = 7$:

$$f_1(7) = 4300 \text{ (replace)}$$

The equation for stage 2 is

$$f_2(n) = \min\{C_0(n + 1) + f_1(n + 1),\quad 9000 - R_s(n) + C_0(1) + f_1(1)\}$$

Since $f_1(n)$ is now known, $f_2(n)$ can be calculated. For example,

$$f_2(1) = \min\{C_0(2) + f_1(2), \quad 9000 - R_s(1) + C_0(1) + f_1(1)\}$$
$$= \min\{2100 - 600, \quad 9000 - 6000 + 1800 - 1900\}$$
$$= \min\{1500, 2900\}$$
$$= 1500 \text{ (retain)}$$

Similar calculations give

$$f_2(2) = 2850 \text{ (retain)}$$
$$f_2(3) = 4200 \text{ (retain)}$$
$$f_2(4) = 5700 \text{ (retain)}$$
$$f_2(5) = 7400 \text{ (replace)}$$
$$f_2(6) = 8000 \text{ (replace)}$$
$$f_2(7) = 8400 \text{ (replace)}$$

Now stage 3 can be evaluated. The equation is

$$f_3(n) = \min\{C_0(n + 1) + f_2(n + 1), \quad 9000 - R_s(n) + C_0(1) + f_2(1)\}$$

This repetitive calculation can be organized as shown in Table 8.2. This shows that with 3 years to go a 3-year-old truck would be retained. However, a truck that is already 4 years old would be replaced and the new truck would be used for the 3-year period.

TABLE 8.2 Stage 3 Calculation

n	$C_0(n + 1) + f_2(n + 1)$	$[9000 - R_s(n)] + [C_0(1) + f_2(1)]$	$f_3(n)$
1	2100 + 2850 = 4950	3000 + 3300 = 6300	4950 (retain)
2	2400 + 4200 = 6600	5000 + 3300 = 8300	6600 (retain)
3	2700 + 5700 = 8400	6000 + 3300 = 9300	8400 (retain)
4	3000 + 7400 = 10,400	6750 + 3300 = 10,050	10,050 (replace)
5	3600 + 8000 = 11,600	7500 + 3300 = 10,800	10,800 (replace)
6	4500 + 8400 = 12,900	8100 + 3300 = 11,400	11,400 (replace)
7		8500 + 3300 = 11,800	11,800 (replace)

Additional understanding of this problem can be obtained from a decision-tree diagram. A three-stage problem would have three layers to represent the decisions at the three stages. It has $2^3 = 8$ distinct decision paths from start to finish because each stage can be decided in two ways. For example, the tree for $N = 3$, $n = 4$ is shown in Fig. 8.10. This diagram shows the optimum decision, for each possible starting point, by a heavy line. The numbers associated with the lines are the

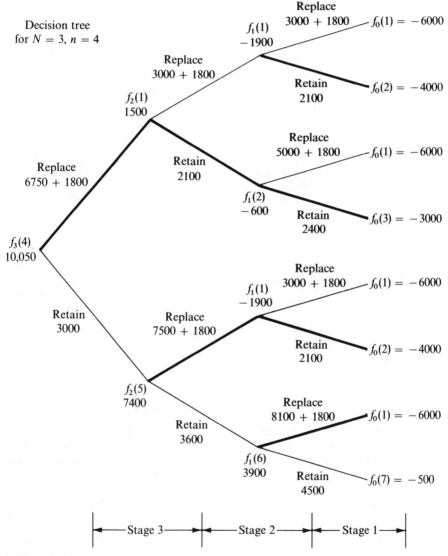

Decision tree
for $N = 3$, $n = 4$

FIGURE 8.10

costs within the year if that decision is followed. The number at each decision point is the cost of the future stages if the optimum decision is made. For example,

$$f_3(4) = 10,050 = 6750 + 1800 + f_2(1)$$
$$= 6750 + 1800 + 2100 + f_1(2)$$
$$= 6750 + 1800 + 2100 + 2400 + f_0(3)$$
$$= 6750 + 1800 + 2100 + 2400 - 3000$$

The whole analysis can be performed on the decision tree. One would begin at the right-hand side, entering the costs of each path. At each decision point the path of least future cost would be selected. This corresponds exactly to the calculations performed according to the dynamic program. The decision tree conveys more clearly the understanding of the process whereas the dynamic program is more efficient for calculation. For example, to solve stage 4 would require doubling the size of the tree. However, the dynamic programming calculation would require only another table (Table 8.3), such as that used for stage 3.

TABLE 8.3   Stage 4 Calculation

n	$C_0(n+1) + f_3(n+1)$	$[9000 - R_s(n)] + [C_0(1) + f_3(1)]$	$f_4(n)$
1	$2100 + 6600 = 8700$	$3000 + 6750 = 9750$	8700 (retain)
2	$2400 + 8400 = 10,800$	$5000 + 6750 = 11,750$	10,800 (retain)
3	$2700 + 10,050 = 12,750$	$6000 + 6750 = 12,750$	12,750 (either)
4	$3000 + 10,800 = 13,800$	$6750 + 6750 = 13,500$	13,500 (replace)
5	$3600 + 11,400 = 15,000$	$7500 + 6750 = 14,250$	14,250 (replace)
6	$4500 + 11,800 = 16,300$	$8100 + 6750 = 14,850$	14,850 (replace)
7		$8500 + 6750 = 15,250$	15,250 (replace)

These calculations can be continued for higher-stage numbers. The results for all stages up through stage 10 are given in Table 8.4. Table 8.4 also shows the optimal decision. The symbol (R) indicates that the truck should be replaced at the start; no symbol indicates that it should be retained another year; (E) indicates that either action is equally good.

This problem is related to the replacement problem of Chap. 2. In that case there was an infinite decision horizon: The truck capacity would be needed indefinitely far into the future. It was found that 5-year replacement cycles were best, with a total cost of $19,500/5 years or $3900/year. In this chapter the replacement problem is solved for all finite decision horizons up to 10 years. This is actually a larger set of problems, but it includes the infinite horizon as a special case. For example, an infinite horizon of 5-year replacement cycles is an infinite repetition of 5-year planning horizons beginning with a 5-year-old truck. Table 8.4 shows that

TABLE 8.4   Values of $f_N(n)$

Value of N	$n = 1$	$n = 2$	$n = 3$	$n = 4$	$n = 5$	$n = 6$	$n = 7$
0	-6000	-4000	-3000	-2250	-1500	-900	-500
1	-1900	-600	450	1500	2700	3900(R)	4300(R)
2	1500	2850	4200	5700	7400(R)	8000(R)	8400(R)
3	4950	6600	8400	10,050(R)	10,800(R)	11,400(R)	11,800(R)
4	8700	10,800	12,750(E)	13,500(R)	14,250(R)	14,850(R)	15,250(R)
5	12,900	15,150	16,200	17,250(E)	18,000(R)	18,600(R)	19,000(R)
6	17,250	18,600	19,950	21,000	22,200(E)	22,800(R)	23,200(R)
7	20,700	22,350	23,700	25,200	26,400	27,150(R)	27,550(R)
8	24,450	26,100	27,900	29,250(R)	30,000(R)	30,600(R)	31,000(R)
9	28,200	30,300	31,950	33,000(E)	33,750(R)	34,350(R)	34,750(R)
10	32,400	34,350	35,700	36,750(E)	37,500(R)	38,100(R)	38,500(R)

$f_5(5) = 18,000$. Since this total cost represents ending with no truck, the value of the 5-year-old truck must be added. Thus

$$f_5(5) + R_s(5) = 19,500$$

which is the total cost of a 5-year cycle. Similarly a 6-year cycle would have total cost

$$f_6(6) + R_s(6) = 22,800 + 900$$
$$= \$23,700$$

The average cost per year of the 6-year cycle would be

$$\frac{23,700}{6} = \$3950$$

as found in Chap. 2.

The dynamic programming method of solving the replacement problem is well suited only for finite-horizon cases. The infinite-horizon case is actually easier and best performed by the methods of earlier chapters.

8.3   GENERAL FORMULATION OF DYNAMIC PROGRAMMING

The two examples of dynamic programming can serve as a basis for generalization. Table 8.5 summarizes their features.

TABLE 8.5   Summary of Two Dynamic Programming Examples

Example	Process	Stage	Decision	State
8.1	Travel	1 day	Next destination	Stop-over city
8.2	Utilized truck capacity	1 year	Retain or replace	Age of current vehicle

As a generalization of these problem structures consider an N-stage process. Each stage has

1. Initial state: S_N describes the state at the start of stage N.
2. Decision: x_N is the decision variable of stage N.
3. Return function: $r_N = r_N(S_N, x_N)$ is the return from stage N if the initial state was S_N and the decision was x_N.
4. State transformation: $S_{N-1} = t_N(S_N, x_N)$ is a function that tells what the state of the process will be at the start of the next stage (stage $N - 1$) as a function of S_N and x_N. Here t_N represents a function.

The process can be represented by a stage diagram, as shown in Fig. 8.11. For example, in the replacement problem the state is

S_N = age of current vehicle at start of stage (before replacement decision)

$S_{N-1} = \begin{cases} S_N + 1 \text{ if vehicle is retained} \\ 1 \text{ if vehicle is replaced} \end{cases}$

$x_N \quad = \begin{cases} 0 \text{ represents decision to retain} \\ 1 \text{ represents decision to replace} \end{cases}$

r_N = operating cost plus replacement cost in stage N

In many problems the total return or value of the process is the sum of the stage returns. Therefore the dynamic programming equation relates the total optimal value of the process with N stages to go $f_N(S_N)$ to the stage N return plus the value of the remaining $N - 1$ stages.

$$f_N(S_N) = \max_{X_N} \{r_N(S_N, x_N) + f_{N-1}(S_{N-1})\}$$

subject to

$$S_{N-1} = t_N(S_N, x_N)$$

Dynamic programming is not itself a method of optimization but rather a method

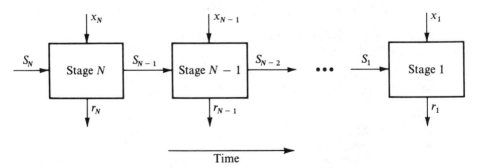

Time

FIGURE 8.11

for decomposing one problem into a set of smaller problems. The method of optimization can be a simple comparison, calculus, linear programming, and so on, whatever is appropriate for the given problem structure. The analyst's choice is not whether to use dynamic programming or some other method of optimization. Rather it is whether to apply that method of optimization directly to the whole multistage problem or to decompose the problem first and apply the appropriate method of optimization to the subproblems. Section 8.4 illustrates the use of linear programming to solve the subproblems; Sec. 8.6 uses calculus.

EXERCISE

A firm operates a rubber plantation of 4 square miles in a country that has just passed a law expropriating, without compensation, all foreign-owned land at the end of 3 years from the present. In the meantime the government will purchase at the beginning of a year any amount of land offered in units of full square miles at the following price:

Square Miles Offered at One Time	Purchase Price ($10,000)
1	4
2	7
3	9
4	10

Land used for rubber production produces a net revenue of $10,000/square mile/year.

(a) Determine the optimum sales and production decisions for the firm if it wishes to maximize total net income over the 4 years.

(b) Show that the optimum sales of land are 0, 1, 3 or 0, 2, 2 or 1, 1, 2. Show that all three give the optimum total revenue of $20,000.

8.4 WAREHOUSE EXAMPLE

The price of a particular commodity of interest varies with time in a predictable way. A warehouse operation attempts to exploit this situation by buying, storing, and selling the commodity at appropriate times. It can buy at cost C_N in month N and sell at price p_N in month N. It is now the beginning of April. The prices for the next 5 months are known and given in Table 8.6.

The warehouse must decide how much to purchase, x_N, and how much to sell, y_N, for each month N. The profitability is limited by the warehouse capacity, which is 10 units of the commodity. Selling precedes buying in each month so that the

TABLE 8.6   Future Commodity Costs and Prices

	April	May	June	July	August
c_N	105	101	95	90	90
p_N	103	102	100	103	105

limitation is on the initial inventory plus the net addition to inventory for each month. The state of the warehouse is the starting inventory S_N for each month. The state transformation is

$$S_{N-1} = t_N(S_N, x_N, y_N)$$
$$= S_N + x_N - y_N$$
$$= \text{inventory at start of month } N - 1$$

There are constraints upon the decision variables: They cannot be negative. Therefore

$$x_N, y_N \geq 0$$

Also, since selling precedes buying, the warehouse cannot sell more than it owns at the start of the month:

$$y_N \leq S_N$$

The ending inventory for the month cannot exceed the warehouse capacity:

$$S_N + x_N - y_N \leq 10$$

or

$$x_N \leq 10 - S_N + y_N$$

The return from each month's operation is the net revenue:

$$r_N = y_N p_N - x_N c_N$$

The total return from N months of operation is the sum of the returns from each month. (Present value discounting would be appropriate here but is ignored for simplicity.) The beginning inventory in April is 5 units of commodity. Assume that the use of this commodity is seasonal and that the season ends at the end of August. Inventory carried beyond this time will have zero value.

This entire problem can be solved as a linear programming problem. But the problem will be decomposed first by dynamic programming and the subproblems will be solved by linear programming. The stages are the months. Let April be stage 5 and August be stage 1 so that the stage number measures the future time remaining. Let $f_N(S_N)$ represent the optimal total return from the next N stages if stage

N begins with inventory level S_N. The dynamic programming equation is

$$f_N(S_N) = \max\{y_N p_N - x_N c_N + f_{N-1}(s_N + x_N - y_N)\}$$

subject to

$$0 \leq y_N \leq S_N$$
$$0 \leq x_N \leq 10 - S_N + y_N$$

The first subproblem to solve is the stage 1 (August) problem because it has no future to follow it:

$$f_1(S_1) = \max\{105y_1 - 90x_1\}$$

subject to

$$0 \leq y_1 \leq S_1$$
$$0 \leq x_1 \leq 10 - S_1 + y_1$$

This is a two-variable linear program and can be solved graphically for all values of S_1 between zero and 10, as shown in Fig. 8.12. The objective function increases with y_1 and decreases with x_1. Therefore the optimal solution is

$$x_1 = 0$$
$$y_1 = S_1$$

The optimal return is

$$r_1 = 105S_1$$

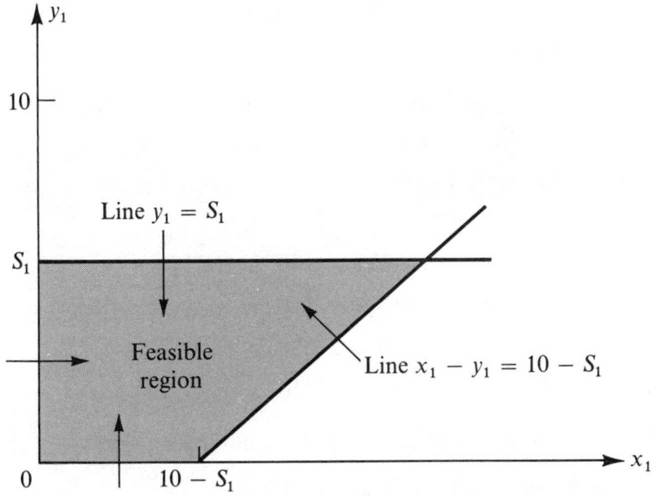

FIGURE 8.12

These conclusions would be true for any value of S_1 between zero and 10.
The stage 2 (July) problem is

$$f_2(S_2) = \max\{103y_2 - 90x_2 + f_1(S_2 + x_2 - y_2)\}$$

subject to

$$0 \le y_2 \le S_2$$
$$0 \le x_2 \le 10 - S_2 + y_2$$

Now $f_1(S_1)$ is known to be $105S_1$. Substitution gives the stage 2 objective function:

$$103y_2 - 90x_2 + 105(S_2 + x_2 - y_2) = 105S_2 - 2y_2 + 15x_2$$

The linear program for stage 2 is shown in Fig. 8.13. The objective function for this stage increases with x_2 and decreases with y_2. The optimal solution can be found by comparing corner-point solutions:

① $x_2 = 0$	$y_2 = 0$	$f_2(S_2) = 105S_2$
② $x_2 = 0$	$y_2 = S_2$	$f_2(S_2) = 103S_2$
③ $x_2 = 10$	$y_2 = S_2$	$f_2(S_2) = 150 + 103S_2$
④ $x_2 = 10 - S_2$	$y_2 = 0$	$f_2(S_2) = 150 + 90S_2$

It is clear that for any $S_2 \le 10$, the optimal solution is at the third corner point.

$$x_2 = 10 \quad y_2 = S_2 \quad f_2(S_2) = 150 + 103S_2$$

The stage 3 problem (June) is

$$f_3(S_3) = \max\{100y_3 - 95x_3 + f_2(S_3 + x_3 - y_3)\}$$

Substitution of $f_2(S_2) = 150 + 103S_2$ gives

$$100y_3 - 95x_3 + 150 + 103(S_3 + x_3 - y_3) = 150 + 103S_3 - 3y_3 + 8x_3$$

The feasible region need not be drawn again; it looks the same. All that changes is the objective function and the subscripts of the variables. Comparison of the four corner points gives

① $x_3 = 0$	$y_3 = 0$	$f_3(S_3) = 150 + 103S_3$
② $x_3 = 0$	$y_3 = S_3$	$f_3(S_3) = 150 + 100S_3$
③ $x_3 = 10$	$y_3 = S_3$	$f_3(S_3) = 230 + 100S_3$
④ $x_3 = 10 - S_3$	$y_3 = 0$	$f_3(S_3) = 230 + 95S_3$

The optimal corner point, for any $S_3 \le 10$, is the third again. Therefore

$$x_3 = 10 \quad y_3 = S_3 \quad f_3(S_3) = 230 + 100S_3$$

This procedure can be continued to solve the May and April subproblems.

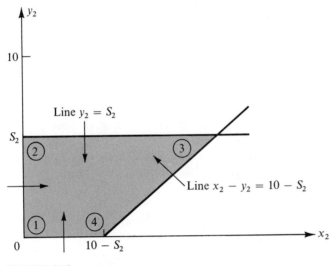

FIGURE 8.13

EXERCISES

1.   Solve the May subproblem and show that $x_4 = 0$, $y_4 = S_4$, and $f_4(S_4) = 230 + 102S_4$.

2.   Solve the April subproblem and show that $x_5 = 0$, $y_5 = S_5$, $f_5(S_5) = 230 + 103S_5$, and $f_5(S) = 745$.

8.5   SIMULTANEOUS-DECISION PROBLEMS

A simultaneous-decision problem is one having several decision variables that will be set at the same point in time.   However, it is often useful to use dynamic programming to decompose the many-variable problems into smaller problems.   It is useful to think of the decisions as being made sequentially in time.   A general problem structure of this type where dynamic programming is useful involves the allocation of a limited resource S among several independent uses or processes.   For example, a company may have budgeted an amount of money S for their national marketing activity.   This amount must then be allocated among their marketing districts.   Let there be N marketing districts and let $r_i(x_i)$ represent the return (profits, sales, or some additive measure of performance) from district i if x_i dollars are allocated for marketing activity in that district.

The simultaneous-decision problem is to maximize

$$\max \sum_{i=1}^{N} r_i(x_i)$$

subject to

$$\sum_{i=1}^{N} x_i \leq S$$

and

$$\text{all } x_i \geq 0$$

This simultaneous-decision problem can be viewed as a sequential, N-stage decision problem. The allocation x_i will be determined sequentially in time. Stage N is when there are N allocations left to be determined subject to budget S. The budget level is the state of the process. Define $f_N(S)$ to be the optimum total return from the N districts as a function of the total budget S.

The N-stage problem can be decomposed into an allocation of an amount x_N to district N and an allocation of the remaining amount $S - x_N$ to the $N - 1$ remaining districts. The dynamic programming equation is

$$f_N(S_N) = \max \{r_N(x_N) + f_{N-1}(S_N - x_N)\} \qquad 0 \leq x_N \leq S_N$$

The determination of $f_{N-1}(S_{N-1})$ is the same kind of problem: It is just a smaller set of districts and another budget level. The last subproblem, which must be solved first, is

$$f_1(S_1) = \max \{r_1(x_1)\} \qquad 0 \leq x_1 \leq S_1$$

The order in which the individual allocations are made does not matter; the sales districts can be listed in any order and the same result will be obtained. However, a judicious ordering can improve the efficiency of calculation. An alternative method for solving this class of problems is that of the Lagrange multiplier. The choice between the two methods depends upon the nature of the functions $r_i(x_i)$ and the decision variables x_i. Dynamic programming is particularly useful when the decision variables are restricted to integer values, as illustrated by the next section.

8.6   LIBRARY SPACE ALLOCATION PROBLEM

A library for periodicals (journals) has limited space. One way to conserve space is to keep only the recent issues of each journal in the high-access area and send all the older issues to some low-cost, low-access area. Suppose that the high-access area has space for 1000 issues of standard size. There are 100 periodicals in the area of interest covered by this library and the ith periodical has an "age" of g_i back issues. The total number of issues in the potential collection is

$$\sum_{i=1}^{100} g_i$$

The ith periodical has a size c_i relative to the standard size. Thus $c_i g_i$ is the

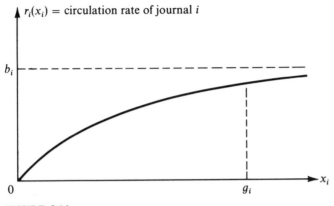

FIGURE 8.14

equivalent number of standard issues for the ith journal if all old issues of that journal are kept. The whole potential collection has total standard size of

$$\sum_{i=1}^{100} c_i g_i$$

Suppose that this total exceeds the available space of 1000 standard issues.

The decision problem for the library is how many back issues x_i to keep for each journal. The decision variables x_i are restricted to $0 \le x_i \le g_i$, and a feasible solution must obey

$$\sum_{i=1}^{100} c_i x_i \le 1000$$

The decision will be based upon circulation of the collection. Suppose that the total circulation rate of journal i depends upon the number of issues held x_i in the following way:

$$r_i(x_i) = b_i(1 - e^{-a_i x_i})$$

This curve increases at a decreasing rate as shown by the graph in Fig. 8.14. This shape represents the fact that older issues have smaller circulation rates than recent issues. Therefore the increase in total circulation obtained by adding older issues is smaller for larger x_i values. This means that the first derivative is positive:

$$\frac{dr_i(x_i)}{dx_i} = b_i a_i e^{-a_i x_i}$$

And the second derivative is negative:

$$\frac{d^2 r_i(x_i)}{dx_i^2} = -b_i a_i^2 e^{-a_i x_i}$$

The parameters b_i and a_i are known for each journal and characterize the interest level in each journal.

The decisions will be made with the objective of maximizing the total circulation rate of the periodicals collection.

$$\max \sum_{i=1}^{100} r_i(x_i)$$

subject to

$$\sum_{i=1}^{100} c_i x_i \leq 1000$$

and

$$0 \leq x_i \leq g_i$$

The dynamic programming equation is

$$f_N(S_N) = \max_{0 \leq x_N \leq g_N} \{b_N(1 - e^{-a_N x_N}) + f_{N-1}(S_N - c_N x_N)\}$$

and

$$c_N x_N \leq S_N$$

If the decision variables are allowed to take on any value within the specified range, calculus can be used to solve these subproblems. Calculus is not practical, however, because of the large number of stages involved. Numerical tabulations of the functions $f_1, f_2, \ldots$, are practical. In the dynamic programming method it is actually easier, as well as more realistic, to restrict the values of the decision variables to be integers. Then the functions need be evaluated only at integer values of their arguments.

PROBLEMS

1. A student has final examinations in three courses. He has just 12 hours available before finals to allocate to review (the remainder of the time is completely committed to current study). He feels that it would be best to break the 12 hours up into three blocks of 4 hours each and to devote each 4-hour block to one particular course. His estimates of his grades, based upon various possible hours devoted to studying each course, are

		Hours		
Course	0	4	8	12
620	D	C	C	B
621	C	C	B	A
622	D	C	B	B

Suppose that he wishes to maximize his term score. Assuming a four-point grade system (A = 4, B = 3, C = 2, D = 1), how many hours should he devote to each course?

Solve this problem by dynamic programming, showing the solution to the sub-problems by use of tables.

2. Consider the problem of deciding on the size of a permanent labor force in a large corporation over the next 4 years. The corporation estimates that it would require 50,000 laborers in the first year, 70,000 in the second, 90,000 in the third, and 60,000 in the fourth. Currently it has a labor force of 40,000. If the labor force for any year exceeds the requirement for that year, the company would lose approximately $10,000 per excess laborer. On the other hand, if the labor size falls short of the requirement figure, additional temporary laborers are recruited and given suitable training. The cost of training in salary is expected to be about $20,000 per person. Because of the labor union, the corporation would try not to fire any permanent worker. Formulate the problem as a dynamic program and find the optimal solution.

3. A student is faced with the problem of selecting eight elective courses from three different departments. He must choose at least one course from each department. His objective is to allocate the eight courses to the three departments so as to maximize his knowledge. He realizes that his knowledge will increase, but at a decreasing rate, as he takes more courses in the same department. On the basis of the available evidence, he measures the acquisition of knowledge on a multipoint scale as follows:

Department	Number of Courses Taken							
	1	2	3	4	5	6	7	8
1	10	25	50	70	80	100	100	100
2	35	40	40	50	60	80	90	100
3	15	30	35	40	70	75	100	100

Note that the student estimates he can acquire the maximum knowledge from department 1 by taking just six courses. An additional course will not improve his knowledge. His problem is to decide how to allocate the eight courses to the three departments so as to maximize his total knowledge points. It is assumed that these courses satisfy the prerequisites for each department and that knowledge points collected from different departments are additive. Formulate the problem as a dynamic program and solve.

4. Chemco is planning a production run of a certain chemical process. The process begins with k pounds of the chemical and goes through N production cycles. At the start of any cycle Chemco can sell d_n pounds of the chemical and obtain a monetary return $r(d_n) = bd_n$ (where $b > 0$) but forgo the use of it during this

cycle. If Chemco retains and uses z_n pounds of the chemical during any cycle, the yield of the process is $(1 + a)z_n$ pounds of the same chemical at the end of that cycle (where $a > 0$). The value of the chemical remaining after the last cycle is zero. It is desired to operate the process in such a way that the total monetary return is as large as possible.

(a) Formulate this problem as a dynamic program, showing the definition of stage, state, and state transformation. (It is not necessary to prove that this decomposition satisfies the sufficient conditions.)

(b) Solve the equations for $N = 3$. Guess the general form of the decision and test that it is true for $N = 4$ also.

5. Suppose that 10 units of production are needed at the end of a 3-week period. A schedule in which x_i units are made in the ith week prior to the date of the requirement has total cost $x_1^2 + 2x_2^2 + 3x_3^2$. This value should be minimized subject to $\sum_{i=1}^{3} x_i = 10$.

(a) Solve by dynamic programming, identifying first the stages, states, and the value function. Use calculus to solve the subproblems.

(b) Solve the same problem by Lagrange multiplier.

(c) Now suppose that the x_i may take on integer values only. Solve again by dynamic programming using an appropriate method of optimization to solve the subproblems.

6. A ship that can carry up to 100 tons is to be loaded. Three different types of cargo are available in any integer quantity. The ith type has weight w_i per (indivisible) unit and gives revenue v_i per unit. These weights and revenues are

Type	Weight (tons)	Revenue
1	49	20
2	50	75
3	51	102

Find the cargo loading that maximizes the revenue.

Chapter 9 DECISIONS UNDER UNCERTAINTY

In Chaps. 1 to 8 the only processes considered were predictable ones. For example, the demand during future inventory cycles was assumed to be reasonably well known. Future operating and replacement costs were assumed to be known in the replacement problem. The poultry farmer's optimum mix of vitamin supplies would, with certainty, satisfy the vitamin needs. The implication was not that these processes were perfectly predictable but rather that the uncertainties were thought to be small enough that they were not the dominant feature of the problem. Uncertainty about these processes would have complicated the problems. However, they are important and useful structures even without the uncertainties that could have been present.

The problems of this chapter, and of most of the subsequent chapters, are problems where uncertainty is the dominant feature of the problem structure. Such problems are not hard to find. For example, the need for insurance would disappear if one could predict the occurrence and size of losses. Exploration for oil and other natural resources would be relatively simple if one knew beforehand where to look. Investment in common stocks would be simple if one knew in advance which stock would have the highest increase in value. Given the existing uncertainties, these problems are deep and fascinating subjects for analysis. Moreover they are also of great practical importance. The problems of the previous eight chapters are those in which operations research has a proven record of success. They will continue to be of great importance. However, it is important also to study problems that have good growth potential, even if the past record is not so extensive. Operations research will become increasingly involved with decision problems under uncertainty if only because they exist and are of great practical importance. The problems are not new. What is relatively new is the presence of an analytic discipline having, to a reasonable extent, the confidence of the decision makers and the access to these problems. The study of uncertainty begins with the description of uncertainty in a precise, analytic way.

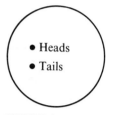

FIGURE 9.1

9.1   DESCRIPTION OF UNCERTAINTY: LIST OF POSSIBLE OUTCOMES

The first step in analytically describing the uncertainty about a future outcome is to list all distinct outcomes that are considered possible. The outcomes in the list must all be mutually exclusive so that only one will actually occur. It is usually agreed that one toss of a coin can result in heads or tails, two distinct possibilities. An exploratory oil well might be considered to have four mutually exclusive possible outcomes: Oil alone, gas alone, both oil and gas, or nothing will be discovered. The number of demands for newspapers at a newsstand during one day might have the possibilities of 50, 51, 52, ..., 150. The market price of the common stock of XYZ Corporation one year from now could be any number between $10 and $1000. The list must contain all possible outcomes and therefore the actual outcome must be one from this list. Furthermore the requirement that the elements of the list be mutually exclusive implies that no more than one element from the list will actually occur.

This list, or set of possible outcomes, is called a *sample space* by convention although the term *possibility space* would be more accurate. A diagram called a *Venn diagram* is often used as a conceptual aid. It has an outside boundary to denote its limits. Inside the boundary it has one point for each possible elementary outcome. For example, the sample space for the toss of one coin is as shown in Fig. 9.1. The sample space for one exploratory oil well is as shown in Fig. 9.2. When the sample

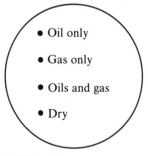

FIGURE 9.2

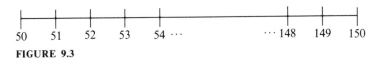

FIGURE 9.3

space of interest is a set of numbers, either an integer or an interval of values, the sample space is usually depicted instead by a line. For example, the number of demands for newspapers has the sample space shown in Fig. 9.3. The market price of the common stock mentioned has a sample space that includes all points in the interval shown in Fig. 9.4.

Remember that these sample spaces are only models of reality. Construction of a list of possible outcomes requires judgment, as does the construction of all models. Two kinds of judgment are required. The first involves the length of the list. Should "landing on the edge" be included as a possible outcome of the toss of a coin? It is a possible outcome. Its exclusion can only be based upon the judgment that it is an extremely unlikely outcome. Another example of this idea is the demand for newspapers. The list of all integer numbers between zero and infinity may appear more accurate. However, the list of integers from 50 to 150 may be a sufficiently good model.

The second kind of judgment involves the level of detail of the sample space. An exploratory oil well may find 10 million barrels of oil or 20 million. These two outcomes are quite different from some viewpoints and not so different from others. The level of detail of the sample space should always be enough to give a complete description of the outcome for the problem at hand. As with any model, an excess of detail only detracts from the power of the model. Although common stock shares are actually traded in units of one-eighth of a dollar, it is mathematically simpler to allow any number (10,1000). In summary, the sample space is a mutually exclusive listing of all possible elementary outcomes of an uncertain situation.

It is often useful to speak of *aggregates,* or sets, of elementary outcomes. For example, the exploratory oil well may produce something of value. The "event" that it does so can occur in three ways: It may produce oil only, gas only, or both. On a more abstract level, an *event* is defined to be a subset of sample space. Thus the whole sample space is an event, and each possible elementary outcome is also an event. It is useful in analysis to use letter symbols for events. For example, define

S: event something happens (whole sample space)
O: event oil alone will be discovered
G: event gas alone will be discovered
B: event both will be discovered

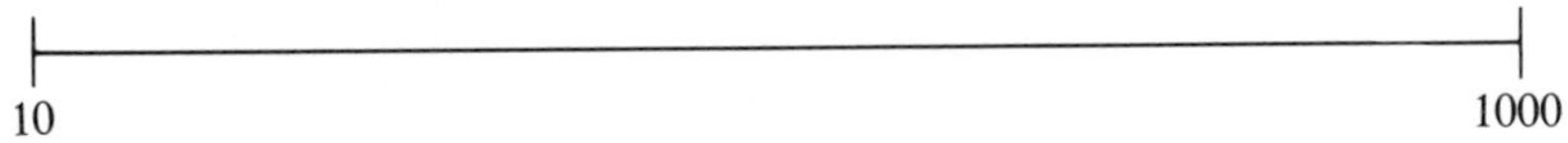

```
|                                                           |
10                                                          1000
```

FIGURE 9.4

D: event the well will be dry (nothing discovered)
V: event something of value will be discovered

Events are shown in Venn diagrams by boundaries that contain the elementary outcomes favorable to that event, as, for example, in Fig. 9.5. An event is said to occur if any one of the elementary outcomes occurs. In this example, V occurs if O, G, or B occurs.

Events are sets. It is useful in set theory to define *unions* and *intersections* of sets because they are also sets. It is similarly useful here to define unions and intersections of events because they too are events. The union of two events A and B is denoted $A \cup B$. It is the event whose elementary outcomes are either in A or in B or in both. The intersection of two events A and B is denoted $A \cap B$. It is the event whose elementary outcomes are only those in both A and B, those common to both. These two definitions can be illustrated using the possible outcomes of the toss of one die. A die is a cube whose six faces are marked with one, two, three, four, five, or six dots. The outcome is the number of dots on the side facing up after the toss. Let e_1, e_2, ..., e_6 represent the six elementary possible outcomes. Let E be the event that the outcome is an even number. Then

$$E = \{e_2, e_4, e_6\}$$

Let H be the event that the outcome is e_5 or e_6. Then

$$H = \{e_5, e_6\}$$

The union of these two events is

$$E \cup H = \{e_2, e_4, e_5, e_6\}$$

The intersection is

$$E \cap H = \{e_6\}$$

This is shown by the Venn diagram in Fig. 9.6.

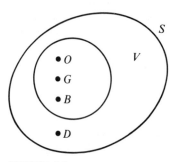

FIGURE 9.5

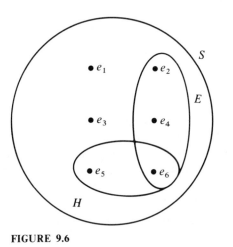

FIGURE 9.6

Another important concept is a relationship between events called *mutual exclusion*. Mutual exclusion has already been used as a relationship between elementary outcomes, meaning that only one of them can occur. As a relationship between two events it similarly means that those two events have no elementary outcomes in common. In set language it is said that they are *disjoint* or that their intersection is *empty*. In the Venn diagram in Fig. 9.7, two mutually exclusive events A and B appear with no overlap. The relationship of mutual exclusion implies that at most one of the events can occur. Knowledge that A has occurred implies that B has not occurred. A final concept is that of a *complementary event*. The complement of event A is denoted $\overline{A}$. It is the event containing all elementary outcomes not in A itself. For example, the event O, that the outcome of the toss of one die is an odd number, is the complement of E previously defined:

$$O \equiv \{e_1, e_3, e_5\} = \overline{E}$$

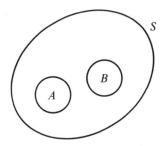

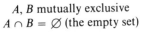

A, B mutually exclusive
$A \cap B = \varnothing$ (the empty set)

FIGURE 9.7

It follows as a general result that the union of any A with its complement contains the whole sample space:

$$A \cup \bar{A} = S$$

9.2   DESCRIPTION OF UNCERTAINTY: PROBABILITY

A *probability* is a number assigned to an event representing the degree of likelihood that that event will occur. The conventional scale has two distinguished points. The probability value zero represents impossible events, those that are certain not to occur. The value 1 represents events that are certain to occur. All numbers within $(0, 1)$ represent intermediate degrees of likelihood, as illustrated in Fig. 9.8.

It is important to realize that probability can represent subjective, personal judgments of relative likelihood. If the operations research analyst wishes to participate in the full range of important decision problems that face the real decision maker of business and government, he must realize that many of their problems involve uncertainties about unique situations. Repeatability is unfortunately not a property of many of these uncertain situations. Experimentation is often impossible or too costly. A great deal of relevant information is contained in the judgment of managers and experts on their staffs. An inability to utilize this kind of information as input to quantitative analysis implies a severe limitation upon the usefulness of quantitative analysis. Indeed the challenge of modern business problems has forced an enlargement of the concept of probability over the past two decades to include subjective judgments about unique uncertainties.

It is beyond the scope of this book to discuss the problem of determining probabilities. This would include both the measurement of subjective probabilities and the statistical techniques of inferring probability values from past observations. However, the examples and problems of this book convey some understanding of the situations in which probability is useful.

A *complete probability description* of an uncertain situation specifies the probability of every one of the elementary outcomes in the sample space. Therefore as many probability numbers are needed as there are elementary outcomes. From these the probabilities of all events can be computed. A complete description of the uncertainty about the outcome of the toss of one die is given by the list of possible outcomes and a corresponding list of their probabilities, as in Table 9.1.

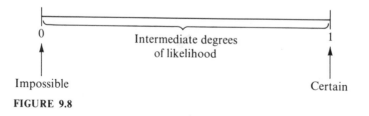

FIGURE 9.8

TABLE 9.1   Complete Probability Description

Outcome	Probability
e_1	$\dfrac{1}{6}$
e_2	$\dfrac{1}{6}$
e_3	$\dfrac{1}{6}$
e_4	$\dfrac{1}{6}$
e_5	$\dfrac{1}{6}$
e_6	$\dfrac{1}{6}$

From this complete description the probability of any event in this sample space can be computed. The fundamental rule is this: *The probability of an event is the sum of the probabilities of the elementary outcomes contained in the event.* This fundamental rule can be expressed in mathematical notation as follows. Given elementary outcomes $e_1, e_2, \ldots,$ and their probabilities $P(e_1), P(e_2), \ldots,$ and any event A such that

$$A = \{e_1, e_2, \ldots, e_n\}$$

the probability of event A is defined to be

$$P(A) = P(e_1) + P(e_2) + \cdots + P(e_n)$$

For example, given the sample space for one toss of a die, the list of probabilities, and the event

$$E = \{e_2, e_4, e_6\}$$

the probability of event E is

$$P(E) = P(e_2) + P(e_4) + P(e_6)$$
$$= \frac{1}{6} + \frac{1}{6} + \frac{1}{6}$$
$$= \frac{3}{6}$$

Similarly, for

$$H = \{e_5, e_6\}$$

$$P(H) = \frac{2}{6}$$

The probability of the intersection event

$$E \cap H = \{e_6\}$$

is

$$P(E \cap H) = \frac{1}{6}$$

The probability of the union event $E \cup H$ can be found from

$$E \cup H = \{e_2, e_4, e_5, e_6\}$$

It is

$$P(E \cup H) = \frac{4}{6}$$

EXERCISES

1. Given the sample space and the following probability description associated with a particular exploratory oil well:

Elementary Outcome	Probability
Oil only	.10
Gas only	.05
Both	.05
Dry	.80

Find the probability of the event that something of value will be discovered.

2. The sample space for the demand for newspapers at a newsstand is given as the set of integers 50, 51, 52, ..., 150. The probability of all 101 elementary outcomes is given to be $\frac{1}{101}$. Find the probability that the demand will be between 90 and 110.

A consequence of the fundamental rule for the probability of an event is that the sum of the probabilities of all elementary events in the sample space must be unity. This simply follows from the requirement that the list of elementary outcomes must contain all possibilities.

$$S = \{e_1, e_2, \ldots\}$$

One of them must occur, and therefore

$$P(S) = 1$$

Then the fundamental rule implies that

$$P(S) = \sum_{\text{all } i} P(e_i)$$

Together these conditions imply that the sum is 1. This is often called the *normalization condition.*

9.3   DESCRIPTION OF UNCERTAINTY: CONDITIONAL PROBABILITY

The sample space with its probabilities is a complete description of uncertainty at one point in time. It is a static description. However, it also contains information about how the probabilities would change with experience. The experience could be the observation of exactly which elementary outcome occurred. This would completely resolve the uncertainty. However, a less complete resolution of the uncertainty is also possible. It might show that some event A has occurred but still leave unresolved which elementary outcome within A has occurred. Experience changes probabilities. By analogy it is the "force" in the "dynamics" of probability. This is represented by *conditional probability.* The new probability of any event B in the sample space, given that event A is known to have occurred, is represented by the notation $P(B \mid A)$. The bar in this notation means "given that" the event following it has occurred. The probability of B given A can be found from the probabilities present in the original sample space by the fundamental rule of conditional probability:

$$P(B \mid A) = \frac{P(B \cap A)}{P(A)} \qquad \text{for events } A \text{ whose } P(A) > 0$$

It is important to consider whether this rule agrees with intuition. It can be viewed as representing a redistribution of the probability in the original sample space. Suppose that the original sample space has two events A and B with probability distributed over it, as shown in the Venn diagram in Fig. 9.9. Consider the four elemen-

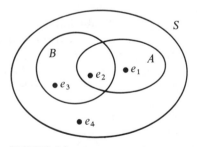

FIGURE 9.9

tary outcomes e_1, e_2, e_3, and e_4. Given that A has occurred, all the probability must be redistributed to lie within the event A. No elementary outcome outside event A can have nonzero probability. Thus

$$P(e_3 \mid A) = 0 \quad \text{and} \quad P(e_4 \mid A) = 0$$

All events such as e_1 and e_2 inside A that previously had nonzero probability should still have nonzero probability. Furthermore it seems intuitively reasonable that they should now have larger probabilities but in the same proportion as before. The fact that their relative likelihood should remain unchanged is expressed by

$$\frac{P(e_1 \mid A)}{P(e_2 \mid A)} = \frac{P(e_1)}{P(e_2)}$$

The requirement that all the redistributed probability should be within A is represented by

$$P(A \mid A) = 1$$

These last two conditions imply that the new probabilities of elementary outcomes within A are found from the old ones by multiplying them all by the same factor $1/P(A)$. Since $0 < P(A) \leq 1$, this factor is not less than 1. The conclusion is that

$$P(e_i \mid A) = \frac{P(e_i)}{P(A)} \quad \text{for } i = 1, 2$$

The new probability of an event B, which may contain many elementary outcomes, is similarly found by taking the set of elementary outcomes that are in common with event A. These are in $A \cap B$. Their probabilities are also multiplied by the same factor to give

$$P(B \mid A) = \frac{P(A \cap B)}{P(A)}$$

Thus the fundamental rule for conditional probability is seen to represent a redistribution of probability from S to A with the property that the relative likelihoods of elementary outcomes within A remain unchanged. The new probability of B, $P(B \mid A)$, may be more or less than $P(B)$ because some of its elementary outcomes may now have zero probability and others may have increased probability.

The calculation of conditional probabilities can be illustrated with the sample space given for one exploratory oil well. The sample space and probabilities are shown in Fig. 9.10. Suppose that something of value has been discovered. The new probabilities of oil and gas are needed. The first step is to compute the probability of the event given to have occurred. Two ways are correct:

$$V = O \cup G \cup B \quad \text{or} \quad V = \bar{D}$$

$$P(V) = P(O) + P(G) + P(B) \quad \text{or} \quad P(V) = 1 - P(D)$$

$$P(V) = .20 \quad \text{both ways}$$

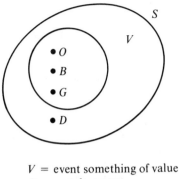

Elementary outcomes	Probability
O: oil only	.10
G: gas only	.05
B: both	.05
D: dry	.80

V = event something of value
S = sample space
FIGURE 9.10

Now the conditional probabilities can be found. Since O, G, and B are elementary outcomes, the conditional probabilities are found by multiplying by the factor

$$\frac{1}{P(V)} = \frac{1}{.20} = 5$$

The result is

$$P(O \mid V) = 5P(O) = .50$$
$$P(G \mid V) = 5P(G) = .25$$
$$P(B \mid V) = 5P(B) = .25$$

Notice that these three probabilities sum to 1.

To illustrate these ideas further, recall the sample space for one toss of a die (see Fig. 9.11). It was previously determined that

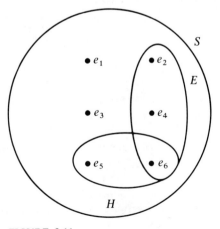

All six elementary outcomes

have probability $\frac{1}{6}$

$E = e_2 \cup e_4 \cup e_6$
$H = e_5 \cup e_6$

FIGURE 9.11

$$P(E) = \frac{3}{6} \qquad P(H) = \frac{2}{6}$$

Also

$$P(E \cap H) = \frac{1}{6}$$

Suppose now that E is given. The new probability of H is

$$P(H \mid E) = \frac{P(H \cap E)}{P(E)} = \frac{1/6}{3/6} = \frac{1}{3}$$

Notice that the probability of H has not changed; it has turned out that $P(H \mid E) = P(H)$. Suppose instead that H is known to have occurred. The new probability of E is

$$P(E \mid H) = \frac{P(E \cap H)}{P(H)} = \frac{1/6}{2/6} = \frac{1}{2}$$

Again it has turned out that $P(E \mid H) = P(E)$. These two cases illustrate the calculation of conditional probabilities. Furthermore they point out the possibility of an interesting relationship between two events: The conditional probability of either event just equals its original probability. Apparently the knowledge that H has occurred does not change the likelihood of occurrence of E.

This relationship between two events turns out to be useful because there are many situations where it is known that the probabilities should not change. For example, if two different coins are to be tossed one after another, it is reasonable to believe that the outcome of the first toss cannot in any way influence the outcome of the second. This relationship is called *independence*. Two events A and B, whose probabilities are not zero, are (mutually) independent if and only if

$$P(A \mid B) = P(A) \qquad \text{or} \qquad P(B \mid A) = P(B)$$

Using the fundamental rule for conditional probability, it can be seen that these two conditions are equivalent (if one is true, then both are true) and that both are equivalent to

$$P(A \cap B) = P(A) \cdot P(B)$$

This yields further insight: Two events must have some overlap, $P(A \cap B) > 0$, in order to be independent. Thus two events that are known to be mutually exclusive have $P(A \cap B) = 0$ by definition and, therefore, they cannot be independent. Furthermore the existence of an overlap is not sufficient for independence between two events; the probability of the overlap must exactly equal the product of the individual event probabilities.

A final example illustrates this. Suppose that every student will receive either a grade of G (for great performance) or a grade of T (for terrible). Furthermore every student has either a mathematical background, event M, or a qualitative background, event Q. It is also given that an individual selected randomly from the class will obtain a grade G with probability $P(G) = .15$. The individual has a qualitative background with probability $P(Q) = .60$. Suppose it is learned that the individual selected does in fact have a qualitative background. What is his probability of a grade of G? Intuition suggests that $P(G \mid Q) \leq P(G)$ because lack of mathematical experience would be a handicap in the course. Not enough information has been given to determine $P(G \mid Q)$. However, suppose it turns out that $P(G \cap Q) = .09$. This would imply that

$$P(G \mid Q) = \frac{P(G \cap Q)}{P(Q)} = \frac{.09}{.60} = .15 = P(G)$$

and therefore that the grade is independent of the student's mathematical background. In this case the background information would not help in predicting the grade because grades of G are received by the same fraction of Q students, 15 percent, as the fraction of all students receiving grade G.

9.4 PROBABILITY CALCULATIONS

Sections 9.1 to 9.3 explained the fundamental concepts and rules of probability. However, the analysis does not always begin with the complete list of probabilities of all elementary outcomes. If it did, the probabilities of all events could always be found by adding the probabilities of the elementary outcomes contained in the event. Since it does not, it is useful to give formulas that more often correspond to the form of the given information.

Union of Two Events A, B

A useful general formula is

$$P(A \cup B) = P(A) + P(B) - P(A \cap B)$$

This results from the consideration that the addition of the two individual probabilities double-counts the intersection event. Therefore it must be subtracted once. When A and B are mutually exclusive, this formula becomes simply

$$P(A \cup B) = P(A) + P(B)$$

Furthermore, when there are several events $A, B, C, \ldots$, the first formula for the union probability $P(A \cup B \cup C \cup \cdots)$ becomes complex. However, when the events are all mutually exclusive, the second formula continues to be simple. Thus in that case

$$P(A \cup B \cup C \cup \cdots) = P(A) + P(B) + P(C) + \cdots$$

Another special case is when all events are mutually exclusive and their union is the whole sample space:

$$A \cup B \cup C \cup \cdots = S$$

Then

$$P(A) + P(B) + P(C) + \cdots = 1$$

Intersection of Two Events A, B

A useful general formula, based upon the rule for conditional probability, is

$$P(A \cap B) = P(A \mid B)P(B) = P(B \mid A)P(A)$$

When A and B are independent, this formula simplifies to

$$P(A \cap B) = P(A) \cdot P(B)$$

Furthermore, when there are several events A, B, C, ..., the first formula for the intersection probability becomes complex. However, when the events are all independent the second formula continues to be simple. Thus in that case

$$P(A \cap B \cap C \cap \cdots) = P(A) \cdot P(B) \cdot P(C) \cdots$$

Expansion Rule

Suppose that there are n events $B_1, B_2, \ldots, B_n$ that are all mutually exclusive and whose union is the whole sample space:

$$B_1 \cup B_2 \cup \cdots \cup B_n = S$$

Suppose also that $P(B_i)$ are all known: $i = 1, 2, \ldots, n$. It is desired to find $P(A)$ for some event A. The knowledge about A is of the form that $P(A \mid B_i)$ is known for all $i = 1, 2, \ldots, n$. This is represented with $n = 3$ by the Venn diagram in Fig. 9.12.

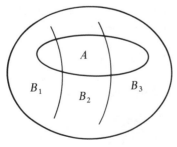

FIGURE 9.12

Now A can be viewed as the union of n pieces that are its intersections with the n B's:

$$A = (A \cap B_1) \cup (A \cap B_2) \cup (A \cap B_3) \cup \cdots \cup (A \cap B_n)$$

Since these pieces are mutually exclusive, the probability of A is

$$P(A \cap B_1) + P(A \cap B_2) + \cdots + P(A \cap B_n)$$

Finally each intersection probability can be replaced, using conditional probability, to yield

$$P(A) = P(A \mid B_1)P(B_1) + P(A \mid B_2)P(B_2) + \cdots + P(A \mid B_n)P(B_n)$$

This expression utilizes the known probabilities to obtain the desired result. It is called the *formula for probability expansion*. The following example illustrates this situation.

Every individual account in a credit card system either pays or defaults for every month his credit card is active. The population of all accounts is made up of two types: Type 1 would pay with probability .60 every month; type 2 would pay with probability .90. It is not easy to determine before granting a credit account which type an applicant is. The prior probability that an individual is of type 1 is .30 before any credit investigation is done. What is the probability that an individual whose type is unknown will pay his account in the first month if granted credit? Let B_1 and B_2 represent the events that the individual is of type 1 or 2, respectively. Let A be the event that he pays his account in the first month. It is known that a type 1 would pay with probability .6. Therefore

$$P(A \mid B_1) = .6$$

Similarly it is known that $P(A \mid B_2) = .9$. Furthermore $P(B_1) = .30$ and $P(B_2) = .70$ because there are only two types. The expansion law is

$$P(A) = P(A \mid B_1)P(B_1) + P(A \mid B_2)P(B_2)$$
$$= (.6)(.30) + (.9)(.70) = .18 + .63 = .81$$

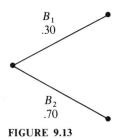

B_1
.30

B_2
.70

FIGURE 9.13

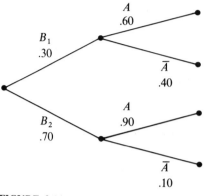

FIGURE 9.14

This can also be represented by a diagram called a *probability tree.* Suppose that chance decides first whether the individual is of type 1 or 2. This decision is represented by a point with two branches, one for each possible outcome. The probabilities are placed on the branches, as shown in Fig. 9.13. The points represent points in time, moving from left to right. For each outcome of the first decision, chance will subsequently decide whether the individual will pay his account or not. These branches are added to the diagram in Fig. 9.14. The probabilities placed on these branches depend upon the first outcome. Thus $P(A \mid B_1)$ is the relevant probability on the A branch following branch B_1. The calculation required is to find the product of the path probabilities for every path from left to right. These joint probabilities are placed at the end of each path, as shown in Fig. 9.15. Finally the probability

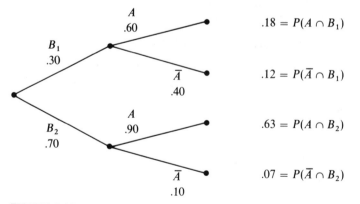

FIGURE 9.15

of A is

$$P(A) = P(A \cap B_1) + P(A \cap B_2)$$
$$= .18 + .63$$
$$= .81$$

Bayes' Rule

Bayes' rule is just a restatement of the fundamental rule for conditional probability:

$$P(A \cap B) = P(B \mid A)P(A) = P(A \mid B)P(B)$$

This is divided by $P(A)$ to obtain an expression for $P(B \mid A)$:

$$P(B \mid A) = \frac{P(A \mid B)P(B)}{P(A)}$$

This is a short form of Bayes' rule. Often there are several B events: B_1, B_2, ..., B_n. The values of $P(A \mid B_i)$ and $P(B_i)$ are often known. Then the probability expansion rule is used for the denominator, and the resulting expression gives $P(B_i \mid A)$ for $i = 1, 2, \ldots, n$:

$$P(B_i \mid A) = \frac{P(A \mid B_i)P(B_i)}{\displaystyle\sum_{i=1}^{n} P(A \mid B_i)P(B_i)}$$

Suppose, in the credit payment illustration, that the individual does pay his first-month charge. This experience constitutes additional information about the individual's type. Before the experience it was known only that the individual was from a population having 30 percent type 1. Therefore the state of knowledge about that individual was summarized by the probability statement

$$P(B_1) = .30$$

After the favorable experience that the individual has paid his account it seems, based on intuition, that the probability that the individual belongs to the less favorable type 1 should have decreased. This new probability $P(B_1 \mid A)$ can be calculated by using Bayes' rule:

$$P(B_1 \mid A) = \frac{P(A \mid B_1)P(B_1)}{P(A \mid B_1)P(B_1) + P(A \mid B_2)P(B_2)}$$
$$= \frac{(.60)(.30)}{(.60)(.30) + (.90)(.70)}$$
$$= \frac{18}{18 + 63} = \frac{18}{81} = \frac{2}{9} = .22$$

As expected, the probability that the individual is of type 1 has decreased from .30 to .22. A similar calculation would have been performed if the experience had instead been a default on the first month. The probability that the individual is of the less favorable type 1, given that experience, is .632—which is more than twice the prior value of .30. This example points out a typical use of Bayes' rule. It is the way to adjust probabilities to reflect experience. The following example has the same structure but is from an entirely different content area.

An oil company is considering the possibility of drilling an exploratory well on a given site. Their chief geologist believes that the probability of finding oil there is .2 and that the probability of a dry outcome is .8. Before making this decision, the company can obtain more evidence by means of an expensive experiment called seismographic recording. This will discover something about the underlying geological structure and will result in the determination that one of three conditions prevails:

Event R_1: no subsurface structure
Event R_2: open subsurface structure
Event R_3: closed subsurface structure

It is known from past experience that the probabilities of these three events given that oil is present are .3, .36, and .34, respectively. If the site is dry, the probabilities of the outcomes are .68, .28, and .04, respectively.

Each of the three possible outcomes of this test would result in a revised probability that oil is present. The task at hand is to compute them. Let O be the event that oil is present and let D be the event that it is not present. It is given that $P(O) = .2$ and $P(D) = .8$. The revised probabilities can all be found from the probability tree in Fig. 9.16.

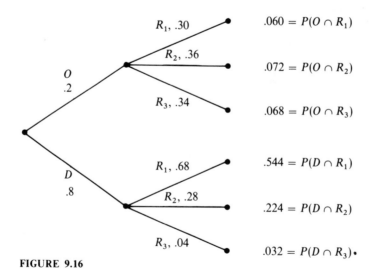

FIGURE 9.16

Three applications of Bayes' rule are made:

$$P(O \mid R_1) = \frac{P(O \cap R_1)}{P(O \cap R_1) + P(D \cap R_1)} = \frac{.060}{.060 + .544} = .099$$

$$P(O \mid R_2) = \frac{P(O \cap R_2)}{P(O \cap R_2) + P(D \cap R_2)} = \frac{.072}{.072 + .224} = .243$$

$$P(O \mid R_3) = \frac{P(O \cap R_3)}{P(O \cap R_3) + P(D \cap R_3)} = \frac{.068}{.068 + .032} = .680$$

Clearly the first and third outcomes would have a great effect upon the probability of oil. In assessing whether or not the experiment should be done, it is important to find the probabilities of these three outcomes. These are the denominators of the three applications of Bayes' rule:

$$P(R_1) = P(O \cap R_1) + P(D \cap R_1) = .060 + .544 = .604$$
$$P(R_2) = P(O \cap R_2) + P(D \cap R_2) = .072 + .224 = .296$$
$$P(R_3) = P(O \cap R_3) + P(D \cap R_3) = .068 + .032 = .100$$

The use of Bayes' rule in this form, with intersection probabilities rather than conditional probabilities, is equivalent and somewhat more useful in conjunction with the use of the probability tree. Section 9.6 considers the decision problem of whether or not to drill for oil under each of the three possible outcomes of the experiment.

EXERCISES

1. Events A and B are mutually exclusive, and A and C are independent. If $P(A) = .5$, $P(B) = .3$, $P(C) = .4$, and $P(B \cap C) = .1$, what is $P(A \mid B \cup C)$? Illustrate your method with a Venn diagram and label the events.

2. Two coins A and B are to be tossed together. List the four possible elementary outcomes. Show the events

$$H_A: \text{coin } A \text{ lands heads up}$$
$$H_B: \text{coin } B \text{ lands heads up}$$

Assign equal probability to all four elementary outcomes. Compute $P(H_A)$. Then compute the probability of H_A given H_B. Are these two events independent?

3. A company owns two similar office buildings. The probability of fire damage in a building of this type during 1 year is .001. The buildings are in different cities. Define the events

$$L_A: \text{fire loss in building } A \text{ during year}$$
$$L_B: \text{fire loss in building } B \text{ during year}$$

Construct the sample space. Assign probabilities to all elementary outcomes based upon the assumption that these two events are independent. Find the probability of no damage during 1 year. Find the probability of the complementary event that there is some loss.

4.   Another company owns four similar buildings. Again assume that the events

$$L_i: \text{fire loss in building } i \text{ during 1 year}$$

are all independent. Compute the probability that there is some loss during the year. Do this without constructing the sample space, but use the complementary event.

5.   Assume that any individual's birthday is equally likely to be on any one of the 365 days of the year. What is the probability that in a group of 5 people there will be at least one pair with the same birthday? Again use the strategy of the complementary event.

6.   In a multiple-choice question an examinee is given a choice among five answers. Suppose that there are only two possibilities: Either he knows the answer, with probability p; or he guesses the answer, with probability $\frac{1}{5}$. If an examinee has answered a question correctly, what is the chance that he really knew the answer and was not guessing?

9.5   EXPECTED VALUE AS A DECISION CRITERION

Sections 9.1 to 9.4 dealt only with the quantitative representation of uncertainty. The problem remains of how to make a decision under uncertainty. It is not possible under uncertainty simply to seek to maximize profits or minimize costs because the profit or cost consequences of the decision are not known at the time the decision must be made. That fixed relationship between decision and consequence has been replaced by a random relationship. Under uncertainty the concept of a "best" decision must be reexamined. No matter how it is defined, a best decision can, under uncertainty, lead to a bad outcome when the uncertainty is resolved. Similarly distressing, a bad decision can lead, by luck, to the best outcome. Yet the decision maker must still try to exert his limited control; he would prefer to be lucky but, having no way to control luck, he must define a criterion for decision and manage his options accordingly.

Decision making under uncertainty has often been likened to gambling. It differs in one essential way from gambling: the business executive does not view the uncertainty as a benefit in itself. The word "gambling" conveys an entertainment value in experiencing the resolution of uncertainty. The analytic criteria for decision under uncertainty to be considered here do not attribute any entertainment value to uncertainty but value it according to the possible gains or losses that may be achieved.

The term *lottery* in this context refers to a chance process that will generate one

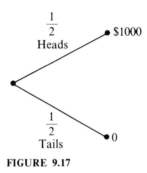

FIGURE 9.17

out of several possible outcomes, each of which has known value to the decision maker. It represents the common nature of uncertain situations—that once the possible outcomes and their probabilities are known, further description of the chance process is not relevant.

Consider a hypothetical lottery based upon the toss of a coin. The coin will be tossed once. If heads results, the decision maker will receive $1000. If tails results, he will receive nothing. This is represented in Fig. 9.17 by a probability tree with the payoff values shown at the ends. The opportunity to play this lottery is clearly valuable. It is necessary to be able to evaluate this lottery in the sense of assigning to it a certain dollar value. This value represents the least money a decision maker who already owns the lottery would sell it for. Also it is the most a decision maker who does not own the lottery would pay to own it. Clearly this dollar value must be between $1000 and $0, which are the best and worst outcomes.

One answer to the questions posed is that the value of the lottery is its *expected-value* payoff and that the criterion for decision under uncertainty is to maximize the expected value of profit or minimize the expected value of cost. The word "expected" is used here as a technical term that means weighting all payoffs by their probabilities and summing the results. The lottery above has the following expected value:

$$\left(\frac{1}{2}\right)(1000) + \left(\frac{1}{2}\right)(0) = \$500$$

This does not represent the value of an "expected outcome" of the toss of one coin. In fact this is not even a possible outcome.

The use of expected value is not the complete answer to the dilemma posed by uncertainty. The next chapter pursues that question further; the remainder of this chapter shows how this criterion is used to make decisions. Consider the following example.

An oil company is considering the possibility of drilling an exploratory well on a given site. Their chief geologist believes that the probability of finding oil there

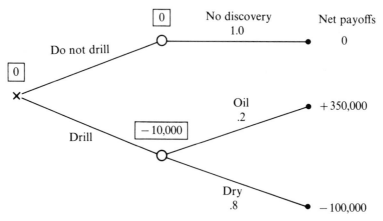

FIGURE 9.18

is .2 and that the probability of a dry outcome is .8. It costs $100,000 to drill the well in any case. If oil is present, it will be worth $450,000. A dry well is worth nothing. Find the expected value of this possible venture.

This problem can be represented by a probability tree. Now, however, something new will be added: The decision maker's decision point will be shown also. This comes first because he must decide whether or not to drill before chance decides the result of drilling. This will now be called a *decision tree* (Fig. 9.18). The decision points are marked ×; the chance points are marked ○. The analysis consists of finding the expected payoff at the chance node and entering that number in a box above the node. The expected payoff here is

$$(.2)(350,000) + (.8)(-100,000) = 70,000 - 80,000$$
$$= -\$10,000$$

Thus the expected profit is actually a $10,000 loss. At the decision point the decision maker has a choice between "do not drill" with expected value 0 and "drill" with expected value −$10,000. The best decision is that having highest expected value: do not drill. This value is finally entered at the decision point.

The following problem has the same structure, but the outcomes are expressed as costs. A firm must purchase a large quantity of a commodity either today or tomorrow. Today's price is $14.50/unit. The firm's purchasing agent believes that tomorrow's price will be either $10 or $20 per unit. He also believes that the higher price is as likely as the lower one. (See Fig. 9.19.) The expected value of tomorrow's price is

$$\left(\frac{1}{2}\right)(10) + \left(\frac{1}{2}\right)(20) = \$15$$

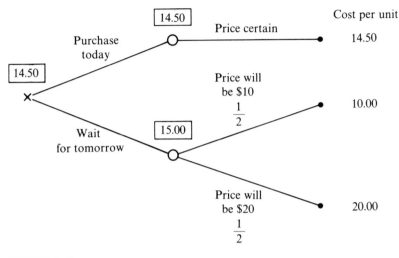

FIGURE 9.19

Comparison with today's certain price of $14.50 implies that the optimum decision is to buy today.

The concept of aversion toward risky situations is relevant to the discussion of decision under uncertainty. The following problem illustrates that the expected-value decision criterion represents a neutral attitude toward risk and therefore, although useful, cannot be the whole answer to the problem of decision under uncertainty. A manager has a choice between

1. A risky contract promising $70,000 with probability .60 and −$40,000 with probability .40

2. A diversified portfolio consisting of two contracts whose outcomes are independent, each of which promises $35,000 with probability .60 and −$20,000 with probability .40

The sample space for the diversified portfolio has four possible outcomes, shown in Table 9.2. Independence of the outcomes of the two contracts enables the probability assignment to be determined. The two middle outcomes can be combined.

TABLE 9.2   Possible Outcomes for Diversified Portfolio

Sample Space	Net Payoff	Probability
Win on both	+70,000	$(.60)^2$ = .36
Win first, lose second	+15,000	$(.60)(.40)$ = .24
Lose first, win second	+15,000	$(.40)(.60)$ = .24
Lose both	−40,000	$(.40)^2$ = .16

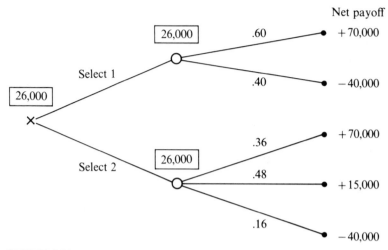

FIGURE 9.20

Figure 9.20 shows the decision tree. Option 1 has expected value

$$(.60)(70,000) + (.40)(-40,000) = 26,000$$

Option 2 has expected value

$$(.36)(70,000) + (.48)(15,000) + .16(-40,000) = 26,000$$

The two options do not differ in expected value. The decision maker following the expected-value criterion is indifferent between the two. However, on an intuitive basis many individuals would have a positive preference for option 2. Such a preference is a manifestation of the aversion toward risk. Quantification of the aversion toward risk is the subject of Chap. 11.

9.6 TWO-STAGE DECISION TREES AND THE VALUE OF INFORMATION

The discussion of decision under uncertainty would be incomplete without considering ways to reduce the uncertainty before making the final decision. A natural response to uncertainty is to perform some experiment, survey, or study to resolve at least partly the uncertainty in time for the decision. This course of action has its own limitations: Gathering information may be impossible or very costly. It is often more economical to make the decision under the existing uncertainty than to expend the effort required to reduce the uncertainty. It is important to study the economics of information. This will be done now for the expected-value decision criterion. Under this criterion, information has an expected value that is the increase in expected values of the process achieved by using the information.

Consider first the possibility of perfect information. Such information would resolve completely the existing uncertainty in time to make the decision. Furthermore there is no possibility that perfect information can be wrong. The expected value of perfect information is denoted EVPI. This will be illustrated by the commodity purchasing example of Sec. 9.5. Let A represent the event that tomorrow's price will be $10. Let $\overline{A}$ be the complementary event that it will be $20. It is known that $P(A) = \frac{1}{2}$, $P(\overline{A}) = \frac{1}{2}$. Perfect information will tell which of these will actually occur. If the information is A, the decision maker will wait to purchase and take advantage of tomorrow's price. The total cost of the process would be $10/unit. Similarly, if the information is $\overline{A}$ he will purchase today and the total cost of the process will be $14.50. However, the information must be evaluated *before* it is received. Therefore these two cases must be weighted by their probabilities of occurrence, which are the same as the probabilities of the events. Hence the expected cost (EC) of the process with perfect information (PI) is

$$\text{EC with PI} = 10 P(A) + 14.50 P(\overline{A})$$

$$= 10\left(\frac{1}{2}\right) + 14.50\left(\frac{1}{2}\right) = 12.25$$

It is already known that the expected cost of the process without the information is $14.50. The difference, a decrease in expected cost, is the EVPI:

$$\text{EVPI} = \text{EC without PI} - \text{EC with PI}$$

$$= 14.5 - 12.25 = 2.25$$

Another way to arrive at this result is to reason that the best decision without information is to purchase today. Information that A is true would switch this decision and save $4.50. Information that $\overline{A}$ is true would not change the decision and would give no savings. The expected savings are

$$\text{EVPI} = \frac{1}{2}\,(4.50) + \frac{1}{2}\,(0) = 2.25$$

The conclusion is that, in an expected-value sense, the perfect information would be worth $2.25 per unit of the commodity. However, perfect information is not likely to be a feasible alternative. The importance of the calculation is that the value of perfect information is a bound upon the value of any imperfect information.

Consider a more realistic source of information. A commodity market expert will, for a fee of $0.15/unit of commodity, predict tomorrow's price. The expert will say either "Tomorrow's price will be $10" (event B) or "Tomorrow's price will be $20" (event $\overline{B}$). The expert is not always right; in fact he is right only 60 percent of the time. This means that the probability of event B, given that the price will actually be $10, is only .60. Similarly the probability of event $\overline{B}$, given that the price will actually be $20, is only .60.

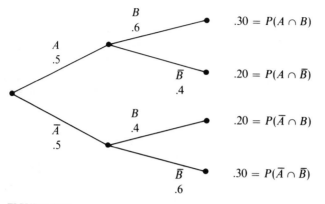

FIGURE 9.21

The information given by the expert will not completely resolve the uncertainty about tomorrow's price. However, it can be used to revise the probabilities of tomorrow's price, by Bayes' rule. Figure 9.21 shows the probability tree. Then

$$P(B) = P(A \cap B) + P(\bar{A} \cap B) = .5$$
$$P(\bar{B}) = P(A \cap \bar{B}) + P(\bar{A} \cap \bar{B}) = .5$$

and

$$P(A \mid B) = \frac{P(A \cap B)}{P(B)} = \frac{.3}{.5} = .6$$

and

$$P(A \mid \bar{B}) = \frac{P(A \cap \bar{B})}{P(\bar{B})} = \frac{.2}{.5} = .4$$

Thus the imperfect prediction that the price will be $10 (event B) raises the probability of that event from .5 to .6. The opposite prediction ($\bar{B}$) would lower it from .5 to .4.

The complete decision problem now has two stages of decision. The sequence of actions is

1. Decision maker decides whether to purchase imperfect information.
2. Chance decides outcome of information.
3. Decision maker makes terminal decision of whether to purchase today or wait.
4. Chance decides tomorrow's price.

A decision tree is constructed for the complete problem. Probabilities of chance events are entered. Net costs are placed at the right for each complete path through the tree. The analysis consists of expected-value calculations and selection of op-

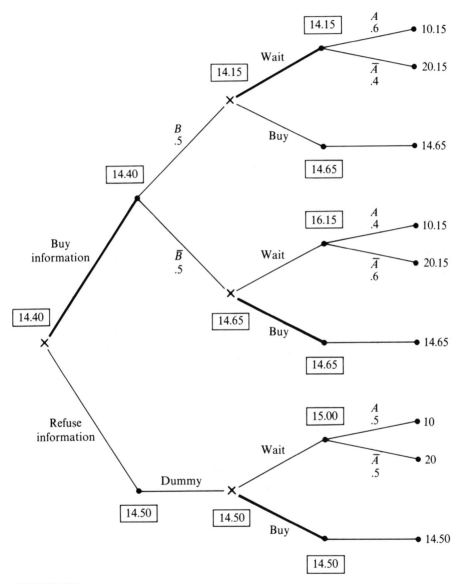

FIGURE 9.22

timum decisions. For example, given B, the expected cost of waiting for tomorrow's price is

$$(.6)(10.15) + (.4)(20.15) = 14.15$$

With the opposite prediction the expected cost is

$$(.4)(10.15) + (.6)(20.15) = 16.15$$

Figure 9.22 is a diagram of the complete tree with the analysis.

The conclusion of the analysis is that the expert's opinion is worth the cost on an expected-value basis. The net gain attributable to the imperfect information is .10 per unit of commodity. This is obtained from the difference $14.50 - 14.40$ in expected costs between not buying and buying the information.

After buying the information, the purchase decision will depend upon the following predication:

If B, then wait and purchase tomorrow.
If $\bar{B}$, then purchase today.

The optimal decisions and their expected costs can be summarized by the tree illustrated in Fig. 9.23.

The same problem structure is present for the oil company deciding whether or not to drill a well. Recall that before making this decision, the company can obtain more evidence by means of an expensive experiment called seismographic recording. This will determine something about the underlying geological structure and will cost $10,000 to perform. Previous calculations using Bayes' rule have indicated that for the three possible test outcomes the revised probability of oil is as shown in Table 9.3.

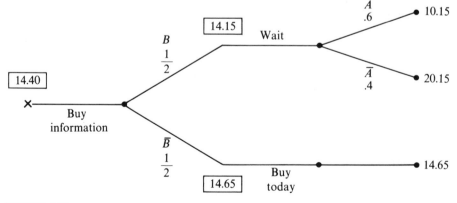

FIGURE 9.23

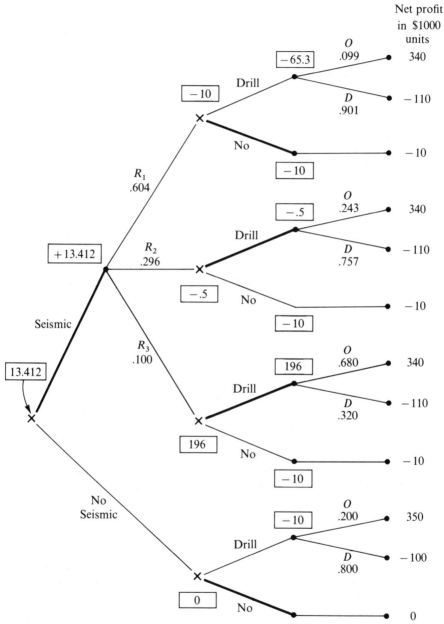

FIGURE 9.24

TABLE 9.3   Revised Probability of Oil

Event	$P(O \mid \text{event})$	$P(\text{event})$
R_1: No subsurface structure	.099	.604
R_2: Open subsurface structure	.243	.296
R_3: Closed subsurface structure	.680	.100

The sequence of action is

1. Decision maker decides whether to buy seismic test.
2. Chance decides outcome of test.
3. Decision maker uses outcome to decide whether to drill.
4. Chance decides whether oil is present.

The complete decision tree is shown in Fig. 9.24. The conclusion of the analysis is that the expected gain from using the seismic recording is $13,412. The well will be drilled if the test outcome is either R_2 or R_3 but not if R_1 results.

Many problems have the same structure as the two just considered. Table 9.4 is a helpful summary for identifying the common elements of this problem structure. Information has value through the possibility that it will improve the terminal decision. The value of information is determined by the analysis.

TABLE 9.4   Summary of Two-stage Decision Problems

Common Elements	Example 1	Example 2
Unknown state of nature	Tomorrow's price	Oil or dry
Terminal decision	Buy today or wait	Drill or not
Source of imperfect information	Ask expert	Take seismic
Possible outcomes of experiment	Expert predicts $10 or $20	R_1, R_2, R_3

Probability description required: 1. Prior probability of unknown state of nature 2. Conditional probability of experimental outcomes given state of nature.

PROBLEMS

1. Airplane flight 311-Y is scheduled to leave for New York tomorrow morning. Fifty seats are now reserved. There may be some cancellations before flight time. Also there may be additional requests for reservations. Suppose that the probabilities of zero, one, or two cancellations are .7, .2, and .1, respectively. Any larger number of cancellations is highly unlikely. The number of new requests will be zero, one, or two with probabilities .8, .15, and .05. Any larger number is unlikely. There are 10 seats unreserved now. Find the probability distribution

of the number of unreserved seats at flight time under the assumption that cancellations and new reservations are independent processes.

2. Suppose that the probability of a student passing an examination is $\frac{4}{5}$, that of the student sitting to his left $\frac{3}{5}$, and that of the student to his right $\frac{1}{5}$. Assuming that none of these students looks at his neighbor's paper, find the probability that, of these three students,

   (a) Exactly two pass the examination.

   (b) The student sitting in the middle passes the examination, given that the student on his right passes it.

3. A company has just completed the development of a new product and must decide whether to introduce it on the market. They believe that their new product will be considered either superior or inferior to the competitor's product, but they do not know which of these two outcomes will occur. The company estimates that the probability of the new product's superiority is .7. A market survey can be taken at considerable cost. It would indicate whether the product is superior to its competitor. The market survey has the following reliability:

   If the product is really superior, the probability that the survey will indicate "superior" is .8.

   If the product is really inferior, the probability that the survey will indicate "superior" is .3.

   What would be the posterior probabilities of the superiority of the new product for each possible outcome of the survey?

4. Every individual account in a credit card system either pays or defaults for every month his credit card is active. The population of all accounts is made up of two types: Type 1 would pay with probability .60 every month; type 2 would pay with probability .90. It is not easy to determine before granting a credit account which type an applicant is. The prior probability that an individual is of type 1 is .30 before any credit investigation is done. The credit screening test can be done once; it classifies each applicant as low (type 1) or high (type 2). Its probability of giving the correct classification is .60 for either type of customer. Find the posterior probability that an applicant is of type 2 for each possible outcome of this test.

5. A patient thinks he may have cancer and consults doctor A, who, after examination, declares that he does not.

   (a) Suppose that doctor A diagnoses cancer in only 60 percent of those patients who have it and never in the case of those who do not. What is the probability of this outcome of the diagnosis? Given the diagnosis, what is the probability that the patient has cancer? Graph this as a function of the prior probability of cancer.

(b)   The patient feels that his doctor is overcautious about diagnosing cancer so he consults a second doctor, B, who declares that he does have cancer. Suppose that B diagnoses cancer in 80 percent of those patients who have it and in 10 percent of those who do not. Suppose that the two opinions are given independently. This means that doctor B's diagnosis depends only upon whether cancer is present and not upon the outcome of A's examination. Graph the posterior probability of cancer as a function of the original prior probability.

6.   An oil company is planning a pipeline to carry oil a distance D miles from the producing wells to the refinery. They want to limit the loss from oil spills resulting from breaks in the pipeline. They plan to place automatic shutoff valves in the pipeline every d miles but must decide what value to use for d. These valves can sense a pressure drop from a break and automatically stop the flow. The loss due to spilled oil is then proportional to just the distance between valves; the cost per mile of spillage is C_s (in $1000) per mile. Therefore the spillage cost of one break is $C_s d$. The cost of the valves is C_v (in $1000) per valve. The total number of pipeline breaks over the projected life of the pipeline is B. Assume that there will be one valve at the start of the line even if it is known that there will be no breaks.

(a)   Find the total cost of the valves plus spillage over the life of the pipeline. It should be a function of the decision variable d, the parameter D, the costs, and the quantity B.

(b)   The number of breaks over the lifetime is unknown. It is believed that there will be either zero, one, or two breaks with probabilities .5, .4, and .1, respectively. Find the expected total cost as a function of d, D, and the costs C_v and C_s.

(c)   Find the expression for the d value that minimizes the expected total cost over the life of the pipeline. Evaluate it using the estimates $C_v = 10$, $C_s = 6$, and $D = 10,000$.

(d)   What would be the value of perfect knowledge of the future number of breaks in time to decide how many valves to use?

7.   Suppose that a population of candidates for insurance is composed of two types: Type A individuals have probability .01 of one accident in 1 year; type B individuals have probability .05 of one accident in 1 year. The whole population has 80 percent type A and 20 percent type B. Assume that the probability of more than one accident is zero for both types. The premium for this type of policy for 1 year is $20. The loss to the insurance company per accident is $1000.

(a)   Suppose that it is not possible to determine the individual's type. For an individual randomly selected from the population, what is the probability of one accident during 1 year? Find the expected profit to the insurance company from a 1-year policy.

(b) Suppose that this individual does have one accident during his first year. Use Bayes' rule to find his posterior probability of one accident during the next year. Find the expected profit to the insurance company for a second 1-year policy. How much more valuable is an individual who has had no accident in his first year? Assume that an individual's type and accident rate do not change with time.

8. The company in Prob. 3 must decide whether to take the survey that costs $.5 million. The company has assessed the consequences of the possible superiority of the product in terms of net profit (in $ million):

	Possible Decisions	
Possible Outcomes	A_1: Market New Product	A_2: Do Not Market New Product
S_1: new product superior to competitor	$5	$1
S_2: new product inferior to competitor	$-.3	$.4

The reason for the net profits if the product is not marketed is that the company can sell the process and patents associated with the new product idea.

(a) Which decision (market or not market) should the company take? What is its expected net profit if it makes its decision without obtaining additional information?

(b) What is the appropriate decision for each outcome of the survey, taking into account the preceding information? What is the expected net profit?

(c) Should the survey be taken?

(d) What is the expected net gain of the survey before it is taken?

9. Suppose that a population of candidates for insurance is composed of two types: Type A individuals have probability .01 of one accident in 1 year; type B individuals have probability .05 of one accident in 1 year. The whole population has 80 percent type A and 20 percent type B. Assume that the probability of more than one accident is zero for both types. The premium for this type of policy for 1 year is $20. The loss to the insurance company per accident is $1000. Suppose that individuals can be classified according to an observable characteristic related to their accident behavior type. Given that an individual is type A, he will be put into class 1 with probability .7 and into class 2 with probability

.3. A type B individual will be put into class 1 with probability .4 and into class 2 with probability .6.

(a) Use Bayes' rule to find the posterior probabilities of types A and B for an individual who has been put into class 1.

(b) The insurance company wishes to maximize expected profit. They will sell a policy only when the expected profit is positive. Find their decision for each outcome of the screening test.

(c) Find the expected contribution to profit if the screening test is used. Should it be used if it costs $2 per applicant to apply?

Chapter 10 RECURRENT DECISION PROBLEMS UNDER UNCERTAINTY

A *random variable* consists of a sample space and probability assignment with the additional property that every possible outcome can be described by a number. The value of the random variable is the number associated with the actual outcome. The probability assignment is now called a *probability distribution.* This concept is useful in operations research problems because numerical values, usually economic values, are often associated with uncertain outcomes.

10.1 DISCRETE RANDOM VARIABLES

Consider a hypothetical lottery based upon the toss of five coins. The lottery will pay its owner $100 for every coin showing heads. It is desired to find the probability distribution of the random variable: $\tilde{z}$ = payoff from the lottery. The tilde notation means that $\tilde{z}$ is a random variable, not a single number, whereas z would denote a particular value realized. The sample space of this random variable is 0, 100, 200, 300, 400, 500—six possibilities. The probabilities associated with these outcomes can be found from the assumptions that each coin has probability $\frac{1}{2}$ of giving heads, and each coin is independent of the others. The probability of all heads is then the product

$$\left(\frac{1}{2}\right)^5 = \frac{1}{32}$$

This is also the probability associated with the outcome zero heads (all tails). The outcome of exactly one heads among the five coins can occur in five distinct ways because the coin showing heads can be any one of the five. The probability of this event is

$$5\left(\frac{1}{2}\right)^n = \frac{5}{32}$$

This, by the symmetry of the problem, is also the probability of exactly four heads among the five coins. A similar counting of the number of ways in which the five coins can give two heads gives a probability of

$$10\left(\frac{1}{2}\right)^n = \frac{10}{32}$$

Again by symmetry this applies also to the outcome of three heads (two tails).

Thus the random variable $\tilde{z}$ has the distribution of probability shown in Table 10.1. Notice that the sum of the probabilities is unity. This probability distribution can be represented by a graph, as shown in Fig. 10.1.

TABLE 10.1 Probability Distribution of $\tilde{z}$

Possible z Values	Probability of z
0	$\frac{1}{32}$
100	$\frac{5}{32}$
200	$\frac{10}{32}$
300	$\frac{10}{32}$
400	$\frac{5}{32}$
500	$\frac{1}{32}$

Any discrete random variable can be represented by a similar graph. Furthermore the probabilities can often be represented by an analytic function called the *probability function* or probability distribution function:

$$f(z) = \text{probability that random variable } \tilde{z} \text{ will take on value } z$$

Since $f(z)$ is a probability, it can have values $0 \leq f(z) \leq 1$. Since some outcome must occur, the probability function must be normalized:

$$\sum_{\text{all } z} f(z) = 1$$

Any random variable has an *expected value* that is an average of all possible values weighted by their probabilities. This is represented by the expectation notation $E(\tilde{z})$:

$$E(\tilde{z}) = \sum_{\text{all } z} zf(z)$$

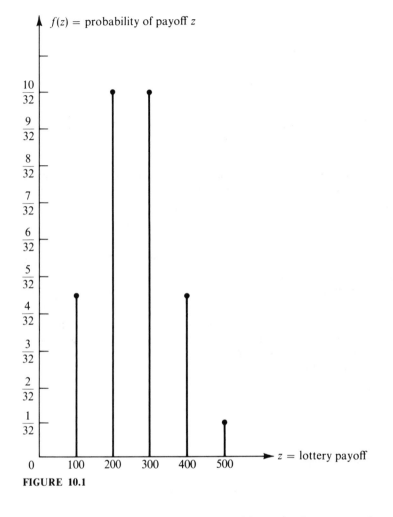

FIGURE 10.1

For example, the lottery based on the toss of five coins has expected payoff

$$E(\tilde{z}) = 0\left(\frac{1}{32}\right) + 100\left(\frac{5}{32}\right) + 200\left(\frac{10}{32}\right) + 300\left(\frac{10}{32}\right) + 400\left(\frac{5}{32}\right) + 500\left(\frac{1}{32}\right)$$

$$= \$250$$

The expected value of a random variable is also called the *mean value* or the *first moment of the distribution.* If a probability distribution had to be summarized by only one number, the most important single number is its expected value or first moment. If allowed just two numbers to characterize a probability distribution, the second most descriptive number is the variance of the distribution. This is a measure of the degree of spread of the distribution about its mean. It is defined by

$$V(\tilde{z}) = E\{[\tilde{z} - E(\tilde{z})]^2\} = \sum_{\text{all } z} [z - E(\tilde{z})]^2 f(z)$$

For example, the variance of the five-coin lottery is

$$V(\tilde{z}) = (-250)^2 \frac{1}{32} + (-150)^2 \left(\frac{5}{32}\right) + (-50)^2 \frac{10}{32} + (50)^2 \frac{10}{32} + (150)^2 \frac{5}{32} + (250)^2 \frac{1}{32}$$

$$= 12{,}500$$

The square root of variance is called the *standard deviation* (SD). Although it measures the same thing, its units are the same as those of the random variable. The standard deviation is conventionally denoted by σ. Here

$$\sigma = \sqrt{V(\tilde{z})} = 111.80$$

The variance is often used as an intuitive measure of "risk." A variance of zero represents a random variable that can take on only one value. Therefore there is no uncertainty about its outcome and so there is no risk. A larger variance means a greater spread in the range of possible outcomes and hence, intuitively, a greater risk. As an example, consider an alternative lottery whose outcome is determined by the toss of only one coin. The payoff will be $500 if heads comes up and zero otherwise. The probability distribution is shown in Fig. 10.2.

The expected value of this random variable is

$$E(\tilde{z}) = 0\left(\frac{1}{2}\right) + 500\left(\frac{1}{2}\right) = 250$$

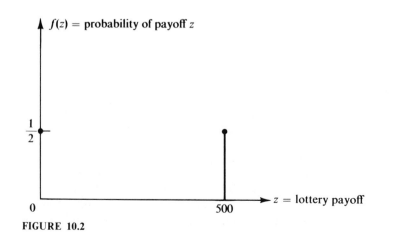

FIGURE 10.2

and

$$V(\tilde{z}) = (-250)^2 \frac{1}{2} + (250)^2 \frac{1}{2} = 62{,}500$$

$$\sigma = \sqrt{V(\tilde{z})} = 250$$

The standard deviation of this lottery is more than double that of the previous lottery while the mean values of both are equal. In many situations real decision makers shown an aversion to risk and would prefer the first lottery over this one. However, under the expected-value decision criterion, a decision maker is represented as being indifferent between these two lotteries. Therefore this criterion represents an attitude of neutrality toward risk. The mathematical representation of aversion toward risk is covered in Chap. 11.

Other characteristics of probability distributions can sometimes be useful. However, a graph of a distribution is usually more useful and conveys more information than any characteristics beyond mean and variance. Many analytic probability distributions are useful for their ability to represent common processes. They contain parameters that enable them to represent a situation of interest. Formulas are available that give their mean and the variance as a function of the parameter values. Some of these analytic distributions are given here along with suggestions on possible applications.

The *binomial distribution* is given by the probability function

$$f(z \mid n,p) = \frac{n!}{z!\,(n - z)!} p^z (1 - p)^{n-z} \qquad \text{for } z = 0, 1, 2, \ldots, n$$

for any parameter values such that $0 < p < 1$ and n is a positive integer. This distribution is applicable whenever there are n independent trials each of which has two possible outcomes. Then the random variable $\tilde{z}$ is the number of trials that result in the outcome which has probability p.

It can be demonstrated, using the binomial expansion, that the expected value of $\tilde{z}$ is

$$E(\tilde{z}) = np$$

and the variance is

$$V(\tilde{z}) = np(1 - p)$$

Table 10.2 gives some possible applications.

The *Poisson distribution* has probability function

$$f(z \mid \lambda) = \frac{\lambda^z e^{-\lambda}}{z!} \qquad \text{for } z = 0, 1, 2, \ldots$$

TABLE 10.2   Application of the Binomial Distribution

n Trials	p = Probability of	Random Variable $\tilde{z}$ = Number of
Sales calls	Sale on one call	Sales
Newspaper subscribers	Cancellation	Cancellations
Individuals in age group	Accident	Accidents
New products	Defect	Defective products

The parameter λ can have any positive value. The mean of this distribution is

$$E(\tilde{z}) = \lambda$$

and the variance is

$$V(\tilde{z}) = \lambda$$

This distribution is applicable when there are many trials but each has a small probability of generating the event being counted. For example, there may be a large number of potential customers each with a small probability of making a purchase within a short time period. The number of sales within that period is a random variable whose distribution may be well approximated by the Poisson distribution. Similarly the number of demands for a service, the number of hydrocarbon or mineral deposits in a large area, the number of accidents in a time period, the number of typographical errors on a page, and many other random variables are found to have the Poisson distribution.

10.2   CONTINUOUS RANDOM VARIABLES[1]

When the possible outcomes can have any number associated with them within a fixed interval of values, a continuous random variable is useful. For example, the future price of a stock traded on the stock market is really an integer multiple of one-eighth of a dollar. However, for many applications it is useful to ignore that knowledge and represent the list of possible future prices as any number between two limits. Similarly most money transactions are made in multiples of $0.01. However, when dealing with hundreds, thousands, or millions of dollars, that fact is of no practical significance. Continuous distributions offer great mathematical convenience in many problems.

Probabilities are now assigned to *intervals* of outcome values rather than to individual outcome values. When probability is spread over an interval, the concept of *density* is the natural way to describe the concentration of probability. Thus $f(z)$

---

[1] This section is essential only for Secs. 10.3, 10.5, and 10.6; for parts of Secs. 11.4 and 11.6 to 11.8; and for Secs. 14.8 and 14.9.

represents a density of probability in the neighborhood of the point z. The probability that the random variable $\tilde{z}$ will fall within the small interval $(z, z + dz)$ is

$$P[\tilde{z} \text{ has outcome in } (z, z + dz)] = f(z)\, dz$$

for small values of dz only. The whole probability distribution is specified by giving the probability density function $f(z)$ for all z values. For all finite intervals, the probability is found as an integral:

$$P[\tilde{z} \text{ has outcome in } (a,b)] = \int_a^b f(z)\, dz$$

Since $f(z)$ is not itself a probability, it can have value exceeding unity over a short interval.

The calculation of the probability associated with any interval (a,b) is performed in terms of the *cumulative probability distribution* $F(x)$, defined by

$$F(x) \equiv P(\tilde{z} < x) = \int_{-\infty}^x f(z)\, dz$$

Then the probability for interval (a,b) is

$$P[\tilde{z} \text{ is in } (a,b)] = \int_{-\infty}^b f(z)\, dz - \int_{-\infty}^a f(z)\, dz = F(b) - F(a)$$

The cumulative distribution function is given by either an analytic expression or a table.

The expected value of a continuous random variable is also found by an integral that is the continuous analog of the summation by which expected value was defined. The expected value $E(\tilde{z})$ of the continuous random variable $\tilde{z}$, having probability density function $f(z)$, which could assign nonzero probability density over the whole interval $(-\infty, \infty)$, is

$$E(\tilde{z}) = \int_{-\infty}^\infty zf(z)\, dz$$

Similarly the variance is found by the integral

$$V(\tilde{z}) = \int_{-\infty}^\infty [z - E(\tilde{z})]^2 f(z)\, dz$$

These two characteristics of a distribution have the same significance for continuous random variables as for discrete random variables.

The graph of a probability density function can be an intuitive device for describing uncertainty (see Fig. 10.3). Suppose a study might show that two proposed risky business projects A and B have the probability density functions of

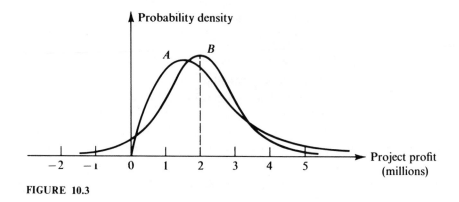

FIGURE 10.3

profit shown in Fig. 10.3. These two projects have the same expected profit. How-ever, the graph shows that project *A* cannot result in a loss although *B* can. *A* has a lower most-likely outcome than *B* because it peaks at about 1.5 compared to 2.0. However, *A* also has higher probability associated with very high profits than does *B*. It is not unusual for managers to be faced with such difficult comparisons of risky projects. Probability density functions are increasingly becoming a part of the language of management. A few highly useful analytic forms will be considered here.

The *uniform density* represents the most uncertainty of density functions whose probability is all contained within the same interval from $z = a$ to $z = b$. The density function is a constant over the interval, implying that no outcome is more likely than any other (Fig. 10.4). The mean of the distribution is given by

$$E(\tilde{z}) = \left(\frac{a + b}{2}\right)$$

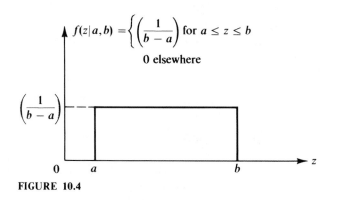

FIGURE 10.4

The variance is

$$V(\tilde{z}) = \frac{(b - a)^2}{12}$$

The cumulative distribution function is found by integration:

$$F(x) = \int_a^x \frac{1}{b - a} \; dz = \frac{x - a}{b - a} \qquad \text{for } a \le x \le b$$

The advantages of this distribution are that it represents extreme uncertainty within given limits and has great mathematical simplicity.

The *exponential probability density* function is given by

$$f(z) = \lambda e^{-\lambda z} \qquad \text{for } z \ge 0$$

The parameter λ can have any positive value. The graph is shown in Fig. 10.5. The cumulative distribution function is

$$F(z \mid \lambda) = \int_0^x \lambda e^{-\lambda z} \; dz = 1 - e^{-\lambda x} \qquad \text{for any } x \ge 0$$

The mean of this distribution is

$$E(\tilde{z}) = \frac{1}{\lambda}$$

The variance is

$$V(\tilde{z}) = \left(\frac{1}{\lambda}\right)^2$$

This probability distribution represents a random variable that can have only positive values. Negative-valued outcomes are not possible. Furthermore lower-

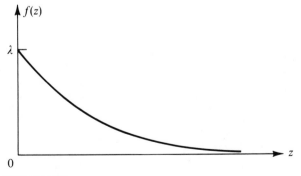

FIGURE 10.5

value outcomes are always more likely than higher values. This distribution is useful for random time intervals. The time between the arrivals of successive customers or demands for service is often observed to have this distribution. The time required for service operations that are not routine may have this distribution.

The *normal distribution* has density function

$$f(z \mid \mu, \sigma^2) = (2\pi\sigma^2)^{-1/2} \exp\left[-\frac{(z - \mu)^2}{2\sigma^2}\right] \quad \text{for } -\infty < z < \infty$$

The parameter μ can have any value whereas the parameter σ can have any positive value. The graph of the density is shown in Fig. 10.6. The mean of this distribution is

$$E(\tilde{z}) = \mu$$

The variance is

$$V(\tilde{z}) = \sigma^2$$

Therefore the standard deviation is σ. One important feature of this distribution is that it is symmetric: The outcome $\mu + y$ has the same probability density as the outcome $\mu - y$, for any y. The standard deviation is particularly meaningful for this distribution. The following statements show how the probability is distributed within σ intervals around the mean:

$$P[\tilde{z} \text{ is in } (\mu - \sigma, \mu + \sigma)] = .683$$
$$P[\tilde{z} \text{ is in } (\mu - 2\sigma, \mu + 2\sigma)] = .955$$
$$P[\tilde{z} \text{ is in } (\mu - 3\sigma, \mu + 3\sigma)] = .997$$

Thus the standard deviation gives a good intuitive grasp of the uncertainty represented by this distribution.

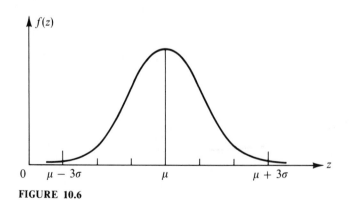

FIGURE 10.6

A transformation from $\tilde{z}$ to a new random variable $\tilde{y}$, defined by

$$\tilde{y} = \frac{\tilde{z} - \mu}{\sigma}$$

is useful for calculation. Since $\tilde{y}$ has zero mean and unit variance, its probability density, called a *standard normal*, is tabulated. The cumulative distribution function $F_s(y)$ of $\tilde{y}$ is also tabulated and used to calculate $F(x)$ for $\tilde{z}$. Then the

$$P[\tilde{z} \text{ is in } (a,b)] = F(b) - F(a)$$

$$= P\left[y \text{ is in } \left(\frac{a - \mu}{\sigma}, \frac{b - \mu}{\sigma}\right)\right]$$

$$= F_s\left(\frac{b - \mu}{\sigma}\right) - F_s\left(\frac{a - \mu}{\sigma}\right)$$

After the arguments of $F_s(\ )$ are calculated, the table is used to evaluate the functions. The normal distribution is one of the most useful analytic distributions. It applies to most situations where symmetry about the mean value is reasonable. Random variables whose values are determined by addition of many independently determined increments will have a probability distribution that is at least approximately normal.

The *gamma distribution* is useful when a nonsymmetric shape is desired. Its density function is

$$f(z \mid a,b) = \frac{a^b z^{b-1} e^{-az}}{(b - 1)!} \qquad \text{for } z \geq 0$$

The parameter a can have any positive value. If the parameter b is a positive integer, $(b - 1)!$ is easily computed. However, positive noninteger values of b are also useful but require a generalization of the factorial function to allow noninteger values. The cumulative probability distribution can be expressed analytically when b has integer value:

$$F(X) = 1 - \sum_{n=0}^{b-1} \frac{e^{-ax}(ax)^n}{n!}$$

If b is not an integer, a table is required. The possible shapes of this density function are shown in Fig. 10.7. The mean of this distribution is

$$E(\tilde{z}) = \frac{b}{a}$$

The variance is

$$V(\tilde{z}) = \frac{b}{a^2}$$

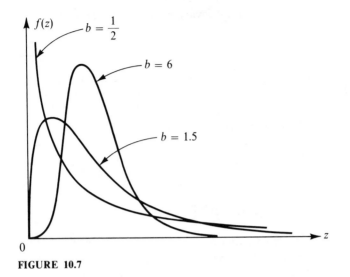

FIGURE 10.7

This distribution is useful for random variables that can have only positive outcomes. Furthermore there are many situations where there is a small but significant probability of very large outcomes. Profits and rates of return from projects, costs, sizes of bids in auctions, and many economic variables have this general nonsymmetric distribution shape.

Consider the following example of the use of probability density functions. Suppose that a risky exploration program has been analyzed. The analysis shows that the probability density function of net profit from the program has

$$\text{Mean} = \$10 \text{ million}$$
$$\text{Variance} = 50 \,(\text{SD} = \$7.1 \text{ million})$$

Suppose that the analytic expression of the density function is given by the gamma probability density. What is the probability associated with the intervals $(-\infty, 2.9)$, $(2.9, 17.1)$, $(17.1, \infty)$?

The parameters of the gamma density are determined from the mean and variance:

$$\frac{b}{a} = 10 \qquad \frac{b}{a^2} = 50$$

The solution is $a = .2, b = 2$. Therefore, because b has integer value, the cumulative probability distribution is given by

$$F(x) = 1 - e^{-ax}(1 + ax) \qquad \text{with } a = .2$$

Now

$$F(17.1) = 1 - e^{-3.42}(4.42)$$
$$= 1 - .1446$$
$$= .8554$$

Also

$$F(2.9) = 1 - e^{-.58}(1.58)$$
$$= 1 - .8845$$
$$= .1155$$

Therefore the probability that the actual profit will exceed 17.1 is $1 - F(17.1) = .1446$. The probability that the actual profit will be between 2.9 and 17.1 is $F(17.1) - F(2.9) = .7399$. The probability that the actual profit will be less than 2.9 is $F(2.9) = .1155$.

Now suppose that the distribution is normal. Then

$$\mu = 10$$
$$\sigma = 7.1$$

The value of y corresponding to $z = 17.1$ is

$$\frac{17.1 - \mu}{\sigma} = \frac{17.1 - 10}{7.1} = +1$$

The value of y corresponding to $z = 2.9$ is

$$\frac{2.9 - \mu}{\sigma} = \frac{2.9 - 10}{7.1} = -1$$

The table of the normal distribution function in Appendix D shows that

$$F_s(+1) = .8413$$
$$F_s(-1) = .1587$$

The interval probabilities are shown in Fig. 10.8.

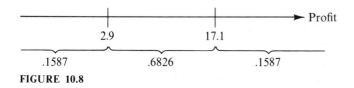

FIGURE 10.8

EXERCISES

1.   A sealed bidding competition is to be held. The company that submits the highest bid will win the lease for the mineral rights to a tract of land. Your firm believes that their uncertainty about the highest bid of all their competitors can be represented by the uniform distribution between $1000/acre and $10,000/acre. Find the expected value of the highest competitor's bid and the probability that the highest competitor's bid exceeds its expected value. What is the probability that your firm will win the lease as a function of its bid B?

2.   An office building has a storage tank for fuel oil used to heat the building. The number of days in which a full tank would be emptied is uncertain because of variations in the weather. Suppose that the tank has just been filled. The number of days until the tank will run dry has a Poisson probability distribution with mean 17 days. If a refill is scheduled for 14 days, what is the probability that the tank will already have run dry by that time?

10.3   EXPECTED-VALUE DECISION MAKING UNDER UNCERTAINTY

There are many important problems whose structure is that of decision under uncertainty. The main purpose of this chapter is to consider a few special cases that are very common and not too difficult mathematically. It is useful to state a general structure of these problems first. The elements of the problem are

x = decision variable
y = parameter or uncontrollable variable
$\tilde{z}$ = random variable at time decision must be made

The model has two parts:

1.   Deterministic part: a conditional objective function that specifies the value of the objective function if the decision is x and the random variable has outcome z. Denote this by $E_c(x, y, z)$.

2.   Probabilistic part: a probability distribution $f(z)$, either a discrete probability function or a continuous probability density function to describe the uncertainty about $\tilde{z}$.

These two parts are combined to form an objective function based upon the expected-value criterion:

$$E(x, y) = \int_{\text{all } z} E_c(x, y, z) f(z) \, dz$$

The objective then is to maximize this objective function:

$$E^* = \max_{\text{all } x} \{E(x, y)\}$$

This formal statement emphasizes the necessity of first determining the value of the objective function as if z were known. The understanding of the problem under certainty must come first.

10.4 THE NEWSBOY INVENTORY PROBLEM

The *newsboy inventory problem* refers to a problem structure rather than a content area. Like the transportation problem, its name conveys little information about its use. It is usually about inventory—but inventory as a structure, not necessarily inventory content. Basically it is in an inventory problem with uncertain demand. However, for simplicity the units in inventory cannot be carried over from one cycle to the next; furthermore each cycle is of fixed duration. The word "newsboy" conveys these conditions. The newsboy selling papers on the city street must decide at the start of the day how many newspapers to stock for the whole day. He does not know exactly what the demand will be at the time he must make this decision: Natural variations in daily demand make it difficult to predict. The inventory cycle length is fixed by the nature of the product, and newspapers cannot be carried over for the next day. Therefore this is actually the simplest inventory problem having the main feature of uncertain demand.

Consider the more plausible problem of a personnel manager in a machine-tool manufacturing company. He must decide how many repairmen to hire to service the plant equipment. Since the plant is operated during the day, the repairmen work on the night shift repairing machines that have failed during the day. Each repairman can repair one machine per shift. If he has x repairmen and the number of machine failures during the day, z, is such that $z > x$, then the extra $z - x$ machines must be repaired during the night shift by an outside contractor at \$150/machine. The wages and benefits of the company repairmen are \$50/day. The number of machine failures in 1 day varies randomly. Experience shows that the probability function of the number of machine failures in 1 day is as shown in Table 10.3.

TABLE 10.3 Probability of z

z	$f(z)$
0	.20
1	.30
2	.30
3	.10
4	.10

The object of the analysis is to decide how many permanent repairmen to hire to minimize the average repair cost per day. The stock of repairmen is like an inventory of service capacity. Machine failures are demands against that inventory. Excess repairmen cost $50 per man of unused capacity. An insufficient supply of repairmen costs $150 per unsatisfied demand.

This problem can be solved by the most direct approach of evaluating all possible solutions: $x = 0, 1, 2, 3,$ or 4. For each possible value of x the actual cost is found for each possible z value. Then the expected cost associated with x is computed. Finally the x having minimum expected cost is found (see Table 10.4).

TABLE 10.4   Calculation of Expected Cost

Decision (x)	Actual Cost Given z					Expected Cost
	$z = 0$	$z = 1$	$z = 2$	$z = 3$	$z = 4$	
0	0	150	300	450	600	$0(.2) + 150(.3) + 300(.3)$ $+ 450(.1) + 600(.1) = 240$
1	50	50	200	350	500	$50(.2) + 50(.3) + 200(.3)$ $+ 350(.1) + 500(.1) = 170$
2	100	100	100	250	400	$100(.2) + 100(.3) + 100(.3)$ $+ 250(.1) + 400(.1) = 145$
3	150	150	150	150	300	$150(.2 + .3 + .3 + .1)$ $+ 300(.1) = 165$
4	200	200	200	200	200	$200(.2 + .3 + .3 + .1 + .1) = 200$

The expected cost is computed by weighting each actual cost for given z by the probability of that z occurring. Comparison of the resulting expected costs shows that $x = 2$ repairmen is optimal. The expected cost associated with this decision is $145/day. It is better by $20/day than the next-best decision, $x = 3$. The probability that an outside repairman will be needed is the probability that the number of failures is three or four. This is $.1 + .1 = .2$.

Any problem of the newsboy type can be analyzed in this way. If the demand is a continuous random variable, however, the summation operation is replaced by an integral. Even for discrete random variables the number of possible decisions and outcomes may be large and this method will not be efficient.

Analysis shows that there is a simple way to find the optimum decision. It also gives a better understanding of the structure and scope of this problem. Again let $\tilde{z}$ represent the number demanded in one cycle and let $f(z)$ be the probability function of $\tilde{z}$. Consider the following costs:

c_1 = cost per unsatisfied demand
c_2 = cost per excess unit

The decision variable is x, the number of units to stock. The objective is to minimize the expected cost of one cycle.

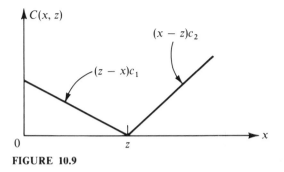

FIGURE 10.9

The derivation of the model begins with the actual cost if x units are stocked and z units are subsequently demanded. Let $C(x,z)$ represent this actual cost:

$$C(x,z) = \begin{cases} (z - x)\,c_1 & \text{if } z \geq x \text{ (excess demand)} \\ (x - z)\,c_2 & \text{if } x > z \text{ (excess supply)} \end{cases}$$

Considered as a function of x for given z, this function has the graph shown in Fig. 10.9.

It is clear that if z is known at the time of the decision the problem is trivial: Order z units and the actual cost will be zero. This would hardly be a problem in the absence of uncertainty of demand. However, the decision must be made before the actual demand is known and, therefore, the next step is to compute the expected cost as a function of the decision variable alone. Thus the expected cost is

$$C(x) = \sum_{z=0}^{\infty} C(x,z) f(z)$$

The function $C(x,z)$ is given in two parts and so the expectation is written next as two summations:

$$C(x) = \sum_{z=0}^{x} (x - z)\, c_2 f(z) + \sum_{z=x+1}^{\infty} (z - x)\, c_1 f(z)$$

This is the model relating the objective function to the decision variable. It is this expression that must be minimized as a function of x. The use of calculus would be inappropriate here because the decision variable can take only discrete values. Furthermore it appears in the limits of summation. However, the derivative condition for optimality can be replaced by a difference condition. (The following derivation of the condition for optimality is not essential to the understanding of its applications.) The conditions for optimality are these: If x is optimal, then

$$C(x) \leq C(x + 1)$$

and also

$$C(x) \leq C(x - 1)$$

To implement this it is necessary to compute $C(x + 1)$. Replacing x by $x + 1$, the expression is

$$C(x + 1) = \sum_{z=0}^{x+1} (x + 1 - z) c_2 f(z) + \sum_{z=x+2}^{\infty} (z - x - 1) c_1 f(z)$$

The term $z = x + 1$ contributes zero in either summation. Therefore shifting it from the first to the second does not alter the value of the expression:

$$C(x + 1) = \sum_{z=0}^{x} (x + 1 - z) c_2 f(z) + \sum_{z=x+1}^{\infty} (z - x - 1) c_1 f(z)$$

Next separate terms to obtain

$$C(x + 1) = \sum_{z=0}^{x} (x - z) c_2 f(z) + \sum_{z=x+1}^{\infty} (z - x) c_1 f(z) + \sum_{z=0}^{x} c_2 f(z) - \sum_{z=x+1}^{\infty} c_1 f(z)$$

Now the first two terms are to be $C(x)$. Therefore

$$C(x + 1) - C(x) = \sum_{z=0}^{x} c_2 f(z) - \sum_{z=x+1}^{\infty} c_1 f(z)$$

Now the second term can be replaced by

$$c_1 \sum_{z=x+1}^{\infty} f(z) = c_1 \left[1 - \sum_{z=0}^{x} f(z) \right]$$

This results from the normalization condition that the sum of $f(z)$ over all z values is unity. Finally the result is

$$C(x + 1) - C(x) = -c_1 + (c_1 + c_2) \sum_{z=0}^{x} f(z)$$

The condition for optimality—that $C(x + 1) \geq C(x)$—translates to the condition that

$$\frac{c_1}{c_1 + c_2} \leq \sum_{z=0}^{x} f(z)$$

By analogy with the results so far,

$$C(x) - C(x - 1) = -c_1 + (c_1 + c_2) \sum_{z=0}^{x-1} f(z)$$

Therefore the condition that $C(x) \leq C(x - 1)$ translates to

$$\sum_{z=0}^{x-1} f(z) \leq \frac{c_1}{c_1 + c_2}$$

The conclusion is that the optimum x^* must satisfy the two conditions

$$\sum_{z=0}^{x^*-1} f(z) \leq \frac{c_1}{c_1 + c_2} \leq \sum_{z=0}^{x^*} f(z)$$

Although the derivation of this result may be considered difficult, the result once derived is easy to use. It is necessary only to compute the function

$$\sum_{z=0}^{x} f(z)$$

for each x until two successive sums just bracket the value of the cost ratio. Then the x associated with the larger sum is the optimum. This can be illustrated by application to the previous example. Excess supply (repairmen) costs \$50/unit: $c_2 = 50$. Excess demand costs \$150/unit, but only \$100 of that could have been saved by having more repairmen $(150 - 50)$. Therefore $c_1 = \$100$. The cost ratio is

$$\frac{c_1}{c_1 + c_2} = \frac{100}{100 + 50} = \frac{2}{3}$$

Now tabulated, $\sum f(z)$ alongside $f(z)$ is shown in Table 10.5.

TABLE 10.5   Calculation of $\sum f(z)$

z	$f(z)$	$\sum f(z)$	
0	.20	.20	
1	.30	.50	
			.66
2	.30	.80	
3	.10	.90	
4	.10	1.00	

Clearly the cost ratio falls between

$$\sum_{z=0}^{1} f(z) \leq \frac{2}{3} \leq \sum_{z=0}^{2} f(z)$$

and so $x^* = 2$. No other solution can satisfy the conditions. In conclusion the analysis has uncovered a simple method for solving problems of this type. It does not tell the value of $C(x)$ directly, but knowledge of x^* means evaluating $C(x)$ for only one value rather than for all values.

10.5   MODIFICATIONS OF THE NEWSBOY PROBLEM

Suppose that the demand $\tilde{z}$ is a continuous random variable with probability density function $f(z)$. Now the decision can also take on any value and calculus can be used. The derivation of the model is unchanged up to the point of finding $C(x)$. It becomes

$$C(x) = \int_0^x (x - z)c_2 f(z)\,dz + \int_x^\infty (z - x)c_1 f(z)\,dz$$

The optimum x^* can be found by taking the derivative of $C(x)$. However, the rule for differentiation of a definite integral is required. The result can almost be guessed by analogy with the discrete case already studied:

$$\int_0^{x^*} f(z)\,dz = \frac{c_1}{c_1 + c_2}$$

As an example of this, consider a gas station that is able to replenish its stock of gas only once each week. It is known that the total sales of gasoline per week is a random variable uniformly distributed between 1800 and 2200 gallons; for example,

$$f(z) = \begin{cases} \dfrac{1}{400} & \text{for } 1800 \leq z \leq 2200 \\ 0 & \text{for all other } z \text{ values} \end{cases}$$

Shortage costs are computed to be \$0.04/gallon; the storage cost for gas unsold at the end of the week is \$0.005/gallon. There is no order cost.

The optimum inventory level is found by computing

$$\int_{1800}^x f(z)\,dz = \int_{1800}^x \frac{1}{400}\,dz = \frac{x - 1800}{400}$$

The cost ratio is

$$\frac{c_1}{c_1 + c_2} = \frac{.04}{.04 + .005} = \frac{8}{9}$$

The equation

$$\frac{x - 1800}{400} = \frac{8}{9}$$

is solved to obtain

$$x^* = 2155 \text{ gallons}$$

The expected-cost function is

$$C(x) = \int_{1800}^x .005(x - z)\frac{1}{400}\,dz + \int_x^{2200} .04(z - x)\frac{1}{400}\,dz$$

This needs to be evaluated only for $x^* = 2155$. However, it is interesting to obtain the whole function, which is

$$C(x) = .0001125 \frac{x^2}{2} - .2425x + 262.25$$

Therefore $C(2155) = .88$.

This leads to an interesting question. The problem as formulated assumes that there is no order cost. Now suppose that there is an order cost of $5/order. If at the end of 1 week 2000 gallons remain in the tank, should you still order? The answer is based upon comparison of the expected cost of the optimal decision with the expected cost of starting the week with the nonoptimal amount in the tank:

$$C(2000) = 2.25$$

The difference, $1.37, is not enough to justify an order to bring the level from 2000 to 2155 gallons. This illustrates that the order cost significantly changes the problem and brings it outside the scope of a newsboy inventory problem.

Another useful modification is the maximization of profit in place of the minimization of cost. Assume the following economic structure:

c = unit cost of items in inventory
p = selling price of items in inventory
d = salvage value of excess units

The actual profit, as a function of x units supplied and z units demanded, is

$$P(x,z) = \begin{cases} x(p - c) & \text{for } z \geq x \text{ (excess demand)} \\ zp + (x - z)d - xc & \text{for } x > z \text{ (excess supply)} \end{cases}$$

This results from the reasoning that when $z > x$, all x units are sold at a profit $(p - c)$ each. However, if $x > z$ the profit is revenue zp plus salvage value of $(x - z)d$ less the cost xc of the units.

This is directly related to the previous formulation. The cost c_1 is the lost profit $p - c$. The cost c_2 is the loss in value of unused units, $c - d$. The cost ratio

$$\frac{c_1}{c_1 + c_2} = \frac{p - c}{(p - c) + (c - d)} = \frac{p - c}{p - d}$$

Similarly $P(x,z)$ can be expressed in terms of c_1 and c_2:

$$P(x,z) = \begin{cases} zc_1 - (z - x)c_1 & \text{for } z \geq x \\ zc_1 - (x - z)c_2 & \text{for } x > z \end{cases}$$

Therefore the expected profit $P(x)$ is related to the expected cost $C(x)$ by

$$P(x) = E(\tilde{z})c_1 - C(x)$$

Now it is clear that $E(\tilde{z})c_1$ is not a function of x. Therefore maximizing $P(x)$ is equivalent to minimizing $C(x)$.

It is important to realize that the problem has been formulated to minimize not the total cost but just that part of total cost which is due to the uncertainty. For example, in the repairman problem the expected number of failures per day is 1.6. Even if you could adjust your work force every day to the level actually required, the expected cost would be $(1.6)(50) = \$80/day$. The additional cost of uncertainty is

$$\sum_{z=0}^{2} 50(2 - z)f(z) + \sum_{z=3}^{4} 100(z - 2)f(z) = 65$$

The total $80 + 65 = 145$ as originally computed.

10.6   A BIDDING PROBLEM

There are other problems with a structure somewhat similar to the newsboy problem. For example, in a sealed-bid auction for a contract that will be awarded to the lowest bidder, the bid is like a supply of money with which to perform the contract. The performance of the contract work is a demand upon that supply of money. Although the structure of the problem is somewhat different, the strategy of analysis is quite similar. This section illustrates a content area where operations research has been very useful. Consider the following problem.

Your firm is entering a bidding competition against a number of other companies to obtain a large government contract. The contract is to be awarded solely on the basis of the *lowest sealed bid submitted*. In the past the lowest competitor's bid (x dollars) on similar projects can be described by a density function $f(x)$. Given that your firm's estimated cost on this project is C dollars, obtain an expression for the expected profit of a bid of B dollars by your firm. (Remember that the lowest bidder is awarded the contract.) Given that

$$f(x) = \begin{cases} 2.5 & 1.9 \leq x \leq \$2.3 \text{ million} \\ 0 & \text{elsewhere} \end{cases}$$

and that $C = \$2$ million, what is the optimum bid B your firm should submit to maximize expected profits?

The analysis begins with an expression for the actual profit if your bid is B and the lowest competitor's bid is x. Call this $P(B,x)$. Then

$$P(B,x) = \begin{cases} 0 & x \leq B \text{ (you lose)} \\ B - C & x > B \text{ (you win)} \end{cases}$$

Let $P(B)$ represent the expected profit if your bid is B:

$$P(B) = \int_{1.9}^{2.3} P(B,x)f(x)\,dx$$

$$= \int_{B}^{2.3} (B - C)f(x)\,dx$$

$$= (B - C) \int_{B}^{2.3} 2.5\,dx$$

$$= (B - C)(2.5)(2.3 - B)$$

For $C = 2.0$, this is

$$P(B) = -2.5B^2 + 10.75B - 11.50$$

Optimization can be performed using the derivative condition

$$\frac{dP(B)}{dB} = -5B + 10.75 = 0$$

$$B^* = \$2.15 \text{ million}$$

A larger bid would give more profit if you won but would decrease your chance of winning. A smaller bid would have greater chance of winning but would give smaller profit. The probability of winning under the optimum bid is

$$\int_{2.15}^{2.3} (2.5)\,dx = (2.5)(2.3 - 2.15) = (2.5)(.15) = .375$$

The profit if you win is $2.15 - 2 = \$.15$ million. Often in bidding situations there is also uncertainty in the cost C of performing the contract. More realistic formulations of bidding problems, which take this into account, are available in the literature.

10.7 A SEARCH PROBLEM

Another useful class of problems under uncertainty involves a process of search. The decision is often the amount of search effort to expend. The return to be achieved from that effort is very uncertain. The decision to halt the search process can be a difficult one to make because of the possibility, which always exists, that a little more effort may have generated a great return. Consider the following problem.

A geological basin is a large area, say 5 million acres, that may contain oil deposits. Oil deposits are called fields and can be discovered only by drilling exploratory wells. The decision to be made is about the number of wells to drill. Consider, for simplicity, that all fields are of the same size. Then the unknown state of nature, prior to any exploration of the basin, is just N, the number of fields present. Furthermore at any later time the unknown state of nature will be the number of fields yet undiscovered.

Suppose that the probability function of N, prior to any exploration, is

$$P(N \mid \lambda) = \frac{\lambda^N e^{-\lambda}}{N!} \qquad \text{for } N = 0, 1, 2, \ldots$$

Let $\lambda = 4$. Thus the probabilities of various N values are as shown in Table 10.6.

TABLE 10.6 Probabilities of N

N	0	1	2	3	4	5	6	7	8	9	10
$P(N \mid 4)$	.0183	.0733	.1465	.1954	.1954	.1563	.1042	.0595	.0298	.0132	.0053

The process of exploration and discovery can be represented in the following way: Given the state of nature N, one exploratory well will discover or not discover each field present independently with probability $1 - e^{-\gamma}$ of discovery and probability $e^{-\gamma}$ of no discovery. Therefore the number of fields discovered n in T wells (trials) is binomially distributed, given the state of nature N:

$$P(n \mid \gamma, T, N) = \begin{cases} \dfrac{N!}{n!\,(N-n)!}\,(1 - e^{-\gamma T})^n (e^{-\gamma T})^{N-n} & \text{for } 0 \le n \le N \\ 0 & \text{for } n > N \end{cases}$$

Note than n can exceed T but the probabilities of such events are small. The parameter γ represents a measure of search efficiency.

The expected number of fields to be discovered by T wells is the mean of the binomial distribution

$$E(n \mid T, N) = N(1 - e^{-\gamma T})$$

Since N is unknown at the time T must be decided, the expected value of N must be taken. The result is

$$E(n \mid T) = \lambda(1 - e^{-\gamma T})$$

Suppose that discovered fields are worth R dollars and that wells cost c dollars each. Then the expected profit from a program of T wells is

$$V(T) = RE(n \mid T) - Tc = R\lambda(1 - e^{-\gamma T}) - Tc$$

The optimum value of T can be found by calculus. The derivative equation is

$$+R\lambda\gamma e^{-\gamma T} - c = 0$$

So

$$e^{-\gamma T} = \frac{c}{R\lambda\gamma}$$

Then

$$\ln e^{-\gamma T} = \ln \frac{c}{R\lambda\gamma}$$

or

$$T^* = \frac{1}{\gamma} \ln \frac{R\lambda\gamma}{c}$$

with

$$\gamma = 0.015$$
$$\lambda = 4.0$$
$$R = \$1.0 \text{ million}$$
$$c = \$.05 \text{ million}$$
$$T^* = (66.67) \ln \frac{(1)(4)(.015)}{.05}$$
$$\ln 1.2 = .18232$$
$$T^* = (66.67)(.182) = 12.15 \text{ wells}$$

Evaluation of the expected profit for 12 and again for 13 shows which adjacent integer is best. Thus T^* is the total amount of search effort to allocate to this basin.

PROBLEMS

1. A real estate appraiser states that a certain house is worth $20,000. Assume that the true value of the house can be represented as a random variable whose mean is the appraised value. Suppose that it has a normal distribution whose standard deviation is 2 percent of the appraised value. What is the probability that the buyer has received a bargain of $1000 or more?

2. A 55-gallon oil drum has an average weight of 47.35 pounds. A tabulation of the actual weights of about 100 drums shows that the variability of drum weights can be described by a normal distribution with mean 47.35 pounds and standard deviation of 1.55 pounds. The product that is put into the drum weighs 7.5 pounds/gallon and has a value of $0.80/gallon. A drum full of product is billed on the basis of total weight less *average* drum weight. Therefore a drum that actually weighs 48.90 pounds has 1.55 pounds of product less than billed, and the customer is shortchanged by $(1.55)(.80/7.5) = \$0.16$. Conversely a drum weighing 45.80 pounds shortchanges the seller by the same amount. What is the probability that the loss to either party in the sale of one drum of product is less than

$0.50? What is the probability that the loss to either party is less than 1 percent of the cost of the 55 gallons billed?

3. Demand for an item is a discrete random variable with a uniform distribution over the range $1 \leq d \leq 6$ units. The cost of having units left over at the end of a stocking period is $1000/unit. The unit cost of being unable to satisfy a demand is $2000.

(a) How many units should be stocked if one wishes to minimize expected costs?

(b) How much would it be worth to know the exact demand in advance?

4. The demand in 1 day for a certain product has the following probability distribution:

Demand per Day (x)	Probability $[f(x)]$
0	.10
10	.15
20	.20
30	.25
40	.15
50	.10
60	.05

At the end of every day an order may be placed to replenish the inventory. There is no order cost. Orders are received in time for the start of the next day. Units that are not used in 1 day are stored overnight for use the next day. There is a storage cost of $5/night/unit. The profit lost by one lost sale is $20.

(a) The inventory operating policy is to order enough units to start every day with exactly Q units. What is the optimum value of this replenishment level?

(b) Under the optimum replenishment level, what is the probability that the demand in 1 day exceeds the supply?

(c) What is the expected total cost of storage plus lost profit for 1 day?

(d) Suppose that it is not possible to determine the value of storage cost directly. The current policy of the firm is to keep a stock of 40 units at the beginning of every period. Find the range of values of the storage cost for which the policy is optimal when the shortage cost remains at $20/unit.

5. You have an appointment in Center City for 9 A.M. on a specific day. The travel time required to get there is 30 minutes on the average but is subject to variation with the following probabilities:

Travel Time, min	Probability
21	.07
24	.08
27	.15
30	.40
33	.15
36	.08
39	.07

You must decide when to leave your house; your decision variable is the number of minutes you will allow for travel. Suppose that you wish to decide on the basis of minimizing expected total cost. You figure that the cost per minute of being early is C and the cost per minute of being late is three times as much: $3C$.

(a) Suppose that you do not know the value of C. Can you find the optimal departure time without it? Do so if possible.

(b) If $C = \$1/\text{minute}$, find the expected cost of the optimal policy.

(c) What is the probability that you will be late under the optimal policy?

6. You are hired as a consultant to the Number 2 Rent-a-Car Agency to determine the optimal number of company-owned cars to have available for renting to customers at Washington Airport. The cost of maintaining a company-owned car at Washington Airport is $3/day. The policy of the company is such that if a company-owned car is not available for renting, the company will obtain a car from the Number 1 agency at a cost of $5/day. The demand for Number 2 cars is uniform between 20 and 30 cars/day. (Noninteger demand is allowed as an approximation.) What is the optimal number of company-owned cars that should be on hand for rental to customers if the object is to minimize *total* cost?

7. A special tube has been designed and built to order for your firm. The builder indicates that if a spare is ordered later it will cost $16,000/tube whereas each spare ordered now will cost $4000/tube. Let the probability of one spare being required during the life of the process be p, the probability of two spares being required during the life of the process be p^2, and the probability of more than two spares being required during the life of the process be zero. (Assume that the carrying cost of spares is zero.) The following alternatives are available:

1. Buy zero spares now at cost of $0.
2. Buy one spare now at cost of $4000.
3. Buy two spares now at cost of $8000.

For what values of p will alternative 1 be preferred? 2 preferred? 3 preferred?

8. Mr. Nyse is a financial specialist. His job is to buy equity shares and sell them to the public. He currently has an opportunity to buy shares of BMI, a large

computing company that is putting out a new stock issue. These shares will sell to the public at $100/share on the opening day. Mr. Nyse can buy them at $94/share now. All transactions are conducted in blocks of 100 shares. The demand for shares is uncertain. Mr. Nyse believes that the number of blocks that will be requested from him can be represented as a random variable $\tilde{z}$ with probability function

$$f(z) = \frac{1}{10} \qquad \text{for } z = 1, 2, 3, \ldots, 10$$

If Mr. Nyse fails to sell his shares on the opening day of the offering, he will be able to sell them on the next day at a discounted price of $92/share. However, if he does not buy enough shares he must buy them from other specialists at a cost of $101/share and still sell them to his customers for $100.

(a) What is Mr. Nyse's expected profit if he can guess correctly the number of shares to be requested from him?

(b) How many shares should he purchase given the uncertainty about the number to be requested?

(c) What is the expected loss (relative to perfect knowledge of the number to be requested) when the optimum purchase is made?

(d) What is the probability that the optimum purchase (under uncertainty) is not the requested number of shares?

9. Suppose that your company is bidding on a contract against a number of competitors. Let p be the company's cost of performing the contract. There is some uncertainty in the value of p. Let l be the lowest bid of all competitors. Naturally this too is uncertain. Your problem is to determine b, your company's bid on the contract. All the sealed bids will be opened at one time and the lowest bidder will win the contract.

Assume that neither the company's cost p nor the lowest competitor's bid l depends upon the bid b. Assume also that you can represent p and l as independent random variables. The probability distribution of p is based upon experience in similar contracts and upon technical considerations involved in this new contract. Suppose that it is a uniform distribution between zero and 1. The probability distribution of the lowest competitive bid is based upon experience in bidding against similar competitors on previous occasions and upon considerations about this particular situation. Suppose that it is a uniform distribution between zero and 2. Finally suppose that the company's objective is to maximize expected profits. Find the optimal bid b.

Chapter 11 DECISIONS UNDER UNCERTAINTY WITH RISK AVERSION

In Chaps. 9 and 10 the criterion for choice under uncertainty was taken to be the expected value of the uncertain profit or cost. This is a sensible and useful criterion for many situations, but it is not difficult to find situations where it is not appropriate, as evidenced by actual behavior. Expected-value decision making cannot explain the behavior of real decision makers in many inportant business problems. The purchasing of insurance, for example, is based upon an aversion to risk that is not explained by the expected value of loss. The insurance company must charge a premium in excess of the expected loss to cover its operating expenses. Many individuals and corporations are willing to pay this premium to avoid the risk of possible loss. Even insurance companies show an aversion to risk by entering into "reinsurance" contracts with other insurance companies.

Investment decisions also give evidence of aversion to risk. Holding a portfolio of investments instead of a single most desirable investment is usually in response to the risk of the investments. Even large business firms often enter into "combines" to pursue risky projects. This action enables them to reduce the risk to each individual firm to an acceptable level. In fact the fundamental forms of business organization, whether partnerships or corporations, can be viewed as a method of reducing the risk borne by an individual.

This chapter shows how aversion to risk can be represented in a quantitative way. Although the empirical phenomena just mentioned cannot be explained by expected-value decision making, they can be explained by a criterion called *expected-utility decision making*. This criterion helps to clarify the limitations of expected-value decision making and to refine one's intuitive appreciation of the difficulties inherent in decision under uncertainty.

11.1 CHOICE AMONG LOTTERIES

A lottery is a chance process that generates one of several possible outcomes, each of which has known value to the decision maker. It represents the essence of the uncertain situation; once the possible outcomes along with their values and probabilities are known, further description of the chance process is not relevant. The essential problem of decision making under uncertainty can be viewed as a choice among alternative lotteries.

Consider the four specific lotteries L1, L2, L3, and L4 shown in Fig. 11.1. A comparison of the first two lotteries indicates that L1 is clearly better than L2: Although both have the same two possible outcomes, L1 has a higher probability of giving the better outcome. This simple comparison is the model behind the expected-

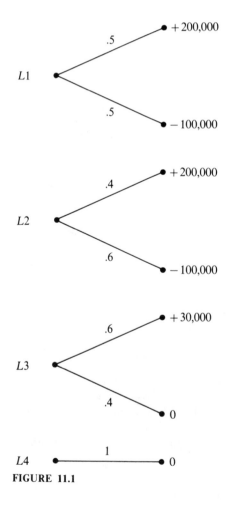

FIGURE 11.1

utility decision criterion; if all lotteries could be transformed to equivalent lotteries, all having a common form such as these, their comparison would be just as simple. The third lottery is not easily compared with the first two because both its outcomes are different from theirs. The fourth lottery gives zero payoff with certainty and has been included only as a reference point.

The expected payoffs of these lotteries are easily computed; they are shown in Table 11.1.

TABLE 11.1 Expected Payoffs

Lottery	Expected Payoff ($)
L1	50,000
L2	20,000
L3	18,000
L4	0

Now suppose that the decision maker is asked his ranking of the lotteries in order of preference. His response, along with the ranking implied by the expected-payoff criterion, is shown in Table 11.2.

TABLE 11.2 Preference Rankings

Lottery	Decision Maker's Rank	Expected-payoff Rank
L1	2	1
L2	4	2
L3	1	3
L4	3	4

His ranking is clearly not in agreement with the expected-payoff ranking. The question arises as to whether this decision maker's preferences are reasonable. But what is the definition of "reasonable"? In fact many individuals would agree with his preferences. A deeper and more practical question is whether there exists a logical, mathematical structure that can represent these preferences. The theory of expected utility demonstrates that there is such a structure and that it can be the basis for consistent decision making under uncertainty.

The basic idea, which will be developed here without proofs, is to construct a standard lottery to facilitate comparisons. Let the notation $L_s(p)$ represent the standard lottery, which has the form shown in Fig. 11.2. Actually this is a whole family of lotteries because the p value must be specified before it represents a specific lottery. This is implied by the functional notation $L_s(p)$. Within this family of lot-

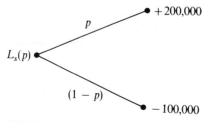

FIGURE 11.2

teries it is easy to compare any two lotteries. The better one is clearly that which has the higher probability of the better outcome.

The purpose of this standard lottery is to facilitate comparison between the given lotteries L1, L2, L3, and L4. It is easy to see that L1 is equivalent to $L_s(.5)$ and that L2 is equivalent to $L_s(.4)$. That much could be observed without any input from the decision maker. However, the difficult task that lies ahead is to determine which p value makes L3 equivalent to an $L_s(p)$. This requires some judgments from the decision maker.

The first question to be asked of the decision maker is what p value makes him indifferent between owning the standard lottery $L_s(p)$ and receiving a payment of $30,000 with certainty. There ought to be such a p value between zero and 1 because $L_s(1)$ is equivalent to a certain +$200,000 while $L_s(0)$ is equivalent to a certain loss of $100,000. Although this is not an easy question to answer, few decision makers would claim that it is too difficult to answer. They are accustomed to making decisions of similar difficulty. There is no "correct" answer to such a question. The answer reflects the decision maker's attitude toward risk and is therefore subjective. It is to be expected that two different decision makers will give different answers.

Suppose that the decision maker answers that he is indifferent between $L_s(.580)$ and the certain receipt of $30,000. This is one piece of information about his attitude toward risk. Suppose further that he expresses indifference between $L_s(.472)$ and a certain payoff of zero. This is another piece of information needed to represent his attitude toward risk. A summary of these responses is given in Table 11.3.

TABLE 11.3   Table of Equivalences

Certain Receipt of	Equivalence between Standard Lottery
− 100,000	$L_s(0)$
0	$L_s(.472)$
+ 30,000	$L_s(.580)$
+ 200,000	$L_s(1.0)$

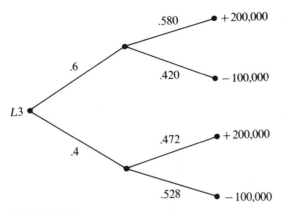

FIGURE 11.3

This information can now be used to construct standard lottery equivalents for L3 and L4. Consider L3 first. The payoffs of L3 can be replaced by their equivalent standard lotteries as shown in Fig. 11.3.

This key step is the substitution of equivalent lotteries. It is justified by the reason that it is only the payoffs and their probabilities which matter in business decision making, not the chance process itself. This two-stage lottery can now be replaced by a one-stage lottery with the same probability for each outcome. The probability of payoff + \$200,000 is

$$(.6)(.580) + (.4)(.472) = .348 + .189 = .537$$

Thus the equivalent lottery is that shown in Fig. 11.4. This has the same form as a standard lottery; therefore L3 is equivalent to $L_s(.537)$.

Now all four lotteries have been found equivalent, for this decision maker, to a standard lottery. The results are summarized in Table 11.4.

TABLE 11.4   Summary of Results

Lottery	Equivalent Standard Lottery
L1	$L_s(.5)$
L2	$L_s(.4)$
L3	$L_s(.537)$
L4	$L_s(.472)$

Now the comparisons between L1, L2, L3, and L4 can be based upon comparisons between their equivalent standard lotteries. The rule for this is simple: The higher the p value, the more desirable the lottery $L_s(p)$. Therefore L3 is the best, L1 is

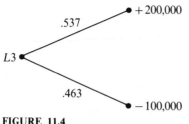

FIGURE 11.4

second best, L4 is next, and L2 is the worst. This analysis agrees with the ranking given by the decision maker and thus represents his attitude toward risk in this situation.

The reader will notice that the word "utility" has not yet been used in the representation of the attitude toward risk. It can now be introduced: "Utility" is just a new name for the p value in the standard lottery. The method so far has associated a standard lottery equivalent with every possible payoff. Thus every possible payoff has a number associated with it that is the p value of the equivalent standard lottery. This p value will now be called the *utility* of the payoff. Thus for every possible payoff x there is an associated number $U(x)$ called the utility of x. This is shown in Table 11.5.

TABLE 11.5 Utility of x

Payoff	Equivalent Standard Lottery	Utility of Payoff
−100,000	$L_s(0)$	$U(-100,000) = 0$
0	$L_s(.472)$	$U(0) = .472$
+30,000	$L_s(.580)$	$U(30,000) = .580$
+200,000	$L_s(1)$	$U(200,000) = 1.0$

The calculation of the p value to be associated with L3 can now be viewed as a calculation of expected utility:

$$(.6)U(30,000) + (.4)U(0) = (.6)(.580) + (.4)(.472) = .537$$

Since this calculation involves multiplying the utility of each possible outcome by the probability of that outcome and summing, it is reasonable to call it a calculation of expected utility.

Finally the decision criterion that the best lottery is the one having the highest p value associated with it can also be restated in terms of expected utility. *The new criterion for decision is that the best lottery is the one having the largest expected utility.* Thus the theory of expected-utility decision making has nothing to say about

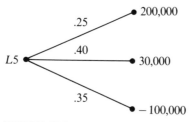

FIGURE 11.5

the inherent "usefulness" of money or of any other measure of the possible consequences. What it does do is to show how to set up a standard that allows for comparison of lotteries and represents the risk attitude of a decision maker. It does not
impose a value system upon a decision maker but rather shows how a decision
maker's own attitude toward risk can be represented mathematically.

Consider one more example of the expected-utility calculation. It is desired to
calculate the expected utility associated with the lottery in Fig. 11.5. The expected
utility of L5 is

$$.25\,U(200,000) + .40\,U(30,000) + .35\,U(-100,000)$$
$$= .25(1.0) + .40(.58) + .35(0) = .482$$

Thus the decision maker will prefer this lottery over L4 or L2 but find it less desirable than L1 and L3 if he remains consistent with his previous preferences.

The evaluation of lotteries that involve possible payoffs other than those already
considered requires more evaluations of the utility function. Each one requires a
response from the decision maker. Suppose that a series of further questions to the
decision maker reveals the evaluations of his utility function as shown in Table 11.6.

TABLE 11.6 Evaluations of
Utility Functions

x	$U(x)$
− 100,000	0
− 50,000	.26
− 40,000	.31
− 25,000	.37
0	.47
+ 15,000	.53
+ 20,000	.55
+ 30,000	.58
+ 35,000	.60
+ 50,000	.65
+ 70,000	.70
+100,000	.79
+200,000	1.00

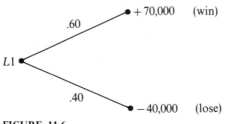

FIGURE 11.6

Recall the simple portfolio problem of Chap. 9. A decision maker has a choice between

1. A risky contract whose outcomes are $70,000 with probability .60 and $-$40,000 with probability .40

2. A portfolio consisting of two contracts whose outcomes are independent, each of which will pay $35,000 with probability .60 and $-$20,000 with probability .40

The lottery diagrams in Figs. 11.6 and 11.7 (taken from Fig. 9.20) illustrate these alternatives.

The risk attitude of this decision maker is represented by his utility function (Table 11.6). The calculation of the expected utilities of these two lotteries will therefore represent his attitude toward them. The expected utility of the first lottery is

$$(.60)\,U(70,000) + (.40)\,U(-40,000) = (.60)(.70) + (.40)(.31) = .544$$

The expected utility of the second lottery is

$$(.36)\,U(70,000) + (.48)\,U(15,000) + (.16)\,U(-40,000)$$
$$= (.36)(.7) + (.48)(.53) + (.16)(.31) = .556$$

The conclusion from this calculation is that the portfolio is clearly preferred by this decision maker. It was shown in Chap. 9 that both lotteries have identical expected payoffs of $26,000. Therefore the preference for L2 must be a result of the decision maker's aversion to risk.

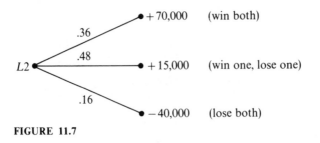

FIGURE 11.7

The second lottery can be viewed as two independent trials of the first lottery but with the payoff determined by averaging the payoffs of the two trials. The lower risk of the second lottery results from its intermediate possible outcome of $15,000 and from the fact that there is less probability associated with the extreme outcomes.

Another intuitive way to compare the risk of these two lotteries having equal expected payoffs is to compare their variances of payoff. The variance for lottery 1 is

$$(.60)(70,000 - 26,000)^2 + .40(-40,000 - 26,000)^2 = 2904 \times 10^6$$

The standard deviation is

$$(2904 \times 10^6)^{\frac{1}{2}} = \$53,900$$

The variance for lottery 2 is

$$(.36)(70,000 - 26,000)^2 + (.48)(15,000 - 26,000)^2 + (.16)(-40,000 - 26,000)^2$$
$$= 1452 \times 10^6$$

The standard deviation is

$$(1452 \times 10^6)^{\frac{1}{2}} = \$38,070$$

The smaller variance of lottery 2 leads to the conclusion, quite independently of the utility comparison, that it has less risk than lottery 1.

EXERCISES

The decision maker must decide whether to undertake a risky project whose profit will be $200,000 with probability .45 but will result in a net loss of $100,000 with probability .55.

1. Show that the expected utility of this project is .45 and that the decision maker would prefer to do nothing.

2. Suppose that the decision maker can find a partner who will share equally in the profit or loss. Show that the expected utility of this option is greater than that of undertaking the whole project. (*Answer:* .4985.)

3. Find the expected utility of a 25 percent share of the project. (*Answer:* .496.)

11.2 ANALYTIC UTILITY FUNCTIONS AND THEIR PROPERTIES

As a practical matter, it is often more useful to use an analytic utility function than to attempt to elicit the complete function from the decision maker. The functional form chosen may have one or more parameters that are determined from the decision maker's responses to a much smaller number of questions.

The following function represents the utility function of Sec. 11.1:

$$U(x) = a - be^{-rx}$$

where

$$a = 1.431$$
$$b = .959$$
$$r = .40 \times 10^{-5}$$

The graph of this utility function is shown in Fig. 11.8.

This functional form is easy to use: It requires only a table of the exponential function. For example, the utility of $30,000 is calculated.

$$rx = (.4 \times 10^{-5})(30,000) = .12$$

and

$$U(30,000) = 1.431 - (.959)e^{-.12}$$
$$= 1.431 - (.959)(.887)$$
$$= .58$$

A moment's reflection upon how utility values have been used in the preceding development will show that they are used *only in comparisons*. Their absolute values never enter into the decision rule. The utility scale is actually arbitrary, like the scales for the measurement of temperature. The scale being used resulted from the choice of the standard lottery. Since the standard lottery was based upon the two payoffs $-100,000$ and $+200,000$, it was a natural result that

$$U(-100,000) = 0$$

and

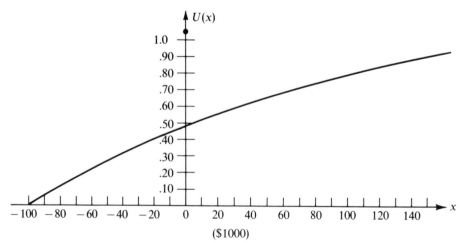

FIGURE 11.8

$$U(200,000) = 1$$

If the standard lottery had been based instead upon $-50,000$ and $+100,000$, the resulting utility function would have appeared different. Denote this utility function by $U_2(x)$. It would have the property that

$$U_2(-50,000) = 0$$
$$U_2(+100,000) = 1$$

If the decision maker's responses to questions based upon this standard lottery are perfectly consistent with his responses to the original standard lottery, then $U_2(x)$ is related to $U(x)$ by

$$U_2(x) = c + dU(x)$$

where c and d are constants. This fact can be proved from the axioms of utility theory but the proof will not be given here. The values of the constants can be determined by the conditions

$$U_2(-50,000) = c + dU(-50,000) = 0$$
$$U_2(100,000) = c + dU(100,000) = 1$$

Thus

$$c + (.26)d = 0$$
$$c + (.79)d = 1$$

The solution is

$$d = 1.886 \qquad c = -.490$$

Therefore

$$U_2(x) = 2.21 - 1.81e^{-rx}$$

The important point is that this utility function, although it appears different, is equivalent to $U(x)$ in the sense that it would make the same decisions.

A more general statement is that any two utility functions $U(x)$ and $U_2(x)$ are equivalent in a decision-making sense if and only if they are related to each other by a positive linear transformation:

$$U_2(x) = c + dU(x) \qquad \text{for some } d > 0$$

This is a formal statement of the fact that the zero point and the unit of measurement of utility are both arbitrary.

In view of this arbitrariness a useful conventional form for the exponential utility function, which is a positive linear transformation of the original utility function, is

$$U(x) = \frac{1}{r}(1 - e^{-rx})$$

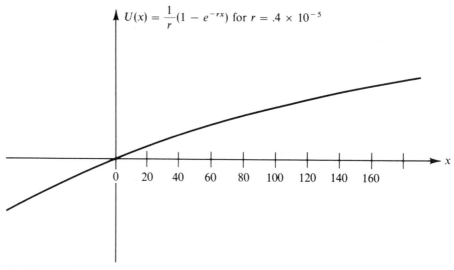

$$U(x) = \frac{1}{r}(1 - e^{-rx}) \text{ for } r = .4 \times 10^{-5}$$

FIGURE 11.9

This is a utility function for any value of r. It is equivalent to the decision maker's utility function when

$$r = .4 \times 10^{-5}$$

One advantage of this form is that the curve passes through the origin: $U(0) = 0$. The graph is shown in Fig. 11.9.

The curve in Fig. 11.9 is bounded from above; it asymptotically approaches the value

$$\frac{1}{r} = 250,000$$

Near the origin it looks much like a straight line. This can be shown mathematically; for x values very much smaller than $1/r$, the quantity rx is very small. Then the standard two-term series expansion for the exponential function shows that e^{-rx} is approximately equal to $1 - rx$. Thus

$$U(x) = \frac{1}{r}(1 - e^{-rx})$$

approaches

$$\frac{1}{r}(rx) = x$$

The meaning of this in practical terms is that for lotteries having small outcomes the decision maker follows approximately the expected-value or risk-neutral decision

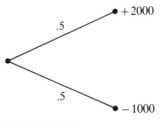

FIGURE 11.10

rule. For example, in Fig. 11.10 the lottery has outcomes that are considered small by this decision maker. The utilities are

$$U(2000) = (250{,}000)(1 - e^{-.8 \times 10^{-2}})$$
$$\cong (250{,}000)(.008)$$
$$= 2000$$
$$U(-1000) = (250{,}000)(1 - e^{+.4 \times 10^{-2}})$$
$$\cong (250{,}000)(-.004)$$
$$= -1000$$

The utility values of the payoffs are approximately equal to the payoffs. Therefore the expected utility, to a close approximation, is the same as the expected payoff:

$$(.5)(2000) + (.5)(-1000) = 500$$

This observation imparts an important understanding of the limitations of the expected-value criterion: It depends upon the decision maker's attitude toward risk. If his attitude can be represented by an exponential utility function, the parameter r must be known. If a lottery has all its payoffs smaller than about 1 percent of $1/r$, expected value and expected utility are in close agreement.

The variance of a lottery or probability distribution has long been used as an intuitive measure of its risk. The mathematical explanation of this, for the exponential utility function, is based upon the series expansion of the exponential function. For small values of rx, the exponential is

$$e^{-rx} = 1 - rx + \frac{(rx)^2}{2} - \frac{(rx)^3}{6} + \cdots$$

If the last term is small enough to be ignored, then

$$U(x) \cong x - \frac{1}{2} rx^2$$

Therefore the expected utility is approximately

$$E\{U(\tilde{x})\} = E(\tilde{x}) - \frac{1}{2}rE(\tilde{x}^2)$$

$$= E(\tilde{x}) - \frac{1}{2}r\left\{V(\tilde{x}) + [E(\tilde{x})]^2\right\}$$

where $V(\tilde{x})$ is the variance of the payoff. For example, the previous lottery has

$$E(\tilde{x}) = 500$$
$$V(\tilde{x}) = (.5)(2000 - 500)^2 + .5(-1000 - 500)^2 = 2.25 \times 10^6$$

The expected utility is approximately

$$500 - \frac{1}{2}(.4 \times 10^{-5})(2.25 \times 10^6 + .25 \times 10^6) = 500 - 5$$

$$= 495$$

The variance thus gives a first-order correction term that brings expected payoff closer to expected utility.

EXERCISES

1.   Use the utility function

$$U(x) = \frac{1}{r}(1 - e^{-rx}) \qquad \text{with } r = .4 \times 10^{-5}$$

to compute the utilities of lotteries L1, L2, L3, and L4 of Sec. 11.1. Show that this utility function leads to the same preference ordering as the original utility function.

2.   For the lottery shown in Fig. 11.10, use the three-term expansion of e^{-rx} for the utility function of Exercise 1 to show that

$$U(2000) = (.25 \times 10^6)(1 - e^{-8 \times 10^{-3}})$$
$$\cong 2000 - 8$$

and

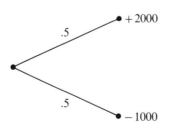

FIGURE 11.10

$$U(-1000) = (.25 \times 10^6)(1 - e^{+4 \times 10^{-3}})$$
$$\cong -1000 - 2$$

Now using this utility approximation, show that the resulting expected utility gives the same result as the approximation based upon the variance.

3.   Analytic utility functions allow the evaluation of utility for any outcome. They also allow the use of calculus. Use the utility function of Exercise 1. Suppose that the decision maker can select any share α between 0 and 100 percent of the risky project whose profit will be $200,000 with probability .45 but will result in a loss of $100,000 with probability .55. Find the share α that maximizes the expected utility. The expected utility, as a function of α, is

$$.45\,U(200,000\alpha) + .55\,U(-100,000\alpha)$$

Show that the optimum share is $\alpha^* = 41$ percent.

11.3   RISK-ADJUSTED VALUE OF A LOTTERY

Consider a decision maker whose current wealth is w. He owns the lottery shown in Fig. 11.11. If the outcome is favorable, his wealth will be $w + 10$; otherwise it will be $w - 2$. His attitude toward risk is represented by a utility function whose argument is the wealth after the outcome of the lottery. Let $U(w)$ be the utility of wealth w. Let $\tilde{z}$ represent the random payoff of the lottery. The expected utility is

$$E\{U(w + \tilde{z})\} = \frac{1}{2}\,U(w + 10) + \frac{1}{2}\,U(w - 2)$$

Given a specific utility function this calculation will result in one number. However, that one number is useful only for comparison and consequently lacks direct meaning. There is a more meaningful way to assign a value to this or any other lottery. This new number is the price that, if offered to the decision maker, would make him indifferent between selling and retaining ownership of the lottery. Let v represent this price. The utility if he sells is $U(w + v)$. Since he is indifferent, both actions must have equal utility. The equation

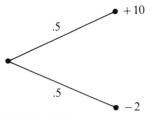

FIGURE 11.11

$$U(w + v) = \frac{1}{2} U(w + 10) + \frac{1}{2} U(w - 2)$$

enables the value of v to be determined. This price v is called the *certainty equivalent value* of the lottery because the decision maker would accept a certain payment of v in return for giving up his ownership of the lottery. A more appropriate name for the quantity v is *risk-adjusted value* because it takes into account the risk of the lottery according to the risk preferences of the decision maker.

A general definition of risk-adjusted value, for any lottery with random payoff $\tilde{z}$ and any utility function, is

$$U(w + v) = E\{U(w + \tilde{z})\}$$

This equation must always have a solution for v because all utility functions are increasing functions of their arguments and therefore must have an inverse function. The risk-adjusted value and its relationship to the expected payoff can be better understood in terms of a graph. Three cases are offered here to represent the three possible general attitudes toward risk.

Case 1: Aversion toward Risk

Suppose that $U(x)$ has the property that, for any two points on the curve, a line drawn between them either lies below the curve or coincides with it. A curve with this property is called *concave*. (An equivalent property is that the second derivative is negative or zero at all points, assuming that it is defined at all points.) The graph in Fig. 11.12 shows the relationship between risk-adjusted value and expected payoff for the example lottery.

The operations in drawing this graph are as follows: Starting with the utility curve, the points $w - 2$ and $w + 10$ are identified. Vertical lines are extended up to determine two points on the utility curve. These two points are connected by a line

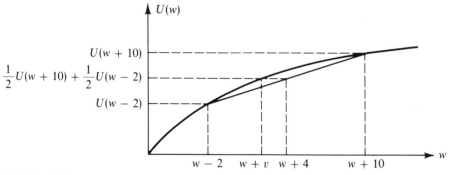

FIGURE 11.12

that is found to lie below the utility curve. Next the expected payoff $w + 4$ is identified and a vertical line is extended up to intersect the straight line. From that intersection point, a horizontal line is extended left to the utility axis. It intersects the utility axis at point a. Since $w + 4$ is the midpoint of the interval on the wealth axis, by geometric construction, the point on the utility axis is the midpoint of the corresponding interval on the utility axis. This point is the expected utility of the lottery. At the point where this horizontal line intersects the utility curve, a vertical line is drawn down to the wealth axis. The line intersects the wealth axis at a point that is $w + v$. The important fact demonstrated by this construction is that

$$w + v \le w + 4$$

or

$$v \le 4$$

One step of generalization is to replace the example lottery by the general form of lottery, as shown in Fig. 11.13. Then if the line is below the utility curve, the construction will show that

$$w + v \le p(w + z_1) + (1 - p)(w + z_2)$$

or

$$v \le pz_1 + (1 - p)z_2 \quad \text{(expected payoff)}$$

It can be shown mathematically, with still greater generality, that for any non-degenerate lottery with random payoff $\tilde{z}$ and any strictly concave utility function, the risk-adjusted value is less than the expected payoff:

$$v < E(\tilde{z})$$

This is important because it gives a useful definition of risk aversion: A decision maker is risk averse if he values all lotteries at less than their expected payoffs. The construction demonstrates that a risk-averse decision maker can be represented by a concave utility function. Such a decision maker will discount all risky lotteries by some positive amount from their expected payoff. The amount of the discount is $E(\tilde{z}) - v$. This is called the *risk premium* or risk discount—the amount the decision

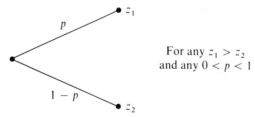

For any $z_1 > z_2$
and any $0 < p < 1$

FIGURE 11.13

maker would pay to transform the risky lottery into a certain receipt of an amount equal to the expected payoff of the lottery.

Case 2: Neutrality toward Risk

Suppose that $U(x)$ has the property that it is linear. Thus for any two points on $U(x)$, the line between them coincides exactly with the function $U(x)$. Repeating the construction of the previous case, it is easy to see that the risk-adjusted value v exactly equals the expected payoff $E(\tilde{z})$ for every lottery. Therefore a linear utility function gives the same decisions as the expected-payoff criterion. A decision maker having a linear utility function is said to be neutral toward risk. He does not care whether he owns a risky lottery or a claim to a certain receipt of an amount equal to the expected payoff of that lottery.

Case 3: Preference toward Risk

Suppose that $U(x)$ has the property that, for any two points on the curve, a line drawn between them lies either above the curve or on it. A curve with this property is called *convex*. (Assuming that it has a second derivative defined at all points, an equivalent property is that its second derivative is nonnegative everywhere.) The graph for this case (Fig. 11.14) shows that the risk-adjusted value v is at least as great as the expected payoff.

Such a decision maker would prefer ownership of a lottery to the receipt with certainty of the expected payoff of the lottery. Such behavior is not in evidence, at least in the world of business. Gambling behavior may be evidence of this type of curve. Many people do buy tickets to real lotteries whose ticket cost exceeds their expected payoff. However, it is not clear that the assumptions of utility theory even apply to gambling because the pleasure derived from that activity may not be wholly represented by the possible payoffs. It may include some entertainment value due to

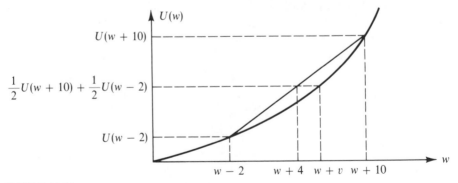

FIGURE 11.14

experiencing the resolution of uncertainty. Other intangible aspects may also be involved.

The risk-adjusted value, or certainty equivalent, of a lottery is directly related to the expected utility of the lottery through the utility function. Therefore the decision criterion of maximizing expected utility can be replaced by the criterion of maximizing the risk-adjusted value. The advantage of the risk-adjusted value is that it is directly meaningful.

11.4 EXPONENTIAL UTILITY

The exponential utility function has the form

$$U(x) = \frac{1}{r}(1 - e^{-rx})$$

This can represent all three attitudes toward risk:

Case 1. For $r > 0$, $U(x)$ is a strictly concave function and represents aversion toward risk. Larger r values represent greater risk aversion in the sense that all risk premiums are larger.

Case 2. For $r = 0$, $U(x) = x$. This represents risk neutrality, also known as expected-value decision making. [The result $U(x) = x$ can be found as a limit or by series expansion of the exponential, as shown in Sec. 11.2.]

Case 3. For $r < 0$, $U(x)$ is a strictly convex function. All risk-adjusted values exceed their corresponding expected payoffs and hence the function encodes a positive preference for risk.

The risk-adjusted value has a simple direct formula in the case of exponential utility. Let $\tilde{z}$ be the random payoff from a lottery and let w be the initial wealth. Then the definition of v is

$$U(w + v) = E\{U(w + \tilde{z})\}$$

For the exponential utility this is

$$\frac{1}{r}\{1 - e^{-r(w+v)}\} = E\left\{\frac{1}{r}[1 - e^{-r(w+\tilde{z})}]\right\}$$

Therefore

$$\frac{1}{r} - \frac{1}{r}e^{-rw}e^{-rv} = \frac{1}{r} - \frac{1}{r}e^{-rw}E\{e^{-r\tilde{z}}\}$$

Algebraic operations give

$$e^{-rv} = E\{e^{-r\tilde{z}}\}$$

The solution for v is

$$v = -\frac{1}{r} \ln [E\{e^{-r\tilde{z}}\}]$$

This is a useful formula because it eliminates the need to compute expected utility first and then transform it to risk-adjusted value. One property of exponential utility which is apparent from this result is that the *risk-adjusted value is not a function of the initial wealth w.* Two properties unique to the exponential utility function are

1. It is the only utility function such that changes in wealth do not change the risk-adjusted value assigned to lotteries.

2. It is the only utility function such that the risk-adjusted value of a set (portfolio) of *independent* lotteries is the sum of their individual risk-adjusted values.

Thus the risk-adjusted value of a lottery under exponential utility does not depend upon the decision maker's wealth or upon whether he owns other lotteries that are independent (in the probability sense) of the lottery.

The exponential utility function is the simplest model of risk aversion. It is not likely to be entirely satisfactory for every situation; however, as in previous chapters, it is useful to begin a study with the models that are the simplest, both conceptually and mathematically. This function will be used for the remainder of this chapter.

The formula given for risk-adjusted value applies to both continuous and discrete random variables. Special-purpose formulas can be given for the important analytic probability distributions. Consider a lottery based upon the binomial distribution. The lottery pays \$$a$ per success. There are n trials, each with probability p of success. The number of successes is the random variable $\tilde{z}$, which has the binomial probability function

$$f(z \mid n,p) = \frac{n!}{z!(n-z)!} p^z (1-p)^{n-z} \qquad \text{for } z = 0, 1, 2, \ldots, n$$

The risk-adjusted value is

$$v = -\frac{1}{r} \ln \left[\sum_{z=0}^{n} e^{-raz} f(z \mid n,p) \right]$$

$$= -\frac{1}{r} \ln \left[\sum_{z=0}^{n} p^z e^{-raz} \frac{n!}{z!(n-z)!} (1-p)^{n-z} \right]$$

$$= -\frac{1}{r} \ln (1 - p + pe^{-ra})^n$$

$$= -\frac{n}{r} \ln (1 - p + pe^{-ra})$$

This result is consistent with the additivity of risk-adjusted values of independent lotteries. The n trials can be viewed as n independent lotteries all having the same risk-adjusted value.

Consider next a lottery based upon the Poisson probability distribution. Again the payoff will be $\$a$ per success. The number of successes $\tilde{z}$ has the Poisson probability function

$$f(z \mid \lambda) = \frac{\lambda^z e^{-\lambda}}{z!} \qquad \text{for } z = 0, 1, 2, \ldots$$

The risk-adjusted value is easily found:

$$v = -\frac{1}{r} \ln \left[\sum_{z=0}^{\infty} e^{-raz} f(z \mid \lambda) \right]$$

$$= -\frac{1}{r} \ln \left(\sum_{z=0}^{\infty} e^{-raz} \frac{\lambda^z e^{-\lambda}}{z!} \right)$$

$$= -\frac{1}{r} \ln \left[\left(e^{-\lambda} e^{+\lambda e^{-ra}} \right) \sum_{z=0}^{\infty} \frac{(\lambda e^{-ra})^z e^{-\lambda e^{-ra}}}{z!} \right]$$

$$= -\frac{1}{r} \ln \left[e^{-\lambda(1 - e^{-ra})} \right]$$

$$= \frac{\lambda}{r} (1 - e^{-ra})$$

Next consider a lottery where the payoff $\tilde{z}$ can be any number, positive or negative, and its probability density is the normal:

$$f(z) = (2\pi\sigma^2)^{-\frac{1}{2}} \exp \left[-\frac{(z - \mu)^2}{2\sigma^2} \right] \qquad \text{for } -\infty < z < +\infty$$

The mean and variance of the payoff are μ and σ^2, respectively. The risk-adjusted value is

$$v = -\frac{1}{r} \ln \left[\int_{-\infty}^{\infty} e^{-rz} f(z) \, dz \right]$$

The algebra required for this integral is long and will not be shown here. The result, however, is very simple:

$$v = \mu - \frac{1}{2} r\sigma^2$$

For a normal distribution and exponential utility, the risk-adjusted value is the expected payoff μ less a risk discount that is proportional to the variance of the distribution and to the risk-aversion parameter.

Consider next a lottery where the payoff $\tilde{z}$ cannot be negative and has a gamma distribution:

$$f(z \mid a,b) = \frac{a^b z^{b-1} e^{-az}}{(b-1)!} \qquad \text{for } z \geq 0$$

The risk-adjusted value is

$$
\begin{aligned}
v &= -\ \frac{1}{r} \ln\left[\int_0^\infty e^{-rz} f(z \mid a,b)\, dz \right] \\
&= -\frac{1}{r} \ln\left[\int_0^\infty e^{-rz}\frac{e^{-az} a^b z^{b-1}}{(b-1)!}\, dz \right] \\
&= -\frac{1}{r} \ln\left[\frac{a^b}{(a+r)^b} \int_0^\infty \frac{(a+r)^b z^{b-1} e^{-(a+r)z}}{(b-1)!}\, dz \right] \\
&= \frac{b}{r} \ln\left(1 + \frac{r}{a} \right)
\end{aligned}
$$

The remainder of this chapter presents applications of these results.

11.5   A BIDDING EXAMPLE

A bidding decision problem was considered in Chap. 10. The criterion for bid selection was the maximization of expected profit. However, in light of the high level of risk in competitive bidding and the relatively large amounts of money involved, it may be more reasonable to maximize expected utility or, equivalently, to maximize the risk-adjusted profit. The following problem is similar to that of Chap. 10 except for the less realistic feature that the opponent's bid is allowed to take on only discrete values for mathematical simplicity.

Your firm is engaged in bidding competition with one other company to obtain a large government contract. The contract is to be awarded solely on the basis of the lowest sealed bid submitted. The competitor's bid ($\$x$) is unknown to you at the time you must decide your bid. The probability, based upon past behavior in similar situations, of competitive bid x is .20 for all values x = \$1.9, 2.0, 2.1, 2.2, and 2.3 million (and zero for all other bid values). The cost of performing the contract is C = \$2 million. Your bid B can be any value but is best restricted to the same set of possible values (each one cent lower to resolve ties in your favor).

The optimum bid depends upon the firm's attitude toward risk. The analysis can be performed in a tabular form. First consider the actual profit as a function of both your bid and your competitor's bid (see Table 11.7).

TABLE 11.7 Your Actual Profit (in $ million)

Your Bid	Competitor's Bid				
	1.9	2.0	2.1	2.2	2.3
1.9	−.1	−.1	−.1	−.1	−.1
2.0	0	0	0	0	0
2.1	0	0	+.1	+.1	+.1
2.2	0	0	0	+.2	+.2
2.3	0	0	0	0	+.3

From this the probability of winning and the profit from winning can be summarized, as in Table 11.8.

TABLE 11.8 Summary of Probabilities and Profits

Your Bid	Probability of Winning	Profit If You Win
1.9	1.0	− .1
2.0	.8	0
2.1	.6	+ .1
2.2	.4	+ .2
2.3	.2	+ .3

The bid that maximizes the expected profit can be found by computing the expected profit associated with each level of B, as in Table 11.9.

TABLE 11.9 Calculation of Expected Profit

Your Bid	Expected Profit
1.9	− .1
2.0	0
2.1	+ .06
2.2	+ .08
2.3	+ .06

The best expected-value decision is $B = 2.2$, which gives an expected profit of $.08 million and a probability .4 of winning.

Now suppose that the decision maker is averse to risk and that his utility function is exponential with parameter $r = 10$ when values are expressed in $1 million units. (This is equivalent to $r = 10^{-5}$ when values are expressed in dollars.) Now for each bid level the risk-adjusted value of profit is computed according to the formula of the preceding section. The calculations are shown in Table 11.10.

TABLE 11.10 Calculation of Risk-adjusted Value of Profit

Your Bid	Risk-adjusted Value for $r = 10$
1.9	$-(.1) \ln (e^{+1}) = -.1$
2.0	$-(.1) \ln (.8e^0 + .2e^0) = 0$
2.1	$-(.1) \ln (.6e^{-1} + .4e^0) = .0476$
2.2	$-(.1) \ln (.4e^{-2} + .6e^0) = .0424$
2.3	$-(.1) \ln (.2e^{-3} + .8e^0) = .0211$

For this level of risk aversion the best bid is $B = 2.1$, which gives a probability .6 of winning and a risk-adjusted profit of \$.0476 million. The expected profit associated with this bid is \$.0600 million; therefore the risk discount is .0600 − .0476 = \$.0124 million.

Other levels of the risk-aversion parameter r can be tried to determine the sensitivity of the optimum bid to the risk-aversion level. Some results are given in Table 11.11.

TABLE 11.11 Comparison of Risk Levels

r Level	Optimum Bid B	Risk-adjusted Value of Bid B
0	2.2	.0800
.25	2.2	.0787
1.0	2.2	.0750
10.0	2.1	.0476

EXERCISES

1. Find the level of r that makes bids 2.1 and 2.2 equally good. (*Answer: r = 6.93.*)

2. Suppose that the competitor's bid is uniformly distributed between \$1.9 and \$2.3 million as in Chap. 10. Find the risk-adjusted value as a function of bid B. The optimum bid would be difficult to obtain because of the form of the derivative with respect to B.

11.6   AN INSURANCE EXAMPLE

A man is considering the purchase of automobile liability insurance. Suppose that a loss will occur with probability .005 within a 1-year period. With probability .995 there will be no loss during the period. Suppose that the insurance premium for full coverage of all losses is \$40 for the year. Suppose first that the size of the loss, if there is one, is \$5000. The expected loss is (.005) (5000) = \$25, considerably less than the premium.

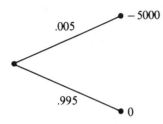

FIGURE 11.15

Given that the man's attitude toward risk is represented by an exponential utility function with parameter $r = 10^{-4}$, should he purchase the insurance? The question is resolved by computing the risk-adjusted value of the lottery shown in Fig. 11.15, which the man would face if he does not purchase the insurance. It is

$$v = -10^4 \ln (.005 e^{+.5} + .995 e^0)$$
$$= -10^4 \ln (1.003244)$$
$$= -\$32.38$$

This means that the risk is perceived as equivalent to a certain loss of \$32.38. This is preferred, however, to the purchase of the insurance policy because that replaces the risk by a certain loss of \$40, which is the premium.

However, this model of the loss possibilities is not realistic. In reality the size of loss, given that a loss occurs, is also a random variable and this makes the situation more risky. Now suppose that the size of loss, given that there is one, is a random variable x with exponential probability density function

$$f(x) = \lambda e^{-\lambda x} \qquad \text{for } x \geq 0 \qquad \text{and} \qquad \lambda = \frac{1}{5000}$$

with mean size \$5000. Now should the insurance be purchased?

The calculation is now more difficult. The process can be viewed as a two-stage lottery. Chance first decides whether there will be a loss. If there will be one, then chance draws a random outcome from the density function of loss size (Fig. 11.16).

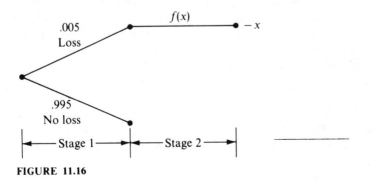

FIGURE 11.16

The expected size of loss is still $25. However, the greater variability of loss size gives greater risk. The risk-adjusted value of this lottery is

$$v = -10^4 \ln \left[.005 \int_0^\infty e^{+rx} f(x)\, dx + .995 e^0 \right]$$

The integral is

$$\int_0^\infty e^{rx} \lambda e^{-\lambda x}\, dx = \lambda \int_0^\infty e^{-(\lambda - r)x}\, dx$$

$$= \frac{\lambda}{\lambda - r}$$

Therefore

$$v = -10^4 \ln \left[.005 \left(\frac{\lambda}{\lambda - r} \right) + .995 \right]$$

Finally, substituting $\lambda = 2 \times 10^{-4}$ and $r = 10^{-4}$, one obtains

$$v = -10^4 \ln (1.005)$$
$$= -\$49.88$$

The more realistic model of possible loss apparently represents a higher risk because it is perceived by this decision maker as equivalent to a certain loss of $49.88. In this case the man would be better off to purchase the insurance because it replaces the risk by a certain loss of only $40.

11.7   A RISK-SHARING EXAMPLE

Sharing of risk is a fundamental way of reducing the risk to each sharing partner. From an empirical viewpoint, sharing seems fundamental to business organization. Corporate organizations are structures for sharing among a large number of partners called shareholders whereas partnerships usually have a small number of partners. Even large corporations enter into combines to undertake large and risky projects. From a mathematical viewpoint, a risky project is represented by a probability distribution of profit. Proportional sharing is a way of modifying the shape of the probability distribution of profit faced by a sharing partner. It is simple to show mathematically that a firm which undertakes half a project instead of the whole project will retain half the expected profit but will face only one-fourth the variance. Since variance is an indicator of risk, it is clear that sharing offers a risk-reducing advantage to risk-averse firms.

Consider a large, risky project with an initial cost of $11.5 million. A study of the possible outcomes indicates that the expected return is $14 million and that the probability distribution of profit is normal with a variance of 20. Let $\tilde{z}$ represent the uncertain profit if the project is undertaken. The firm has an attitude toward risk that is represented by an exponential utility function with parameter $r = .5$ when values are expressed in $1 million units. The risk-adjusted value of the whole project is found from the formula given in Sec. 11.4:

$$v = \mu - \frac{1}{2} r \sigma^2$$

$$= (14 - 11.5) - \frac{1}{2} (.5)(20)$$

$$= 2.5 - 5$$

$$= - 2.5$$

The meaning of this result is that the firm would prefer to do nothing rather than undertake this highly risky project by itself.

Now consider the possibility of undertaking the project in some form of partnership with other firms, assuming that other firms would be willing to do so. Suppose that the firm could retain a share α of both costs and returns from the project in some combination with other sharing partners. The profit to the firm, $\tilde{y}$, would be equal to $\alpha \tilde{z}$. The expected profit would be

$$E(\tilde{y}) = E(\alpha \tilde{z})$$

$$= \alpha E(\tilde{z})$$

The variance of the firm's profit would be

$$V(\tilde{y}) = E\{(y - E(\tilde{y}))^2\}$$

$$= E\{(\alpha z - \alpha E(\tilde{z}))^2\}$$

$$= E\{\alpha^2 (z - E(\tilde{z}))^2\}$$

$$= \alpha^2 V(\tilde{z})$$

Furthermore it can be proved that the probability distribution of $\tilde{y}$ is also of the normal type. Therefore the risk-adjusted value to the firm of share α, denoted $v(\alpha)$, is

$$v(\alpha) = \alpha \mu - \frac{1}{2} r \alpha^2 \sigma^2$$

$$= 2.5\alpha - 5\alpha^2$$

For example, a share $\alpha = \frac{1}{2}$ would have risk-adjusted value

$$v\left(\frac{1}{2}\right) = \frac{1}{2} (2.5) - \frac{1}{4} (5)$$

$$= 1.25 - 1.25 = 0$$

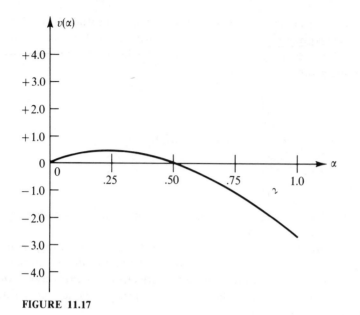

FIGURE 11.17

The risk-adjusted value can be considered to be a function of share α. The graph is shown in Fig. 11.17.

If all values of α between zero and 1 are feasible in the sense that partners are available to take the complementary share $1 - \alpha$, then the optimum share is the one that maximizes $v(\alpha)$. This can be found by calculus:

$$\frac{dv(\alpha)}{d\alpha} = 2.5 - 10\alpha = 0$$

$$\alpha^* = .25$$

The 25 percent share of the project has risk-adjusted value

$$v(.25) = (.25)(2.5) - (.0625)5$$

$$= \$.3125 \text{ million}$$

The firm would prefer to take a 25 percent share of the project. This share has the preferred balance of risk and expected return given the risk preferences of the firm. Sharing is a method of transforming the risk characteristics of the project to suit the risk preferences of the firm.

EXERCISE

Suppose that the project of this section has a gamma distribution of return with expected return 14 and variance 20. The parameter values are $b = 9.8$ and

$a = .7$. The risk-adjusted value of share α is

$$v(\alpha) = \frac{b}{r} \ln \left(1 + \frac{r\alpha}{a} \right) - 11.5\alpha \qquad \text{for } r = .5$$

Find the optimum share and its risk-adjusted value. (*Answer:* $\alpha^* = .304$, $v(\alpha^*) = .355$.) Why, in an intuitive sense, is the gamma case more favorable to the decision maker than the normal?

11.8   A PORTFOLIO EXAMPLE

Suppose that an investor has an amount C dollars of capital to invest in two common stock investment opportunities that are not independent in a probability sense. The investment will be held for 1 year. The return per dollar invested in stock i is $1 + \tilde{x}_i$, where $\tilde{x}_i$ is a random variable. The total return at the end of the year is

$$c_1(1 + \tilde{x}_1) + c_2(1 + \tilde{x}_2)$$

where c_1 and c_2 are the amounts of money invested in stocks 1 and 2, respectively. If the initial capital is not all invested, the remainder $(C - c_1 - c_2)$ is deposited in the bank for 1 year and will return $1 + I$ per dollar invested, where I is the riskless interest rate. The total return is

$$(C - c_1 - c_2)(1 + I) + c_1(1 + \tilde{x}_1) + c_2(1 + \tilde{x}_2)$$
$$= C + CI + c_1(\tilde{x}_1 - I) + c_2(\tilde{x}_2 - I)$$

The profit, or net return, is found by subtracting the initial capital C to get

$$\text{Profit} = CI + c_1(\tilde{x}_1 - I) + c_2(\tilde{x}_2 - I)$$

Notice that for $c_1 + c_2 > C$ these expressions would represent borrowing the amount $c_1 + c_2 - C$ at interest rate I for 1 year and repaying $(c_1 + c_2 - C)(1 + I)$ at the end of the year.

Suppose that $\tilde{x}_1$ and $\tilde{x}_2$ are jointly normally distributed. This means that the joint probability density of x_1 and x_2 is the bivariate normal density

$$f(x_1, x_2) = \frac{1}{2\pi\sigma_1\sigma_2(1 - \rho^2)}$$
$$\exp \left\{ -\frac{1}{2(1 - \rho^2)} \left[\frac{(x_1 - \mu_1)^2}{\sigma_1^2} - 2\rho \frac{(x_1 - \mu_1)(x_2 - \mu_2)}{\sigma_1\sigma_2} + \frac{(x_2 - \mu_2)^2}{\sigma_2^2} \right] \right\}$$

The parameters μ_i, σ_i^2 are the unconditional mean and variance of $\tilde{x}_i$ for $i = 1$ and 2. The parameter ρ is a number in $-1 \leq \rho \leq 1$ that measures the degree of correlation between the two random variables. If they are independent random variables, then

$\rho = 0$. For $\rho > 0$ the two random variables tend to go in the same direction whereas when $\rho < 0$ they tend to go in opposite directions.

The investment opportunity is evaluated by computing the risk-adjusted value of the profit. Let $\tilde{y}$ be the profit:

$$\tilde{y} = CI + c_1(\tilde{x}_1 - I) + c_2(\tilde{x}_2 - I)$$

It can be shown that this random variable has a (univariate) normal distribution with expected value

$$E(\tilde{y}) = CI + c_1(\mu_1 - I) + c_2(\mu_2 - I)$$

and variance

$$V(\tilde{y}) = c_1^2\sigma_1^2 + 2c_1c_2\rho\sigma_1\sigma_2 + c_2^2\sigma_2^2$$

Therefore the risk-adjusted value is[1]

$$v(c_1,c_2) = CI + c_1(\mu_1 - I) + c_2(\mu_2 - I) - \frac{1}{2}r(c_1^2\sigma_1^2 + 2c_1c_2\rho\sigma_1\sigma_2 + c_2^2\sigma_2^2)$$

The decision problem is to find the investment allocations c_1 and c_2 that maximize this risk-adjusted value. If borrowing were not allowed, the constraint

$$c_1 + c_2 \leq C$$

would be imposed. If "short" investment positions were not allowed, the non-negativity constraints

$$c_1 \geq 0 \qquad c_2 \geq 0$$

would also be imposed.

A numerical example of this situation is

Stock 1: $\mu_1 = .068$, $\sigma_1^2 = .0009$ ($\sigma_1 = .03$)

Stock 2: $\mu_2 = .056$, $\sigma_2^2 = .0004$ ($\sigma_2 = .02$)

Interest rate: $I = .04$

Risk-aversion level: $r = .01$

Initial capital: $C = \$5000$

The objective function, after substitution of these numbers, becomes

$$v(c_1,c_2) = 200 + .028c_1 + .016c_2 - \frac{1}{2}10^{-6}(9c_1^2 + 12\rho c_1c_2 + 4c_2^2)$$

Here the value of ρ has been left unspecified in order to study the effects of correla-

---

[1]Knowledge of the bivariate normal distribution is not essential for understanding this result. Given the expected value and the variance of the single random variable $\tilde{y}$ and that its probability distribution is normal, the result follows.

tion. Now the reader will recognize that this optimization problem has already been studied in Chap. 3. There is a slight difference in notation; the decision variables there, x_1 and x_2, correspond to the decision variables here, c_1 and c_2. Also the constant return, 200, does not appear in the Chap. 3 objective function. The results shown in Chap. 3 are not repeated here but should be reviewed as part of this chapter.

PROBLEMS

1. Consider a lottery whose payoff $\tilde{z}$ is a continuous random variable with mean $1000, standard deviation $1000, and a normal probability distribution. The one-sigma range implies that there is a probability .158 of experiencing a loss. The three-sigma range of outcomes is from $-$2000 to $+$4000. A risk-averse decision maker may actually prefer not to play this lottery, even at no cost, because of the risk involved. Suppose that he is offered a modified lottery consisting of n plays of the basic lottery with payoff computed by averaging the individual payoffs. Thus his payoff $\tilde{y}$ is

$$\tilde{y} = \frac{1}{n} (\tilde{z}_1 + \tilde{z}_2 + \cdots + \tilde{z}_n)$$

   This has mean $E(\tilde{y}) = E(\tilde{z})$ and variance $V(\tilde{y}) = 1/n[V(\tilde{z})]$ and a normal probability distribution. A risk-averse decision maker would wish to make n as large as possible because it reduces the variance. A risk-neutral decision maker would not care what n value is used because it does not change the expected payoff.

   (a) Suppose that the extra repetitions can be made but at a cost of $1 per repetition. Thus a decision maker who wants n repetitions will pay $$(n - 1)$ to have this modified lottery with n repetitions. Show that a decision maker with exponential utility function with parameter $r = .002$ would prefer 32 trials.

   (b) Suppose that the decision maker's r value is unknown, and that when offered this opportunity he responds that he prefers $n = 100$ trials. What does this tell you about his r value?

2. A special tube has been designed and built to order for your firm. The builder indicates that if a spare is ordered later it will cost $16,000/tube whereas each spare ordered now will cost $4000/tube. Let the probability of one spare being required during the life of the process be .30, the probability of two spares being required during the life of the process be .09, and the probability of more than two spares being required during the life of the process be zero. (Assume that the carrying cost of spares is zero.) The following alternatives are available:

   1. Buy zero spares now at cost of $0.
   2. Buy one spare now at cost of $4000.
   3. Buy two spares now at cost of $8000.

The risk attitude of your firm is represented by the utility function $U(x)$ for wealth x. It has the exponential form

$$U(x) = \frac{1}{r}(1 - e^{-rx})$$

Find the optimum number of spares and the risk-adjusted value of the optimum for three cases: $r = 0$, $r = .10$, and $r = .25$ (when value is expressed in $1000 units). The analysis can be arranged in a table showing the risk-adjusted value of each alternative for each r value.

3. An oil company is planning a pipeline to carry oil a distance D miles from the producing wells to the refinery. They want to limit the risk of oil spills resulting from breaks in the pipeline. They plan to place automatic shutoff valves in the pipeline every d miles but must decide what value to use for d. These valves can sense a pressure drop from a break and automatically stop the flow. The loss due to spilled oil is then proportional to just the distance between valves; the cost per mile of spillage is c_s (in $1000) per mile. Therefore the spillage cost of one break is $c_s d$. The cost of the valves is c_v (in $1000) per valve. The total number of pipeline breaks over the projected life of the pipeline is B.

   (a) Find the total cost of the valves plus spillage over the life of the pipeline. It should be a function of the decision variable d, the parameter D, the costs, and the quantity B.

   (b) The number of breaks over the lifetime is unknown. It is believed there will be either zero, one, or two breaks with probabilities .5, .4, and .1, respectively. Find the expected total cost as a function of d, D, and the costs c_v and c_s. Find the expression for the d value that minimizes the expected total cost over the life of the pipeline. Evaluate it using the estimates $c_v = 10$, $c_s = 6$, $D = 10,000$.

   (c) Find the risk-adjusted value of the total cost over the life of the pipeline for a risk-averse company having exponential utility function with parameter $r = 10^{-3}$ (when values are expressed in $1000 units). Evaluate this for the d that minimizes expected total cost and evaluate it again for a larger or smaller d depending upon the effect you think will result from the risk aversion.

4. As a special case of the portfolio example of Sec. 11.8, suppose that there is just one stock with $\mu = .12$ and $\sigma^2 = .0001$ ($\sigma = .01$). The interest rate is $I = .10$ and borrowing is allowed. The risk-aversion parameter is $r = .01$ and the initial capital is $5000 again. How much should the investor borrow and how much should he invest? What is the expected profit of the investment that maximizes his risk-adjusted value and what is its variance? Compare this to the case where the investor is not allowed to borrow. By what factor has borrowing magnified his expected profit?

5. In an "incentive contract" the contractor and contractee negotiate a target cost p, a profit rate α, and a sharing or incentive rate β. If the actual cost is c, the contractor makes a profit

$$\alpha p + \beta(p - c)$$

after receiving payment $(1 + \alpha)p - (1 - \beta)(p - c)$ from the contractee. Thus the contractor pays fraction β of a cost overrun. He has an incentive to reduce costs, if possible, because he will benefit by fraction β of a savings over the target cost. Thus both parties share in the risk inherent in the uncertainty of the cost. The contractor would usually prefer $\beta = 0$, which is called a *cost plus fixed fee* contract. The contractee would usually prefer $\beta = 1$, a *fixed-price* contract.

Study the preference of a contractor having exponential utility with parameter r and a normal probability distribution of actual cost c having mean μ and variance σ^2. Consider $0 \leq \alpha < 1, 0 \leq \beta \leq 1, p > 0$, and $\mu > 0$. Find the contractor's optimum β value and the range of β values for which his risk-adjusted profit is positive, considering both $\mu < p$ and $\mu \geq p$. Derive an expression for the β value at which the contractor is indifferent between accepting the contract or rejecting it. By how much must the target cost exceed the contractor's expected cost so that the contractor would *prefer* to have a fixed-price contract? Evaluate all these for $p = 100, \sigma^2 = 64, r = .5$ (all values in $ millions), $\alpha = .08$, and for three values of μ: 90, 100, and 110 million.

6. Exploration for new oil fields is a risky process. A well is drilled, resulting in either a discovery or a dry well of no value. The variance of return may be of the order of five times the expected return, and the probability distribution of profit typically has a long right tail. The financial action often used to control risk is that of sharing. Even major oil companies find it useful to form combines to drill single wells in new regions such as the offshore or Arctic areas.

For a simple approach to this problem, consider a company with exponential utility function desiring to find the optimum share α with which to participate in both the costs and returns. Their risk-aversion level is $r = .1$ (all values in $ millions). Ignore the effects of taxation, for simplicity. Consider the following three models of exploration, when the value of a dry well is zero and the cost of the lottery is c.

1. Exploration is a simple lottery with probability of discovery p and probability of a dry well $(1 - p)$. The value of success is v.

2. Exploration is a single draw from a gamma distribution having mean b/a and variance b/a^2.

3. Exploration is a lottery with probability p of discovery and $(1 - p)$ of a dry well. If a field is discovered, its value is a draw from a gamma distribution with mean b/a and variance b/a^2.

For parameter values $r = .1$ and $c = \$.5$ million,

$$\text{Model 1: } p = \frac{1}{10}, v = 10$$

$$\text{Model 2: } b = .2, a = .2$$

$$\text{Model 3: } p = \frac{1}{10}, b = 2, a = \frac{1}{5}$$

For each of the three models find (a) the expected profit. (b) Find the risk-adjusted value (RAV) of the whole venture ($\alpha = 1$). (c) Find the risk-adjusted value of share α and find the best share for the first two models.

Table of Results

Model	Expected Profit	Variance	RAV of Whole Project	Best Share	RAV of Best Share
1	$\frac{1}{2}$	9	.156	.75	.167
2	$\frac{1}{2}$	5	.311	1.0	.311
3	$\frac{1}{2}$	14	.071	.56	.118

Chapter 12

GAME THEORY

Game theory deals with making decisions under conflict caused by opposing interests. Previous chapters have concerned decisions in a context where the consequences of the decision maker's actions are either deterministic (predictable) or could be represented as being determined by a chance mechanism described by probabilities. These consequences had the attribute of predictability, at least in a probabilistic sense. They may have been determined partly by many other people and organizations pursuing their own interests. However, their interests may not have been in direct conflict with those of the decision maker. Furthermore the consequences may have been determined by the aggregate behavior of a large number of other individuals and organizations. Such aggregate behavior is often well represented by a deterministic or probabilistic description of the world faced by the decision maker.

There are important decision problems where the consequences of the decision maker's actions are determined partly by a few other decision makers whose interests are in direct conflict. Such problems are usually difficult to solve but are important from a conceptual viewpoint. Quantitative analysis is seldom applied to problems of this type. However, the precise nature of quantitative reasoning is useful in developing a precise understanding of such problems. The understanding will be useful even when the analysis is not carried out in a quantitative fashion.

Many business problems involve competition between decision makers. Competition is usually a combination of conflict and cooperation. However, the purpose of game theory is to model conflict. For simplicity it excludes elements that would lead to cooperation and concentrates solely upon situations of direct conflict. This is necessary to achieve an understanding of conflict; however, it also restricts the apparent usefulness of the subject. A more appropriate name for game theory would be the "theory of conflict." The name "game theory" suggests that it is about games —activities designed for entertainment value. Real games possess an element of cooperation because they entertain players who cooperate to the extent of being willing to participate. Game theory takes no entertainment value or motive into account.

12.1   TWO-PERSON–ZERO-SUM GAMES

Game theory begins with the simplest situation involving direct conflict. It makes many assumptions that may appear unrealistic but are useful for simplifying the problem. The first assumption is that there are only two players, A and B. The second assumption is that of direct conflict; the zero-sum property means that the payoff to A and the payoff to B together sum to zero. This means that A's gain is B's loss and vice versa. The two players are "splitting a fixed pie" and so there is no motivation for cooperation. The game is given the simplest time structure possible; there is just one play and then the problem is over. It is not a series of repetitions. The payoffs to both players, as determined by the actions of both, are made right after the single play.

The decisions of both players are made individually, prior to the play, with no communication between them. The decisions are made simultaneously and also announced simultaneously so that neither player has an advantage resulting from direct knowledge of the other player's decision. Each player has a list of possible courses of action from which he can select. These can be represented by subscripted letters:

List for player A: $A_1, A_2, \ldots, A_m$
List for player B: $B_1, B_2, \ldots, B_n$

The numbers n and m need not be equal. However, it is important to assume that each player knows not only his own list of possible courses of action but also that of his opponent.

One play of the game consists of a simultaneous selection of one A_i by player A and one B_j by player B. The payoff is then determined. It is α_{ij} for player A and $-\alpha_{ij}$ for player B. Clearly these two payoffs sum to zero. There are $n \times m$ possible payoffs, represented by Table 12.1.

TABLE 12.1   Payoff Table

	B_1	B_2	B_3	$\cdots$	B_n
A_1	α_{11}	α_{12}	α_{13}		α_{1n}
A_2	α_{21}	α_{22}	α_{23}		α_{2n}
A_3	α_{31}	α_{32}	α_{33}		α_{3n}
$\vdots$					
A_m	α_{m1}	α_{m2}	α_{m3}		α_{mn}

TABLE 12.2   Two-person–Zero-sum Game

	B_1	B_2	B_3	B_4
A_1	38	32	28	31
A_2	36	33	34	35
A_3	26	31	35	36

If it were not a zero-sum game, it might be necessary to use two such tables—one for the payoff to A and the other for the payoff to B. However, in a zero-sum game it suffices to show only the payoff to one of the players. The convention is to show the payoff to A, knowing that it is also the loss to B. This does not imply, however, that A "always wins" and B "always loses." Negative values of α_{ij} are possible and represent outcomes where B gains and A loses.

One final and vital assumption is that both players know the whole payoff table. They know not only the possible payoffs to themselves but, equally well, they know those of their opponents. Again this assumption is restrictive. It is made not because it is the most likely case but because any other assumption would lead to a much more difficult problem. An example of a two-person–zero-sum game is shown in Table 12.2.

The payoff table (Table 12.2) completely describes a game of this type. Here player B has $n = 4$ courses of action; player A has $m = 3$ courses of action. The payoffs to A happen to be all positive numbers. Therefore it is certain that A will gain something between a minimum of 26 and a maximum of 38. Player B will lose the corresponding quantity. However, the exact size of this transfer of value from B to A is determined by the decisions of both players.

12.2   NATURE OF A SOLUTION

There are two questions to be answered by game theory:

How *will* the players behave?
How *should* the players behave?

These two questions must be answered simultaneously. Consider the viewpoint of one decision maker, A. He must decide how he *should* behave. He sets his objective as the maximization of his expected gain. Yet his gain is determined not only by his choice of action but also by that of his opponent. Therefore he cannot decide how he should behave without simultaneously deciding how his opponent *will* behave.

The basic problem of game theory is to determine what the opponent will do. Decision maker A needs a model of his opponent, decision maker B. Two choices are obvious. One is to model his opponent as a chance mechanism and assign probabilities to the possible actions of B. This would lead to a problem of decision under uncertainty. The other choice is to model the opponent as an intelligent, knowledgeable individual acting in pursuit of his own interests, a "rational" opponent. This is a more reasonable assumption in situations that obey all the preceding assumptions. Furthermore it will be seen that the assumption of a rational opponent is a conservative assumption in the sense that a rational opponent is the hardest to play against. An opponent who is simply a chance mechanism could not give a lower expected gain to decision maker A.

Although a rational opponent is the most demanding upon A's expected gain, he is also easier to understand. It is easier to predict the behavior of a rational opponent than that of an irrational one; in many cases there is just one way to be rational whereas there are many ways of being irrational. It is a key result of game theory that it is possible to predict, either deterministically or probabilistically, what the rational opponent *will* do and therefore to decide what decision maker A *should* do to maximize his expected payoff.

12.3   SOLUTIONS FOR GAMES WITH A SADDLE POINT

Although the term *saddle point* will become clear only at the end of this section, it means that the optimal solution to the game has the property that you can predict with certainty what the opponent's course of action will be. Not all games possess such a solution, but it is an important starting point in understanding game theory.

The first step in solving a game problem is to find A's best solution assuming that B would know it in advance and counter it. This is called A's *best nonsecret strategy*. The reasoning is simple and is represented by rows in Table 12.3 for the specific game already shown.

The first row in Table 12.3 shows that if A selects his first course of action and B knows this choice in advance, B would select this third course of action, B_3, to limit his loss to 28. After repeating this reasoning for A_2 and again for A_3, A can finally select his best nonsecret strategy. It is A_2 because A_2 has the greatest payoff for A. He knows that B will select B_2 and the payoff will be 33.

The next step is to find decision maker B's best nonsecret strategy. A similar table can be used (see Table 12.4). If B selects B_2 and A knows this choice in advance, A would select A_2 and B would lose 33. However, 33 is the smallest loss attainable from a nonsecret strategy. Therefore it is B's best nonsecret strategy.

TABLE 12.3   *A*'s Best Nonsecret Strategy

If A Selects	B Would Select	A Would Receive
A_1	B_3	28
A_2	B_2	33*
A_3	B_1	26

TABLE 12.4   *B*'s Best Nonsecret Strategy

If *B* Selects	*A* Would Select	*B* Would Lose
B_1	A_1	38
B_2	A_2	33*
B_3	A_3	35
B_4	A_3	36

It is perhaps not yet clear to the reader why the best nonsecret strategy is at all relevant to the problem, because the selections are in fact made without knowledge of the opponent's choice. However, there is a compelling reason: If game theory can tell player *A* how he should behave, it also tells player *B* how player *A* will behave. In other words, if a solution of this type exists it must be a nonsecret solution. Therefore the best nonsecret solutions, if they coincide, are the best solutions to the game. For this specific game the best nonsecret strategies do coincide:

A's best nonsecret strategy is A_2, expecting *B* to select B_2.
B's best nonsecret strategy is B_2, expecting *A* to select A_2.

Each player expects the other to do what is in fact his best nonsecret strategy. When these coincide, the game is said to have a *saddle-point* or deterministic solution. The word "deterministic" means here that player *A* can predict with certainty that *B* will select B_2 if he is confident that the assumptions of the game model are true (that *B* is rational, that the payoffs in the table are perceived by *B* to be the correct payoffs, and so forth). If the best nonsecret strategies do not coincide, then there does not exist a deterministic solution. The nature of the solution for that case is shown in the next section.

The term *saddle-point solution* is also useful because it indicates a property of the solution that makes the solution method much faster. A saddle-point solution exists if one cell in the table is the smallest entry in its row and simultaneously the largest entry in its column. The efficient method of solution is

1.   For each row find the smallest entry and mark it with a *B* because it is *B*'s best countermove if *B* knew that *A* would select that row. If the smallest entry is not unique, mark all equal ones.

2.   For each column find the largest entry and mark it with an *A* because it is *A*'s best countermove if *A* knew that *B* would select that column. If the smallest entry is not unique, mark all equal ones.

3.   If at least one entry has been marked with both an *A* and a *B*, it is a saddle-point solution. If no entry is marked twice, there exists no saddle-point solution.

TABLE 12.5   Calculations for Saddle-point Solution

	B_1	B_2	B_3	B_4
A_1	38^A	32	28^B	31
A_2	36	33^B_A	34	35
A_3	26^B	31	35^A	36^A

The result is illustrated in Table 12.5.

The conclusion of this efficient method is that there is a saddle-point (deterministic) solution. A will select A_2 and B will select B_2 and the payoff will be a transfer of 33 units from B to A. Both players, believing that this model accurately describes the problem, can confidently predict the outcome and the value of the game.

Suppose, in this situation, that some communication is allowed prior to the final decisions and determination of outcome. Each player will attempt to test the rationality of his opponent by bluffing. For example, B may lead off with the statement that "I plan to select B_1." He reasons that if A believed him, A would plan to select A_1. If B believes that A believes his statement, he will pick B_3 to reduce his loss to 28. However, it is in A's interest to pretend to believe B's statement because, if he appears to believe it, he can expect B to select B_3. Meanwhile A can plan to select A_3 and expect a payoff of 35. There is no equilibrium to this chain of reasoning. Neither player can be confident that his opponent will do as he says, because it would be against that opponent's self-interest. The only credible communication that B could make is "I plan to select B_2." However, that communication is unnecessary because A already knows that a rational opponent will select B_2. Thus it appears that the possibility of communication has no effect upon the solution of the game if each player believes in the rationality of his opponent.

12.4   EXAMPLE AND COMPARISON WITH A CHANCE MECHANISM

Consider the following game in which both decision makers A and B have two possible courses of action, as shown in Table 12.6:

TABLE 12.6 Game against a Chance Mechanism

	B_1	B_2
A_1	4^B_A	5^A
A_2	2	1^B

The search for a saddle point reveals that the best nonsecret strategy of each player is to select his first course of action.

Suppose that decision maker A wishes to model his opponent as a chance mechanism rather than a rational opponent. This means he will specify a probability y_1 that the chance mechanism will select course of action B_1. Let y_2 represent the probability that the chance mechanism will select B_2. These two events are mutually exclusive and are the only possible outcomes. Therefore the probabilities must obey

$$y_1 + y_2 = 1 \quad \text{or} \quad y_2 = 1 - y_1$$

The expected payoff of this game against chance, if A selects A_1, is

$$4y_1 + 5(1 - y_1)$$

If A selects A_2, his expected payoff is

$$2y_1 + (1 - y_1)$$

For example, if decision maker A believes that chance is equally likely to select B_1 or B_2, the expected values are 4.5 for A_1 and 1.5 for A_2. He would select A_1 and expect to gain 4.5.

It is interesting to compare the two possible views of decision maker A about the nature of his opponent. If B is a rational opponent then A can expect the payoff of 4, whereas he can expect a payoff of 4.5 if his opponent is a chance mechanism having $y_1 = \frac{1}{2}$. Apparently it is worse to play against a rational opponent. It is easy to show that the chance mechanism cannot be a worse opponent than a rational opponent for any value of y_1. This is true because

$$4y_1 + 5(1 - y_1) > 2y_1 + (1 - y_1) \quad \text{for any } 0 \leq y_1 \leq 1$$

and therefore A would select A_1 for any value of y_1. Also the smallest possible value of

$$4y_1 + 5(1 - y_1)$$

is the value 4, attained when $y_1 = 1$. Thus the worst possible chance mechanism has $y_1 = 1$ and therefore behaves just like a rational opponent who would also select B_1 with probability 1. Thus a rational opponent is like the least favorable chance mechanism; all other chance mechanisms, $y_1 < 1$, would be a more desirable opponent.

A formal statement of this problem of finding the least favorable chance mechanism for this game is a two-variable linear program. Let v represent the expected payoff to player A (and expected loss to player B). Then

$$\min v$$

subject to

$$4y_1 + 5(1 - y_1) \le v$$
$$2y_1 + (1 - y_1) \le v$$
$$y_1 \le 1$$

and

$$y_1 \ge 0$$

Notice that v is not restricted to be nonnegative.

EXERCISES

1. Show that the optimum solution to the preceding linear program is $y_1 = 1$ and $v = 4$. Therefore the worst possible chance mechanism will select B_1 with probability 1 and the expected payoff is 4. Use a graphic method.

2. Formulate a linear program to find the worst chance mechanism to be A's opponent in the game of Sec. 12.1. Since B has four courses of action, there must be four probabilities y_1, y_2, y_3, and y_4 that sum to 1.

12.5 GAMES WITHOUT A SADDLE POINT

Many games do not have a saddle-point solution. However, they still have a solution. It is important to understand the nature of a solution in this case. Consider the game in Table 12.7.

A search for a saddle point quickly shows that there is none. Look at this problem from decision maker A's viewpoint. If game theory told him to select A_1, it would also tell his opponent that he will select A_1. Then B would select B_1, the least favorable outcome to A. If it told him to select A_2, then B would know to select B_2. There would be no way for A to obtain the favorable outcomes of cells (A_2, B_1) and A_1, B_2. There cannot be a deterministic solution to this game because the information it would give to B about A's decision can always be used to B's advantage.

If there is to be a solution to this game, it must tell A how to decide without simultaneously telling B what A will decide. A solution must have the property that it is a procedure to make a decision while protecting the information about what the

TABLE 12.7   Game without
a Saddle Point

	B_1	B_2
A_1	-5^B	6^A
A_2	4^A	-3^B

decision will be. The only way to accomplish this is by a chance mechanism called a *random strategy*. Game theory can tell decision maker A to select A_1 with probability x_1 and select A_2 with probability x_2 (such that $x_1 + x_2 = 1$). This tells A how to decide without telling B what decision will be made.

Operationally this can be implemented using any standard chance mechanism such as a random number table. A random number between zero and 1 will be drawn by chance from the table. If the number is less than x_1, the decision is A_1. If the number exceeds x_1, then A_2 is selected. This is a perfectly well-defined procedure for making the decision. It is a superior solution compared to any deterministic solution because it gives decision maker A a higher expected payoff. Player B can know these probabilities but is denied perfect predictability of decision maker A's action.

Game theory determines the best values of x_1 and x_2—A's best nonsecret random strategy. When A has just two possible courses of action, as in this example, there is just one unknown to be determined: x_1. Since the two probabilities must sum to 1, x_2 can be found by $x_2 = 1 - x_1$. The method of solution is to consider the expected payoff to A of each of B's possible courses of action as functions of x_1, which is the decision variable of this problem. If B picks B_1, the expected payoff to A is

$$-5x_1 + 4(1 - x_1)$$

If B picks B_2, the expected payoff to A is

$$6x_1 - 3(1 - x_1)$$

Player B will know the x_1 value in advance and select B_1 or B_2 depending upon which of these expected payoffs to A is smaller for the given x_1 value. This choice is easily understood from the graph of these two functions of x_1 in Fig. 12.1. The line marked B_1 is the expected payoff to A if B selects B_1. Similarly B_2 is shown. For any particular value of x_1, one line is lower than the other. There is one point where both lines have the same height. This is found by equating the expected payoffs of the two courses of action and solving for x_1:

$$-5x_1 + 4(1 - x_1) = 6x_1 - 3(1 - x_1)$$
$$4 - 9x_1 = -3 + 9x_1$$
$$x_1 = \frac{7}{18} = .388$$

For $x_1 < .388$, the line B_2 is lower and so B would select B_2 for all such x_1 values. For $x_1 > .388$, the line B_1 is lower and B would select B_1 for all such x_1 values. The expected payoff to A from B's best counterstrategy is the line B_2 for $0 \leq x_1 < .388$ and the line B_1 for $.388 < x_1 \leq 1$. Finally, A must select the best value of x_1. Clearly the value $x_1 = .388$ gives the greatest expected payoff to A.

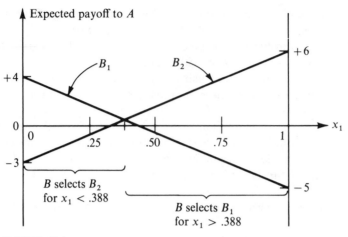

Expected payoff to A

B_1

B_2

$+6$

$+4$

0

$.25$ $.50$ $.75$ 1 x_1

-3

-5

B selects B_2
for $x_1 < .388$

B selects B_1
for $x_1 > .388$

FIGURE 12.1

Thus A's best nonsecret random strategy is $x_1 = .388$ and $x_2 = 1 - .388 = .612$. Let v denote the expected payoff to A of the optimum nonsecret random strategy. It is found from the height of either line at $x_1 = .388$:

$$v = -5(.388) + 4(.612) = .50$$

Also,

$$v = 6(.388) - 3(.612) = .50$$

If there had been no intersection of the two curves for an x_1 value in $(0,1)$, one of B's courses of action would have been best for all x_1 values. The line for that course of action would be highest at either $x_1 = 0$ or $x_1 = 1$ (or, if the line is level, at both). This would imply that a saddle-point solution exists.

The next step is to solve for B's best nonsecret random strategy. He also wishes to prevent his opponent from knowing his actual decision in advance. His strategy will be represented by y_1, the probability that he will select course of action B_1. Then the probability that he will select B_2 is $y_2 = 1 - y_1$. The easiest, most direct way to find y_1 comes from the knowledge that the expected loss to B if A picks A_1 is

$$-5y_1 + 6(1 - y_1)$$

Now the expected loss to B is also the expected gain to A, which is known to be .50. Therefore y_1 can be determined from

$$-5y_1 + 6(1 - y_1) = .5$$
$$5.5 = 11y_1$$
$$y_1 = .50$$

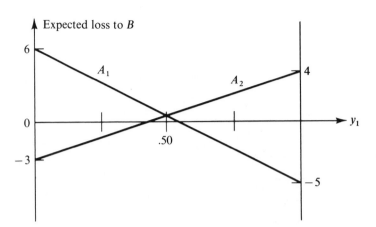

FIGURE 12.2

Therefore B's best nonsecret random strategy is $y_1 = .50$, $y_2 = .50$ and his expected loss is .50.

The difficult way to find B's best nonsecret random strategy is to repeat a whole analysis similar to that done for A. This would be necessary only if the analysis for A had not already been done. It will be done here to emphasize the symmetry of the problem and to show the method one more time. The expected loss to B is

$$-5y_1 + 6(1 - y_1) \qquad \text{if } A \text{ selects } A_1$$

and

$$4y_1 - 3(1 - y_1) \qquad \text{if } A \text{ selects } A_2$$

These are graphed as a function of y_1 in Fig. 12.2. The two expressions are equated to solve for the y_1 point where the lines cross:

$$-5y_1 + 6(1 - y_1) = 4y_1 - 3(1 - y_1)$$

The solution is

$$y_1 = .50$$

The expected loss to B is (also) v:

$$v = -5(.50) + 6(.50) = .50$$

12.6 DOMINANCE

If one course of action is better than or as good as another for all possible courses of action of the opponent, then the first is said to "dominate" the second course of action. The dominated course of action can be simply discarded because it is of no

TABLE 12.8

	B_1	B_2	B_3	B_4	B_5
A_1	4	4	2	-4	-6^B
A_2	8	6^A	8^A	-4^B	0
A_3	10^A	2^B	4	10^A	12^A

TABLE 12.9

	B_2	B_3	B_4	B_5
A_1	4	2	-4	-6
A_2	6	8	-4	0
A_3	2	4	10	12

value. This idea can be used to reduce the size of a game. However, this is useful only when the game does not have a saddle point because a saddle point, when present, is easy to find. When there is no saddle point present it is important to try to reduce the size of the game by dominance. For example, consider the game in Table 12.8.

A search has shown that no saddle point is present. A search for dominance shows that B_2 dominates B_1 and so B_1 can be discarded. The new table is shown in Table 12.9. A search of this table reveals that A_2 dominates A_1. A_1 can be discarded to give Table 12.10.

There may be new dominance relationships in Table 12.10 that were not present before. For example, B_2 now dominates B_3 whereas it did not do so in Table 12.8. Similarly, B_4 now dominates B_5. Both B_3 and B_5 are discarded to give Table 12.11.

TABLE 12.10

	B_2	B_3	B_4	B_5
A_2	6	8	-4	0
A_3	2	4	10	12

TABLE 12.11

	B_2	B_4
A_2	6	-4
A_3	2	10

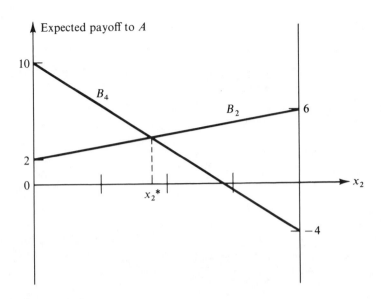

FIGURE 12.3

Thus dominance has reduced a 3 × 5 game to a 2 × 2 game that can be solved by the method of the previous section. Let x_i be the probability with which A should select A_i for $i = 1, 2,$ and 3. Then it is known already that $x_1 = 0$. Therefore $x_2 + x_3 = 1$. It remains to solve for x_2, A's best nonsecret random strategy. It can be found as follows. If B selects B_2, the expected payoff to A is

$$6x_2 + 2(1 - x_2)$$

If B selects B_4, it is

$$-4x_2 + 10(1 - x_2)$$

The graph is shown in Fig. 12.3. The equation that determines the best x_2 is

$$6x_2 + 2(1 - x_2) = -4x_2 + 10(1 - x_2)$$

The solution is

$$x_2 = \frac{4}{9}$$

Therefore

$$x_3 = \frac{5}{9}$$

The expected payoff to A is

$$6\left(\frac{4}{9}\right) + 2\left(\frac{5}{9}\right) = \frac{34}{9} = 3.78$$

The best nonsecret random strategy for B has $y_1 = 0$, $y_3 = 0$, $y_5 = 0$, and $y_2 + y_4 = 1$. The value of y_2 can be obtained from

$$6y_2 - 4(1 - y_2) = \frac{34}{9}$$

The solution is $y_2 = \frac{7}{9}$. Therefore $y_4 = \frac{2}{9}$.

12.7   2 × n GAMES

The difficulty in solving a game (having no saddle-point solution) is determined by the smaller of the game's two dimensions. If A has only two courses of action, the statement implies that B also will use no more than two. This implies that all $2 \times n$ games can be easily solved by the methods of Sec. 12.5. This will be demonstrated for the game in Table 12.12.

A's best nonsecret random strategy (x_1, x_2) is described by one number, x_1. B's best nonsecret random strategy is described by four numbers, y_1, y_2, y_3, and y_4, where y_5 is determined by $y_5 = 1 - y_1 - y_2 - y_3 - y_4$. Clearly it is easiest to solve first for the strategy having the smallest number of variables.

To determine x_1 it is necessary to consider all of B's possible choices. The expected payoff to A is

$$\begin{array}{ll} 4x_1 - 4(1 - x_1) & \text{if } B \text{ selects } B_1 \\ -2x_1 + 8(1 - x_1) & \text{if } B \text{ selects } B_2 \\ 10x_1 - 6(1 - x_1) & \text{if } B \text{ selects } B_3 \\ -4x_1 + 2(1 - x_1) & \text{if } B \text{ selects } B_4 \\ 12x_1 + 0(1 - x_1) & \text{if } B \text{ selects } B_5 \end{array}$$

These can all be graphed as a function of x_1, as illustrated by Fig. 12.4. From this graph it is immediately clear that for x_1 values near zero, B would select B_3, for intermediate values he would select B_1, and for values near 1 he would select B_4. He would never select B_2 or B_5. Actually this much could have been determined by the

TABLE 12.12   2 × n Game

	B_1	B_2	B_3	B_4	B_5
A_1	4	−2	10	−4	12
A_2	−4	8	−6	2	0

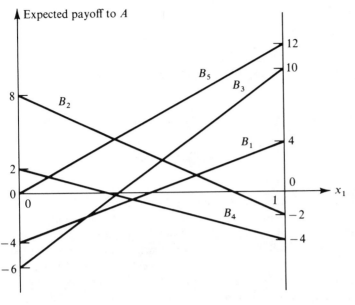

FIGURE 12.4

use of dominance. B_2 is dominated by B_4 and B_5 is dominated by B_3. Therefore they can be discarded and both y_2 and y_5 can be set to zero.

The next observation from the graph is that the intersection of B_1 with B_4 is higher than the intersection of B_1 with B_3. Therefore it is the intersection of B_1 with B_4 that determines x_1:

$$4x_1 - 4(1 - x_1) = -4x_1 + 2(1 - x_1)$$

$$x_1 = \frac{3}{7}$$

and so

$$x_2 = \frac{4}{7}$$

The expected payoff to A is

$$v = 4\left(\frac{3}{7}\right) - 4\left(\frac{4}{7}\right) = -\frac{4}{7}$$

A further conclusion is that B will never use B_3. His best random strategy will use only B_1 and B_4.

The solution for B's best random strategy is now easy. It is known that B_2, B_3, and B_5 will not be used. Therefore y_2, y_3, and y_5 are zero. That leaves y_1 and y_4

to be determined. Since $y_1 + y_4 = 1$, there remains only y_1 to be determined. If A selects A_1, the expected loss to B is

$$4y_1 - 4(1 - y_1)$$

and this must equal the expected payoff to A, which is $-\frac{4}{7}$. Therefore

$$4y_1 - 4(1 - y_1) = -\frac{4}{7}$$

The solution for y_1 is

$$y_1 = \frac{3}{7}$$

Therefore $y_4 = \frac{4}{7}$ and the solution is complete.

In conclusion, when A has only two courses of action an optimum solution for x_1 is always at the intersection of two of B's courses of action. (Even if three of B's courses of action intersected at one point, only two of them would be used.) A similar reasoning would apply to $3 \times n$ games. However, the graphic method used so far is convenient only for two courses of action. For games whose smallest dimension is greater than 2 and cannot be reduced by dominance, a new method must be considered that is generally useful for any dimensions.

12.8   SOLUTION OF GAMES BY LINEAR PROGRAMMING

A general statement of the two-person–zero-sum game is that A has m courses of action $(A_1, A_2, \ldots, A_n)$ and B has n courses of action $(B_1, B_2, \ldots, B_n)$, where m and n are not necessarily equal. The payoff to A if he selects A_i and B selects B_j is α_{ij}. The loss to B is also α_{ij}. A's best random strategy is specified by $x_1, x_2, \ldots, x_m$; B's best random strategy is $y_1, y_2, \ldots, y_n$. Determining A's best random strategy can be formulated as a linear program with $m + 1$ decision variables $(x_1, x_2, \ldots, x_m)$ and v, where v is the expected payoff to A:

$$\max v$$

subject to

$$\alpha_{11} x_1 + \alpha_{21} x_2 + \alpha_{31} x_3 + \cdots + \alpha_{m1} x_m \geq v$$
$$\alpha_{12} x_1 + \alpha_{22} x_2 + \alpha_{32} x_3 + \cdots + \alpha_{m2} x_m \geq v$$
$$\vdots$$
$$\alpha_{1n} x_1 + \alpha_{2n} x_2 + \alpha_{3n} x_3 + \cdots + \alpha_{mn} x_m \geq v$$
$$x_1 + x_2 + \cdots + x_m = 1$$

and

$$x_1, x_2, \ldots, x_m \geq 0$$

There are n inequality constraints. The jth constraint states that the expected payoff to A if B selects B_j cannot be less than v because B will pick his best counterstrategy. The last constraint is an equality constraint: The probabilities must sum to 1. The x's must be nonnegative because they are probabilities. However, the variable v is *not* restricted to be nonnegative. This can be a difficulty when using the standard simplex method because it constrains all variables to be nonnegative. It is not a problem when all α_{ij} are nonnegative because v cannot then be negative. Therefore the nonnegativity problem can be prevented by adding a constant c to all cells in the α_{ij} table such that the resulting table contains all nonnegative entries. This c would be subtracted from the final v value as a last step to recover the true v, which may be negative. The equality constraint can be used for substitution to eliminate one variable if the nonnegativity of the eliminated variable is enforced by a constraint. Otherwise the method of artificial slack variables could be used on the equality constraint.

The solution for $x_1, x_2, \ldots, x_m$ and v can be used to obtain the solution for $y_1, y_2, \ldots, y_n$. Suppose that the first $r \le m$ of the x's are greater than zero and the others are zero. Then the y's can be determined as the solution of simultaneous linear equations. If the jth constraint is satisfied as an equality in the optimal solution, then $y_j > 0$, which means that B may use B_j. If the jth constraint is satisfied as an inequality in the optimal solution, then $y_j = 0$ and B would never use B_j. This reasoning determines which r of the n y values must be solved for.

It is also possible to solve for B's best random strategy as a linear programming problem:

$$\min v$$

subject to

$$\alpha_{11} y_1 + \alpha_{12} y_2 + \alpha_{13} y_3 + \cdots + \alpha_{1n} y_n \le v$$
$$\alpha_{21} y_1 + \alpha_{22} y_2 + \alpha_{23} y_3 + \cdots + \alpha_{2n} y_n \le v$$
$$\vdots$$
$$\alpha_{m1} y_1 + \alpha_{m2} y_2 + \alpha_{m3} y_3 + \cdots + \alpha_{mn} y_n \le v$$
$$y_1 + y_2 + \cdots + y_m = 1$$

and

$$y_1, y_2, \ldots, y_m \ge 0$$

Here the jth inequality represents the expected loss to B if A selects A_j. These expected losses cannot exceed the value of the game because the value of the game is determined by A's selection of the best course of action. Finally B is seeking to minimize v, his expected loss. This is the same linear program used in Sec. 12.4 to

TABLE 12.13   Payoff Table

A	B 1	2	3
1	-1^B	1	1
2	2	-2^B	2^A
3	3^A	3^A	-3^B

find the probabilities $y_1, y_2, \ldots, y_n$ that are least favorable to player A. If this linear program is solved first, then its results, knowledge of which variables are positive and which constraints hold as equalities, may be used to solve for A's best random strategy as a set of linear equations rather than by solving A's linear program.

Consider the following example. The two players A and B must each select a number out of 1, 2, or 3. If both have chosen the same number, A will pay B the amount of the chosen number. Otherwise A receives the amount of his own number from B. The payoff table for this game is shown in Table 12.13.

A search indicates that there is no saddle-point solution. The linear program for A's best random strategy, x_1, x_2, x_3, is

$$\max v$$

subject to

$$-x_1 + 2x_2 + 3x_3 \geq v$$
$$x_1 - 2x_2 + 3x_3 \geq v$$
$$x_1 + 2x_2 - 3x_3 \geq v$$
$$x_1 + x_2 + x_3 = 1$$

and

$$x_1, x_2, x_3 \geq 0$$

The optimal v could be negative because the payoff table does contain negative payoffs. However, if the number 3 is added to all α_{ij}'s, then all will be nonnegative. Then define $v' = v + 3$ or $v = v' - 3$. The problem can be rewritten with all nonnegative variables as

$$\max v' - 3$$

subject to

$$2x_1 + 5x_2 + 6x_3 \geq v'$$
$$4x_1 + x_2 + 6x_3 \geq v'$$
$$4x_1 + 5x_2 \geq v'$$

$$x_1 + x_2 + x_3 = 1$$
$$x_1, x_2, x_3, v' \geq 0$$

It is best with hand calculation to eliminate the equality constraint by substituting

$$x_3 = 1 - x_1 - x_2$$

and replacing the nonnegativity condition $x_3 \geq 0$ by

$$x_1 + x_2 \leq 1$$

The resulting problem is

$$\max v' - 3$$

subject to

$$4x_1 + x_2 + v' \leq 6$$
$$2x_1 + 5x_2 + v' \leq 6$$
$$4x_1 + 5x_2 - v' \geq 0$$
$$x_1 + x_2 \qquad \leq 1$$

and

$$x_1, x_2, v' \geq 0$$

Slack variables are then used to convert the four inequality constraints to equalities. The problem becomes

$$\max v' - 3$$

subject to

$$4x_1 + x_2 + v' + s_1 = 6$$
$$2x_1 + 5x_2 + v' + s_2 = 6$$
$$4x_1 + 5x_2 - v' - s_3 = 0$$
$$x_1 + x_2 + s_4 = 1$$

The initial BFS will have basic variables s_1, s_2, s_3, s_4 and zero variables x_1, x_2, v'. This corner point is degenerate because the third constraint passes through the origin. However, the degeneracy gives no trouble. The first tableau of the simplex method is

Pivot

	Const.	x_1	x_2	v'	Ratio	
E	-3	0	0	1		
s_1	6	-4	-1	-1	-6	
s_2	6	-2	-5	-1	-6	
s_3	0	4	5	-1	-0	Pivot
s_4	1	-1	-1	0	∞	

The next tableau shows no gain in objective because of the degeneracy:

	Const.	x_1	x_2	s_3	Ratio	
			Pivot			
E	-3	$+4$	5	$\top 1$		
s_1	6	-8	-6	$+1$	-1	
s_2	6	-6	-10	$+1$	$-\dfrac{6}{10}$	Pivot
v'	0	$+4$	$+5$	-1	0	
s_4	1	-1	-1	0	-1	

The next tableau is

	Const.	x_1	s_2	s_3	Ratio	
		Pivot				
E	0	1	$-\dfrac{1}{2}$	$-\dfrac{1}{2}$		
s_1	$\dfrac{24}{10}$	$-\dfrac{44}{10}$	$+\dfrac{6}{10}$	$+\dfrac{4}{10}$	$-\dfrac{24}{44}$	Pivot
x_2	$\dfrac{6}{10}$	$-\dfrac{6}{10}$	$-\dfrac{1}{10}$	$+\dfrac{1}{10}$	-1	
v'	3	1	$-\dfrac{1}{2}$	$-\dfrac{1}{2}$	$+3$	
s_4	$+\dfrac{4}{10}$	$-\dfrac{4}{10}$	$+\dfrac{1}{10}$	$-\dfrac{1}{10}$	-1	

The next tableau gives the optimal solution:

	Const.	s_1	s_2	s_3	Ratio
E	$\dfrac{6}{11}$	$-\dfrac{10}{44}$	$-\dfrac{4}{11}$	$-\dfrac{9}{22}$	
x_1	$\dfrac{6}{11}$	$-\dfrac{10}{44}$	$\dfrac{6}{44}$	$\dfrac{1}{11}$	
x_2	$\dfrac{3}{11}$	$+\dfrac{6}{44}$	$-\dfrac{2}{11}$	$\dfrac{1}{22}$	
v'	$\dfrac{39}{11}$	$-\dfrac{10}{44}$	$-\dfrac{4}{11}$	$-\dfrac{9}{22}$	
s_4	$\dfrac{2}{11}$	$+\dfrac{4}{44}$	$+\dfrac{1}{22}$	$-\dfrac{7}{110}$	

The result is

$$x_1 = \frac{6}{11}$$

$$x_2 = \frac{3}{11}$$

$$x_3 = \frac{2}{11}$$

and

$$v = \frac{6}{11}$$

The first three constraints hold as equalities in the optimal solution. Therefore it is known that B uses all three of his courses of action. The best random strategy for B can be found from these results by solving three simultaneous equations in three unknowns. The ith equation represents the expected loss to B if A uses A_i. All these must equal the expected gain to A that is known. The equations are

$$-y_1 + y_2 + y_3 = \frac{6}{11}$$

$$2y_1 - 2y_2 + 2y_3 = \frac{6}{11}$$

$$3y_1 + 3y_2 - 3y_3 = \frac{6}{11}$$

The solution is

$$y_1 = \frac{5}{22}$$

$$y_2 = \frac{4}{11}$$

$$y_3 = \frac{9}{22}$$

This completes the solution to the game problem.

It is possible to begin the analysis of the game by first finding B's optimal strategy. The linear program is

$$\min v$$

subject to

$$-y_1 + y_2 + y_3 \leq v$$
$$2y_1 - 2y_2 + 2y_3 \leq v$$
$$3y_1 + 3y_2 - 3y_3 \leq v$$
$$y_1 + y_2 + y_3 = 1$$

and

$$y_1, y_2, y_3 \geq 0$$

Again v could be negative because some α_{ij} are negative. This problem is circumvented by adding 3 to all payoffs and defining $v' = v + 3$. Also the substitution

$$y_3 = 1 - y_1 - y_2$$

is made and the constraint

$$y_1 + y_2 \leq 1$$

is added to ensure the nonnegativity of the substituted variable. The problem becomes

$$\min v' - 3$$

subject to

$$2y_1 + v' \geq 4$$
$$6y_2 + v' \geq 5$$
$$6y_1 + 6y_2 + v' \leq 0$$
$$y_1 + y_2 \leq 1$$

and

$$y_1, y_2, v' \geq 0$$

EXERCISES

1. In the game of matching pennies, each of two players A and B puts down a penny with either heads or tails up without showing his opponent. The pennies are then uncovered. A receives both pennies if they both show the same side. Otherwise B gets both. Formulate the payoff table and solve the game by linear programming. Show that the expected value of the game is zero and that both players should select heads or tails with equal probabilities.

2. Solve the game

1	2	4
4	2	1

by linear programming. Show that the expected value of the game is 2 and that A has two equally good solutions: $(\frac{2}{3}, \frac{1}{3})$ and $(\frac{1}{3}, \frac{2}{3})$. Show that B will always select his second course of action.

12.9 GAME EXAMPLE

A small branch bank A has been serving a growing market consisting of four small population centers located along an interstate highway. These centers are all about 6 miles apart along the highway. The total population is distributed among the four centers as shown in Fig. 12.5.

These centers have grown considerably since bank A's office opened a few years ago. The bank has had the whole market to itself up to now. However, there is reliable news that their major competitor, bank B, plans to enter this market and is now considering which center to locate in. Bank A needs a larger permanent office in any case and can consider relocating in any one of the population centers.

Both banks are aware that the market split will be determined mainly by travel distance and partly by loyalty, according to the following model. If bank A is nearer than bank B to a population center, it will capture 80 percent of that center's business. If both are equally distant from a center, bank A will capture 60 percent of that business. If bank B is nearer than A to a population center, it will capture 60 percent and bank A will get 40 percent of that center's business. Both banks are considering their alternatives in light of their competitor's possible alternatives. What will happen?

The analysis begins with the listing of each competitor's alternative courses of action. Each bank can locate in any one of the four population centers. These courses of action are denoted A_1, A_2, A_3, A_4 and B_1, B_2, B_3, B_4. The payoffs to bank A associated with each of the 16 possible joint outcomes must be calculated next. This is done in Table 12.14. The first column shows the outcome. The next shows the implied positions. The last column shows the percentage of the total market that will be obtained by bank A. This is based upon the rules that A will capture

 80 percent   if closer

 60 percent   if equally distant

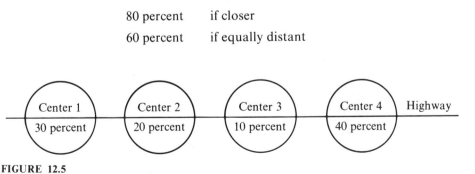

FIGURE 12.5

TABLE 12.14   Payoffs to Bank A

	Joint Outcome	Bank Positions				Calculation of Bank A's Market Share (%)	Result (%)
		C_1 (30%)	C_2 (20%)	C_3 (10%)	C_4 (40%)		
1	A_1, B_1	A, B	...	...	...	$(.6)(100) = 60$	60
2	A_2, B_1	B	A	...	...	$(.8)(70) + (.4)(30) = 56 + 12$	68
3	A_3, B_1	B	...	A	...	$(.8)(50) + (.6)(20) + (.4)(30) = 40 + 12 + 12$	64
4	A_4, B_1	B	...	...	A	$(.8)(50) + (.4)(50) = 40 + 20$	60
5	A_1, B_2	A	B	...	...	$(.8)(30) + (.4)(70) = 24 + 28$	52
6	A_2, B_2	...	A, B	...	...	$(.6)(100) = 60$	60
7	A_3, B_2	...	B	A	...	$(.8)(50) + (.4)(50) = 40 + 20$	60
8	A_4, B_2	...	B	...	A	$(.8)(40) + (.6)(10) + (.4)(50) = 32 + 6 + 20$	58
9	A_1, B_3	A	...	B	...	$(.8)(30) + (.6)(20) + (.4)(50) = 24 + 12 + 20$	56
10	A_2, B_3	...	A	B	...	$(.8)(50) + (.4)(50) = 40 + 20$	60
11	A_3, B_3	...	...	A, B	...	$(.6)(100) = 60$	60
12	A_4, B_3	...	...	B	A	$(.8)(40) + (.4)(60) = 32 + 24$	56
13	A_1, B_4	A	...	...	B	$(.8)(50) + (.4)(50) = 40 + 20$	60
14	A_2, B_4	...	A	...	B	$(.8)(50) + (.6)(10) + (.4)(40) = 40 + 6 + 16$	62
15	A_3, B_4	...	...	A	B	$(.8)(60) + (.4)(40) = 48 + 16$	64
16	A_4, B_4	...	...	...	A, B	$(.6)(100) = 60$	60

and

$$40 \text{ percent} \qquad \text{if farther away}$$

To represent the payoff to A so that it is also the loss to B, it is necessary to use market share in excess of 50 percent. Thus if A obtains 64 percent of the market, this will appear in the payoff table as 14, which is a gain beyond 50 percent to A and a loss from 50 percent to B. The payoff table for the game is shown in Table 12.15.

The search for a saddle point reveals that both banks will choose to locate in either center 2 or 3. Although these interior centers have much smaller populations than the outer centers, the solution allows both banks to protect themselves from a large loss.

TABLE 12.15   Payoff Table

	B_1	B_2	B_3	B_4
A_1	10	2^B	6	10
A_2	18^A	10^B_A	10^B_A	12
A_3	14	10^B_A	10^B_A	14^A
A_4	10	8	6^B	10

PROBLEMS

1. A new shopping mall is being planned for a suburban town. The two main department store chains in the whole metropolitan area, store A and store B, are currently splitting the market in and around that town because the residents travel to their stores in nearby towns. If only one of the stores goes into the new mall, it will capture 90 percent of that market; if both go into the mall, they will continue to split the market evenly. The game matrix, showing market share to store A in excess of 50 percent, is

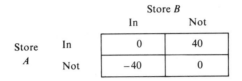

What will happen?

2. Two gas stations across from each other share a market of several city blocks. Although they both sell essentially the same product, there are two distinct price levels: the normal level and the "price war" level. If both have the same price, they will split the market evenly. If one is high while the other is low, the low-price station will get 70 percent of the business. They set their prices every day. However, consider one day in isolation from the others and then see if the result is reasonable. Find the game theory solution and discuss from your experience whether it is reasonable. If it is not, what assumption is being violated?

3. A military missile whose strategic objective is deterrence against a potential enemy's first strike is mobile and can be located at either point 1 or point 2. The potential enemy can aim his first-strike missile at either point 1 or point 2 in hopes of destroying the defensive missile. This is a game with payoffs measuring the number of surviving missiles of the defender.

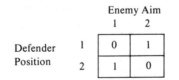

Find the optimal strategies using the graphic method.

4. In a duopolistic market, two competitors compete for profit with promotional effort as their only controllable variables. Each competitor has the option of increasing or decreasing the promotional expenditure or staying at the normal level. The expected increase in profit of competitor 1 under various situations is shown here (in $1000 units):

Competitor 1	Competitor 2		
	Increase	Normal	Decrease
Increase	− 200	− 20	30
Normal	− 50	0	− 10
Decrease	+ 80	10	50

Assuming a zero-sum game, find the optimal strategy of each competitor.

5. Solve the game described by the following matrix:

	B_1	B_2	B_3
A_1	4	4	3
A_2	8	1	7
A_3	− 1	2	− 1

6. Two politicians are running against each other for a particular office. Campaign plans must now be made for the final two days before the election. Polls indicate that the anticipated election result currently is a toss-up. Both politicians plan to campaign in two key areas having 10,000 and 5000 votes, respectively. To avoid wasting campaign time, they plan to travel at night and spend an integer number of days (0, 1, or 2) in the respective areas. However, they are uncertain how they should divide the two available days among these areas.

For either area, it is estimated that both politicians will get 50 percent of the vote if they spend the same number of days there. However, if one politician spends no time in the area, the other will get 55 and 58 percent of the vote if he spends one and two days there, respectively. If either spends one day there, the other will get 53 percent of the vote in the area by being there two days. However, since the necessary arrangements must be made in advance, neither politician will learn his opponent's campaign schedule until after he has finalized his own. Formulate and solve this problem.

7. The management of a corporation is in the process of deciding whether to agree to negotiate with the striking union now or to delay. The decision is difficult because the management does not know the union leadership's position. The union leaders may be adamant and insist on their original demands, they may be ready to compromise, or they may be ready to yield and accept the original management offer. The matrix of payoffs to management, as management sees

it, is (in $1 million units)

	Union Position		
	B_1 Adamant	B_2 Compromise	B_3 Yield
A_1 Negotiate	-2	1	2
A_2 Delay	5	-2	-3

(*a*)   Solve management's problem.

(*b*)   What should be the union's strategy?

(*c*)   Discuss the implications of a conclusion to adopt a random strategy.

Chapter 13

STOCHASTIC PROCESSES

A stochastic process is a chance process with a time dimension. Instead of just one random variable $\tilde{S}$ to describe the outcome, there is a whole series of random variables $\tilde{S}_1, \tilde{S}_2, \ldots$, where $\tilde{S}_i$ is associated with time i. It is often claimed that the market price of a share of common stock obeys a "random walk." A random walk is a special case of a stochastic process. Thus the concept of a stochastic process helps to clarify the nature of the stock market. This is just one example of an area where the concept of a stochastic process has an important impact.

Stochastic service systems are characterized by the inability to schedule the timing of demands for service. Often the time required to give service is also unpredictable. Both types of random variation imply the need for additional service capacity. The theory of *queuing*, or waiting lines, shows how the service capacity required is related to the characteristics of these random variations. This chapter examines the concept of a stochastic process. The primary goal is the understanding of the concept rather than the acquisition of tools for calculation.

13.1 A MARKOV PROCESS

The *state space* of a stochastic process is a list of possible outcomes at any point in time. It is essentially a new name for *sample space*. At every point in time the process is in exactly one of its possible states. Consider for illustration a process familiar to all: the weather. Since the goal of the discussion is the understanding of a stochastic process and not weather itself, a simple representation of weather is used. Every day will be classified as either rain (sometime during the day) or clear (no rain during the day). These will be the possible outcomes, the state space, of the stochastic process:

R: rain sometime
C: no rain

Every day is an observation of this process. Let the days be numbered such that day 0 is today, day 1 is tomorrow, and so forth. Then the event R_n is the event of rain on day n. A *realization,* or history, of this stochastic process is a string of observations:

$$R_0, R_1, C_2, C_3, C_4, R_5, C_6, C_7, C_8, R_9, \ldots$$

Thus a stochastic process has a state space and a time structure. The state space can have any number of states. The market price of a stock might be represented by a continuous interval of possible prices. The time structure defines the time points when the process can be observed. For example, the price of a stock might be observed at the close of trading every day.

Once the state space and time structure have been described, it is necessary to consider how the uncertainty about the state at one time is related to the uncertainty at other times. The example of weather is useful because there is an intuitive notion of "persistence" of weather patterns. Knowledge of today's weather ought to be useful for predicting tomorrow's weather. It ought to be more useful than knowledge of only yesterday's weather.

If there were no relationship between the uncertainties about the weather on two adjacent days, events R_n and R_{n+1} would be independent. The process could then be described by one number, the probability of rain on each day (ignoring seasonal effects):

$$P(R_n) = P(R_{n+1}) = p \qquad \text{for all } n$$

However, intuition suggests that this model is too simple because it ignores the notion of persistence. The simplest model that captures the essence of this idea is the Markov process model. This is based upon the idea that today's weather is the most useful fact in predicting tomorrow's weather. In fact it assumes that the whole history of previous weather up to and including today's weather would be no more useful than the knowledge of only today's weather. This may or may not be a good model of weather. However, it is instructive to explore its implications. The Markov process is only a special case of stochastic processes, but it is broad enough for the purposes of this chapter.

The Markov model of any process is described by conditional probabilities. In this case there are four (the following numerical values are for illustration only):

$$P(C_n \mid C_{n-1}) = .8 \qquad P(R_n \mid C_{n-1}) = .2$$
$$P(C_n \mid R_{n-1}) = .4 \qquad P(R_n \mid R_{n-1}) = .6$$

The first row gives the probabilities of each state for the case when C_{n-1} is known. The second row gives the corresponding probabilities for the case when R_{n-1} is known. This information is a complete description of the Markov model and can be conveniently expressed in a table or matrix form (Table 13.1). It is often called the *transition matrix.*

TABLE 13.1 Matrix of
Conditional Probabilities

	C_n	R_n
C_{n-1}	.8	.2
R_{n-1}	.4	.6

The meaning of this model can be described in terms of the observation of the process. Suppose that the following 10-day history is known:

$$R_0, R_1, R_2, C_3, C_4, C_5, C_6, C_7, C_8, R_9$$

There are six observations of C. Of these, five were followed by C and one was followed by R. There were three observations of R followed by a known outcome. Of these, one was followed by C and the other two by R. Thus there were five C, C pairs out of six possible; one C, R pair out of six possible; one R, C pair out of three possible; and two R, R pairs out of three possible. These counts are summarized in Table 13.2. If the model correctly describes the process generating these observations, then in a large sample, perhaps 1000 days, the percentage associated with each possible pair should come close to the probabilities in the matrix.

In general a Markov process having N states can be described by N^2 probabilities, which can be expressed in an $N \times N$ matrix. The goal of this model is to make a probabilistic prediction of the state of the process at some future time. The question, for example, might be the probability of rain 3 days from now given that it is raining today. More generally it is desired to find $P(C_n)$ and $P(R_n)$ for any n value. The probability expansion rule is useful here. It gives

$$P(C_n) = P(C_n \cap C_{n-1}) + P(C_n \cap R_{n-1})$$

This is based upon the fact that C_{n-1} and R_{n-1} are two mutually exclusive events whose probabilities sum to 1. Similarly

$$P(R_n) = P(R_n \cap C_{n-1}) + P(R_n \cap R_{n-1})$$

The intersection probabilities can now be expressed in terms of conditional proba-

TABLE 13.2 Number
of Observations

C, C	C, R
$\frac{5}{6} = .83$	$\frac{1}{6} = .17$
R, C	R, R
$\frac{1}{3} = .33$	$\frac{2}{3} = .67$

bilities as in the probability expansion rule. The result is

$$P(C_n) = P(C_n \mid C_{n-1})P(C_{n-1}) + P(C_n \mid R_{n-1})P(R_{n-1})$$
$$P(R_n) = P(R_n \mid C_{n-1})P(C_{n-1}) + P(R_n \mid R_{n-1})P(R_{n-1})$$

These equations for $P(C_n)$ and $P(R_n)$ are useful because they involve the known conditional probabilities. After their values are inserted, the two equations are

$$P(C_n) = .8P(C_{n-1}) + .4P(R_{n-1})$$
$$P(R_n) = .2P(C_{n-1}) + .6P(R_{n-1})$$

This apparently is a set of two linear equations for $P(C_n)$ and $P(R_n)$ in terms of $P(C_{n-1})$ and $P(R_{n-1})$. Further simplification is possible. It is known that

$$P(C_n) + P(R_n) = 1 \qquad \text{for any } n$$

Therefore

$$P(R_{n-1}) = 1 - P(C_{n-1})$$

Substitution leaves one equation:

$$P(C_n) = .4 + .4P(C_{n-1})$$

Now the task of obtaining solutions for $P(C_1)$, $P(C_2)$, ..., can begin. The initial state of knowledge that it is raining today is expressed as

$$P(C_0) = 0 \qquad P(R_0) = 1$$

This implies that

$$P(C_1) = .4 + .4(0) = .4 \qquad \text{so } P(R_1) = .6$$

and then

$$P(C_2) = .4 + .4P(C_1)$$
$$= .4 + .16 = .56 \qquad \text{so } P(R_2) = .44$$

Then

$$P(C_3) = .4 + .4(.56) = .624 \qquad \text{so } P(R_3) = .376$$

This process of successive solution can be continued as far out as desired. The results up to $n = 10$ are shown in Table 13.3.

These probabilities are called *transient* because they are a function of time as represented by n. Consider them as a function of n, which represents time into the future. Our intuition says that the knowledge of today's weather should be useful for predicting tomorrow's weather, somewhat less useful for predicting the next day's weather, and almost useless for predicting the weather beyond a few days into the future. This is exactly what the results show: The probability of C jumps up to .624

TABLE 13.3 Transient Probabilities Given R_0

n	$P(C_n)$	$P(R_n)$
0	0	1
1	.4	.6
2	.56	.44
3	.624	.376
4	.650	.350
5	.660	.340
6	.664	.336
7	.667	.333
8	.667	.333
9	.667	.333
10	.667	.333

for day 3 and then changes very little afterward. The value of $P(C_n)$ approaches a constant value for all future days.

Suppose the initial knowledge is that today is clear. This implies that

$$P(C_0) = 1$$

and requires another whole set of calculations. The result is given in Table 13.4.

Table 13.4 shows that $P(C_n)$ approaches the same constant value regardless of the initial knowledge as n gets large. These constant values are known as *steady-state probabilities*. They can be determined directly without the repetitive calculations previously performed. On the assumption that the probabilities will approach a constant value, for example,

$$P(C_n) = P(C_{n-1}) = P(C) \qquad \text{for large } n$$

the equation can be solved directly for $P(C)$:

TABLE 13.4 Transient Probabilities Given C_0

n	$P(C_n)$	$P(R_n)$
0	1	0
1	.8	.2
2	.72	.28
3	.688	.312
4	.675	.325
5	.670	.330
6	.668	.332
7	.667	.333
8	.667	.333

$$P(C) = .4 + .4P(C)$$
$$.6P(C) = .4$$
$$P(C) = \frac{2}{3}$$

Clearly this is a much more efficient method if only the steady-state probabilities are required.

Some Markov process problems are about timing and transient conditions. They require the transient probabilities, and the repetitive process of solution given the initial knowledge is necessary. Many other problems require only the steady-state probabilities, and the direct method of solution is preferred. Both types of problems will be illustrated here. The next section shows a decision problem involving the transient probabilities.

13.2   EXAMPLE OF A TIMING DECISION

A movie producer films outside scenes for western movies every day during an extended period in the summer. This activity is highly dependent upon the weather; filming cannot be done in the rain. The producer must schedule his work force in advance for each day. He can schedule work for a day and then call it off in the morning if it is raining. If he schedules no work for that day and it turns out to be a clear day, he can request his work force to come on short notice. Either calling off scheduled work or requesting unscheduled work requires extra wage expenses according to union contract rules. The normal wage cost for a scheduled day of work is $1000. The value of a day of work is about $3000. If work is called off on a day it was scheduled, there is a wage cost of $500. Although no work is done, this cost is a compensation for the deviation from the schedule. Similarly a day's work on short notice costs $1500 in wages. This represents the normal wage rate plus compensation for deviation from the schedule. This is summarized in Table 13.5.

The schedule must be made in advance for each day. It is important to know how far in advance this schedule decision must be made because the value of the

TABLE 13.5   Profit from 1 Day

Weather	Work Scheduled	No Work Scheduled
Rain	Call off work on short notice: Profit = −500	No cost or revenue: Profit = 0
Clear	Work on schedule: Profit = 3000 − 1000 = 2000	Work on short notice: Profit = 3000 − 1500 = 1500

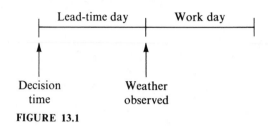

FIGURE 13.1

weather information at the decision time is smaller for longer lead times. Three cases will be considered.

Case 1: 1-day Lead Time

Suppose the work force must be told a full day in advance whether the schedule calls for work or no work. Figure 13.1 illustrates the timing. At the decision time the current day's weather is known: It is either C_0 or R_0. Based upon that information, the decision must be made whether or not to schedule work for the next day. The probability of rain on the workday is $P(R_1)$. The expected profit from the workday can be expressed as a function of $P(R_1)$ for each of the two possible decisions:

Decision	Expected Profit
Schedule work	$-500P(R_1) + 2000[1 - P(R_1)]$
Schedule no work	$0P(R_1) + 1500[1 - P(R_1)]$

The expected profit from each decision can be graphed as a function of $P(R_1)$ (see Fig. 13.2).

It can be seen from Fig. 13.2 that when $P(R_1)$ is small the best decision is to schedule work. When $P(R_1)$ is large it is best to schedule no work. The value of $P(R_1)$ that makes both decisions equally good is found by

$$-500P(R_1) + 2000[1 - P(R_1)] = 1500[1 - P(R_1)]$$

The solution of this equation for $P(R_1)$ determines that $P(R_1) = .50$ is the indifference point. The values of $P(R_1)$ have previously been determined for each initial condition. Therefore with a 1-day lead time the optimal decision rule is as shown in Table 13.6.

Case 2: 2-day Lead Time

With a 2-day lead time the relevant probability is $P(R_2)$. Previous results show that $P(R_2) = .28$ if the weather is clear at time zero and $P(R_2) = .44$ if the weather

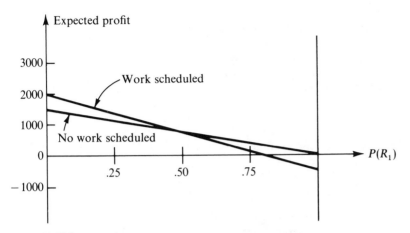

FIGURE 13.2

is R_0. Otherwise the analysis is the same. The optimal decision rule is shown in Table 13.7.

Case 3: 1-week Lead Time

With a 1-week lead time the relevant probability of rain on the workday is $P(R_7)$. Previous results showed that $P(R_7)$ is very close to $\frac{1}{3}$ regardless of whether the initial condition is R_0 or C_0. Since this value is less than .5, the best decision is to schedule work for the day. The expected profit is

$$-500\left(\frac{1}{3}\right) + 2000\left(\frac{2}{3}\right) = 1167$$

TABLE 13.6   Optimal Decision Rule with 1-day Lead Time

Weather at Decision Time	$P(R_1)$	Best Decision	Expected Profit
R_0	.6	Schedule no work	$+1500(.4) = 600$
C_0	.2	Schedule work	$-\ 500(.2) + 2000(.8) = 1500$

TABLE 13.7   Optimal Decision Rule with 2-day Lead Time

Weather at Decision Time	$P(R_2)$	Best Decision	Expected Profit
R_0	.44	Schedule work	$-500(.44) + 2000(.56) =\ \ 900$
C_0	.28	Schedule work	$-500(.28) + 2000(.72) = 1300$

A comparison of different lead times can now be made. A work schedule decision must be made for each of the many possible workdays. For each one there is a corresponding decision day that is either R_0 or C_0. The steady-state probabilities show that the probability of R_0 on a typical decision day is $\frac{1}{3}$. Therefore the average profit under the 1-day lead-time condition is

$$600 \left(\frac{1}{3}\right) + 1500 \left(\frac{2}{3}\right) = 1200$$

Under the 2-day lead time the average daily profit is

$$900 \left(\frac{1}{3}\right) + 1300 \left(\frac{2}{3}\right) = 1167$$

This figure is less because the additional lead time makes the initial weather information less valuable for prediction of weather on the workday. Under the 1-week lead time the average daily profit is also 1167:

$$-500 \left(\frac{1}{3}\right) + 2000 \left(\frac{2}{3}\right) = 1167$$

In fact any lead time greater than 1 day gives the same results. This can be seen from the transient probabilities, which show that the probability of rain is less than .5 for any lead time greater than 1 day. Therefore the decision is the same regardless of the weather at decision time for any lead time greater than 1 day. One conclusion which can be drawn from this example is that the influence of the initial conditions in a Markov process can be very small.

13.3. ANOTHER TIMING EXAMPLE

A fire extinguisher service company works under contract to service all fire extinguishers in large factories and office buildings. Each extinguisher has a required pressure level that must be maintained for proper operation. The service company sends its men periodically to each customer to inspect and recharge all extinguishers in the building. The service company has a pricing problem: For each new potential customer, it must propose a contract that will specify both the inspection period and the service charge, given the type of extinguishers and the number present. The pricing decision is based upon the estimates that the worth to the customer is $0.20 per day for every extinguisher that is up to required pressure, but it is equivalent to a $0.80 loss per day for every extinguisher below required pressure. Furthermore the pressure loss process is a Markov process. Each extinguisher is either above (state A) or below (state B) its required pressure. An extinguisher which is in state A at the start of a week has probability .05 of falling below pressure during 1 week. Once it drops below pressure it will remain below. All extinguishers are in state A at the completion of one periodic inspection. Consider a large office building having 100 extinguishers. The total charge for one inspection and service would be $100. What inspection period (in weeks) would maximize the net worth to the customer?

The Markov process has two states: A and B. The starting condition is that $P(A_0) = 1$. The matrix of conditional probabilities is

	A_n	B_n
A_{n-1}	.95	.05
B_{n-1}	0	1

The equation relating $P(A_n)$ to $P(A_{n-1})$ is

$$P(A_n) = .95 P(A_{n-1})$$

This, together with the initial condition, gives the probability that the extinguisher will still be in state A at time n weeks after the last inspection, as shown in Table 13.8.

TABLE 13.8 Transient Probabilities

n	$P(A_n)$	$P(B_n)$
0	1	0
1	.95	.05
2	.9025	.0975
3	.8574	.1426
4	.8145	.1855
5	.7738	.2262
6	.7351	.2649

The expected worth of the first week is

$$W(1) = + (100)(7)[.20(.95) - .80(.05)]$$
$$= \$105$$

This takes into account the expected worth produced by 100 extinguishers during 7 days a week: $105. The benefit from the second week is

$$W(2) = 700 \cdot [.20(.9025) - .80(.0975)]$$
$$= \$71.75$$

A criterion for selecting the inspection period is to maximize the expected net worth per week. The calculations are shown in Table 13.9.

The net benefit per week to the customer is maximized by an inspection period of 3 weeks. The customer's expected worth is $216.93 less the cost of $100 for the

TABLE 13.9   Calculations for Expected Net Worth

n	Expected Worth of Week n	Cumulative Expected Worth	Net Worth of First n Weeks	Average over n Weeks
1	105.00	105.00	5.00	5.00
2	71.75	176.75	76.75	38.37
3	40.18	216.93	116.93	38.98
4	10.15	227.08	127.08	31.77

inspection. This pricing policy enables the service company to offer the best value for the estimated cost of service.

13.4   DIRECT SOLUTION FOR STEADY-STATE PROBABILITIES

A Markov process that has N states, $s_1, s_2, \ldots, s_N$, can be described by N^2 probabilities. Let

$$p_{ij} = P(s_j \text{ at time } n \mid s_i \text{ at time } n - 1)$$

for $i = 1, 2, \ldots, N$ and $j = 1, 2, \ldots, N$. This can be organized in a matrix:

	s_1	s_2	s_3	$\cdots$	s_N
s_1	p_{11}	p_{12}	p_{13}		p_{1N}
s_2	p_{21}	p_{22}	p_{23}		p_{2N}
$\vdots$					
s_N	p_{N1}	p_{N2}	p_{N3}		p_{NN}

The probabilities in every row must sum to 1:

$$\sum_{j=1}^{N} p_{ij} = 1 \qquad \text{for } i = 1, 2, \ldots, N$$

There are generally N equations for the probabilities:

$$P(s_j \text{ at time } n) = \sum_{i=1}^{N} P(s_i \text{ at time } n - 1) \, p_{ij} \qquad \text{for } j = 1, 2, \ldots, N$$

This represents the reasoning that the process can be in s_j in N different ways, each corresponding to a possible state in the previous time period. The N equations just shown are not all independent because all rows must sum to 1.

This set of effectively $N - 1$ equations can be used to solve for either the transient or the steady-state probabilities. The transient probabilities are solved iteratively starting with an initial condition. The steady-state probabilities can be solved directly. Assuming their existence, then

$$P(s_j \text{ at time } n) = P(s_j \text{ at time } n - 1) = P(s_j) \qquad \text{for all large } n$$

The set of equations becomes

$$P(s_1) = P(s_1)p_{11} + P(s_2)p_{21} + \cdots + P(s_N)p_{N1}$$
$$P(s_2) = P(s_1)p_{12} + P(s_2)p_{22} + \cdots + P(s_N)p_{N2}$$
$$\vdots$$
$$P(s_N) = P(s_1)p_{1N} + P(s_2)p_{2N} + \cdots + P(S_N)p_{NN}$$

Any one of this set of N equations can be discarded because its information is contained in the other $N - 1$ equations. However, there is another requirement: The steady-state probabilities must also sum to 1:

$$\sum_{j=1}^{N} P(s_j) = 1$$

This becomes the Nth equation in a set of N linear equations in N unknowns.

13.5 EXAMPLE OF SOLUTION FOR STEADY-STATE PROBABILITIES

Consider a product having the following characteristics. It is widely considered to be a necessity (like a TV receiver) and so each customer will always have one. The life of the product is unpredictable; it can fail in a sudden way. Each customer will buy a new unit when his current unit fails. A study of replacement rates for units of various ages gives the following probability description of the failure and replacement process:

Age of Current Unit (in years)	Probability of Replacement in Next Year
0	.10
1	.15
2	.22
3	.50
4	1.00

These are conditional probabilities of failure during the next year given that the current unit has not failed by the current age. They show that no units are older than 5 years because they will all fail during their fifth year if they have not failed already.

The market for this product has been relatively stable over the past several years. The manufacturer has an estimate of the current size of the market. He is considering the introduction of a new improved version of the product. He therefore wishes to know the age distribution of the current units owned by the population of customers.

This question is answered by a Markov process model. The states of the process are the possible current ages of the unit owned by one typical customer. Let s_0, s_1, s_2, s_3, s_4 represent these states. The time period of the process is 1 year. Every year the current unit either ages by 1 year or it fails and is replaced by a new unit. If the current unit is 4 years old at the start of the year, it will fail during the year with probability 1 and be replaced by a new unit. The matrix of conditional probabilities is

	s_0	s_1	s_2	s_3	s_4
s_0	.10	.90	0	0	0
s_1	.15	0	.85	0	0
s_2	.22	0	0	.78	0
s_3	.50	0	0	0	.50
s_4	1.0	0	0	0	0

The numbers in the first column are the failure probabilities given by the study. The remaining numbers in each row have been determined by the necessity that the sum of the probabilities in each row sum to unity.

The fact that the market has been stable over the past several years implies that the typical customer has been using and purchasing the product for a reasonably long time. Therefore the state probabilities required are the steady-state probabilities. Let $P(s_i)$ represent these probabilities for $i = 0, 1, 2, 3, 4$. The equations for direct solution of these probabilities are

$$P(s_0) = .10P(s_0) + .15P(s_1)$$
$$+ .22P(s_2) + .50P(s_3) + P(s_4)$$
$$P(s_1) = .90P(s_0)$$
$$P(s_2) = .85P(s_1)$$
$$P(s_3) = .78P(s_2)$$
$$P(s_4) = .50P(s_3)$$

and

$$P(s_0) + P(s_1) + P(s_2) + P(s_3) + P(s_4) = 1.0$$

Any one of the first five equations can be discarded; the first is a good choice. Every succeeding equation relates $P(s_i)$ to $P(s_{i-1})$. Successive substitutions give

$$P(s_1) = .90\,P(s_0)$$
$$P(s_2) = (.85)(.90)\,P(s_0) = .765\,P(s_0)$$
$$P(s_3) = (.78)(.85)(.90)\,P(s_0) = .5967\,P(s_0)$$
$$P(s_4) = (.50)(.78)(.85)(.90)\,P(s_0) = .29835\,P(s_0)$$

The normalization equation is used next to give

$$P(s_0)(1 + .9 + .765 + .5967 + .29835) = 1$$

Therefore

$$P(s_0) = \frac{1}{3.56} = .281$$

Then

$$P(s_1) = (.9)(.281) = .253$$
$$P(s_2) = (.765)(.281) = .215$$
$$P(s_3) = (.5967)(.281) = .167$$
$$P(s_4) = (.29835)(.281) = .084$$

If the manufacturer does not introduce the new product, the probability that this typical customer will make a purchase during the next year can be found. It is just the probability that the process will be in state s_0 at the end of this year:

$$.10\,P(s_0) + .15\,P(s_1) + .22\,P(s_2) + .50\,P(s_3) + P(s_4) = P(s_0) = .281$$

EXERCISES

1.   It is estimated that the probability that a customer will purchase a new improved product during the next year is the following function of the age of his current unit:

Age of Current Unit (in years)	Probability of Replacement by New Improved Product
0	.20
1	.30
2	.50
3	.80
4	1.00

These probabilities represent both the possibility of replacement due to failure of the current unit and replacement due to the higher desirability of the new product. What is the probability that this typical customer will purchase a new unit during the next year when the new product is available?

2.   A car rental company rents cars out on yearly contracts. Each year the customer has an option to extend the contract another year until the car is 5 years old. Suppose the probability of contract renewal at the end of the ith year is:

Year	Probability of Renewal at Year End
First	.9
Second	.8
Third	.5
Fourth	.3
Fifth	0

Suppose that each customer will always either renew his current contract or take a contract on a new car. What is the steady-state probability distribution of the age of a typical customer's current car?

13.6   STOCHASTIC STOCK PRICE MODEL

The future price of a stock openly traded on a stock market is an uncertain quantity. A speculator can buy or sell (or sell "short") shares at the current price. He anticipates making the opposite transaction at a future date to obtain a profit. A speculator will sell if he expects the future price to be lower than the current price. He will buy if he expects the future price to be higher. At the time he makes his transaction decision the uncertainty of the future price can be represented by a probability distribution. This probability distribution should depend at least upon the current price of the stock. The assumption that it depends only upon the current price leads to a Markov model.

The state of the process is the current price of the stock. Although the stock can have many different price levels, it is useful to simplify the process by considering only a small number of possible prices. Suppose that the price can only be $10, $20, $30, $40, or $50 per share. The assumption that the price can neither exceed $50 nor go lower than $10 is often described as *price barriers*.

The time period of the process must be selected. In fact the stock can be traded at almost any point in time while the market is open. To obtain a simpler model it is assumed that the speculator will trade only at one fixed point in time during each day. Therefore he is interested only in the one price at that time of day. The period of the process is 1 day.

For this state space and time structure, consider the following matrix of conditional probabilities:

	s_{10}	s_{20}	s_{30}	s_{40}	s_{50}
s_{10}	.60	.20	.10	.05	.05
s_{20}	.25	.55	.10	.05	.05
s_{30}	.10	.15	.50	.15	.10
s_{40}	.05	.05	.10	.55	.25
s_{50}	.05	.05	.10	.20	.60

Each row is associated with a current stock price and gives the probability distribution for the next day's price. Examination of the probabilities within the rows shows that the most likely next day's price is equal to today's current price.

Suppose that the speculator wishes to consider purchasing one share given that the current price is $30. If he plans to sell 1 day later, what is his expected profit? Let $E(x,n)$ represent the expected profit from the purchase at a current price of x with the intention of selling n days later. Then

$$E(30,1) = -30 + (.10)(10) + (.15)(20) + (.50)(30) + (.15)(40) + (.10)(50)$$
$$= -30 + 30 = 0$$

Similar calculations for other current price levels yield the results shown in Table 13.10.

These results imply that some profit can be expected by a speculator when the current price is near the barriers. However, when it is in the middle of its price range the uncertainty about the future price is such that no profit can be expected. This model is an example of a *random walk with reflecting barriers.* Although this particular model serves only as an illustration of an application of the Markov process, there is some basis in financial theory for the general implications shown. A simple explanation is that if a large number of speculators all have a positive expectation of profit, their resulting transactions will tend to move the price toward the level that would reduce their expectation to zero.

Suppose that the speculator plans to buy and hold the stock until the second day.

TABLE 13.10 Calculation of Expected Profit

Current State	Expected Value of Tomorrow's Price	Expected Profit
s_{10}	17.5	$17.5 - 10 = 7.5$
s_{20}	21	$21 - 20 = 1.0$
s_{30}	30	$30 - 30 = 0$
s_{40}	39	$39 - 40 = -1.0$
s_{50}	42.5	$42.5 - 50 = -7.5$

To compute the expected profit for this strategy, it is necessary first to compute the state probabilities for the second day based upon some initial state. Suppose that the initial state is s_{10}. Let $P_2(s_i)$ represent the state probabilities for the second day. Then

$$P_2(s_{10}) = (.60)(.60) + (.20)(.25) + (.10)(.10) + (.05)(.05) + (.05)(.05) = .425$$
$$P_2(s_{20}) = (.60)(.20) + (.20)(.55) + (.10)(.15) + (.05)(.05) + (.05)(.05) = .250$$
$$P_2(s_{30}) = (.60)(.10) + (.20)(.10) + (.10)(.50) + (.05)(.10) + (.05)(.10) = .140$$
$$P_2(s_{40}) = (.60)(.05) + (.20)(.05) + (.10)(.15) + (.05)(.55) + (.05)(.20) = .0925$$
$$P_2(s_{50}) = (.60)(.05) + (.20)(.05) + (.10)(.10) + (.05)(.25) + (.05)(.60) = .0925$$

The expected profit is

$$E(10,2) = -10 + (.425)(10) + (.250)(20) + (.140)(30) + (.0925)(40) + (.0925)(50)$$
$$= -10 + 21.775$$
$$= 11.775$$

EXERCISE

Compute $E(30,2)$, the expected profit from the purchase of one share at the current price of \$30 with the plan to hold until the second day. Show that $E(30,2) = 0$.

PROBLEMS

1. A customer decides every month whether or not to place an order for a certain product. From the manufacturer's viewpoint the customer's purchasing behavior can be viewed as a stochastic process. The probability that the customer will place an order depends upon whether he placed one last month. This is the state of the process. The Markov matrix is

	Order This Month	No Order This Month
Order Last Month	.2	.8
No Order Last Month	.7	.3

(a) Suppose it is known that the customer did not place an order last month. Find the probability that he will order this month, next month, and so on for a total of six future months. Graph these probabilities as a function of time.

(*b*) Suppose that the manufacturer will get the order if his salesman makes a call at the start of a month in which an order will be placed. If the salesman is not there, this order will be placed with a different manufacturer. What is the purchase probability from the viewpoint of a salesman who knows about this process but, because of the large number of customers he services, cannot remember the customer's past actions?

2. Consider a military missile whose strategic objective is deterrence against a first strike by a potential enemy. Its success in filling this role depends upon how well it is protected against a first strike. One method of protection is a blastproof enclosure. Another concept of protection is random movement. The uncertainty of the missile's position gives it a chance of surviving a first strike. Intentional randomness is a way to protect information.

Suppose that a mobile missile carrier moves randomly between four supply stations A, B, C, and D, which are at the corners of a large square. It can travel the side of the square in 1 day. These stations are far enough apart that a strike against the wrong station will not damage the missile. Every time the missile arrives at a station, a decision is made of which adjacent corner to move to next or whether to remain at the current station for a full day. The following diagram gives the possible movements and their probabilities:

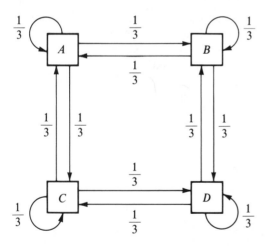

The missile is considered to be at the closest station. Therefore it must be at A, B, C, or D. Find the probabilities that the missile is at A, B, C, or D for an enemy who cannot observe its position but knows that this process has been going on for a long time.

3. A component of a machine is subject to frequent failure. If it fails in a partic-

ular week, the probability that it will not fail the next week is .9. If it does not fail in a particular week, the probability of failure the next week is .3. In the long run, in what proportion of the weeks will the component fail?

4. The economy can be in one of three distinct states at a given time: a boom state, a stable state, or a bust state. The probability matrix describing the economy's movement from state to state is as follows:

From	(To)		
	Boom	Stable	Bust
Boom	$\dfrac{1}{2}$	0	$\dfrac{1}{2}$
Stable	$\dfrac{1}{2}$	$\dfrac{1}{2}$	0
Bust	0	$\dfrac{1}{2}$	$\dfrac{1}{2}$

Given that the economy is currently in a boom state, what is the probability it will be in a bust state after two transitions? A boom state?

5. The Convenience Foods Corporation markets its products through many brand-name franchise outlets. The yearly sales of each of these outlets fluctuate widely. The sales of each outlet will be either low (200,000 pounds), medium (400,000 pounds), or high (600,000 pounds). The best predictor of next year's sales, for any outlet, is found to be the current year's sales. The probabilities of each yearly sales level are given by the following table:

Previous Year's Sales	Yearly Sales		
	L	M	H
L	.5	.5	0
M	.2	.5	.3
H	0	.5	.5

(a) Find the expected value of next year's sales for each possible value of the current year's sales.

(b) Find the expected value of sales in the year after next for an outlet whose current sales are low.

(c) Find the probabilities of each possible sales level for a period far into the future. From these find the expected value of the long-run yearly sales rate.

6. There are three major producers of a certain product: CH, FO, GM. A consumer purchases 1 unit of the product each period. The consumer's transaction matrix regarding from whom he purchases the product in period $n + 1$, given that he purchased the product from one of the firms in period n, is

	CH	FO	GM
CH	.7	.1	.2
FO	.1	.6	.3
GM	.2	0	.8

If a firm fails to maintain a long-run market share of more than 15 percent, its financial position will be in jeopardy. Are any of the three firms in this position?

7. The demand for cameras at a camera shop is as follows:

Weekly Demand	Probability
2	.25
3	.12
4	.30
5	.13
6	.10
7	.10

Cameras can be ordered only at the end of each week, and delivery is effectively immediate. The inventory policy is to replenish the inventory level to 7 units at the end of each week when the level on hand has fallen to 4 or less but to refrain from ordering if the level is 5 or more. What are the long-term probabilities of various inventory levels just after replenishment? State your assumptions.

8. An automatic machine produces units at a rate of 1 unit/hour. The adjustment of the machine is critical and "wanders" during the day, as evidenced by the output; the units produced are either acceptable, reworkable, or unacceptable. Past data show that if the last unit produced was acceptable, the next one is acceptable with probability .8, reworkable with probability .2, and unacceptable with probability zero. If the last unit was reworkable, the next is either acceptable, reworkable, or unacceptable with probabilities .6, .3, and .1. If the last unit was unacceptable, the corresponding probabilities for the next unit are 0, .2, and .8

   (a) If the machine is never adjusted, what is the long-run fraction of time spent producing the three types of output?

(*b*)   Suppose that an adjustment is made instantaneously following every output of an unacceptable unit. Then the next output will be acceptable with certainty. On this basis what long-run fraction of the units are of the three types?

9.   A new state lottery is to be designed with a "tortoise and hare race" theme. On every day either the tortoise or the hare will be ahead. If the tortoise was ahead yesterday, the probability that the hare will be ahead today is .70. If the hare was ahead yesterday, the probability that the tortoise will be ahead today is .8. Every morning at 8 A.M. the result is generated by using a computer to simulate the outcome of a Markov process, and the leader is announced.

After the day's results have been announced, the sale of tickets begins. Tickets can be purchased for either the tortoise or the hare, but the prices depend upon which is ahead today. All tickets will pay $2 if they win. The tickets specify a resolution date. For example, a $2 ticket on the hare to be ahead 3 days from the purchase time will pay out $2 if the hare is ahead on that date. The cost of the ticket is set to be the expected payoff to the holder plus a $0.10 markup for the lottery's profit. In this example the ticket cost is $1.15 if the tortoise is ahead today and $0.90 if the hare is ahead today.

Suppose that the tortoise is ahead today. Find the ticket costs the lottery commission should set so that the state has an expected profit of $0.10 on every ticket sold. Fill in the following table:

Resolution Date	Ticket Price When Tortoise Leading	
	Tortoise	Hare
Tomorrow		
2 days away		
3 days away		
4 days away		

On what fraction of the days is the hare ahead in the long run?

Chapter 14

STOCHASTIC SERVICE SYSTEMS

Queuing (waiting in line) is one of the earliest problem structures identified by operations research. The term *stochastic service system* is somewhat more self-explanatory. The basic elements of this problem structure are

1. Customers, or units, which require service. They are considered identical in their statistical properties.

2. Servers, or service capacity, which perform service operations.

3. Inability to schedule the demands for service and hence unpredictable timing.

4. Lack of predictability of the time duration of the service operation. Often there is a wide variability of service durations.

If the service time for each demand were known in advance and demands could be scheduled, a certain amount of service capacity would be required. Sometimes this predictability is theoretically possible but available only at a prohibitive cost. Given the variability of the timing of demands and of the duration of their service, a considerably greater service capacity will be required. Even with this larger service capacity it may be necessary for customers to queue for their service. These effects are due entirely to the variability in the process. Analysis shows how much service capacity is required as a function of the characteristics of the process and how much waiting the average customer will experience.

The queuing structure applies to problems from a wide diversity of content areas. Table 14.1 gives some suggestions. Not all these demand processes may be totally unpredictable to the server. Yet they may be unpredictable on the time scale of interest. For example, airplane flights usually follow a planned schedule but airplane arrivals at an airport may be unpredictable on the time scale of minutes, which is the magnitude of time required for the landing operation.

TABLE 14.1   Examples of Queuing

Arriving Customers	Servers	Queue (Where Applicable)
Ships	Harbor and docking facilities	
Trucks	Loading crews and facilities	
Shoppers	Checkout counters	Line
Computer programs	Computer central processor and core	Drum or disk storage
Telephone calls	Telephone office switching circuits	No waiting allowed
Airplanes	Runways	"Stack"
Automobiles	Intersection of streets	Street
Library borrowers	Library books	Waiting list
Machine failures	Repairmen	
Medical patients	Hospital beds	Waiting room
Automobiles	Parking lots	
Electronic messages	Transmission lines	"Buffers"
Fires	Firemen and equipment	

14.1 EXAMPLE OF A SINGLE-SERVER QUEUE

Consider a gas station that has just one gas pump and space sufficient for a maximum of two cars to wait for service. There can be at most three cars in the system: two waiting and one receiving service. Suppose that cars arrive irregularly at an average rate of 20 cars/hour. The notation for arrival rate is

$$\lambda = 20 \text{ cars/hour}$$

This rate is equivalent to one car every 3 minutes on the average. Suppose also that the service rate is 40 cars/hour while the server (the gas pump) is continuously busy. In other words one service takes 1.5 minutes on the average. The notation is

$$\mu = 40 \text{ cars/hour}$$

Notice that the station has double the capacity it would need if every service took exactly 1.5 minutes and every interarrival time were exactly 3 minutes. With such perfect timing the station would need no waiting space and no customer would have to wait for service.

This problem will be analyzed as a Markov process. The state of the process is the number of cars present in the station, either receiving service or waiting. This number can be either 0, 1, 2, or 3. It is understood that the server is busy whenever there is a car in the station. It is idle only when the station is empty.

Now it is necessary to select a time period of the process. There is no natural time period at which cars enter or leave this system. The time period is selected according to the criterion that it be small enough that at most one car can enter or leave the station during that period. For example, a period of 1 second seems intuitively reasonable. The chance of two events during such a small interval would be very small. A smaller period could be selected. However, it will be seen that the results are not sensitive to this choice.

Let p_a be the probability that one car will arrive during 1 second. Assuming that all arrivals are randomly distributed in time, this is

$$P(\text{one arrival in 1 sec}) = \frac{20}{3600} = p_a$$

because there are 3600 seconds in 1 hour. The probability of two or more arrivals during 1 second is of the order of magnitude of the square of this number. This is very small and will be treated as zero. This is reasonable because otherwise the time period could be made still smaller, say 10^{-3} second. This would decrease the probability of two arrivals by a factor of $(10^{-3})^2 = 10^{-6}$. Finally the probability of no arrival during 1 second is

$$P(\text{no arrival in 1 sec}) = 1 - p_a = 1 - \frac{20}{3600}$$

Considering the service process, clearly the events of interest are service completions because they move the process to a different state. While a service is in progress the probability of a service completion during 1 second, denoted p_s, is

$$P(\text{one service completion in 1 sec}) = \frac{40}{3600} = p_s$$

and

$$P(\text{no service completion in 1 sec}) = 1 - p_s = 1 - \frac{40}{3600}$$

These hold only while the server is busy. It is clear that two service completions cannot occur during 1 second. The assumption is that the service completion instant is randomly distributed in time and does not depend upon the length of time the current service has already taken. This is explained in more detail in Sec. 14.8.

A Markov probability matrix can now be constructed. If the process is in s_0 at the start of 1 second, the state can change only if an arrival occurs during that second. This would bring the system to s_1. No other events are possible. Therefore the first row of the matrix is

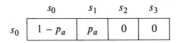

	s_0	s_1	s_2	s_3
s_0	$1 - p_a$	p_a	0	0

When the system is in s_1 two events are possible: A service completion event during the second would bring the system to s_0; an arrival would bring it to s_2. The probability of no event occurring is

$$(1 - p_a)(1 - p_s) = 1 - p_a - p_s + p_a p_s$$

However, the last term in this expression is so small that it is left off. The second row is

	s_0	s_1	s_2	s_3
s_1	p_s	$1 - p_a - p_s$	p_a	0

Similarly the third row is

	s_0	s_1	s_2	s_3
s_2	0	p_s	$1 - p_a - p_s$	p_a

The last row is for s_3. When there are three cars in the system it is completely full. No arrivals can fit in the system. Customers who would otherwise wait will pass by and be lost. A service can happen and this would bring the system to s_2 at the end of the time period.

The complete Markov matrix is

	s_0	s_1	s_2	s_3
s_0	$1 - p_a$	p_a	0	0
s_1	p_s	$1 - p_a - p_s$	p_a	0
s_2	0	p_s	$1 - p_a - p_s$	p_a
s_3	0	0	p_s	$1 - p_s$

Now consider the purpose of the analysis. Usually it is to decide the number of servers or waiting spaces or some other long-run characteristic of the system. In this case the steady-state probabilities are appropriate. Let them be represented by P_0, P_1, P_2, and P_3 for the successive states. The equations for them are

$$P_0 = (1 - p_a) P_0 + p_s P_1$$
$$P_1 = p_a P_0 + (1 - p_a - p_s) P_1 + p_s P_2$$
$$P_2 = p_a P_1 + (1 - p_a - p_s) P_2 + p_s P_3$$
$$P_3 = p_a P_2 + (1 - p_s) P_3$$

Also,

$$P_0 + P_1 + P_2 + P_3 = 1$$

This set of four equations has a special structure that is easy to solve. The first equation simplifies to

$$p_a P_0 = p_s P_1$$

Solving for P_1,

$$P_1 = \frac{p_a}{p_s} P_0$$

The second equation simplifies to

$$0 = p_a P_0 - (p_a + p_s) P_1 + p_s P_2$$

Substitution of $p_a P_0 = p_s P_1$ results in cancellation of two terms to yield

$$p_a P_1 = p_s P_2$$

or

$$P_2 = \frac{p_a}{p_s} P_1$$

Using the previous equation to replace P_1, the result in terms of P_0 is

$$P_2 = \left(\frac{p_a}{p_s}\right)^2 P_0$$

Similar operations on the third equation give the result

$$P_3 = \frac{p_a}{p_s} P_2 = \left(\frac{p_a}{p_s}\right)^3 P_0$$

The next equation contains no new information. The normalization equation is

$$P_0 + P_1 + P_2 + P_3 = 1$$

After substitution, it is

$$P_0 \left[1 + \frac{p_a}{p_s} + \left(\frac{p_a}{p_s}\right)^2 + \left(\frac{p_a}{p_s}\right)^3 \right] = 1$$

Therefore

$$P_0 = \frac{1}{1 + p_a/p_s + (p_a/p_s)^2 + (p_a/p_s)^3}$$

The algebra of the solution is now complete; it remains only to substitute numbers.

However, a crucial result can now be recognized: The steady-state probabilities depend only upon the ratio

$$\frac{p_a}{p_s}$$

and not upon the absolute value of either p_a or p_s. Therefore it does not matter whether 1 second or one-tenth of 1 second or any other small time period is selected to represent the process so long as it is small enough that the occurrence of two events during the period has small probability. This can be made exactly true if the time period approaches zero in a limiting sense.

The ratio p_a/p_s can be replaced by

$$\frac{p_a}{p_s} = \frac{\lambda}{\mu}$$

because p_a and p_s were both divided by the same quantity. The equation is now rewritten as

$$P_1 = \frac{\lambda}{\mu} P_0$$

$$P_2 = \frac{\lambda}{\mu} P_1 = \left(\frac{\lambda}{\mu}\right)^2 P_0$$

$$P_3 = \frac{\lambda}{\mu} P_2 = \left(\frac{\lambda}{\mu}\right)^3 P_0$$

and

$$P_0 = \frac{1}{1 + \lambda/\mu + (\lambda/\mu)^2 + (\lambda/\mu)^3}$$

Now, to return to the example,

$$\frac{\lambda}{\mu} = \frac{20}{40} = \frac{1}{2}$$

Therefore

$$P_0 = \frac{1}{1 + \frac{1}{2} + \frac{1}{4} + \frac{1}{8}} = \frac{8}{8 + 4 + 2 + 1} = \frac{8}{15}$$

and

$$P_1 = \frac{4}{15} \qquad P_2 = \frac{2}{15} \qquad P_3 = \frac{1}{15}$$

It can now be seen that the server is idle *more* than half the time. Furthermore, during 20 percent of the time there are one or more customers waiting for service. The station is completely full 6.6 percent of the time and therefore some customers are being lost entirely. This seems a poor performance for a system that has twice the capacity it would need under perfect timing. Clearly this inefficiency must be due to the imperfect timing of arrivals and the variability of service duration.

Suppose that the station receives an average profit of $1.50 per service. Since the average service takes 1.5 minutes, this is equivalent to a profit rate of $1/minute while the server is busy. However, the server is not always busy. The average profit rate is

$$\$1(1 - P_0) = \frac{7}{15} \text{ dollar/minute}$$

$$= \$28/\text{hour}$$

The amount of profit being lost because of insufficient capacity can easily be found. If no customers were ever turned away, the profit rate would be

$$20 \text{ cars/hour} \times \$1.5/\text{car} = \$30/\text{hour}$$

The difference, $30 - 28 = 2$, is the loss, in dollars per hour, due to insufficient capacity. This can also be found by taking the probability P_3 that the station is full, times the arrival rate, to get the rate at which customers are turned away:

$$\frac{1}{15} \times 20 \text{ cars/hour} = \frac{4}{3} \text{ cars/hour}$$

This, multiplied by $1.5/car, gives the same $2/hour loss rate due to insufficient capacity.

14.2 SINGLE SERVER WITH N – 1 WAITING SPACES

One way to increase the profit of the gas station is to add additional waiting spaces. In reality this may have a limited value because drivers are reluctant to wait for the service of more than a few cars; they would be likely to go to a different station or come back later. However, for the purpose of illustration it is assumed here that cars will not be deterred at all by the prospect of waiting. They will wait, if necessary, so long as there is space for them to enter the station.

The addition of one waiting space augments by 1 the number of states of the Markov process. The states are now s_0, s_1, s_2, s_3, and s_4. The Markov matrix is

	s_0	s_1	s_2	s_3	s_4
s_0	$1 - p_a$	p_a	0	0	0
s_1	p_s	$1 - p_a - p_s$	p_a	0	0
s_2	0	p_s	$1 - p_a - p_s$	p_a	0
s_3	0	0	p_s	$1 - p_a - p_s$	p_a
s_4	0	0	0	p_s	$1 - p_s$

The first three rows are the same as the previous matrix. The steady-state equations have the same structure as before and give the following results:

$$P_1 = \frac{\lambda}{\mu} P_0$$

$$P_2 = \frac{\lambda}{\mu} P_1 = \left(\frac{\lambda}{\mu}\right)^2 P_0$$

$$P_3 = \frac{\lambda}{\mu} P_2 = \left(\frac{\lambda}{\mu}\right)^3 P_0$$

$$P_4 = \frac{\lambda}{\mu} P_3 = \left(\frac{\lambda}{\mu}\right)^4 P_0$$

$$P_0 = \left[1 + \frac{\lambda}{\mu} + \left(\frac{\lambda}{\mu}\right)^2 + \left(\frac{\lambda}{\mu}\right)^3 + \left(\frac{\lambda}{\mu}\right)^4\right]^{-1}$$

Applying this to the gas station, the steady-state probabilities are

$$P_0 = \left(1 + \frac{1}{2} + \frac{1}{4} + \frac{1}{8} + \frac{1}{16}\right)^{-1} = \frac{16}{16 + 8 + 4 + 2 + 1} = \frac{16}{31}$$

$$P_1 = \frac{8}{31} \qquad P_2 = \frac{4}{31} \qquad P_3 = \frac{2}{31} \qquad P_4 = \frac{1}{31}$$

With this extra waiting space the fraction of time the system is full has been cut approximately in half, from $1/15$ to $1/31$. The fraction of time the server is idle has been reduced from $8/15$ to $16/31$, or from 53.3 to 51.6 percent. This is a significant change because it could never be less than 50 percent. The average profit rate is increased to

$$\$1(1 - P_0) = \frac{15}{31} \text{ dollar/minute}$$

$$= \$29.03/\text{hour}$$

Therefore the extra waiting space is generating an additional profit of 29.03 − 28.00 = \$1.03/hour. The rate at which customers are turned away for lack of waiting space is now

$$\frac{1}{31} \times 20 \text{ cars/hour} = .66 \text{ car/hour}$$

Waiting spaces serve an important function in stochastic service systems. If the demands are willing to wait for service, the waiting space transforms the actual time pattern of demands into one that fits the server's availability.

The two previous cases of two and three waiting spaces can be generalized to $N - 1$ waiting spaces. Now the maximum number in the system is N. There are

$N + 1$ states: $s_0, s_1, \ldots, s_N$. It is not necessary to write this matrix because it would be similar to the previous cases. The resulting expressions for the steady-state probabilities can be written by analogy:

$$P_n = \frac{\lambda}{\mu} P_{n-1} = \left(\frac{\lambda}{\mu}\right)^n P_0 \quad \text{for } n = 1, 2, \ldots, N$$

and

$$P_0 = \left[1 + \frac{\lambda}{\mu} + \left(\frac{\lambda}{\mu}\right)^2 + \cdots + \left(\frac{\lambda}{\mu}\right)^N\right]^{-1}$$

This contains a geometric series. The sum of the first N terms of a geometric series is known. Substitution gives

$$P_0 = \frac{1 - \lambda/\mu}{1 - (\lambda/\mu)^{N+1}}$$

This expression holds true even if there is insufficient service capacity, $\mu < \lambda$, because a finite series must give a finite result. However, when this occurs the probabilities of high numbers of customers in the system will be large.

This result is useful and can be applied directly to many single-server systems without writing the Markov matrix. Applying this to the gas station problem, it is now possible to express the average profit rate as a function of N:

$$\text{Average profit rate} = \$1 (1 - P_0) = \frac{\lambda/\mu [1 - (\lambda/\mu)^N]}{1 - (\lambda/\mu)^{N+1}}$$

Here λ/μ can be replaced by $\frac{1}{2}$ and the expression can be evaluated for successive

TABLE 14.2 Average Profit Rate as a Function of N

System Size (N)	Waiting Spaces $(N - 1)$	Average Profit Rate $[\$60 (1 - P_0)/\text{hour}]$	Incremental Gain $(\$/\text{hour})$
1	0	$(60) \dfrac{1}{3} = 20$	....
2	1	$(60) \dfrac{3}{7} = 25.68$	5.68
3	2	$(60) \dfrac{7}{15} = 28.00$	2.32
4	3	$(60) \dfrac{15}{31} = 29.03$	1.03
5	4	$(60) \dfrac{31}{63} = 29.52$	.49
6	5	$(60) \dfrac{63}{127} = 29.76$	.24

N values from $N = 1$ (no waiting spaces) on up. The results up to $N = 6$ are shown in Table 14.2. This clearly shows that the average profit rate is always increasing as a function of N, but at a decreasing rate. If the cost of a waiting space expressed on a per unit time basis is a constant for each space, there will be an optimum number of waiting spaces that maximizes the net profit.

14.3 SINGLE SERVER WITH NO SPACE LIMIT

Often a queuing system has no effective space limit. For example, a toll booth on a highway has the whole road behind it for cars to wait for toll collection. The steady-state probabilities for this case can be obtained easily from the previous section by allowing N to approach infinity.

As N approaches infinity in the sense of a mathematical limiting process, the term $(\lambda/\mu)^{N+1}$ approaches zero if and only if the service capacity exceeds the demand: if $\lambda < \mu$. In this case the ratio λ/μ is less than unity. Otherwise there exists no steady state; the queue would grow larger and larger without any limit. With sufficient extra capacity the server can always catch up after a period of high demand. In the limit,

$$P_0 = \lim_{N \to \infty} \left[\frac{1 - \lambda/\mu}{1 - (\lambda/\mu)^{N+1}} \right] = 1 - \frac{\lambda}{\mu} \qquad \text{if } \lambda < \mu$$

The other steady-state probabilities are given by

$$P_n = \left(\frac{\lambda}{\mu}\right)^n \left(1 - \frac{\lambda}{\mu}\right) \qquad \text{for } n = 0, 1, 2, \ldots$$

This is a normalized probability function for the discrete random variable $\tilde{n}$, the number in the system. It is called the *geometric probability distribution*. The normalization can be verified by using the sum of a complete geometric series:

$$\sum_{n=0}^{\infty} P_n = \left(1 - \frac{\lambda}{\mu}\right) \sum_{n=0}^{\infty} \left(\frac{\lambda}{\mu}\right)^n = \left(1 - \frac{\lambda}{\mu}\right)\left(\frac{1}{1 - \lambda/\mu}\right) = 1$$

These results can be applied to the gas station example under the assumption that customers will wait if waiting space is available. Suppose that the gas station has the opportunity to expand by purchasing the adjacent lot. The lot can be paved to give several additional waiting spaces. The analysis will be performed as if there were no queue limit and then checked to see if 10 or more spaces would actually be used.

The steady-state probabilities for $\lambda/\mu = \frac{1}{2}$ are

$$P_n = \left(\frac{1}{2}\right)^{n+1} \qquad \text{for } n = 0, 1, 2, \ldots$$

Therefore the average profit rate is

$$\$1(1 - P_0) = \frac{1}{2} \text{ dollar/minute}$$

$$= \$30/\text{hour}$$

This is reasonable in light of the fact that no customers would ever be turned away. The service rate of the system is then just equal to the demand rate, $\lambda = 20$ cars/hour. With a profit per customer of $1.50, this also gives an average profit rate of $30/hour.

The probability that 10 or more spaces are actually being used at a typical point in time can be found from the steady-state probabilities:

$$\sum_{n=10}^{\infty} P_n = 1 - \sum_{n=0}^{9} \left(\frac{1}{2}\right)^{n+1}$$

$$= 1 - \left(\frac{1}{2} + \frac{1}{4} + \frac{1}{8} + \frac{1}{16} + \frac{1}{32} + \frac{1}{64} + \frac{1}{128} + \frac{1}{256} + \frac{1}{512} + \frac{1}{1024}\right)$$

$$= \frac{1}{1024} = .000975$$

From this it is possible to conclude that, although the waiting space is not extremely large, it is nevertheless effectively very large. It is large enough that the analysis based upon no space limit is extremely close to that obtained by using an upper limit of $N = 9$.

Another measure of the usage of the waiting spaces is the average number in the system. This is also found from the steady-state probabilities. It is just the expected value of the random variable $\tilde{n}$. The standard notation for this is L:

$$L = \sum_{n=0}^{\infty} nP_n = \left(1 - \frac{\lambda}{\mu}\right) \sum_{n=0}^{\infty} n\left(\frac{\lambda}{\mu}\right)^n$$

This sum has a simple analytic expression. First write it as

$$L = \frac{\lambda}{\mu}\left(1 - \frac{\lambda}{\mu}\right) \sum_{n=0}^{\infty} n\left(\frac{\lambda}{\mu}\right)^{n-1}$$

The summation part of this expression is actually the derivative of the geometric series

$$\frac{d}{dx}\left(\sum_{n=0}^{\infty} x^n\right) = \sum_{n=0}^{\infty} nx^{n-1}$$

Having recognized this fact, one can now differentiate the expression for the sum of a geometric series:

$$\frac{d}{dx}\left(\frac{1}{1-x}\right) = \left(\frac{1}{1-x}\right)^2$$

Therefore, applying this to the expression for L, one obtains

$$L = \frac{\lambda/\mu}{1 - \lambda/\mu}$$

The average number of cars in the gas station is

$$L = \frac{1/2}{1 - (1/2)} = 1$$

The average number of customers in the system, L, is a function of the ratio λ/μ. When this ratio is $1/2$ or smaller the value of L will be 1 or smaller. Thus a service capacity of twice that required under perfect coordination of demands with server availability would give a reasonably high level of service. It is interesting to see how rapidly the number in the system grows as the ratio of λ/μ increases beyond $1/2$ (see Fig. 14.1).

When λ/μ is .9, the value of L is 9. As λ/μ increases from .9 the curve grows very steeply. The formula for L shows that L approaches infinity as λ/μ approaches 1. This means that because of the lack of coordination of demands with service the queue grows indefinitely large when there is no excess service capacity. The steady-state analysis does not tell how rapidly the queue grows, but it is clear that this is an insufficient level of service capacity for most queuing situations.

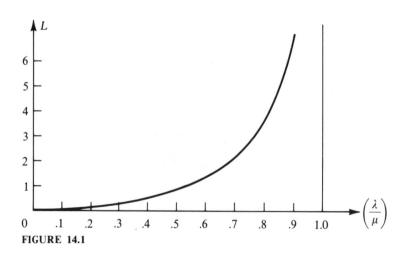

FIGURE 14.1

Another measure of performance is the average number in the waiting line. This is represented by the notation L_q:

$$L_q = 0P_0 + 0P_1 + 1P_2 + 2P_3 + \cdots$$

$$= \sum_{n=1}^{\infty} (n-1)P_n = \sum_{n=0}^{\infty} nP_n - \sum_{n=1}^{\infty} P_n$$

$$= L - (1 - P_0) = \frac{\lambda/\mu}{1 - \lambda/\mu} - \frac{\lambda}{\mu}$$

$$= \frac{\lambda}{\mu} \frac{\lambda/\mu}{1 - \lambda/\mu}$$

The average number of cars waiting for service in the gas station is

$$L_q = \frac{1}{2} \frac{1/2}{1 - 1/2} = \frac{1}{2}$$

The average waiting time until service begins is also an important measure of the performance of a stochastic service system. For the single-server queue with no space limit, it is denoted by W_q. It is derived from the following reasoning. If the customer arrives when there are n customers already in the system, his waiting time is the time of service of those n customers ahead of him. The average time of one service is $1/\mu$. Therefore his average waiting time is n/μ if there are n in the system. This reasoning appears to ignore the fact that the unit currently being served has already received some service. It turns out that this does not matter; the statement is exactly true in the case where the service system can be represented by a Markov process. The average wait for service is obtained by weighing the quantity n/μ by the probability of there being n in the system:

$$W_q = \sum_{n=0}^{\infty} \frac{n}{\mu} P_n = \frac{1}{\mu} \sum_{n=0}^{\infty} nP_n$$

$$= \frac{1}{\mu} L = \frac{1}{\mu} \frac{\lambda/\mu}{1 - \lambda/\mu}$$

In the gas station example the average wait for service is

$$W_q = \frac{1}{40} \frac{1/2}{1 - 1/2} = \frac{1}{40} \text{ hour} = 1.5 \text{ minutes}$$

Thus the average wait for service happens to equal the average duration of one service. This is not unrealistic for a busy service station.

A final measure of service performance is the total waiting time in the system, denoted by W. It is the sum of the average wait for service plus the average duration of service:

$$W = W_q + \frac{1}{\mu}$$

$$= \frac{1}{\mu}\left(\frac{\lambda/\mu}{1 - \lambda/\mu}\right) + \frac{1}{\mu} = \frac{1}{\mu}\left(\frac{\lambda/\mu}{1 - \lambda/\mu} + 1\right)$$

$$= \frac{1}{\mu}\left(\frac{1}{1 - \lambda/\mu}\right) = \frac{1}{\mu - \lambda}$$

For this gas station it is

$$W = \frac{1}{40 - 20} = \frac{2}{40} \text{ hour} = 3 \text{ minutes}$$

14.4 SUMMARY FOR SINGLE SERVER

The single server with no space limit has a steady-state solution if and only if $\lambda < \mu$. It is

$$P_n = \left(\frac{\lambda}{\mu}\right)^n \left(1 - \frac{\lambda}{\mu}\right) \qquad \text{for } n = 0, 1, 2, \ldots$$

The following average quantities are useful measures of performance:

L = average number of units in system
L_q = average number of units waiting for service
W_q = average waiting time until service begins
W = average time in system

The following table gives expressions for these quantities and shows some relationships between them:

$$\boxed{L = \frac{\lambda/\mu}{1 - \lambda/\mu}} \qquad L = \lambda W \qquad \boxed{W = \frac{1}{\mu}\,\frac{1}{1 - \lambda/\mu}}$$

$$L_q = \frac{\lambda}{\mu} L \qquad\qquad W = W_q + \frac{1}{\mu}$$

$$L_q = L - (1 - P_0) \qquad\qquad W_q = \frac{\lambda}{\mu} W$$

$$\boxed{L_q = \frac{(\lambda/\mu)^2}{1 - \lambda/\mu}} \qquad L_q = \lambda W_q \qquad \boxed{W_q = \frac{1}{\mu}\,\frac{\lambda/\mu}{1 - \lambda/\mu}}$$

The relationship $L = \lambda W$ can be seen to be correct mathematically. It has a more intuitive meaning, however: λW is the average number of customers who arrive during the total time W that one typical customer spends in the system. This should be equal, on the average, to the number L who were in the system when the customer arrived. Similarly $L_q = \lambda W_q$ simply says that as one enters service he can expect to see the same number waiting behind him, λW_q, as the average number he saw waiting ahead of him when he arrived.

The expressions summarized in this section apply only to the single-server system with unlimited waiting space and only when the system has the Markovian properties assumed. When there is a limit upon the number of waiting spaces, similar expressions can be derived. The general expressions appear more complex but are easily derived from the same principles when they are needed. For a single-server system having the Markovian property and $N - 1$ waiting spaces, the average number in the system can be found from

$$L = 0P_0 + 1P_1 + 2P_2 + \cdots + NP_N$$

The average number in the queue is

$$L_q = 0P_0 + 0P_1 + 1P_2 + 2P_3 + \cdots + (N - 1)P_N$$

The average wait in queue, for an arrival who actually is able to enter the system, is

$$W_q = \frac{1/\mu [1P_1 + 2P_2 + \cdots + (N - 1) P_{N-1}]}{1 - P_N}$$

and the average time in the system is

$$W = \frac{1}{\mu} + W_q$$

and the rate of arrivals turned away by lack of waiting space is λP_N.

EXERCISES

1. Customers arrive at a telephone booth with an average time of 10 minutes between one arrival and the next. The length of a phone call varies considerably. The average is 3 minutes. The telephone company will install a second booth when convinced that an arrival would expect to have to wait at least 3 minutes for the phone.

(a) By how much must the flow of arrivals be increased to justify a second booth?

(b) Suppose that the company's criterion for installation of a second booth is changed. They will install it when the probability of having to wait at all exceeds $1/2$. By how much must the flow of arrival be increased to justify a second booth under this criterion?

2.   The public library has a waiting list for each book in its collection of popular new books. Their policy is to limit the length of each book's waiting list because many people will lose interest in obtaining a book after waiting several weeks for it. Consider a book having a request rate of 10 requests per week. There is only one copy of the book. The average time a borrower will keep the book is 1 week. The library wants to limit the length of the waiting list so that the average waiting time of a person who is allowed on the list is no more than 3 weeks. Show that they should have three spaces on the list. Do this by evaluating both three spaces and four spaces. Also find the probability that a request will not be rejected. Find the rate at which requests will be rejected. Find the fraction of time the book is not in use.

14.5   MULTIPLE SERVERS AND STATE-DEPENDENT ARRIVAL RATES

Two questions have so far gone unanswered in the study of the gas station. The first regards the value of adding extra servers (gas pumps). The second is how to reconsider the value of both servers and waiting spaces when it is known that the arrival rate to the station is smaller when more cars are already in the station than when it is empty.

Both these questions can be answered by an extension of the Markovian model already considered. The power of this model can be greatly increased at a small cost in mathematical difficulty by allowing both the service rate and the arrival rate to depend upon the current state of the system. Define

λ_n = arrival rate when system is in state n,   for $n = 0, 1, 2, \ldots$

μ_n = service rate when system is in state n,   for $n = 0, 1, 2, \ldots$

The idea which remains unchanged is that the state still represents the number of customers in the system. Furthermore an arrival event still increases the current state by 1 and a service completion event still decreases the current state by 1. Thus the state space is still $s_0, s_1, s_2, \ldots$, and the state can only be changed by 1 unit within a very small instant of time.

This method is correct whether or not there is an upper limit upon the number of states. However, as a beginning let N be the largest possible state number and let $\lambda_N = 0$ so that an arrival cannot enter the system when it is already in its highest state. Also $\mu_0 = 0$ represents the fact that no service can occur when there is no customer in the system.

The time period of the process is again selected to be small enough that two or more events cannot occur within one time period. Let m be the number of such periods within the time unit of the problem. Thus if event rates are expressed in number per hour and the time period is chosen to be 1 second, then $m = 3600$ seconds/hour. The Markov matrix is

	s_0	s_1	s_2	s_3	$\cdots$	s_{N-2}	s_{N-1}	s_N
s_0	$1 - \dfrac{\lambda_0}{m}$	$\dfrac{\lambda_0}{m}$	0	0		0	0	0
s_1	$\dfrac{\mu_1}{m}$	$1 - \dfrac{\mu_1}{m} - \dfrac{\lambda_1}{m}$	$\dfrac{\lambda_1}{m}$	0		0	0	0
s_2	0	$\dfrac{\mu_2}{m}$	$1 - \dfrac{\mu_2}{m} - \dfrac{\lambda_2}{m}$	$\dfrac{\lambda_2}{m}$		0	0	0
$\vdots$								
s_{N-1}	0	0	0	0		$\dfrac{\mu_{N-1}}{m}$	$1 - \dfrac{\mu_{N-1}}{m} - \dfrac{\lambda_{N-1}}{m}$	$\dfrac{\lambda_{N-1}}{m}$
s_N	0	0	0	0		0	$\dfrac{\mu_N}{m}$	$1 - \dfrac{\mu_N}{m}$

The ith row has all zero entries except for μ_i/m, $(1 - \mu_i/m - \lambda_i/m)$, and λ_i/m in the three columns corresponding to states s_{i-1}, s_i, and s_{i+1}, respectively. This is true for all rows except the first and last.

The equations for the steady-state probabilities are no more difficult for this matrix than for the preceding ones:

$$P_n = \frac{\lambda_{n-1}}{\mu_n} P_{n-1} \qquad \text{for } n = 1, 2, \ldots, N$$

and

$$\sum_{n=0}^{\infty} P_n = 1$$

Again the result depends not upon m but only upon ratios. Successive substitutions now give

$$P_n = \frac{\lambda_{n-1}}{\mu_n} P_{n-1} = \frac{\lambda_{n-1}}{\mu_n} \frac{\lambda_{n-2}}{\mu_{n-1}} P_{n-2} = \cdots$$

$$P_n = \frac{\lambda_{n-1}}{\mu_n} \frac{\lambda_{n-2}}{\mu_{n-1}} \cdots \frac{\lambda_0}{\mu_1} P_0 \qquad \text{for } n = 1, 2, \ldots, N$$

Clearly this result coincides with the previous result when all λ's and μ's are equal; this would be

$$P_n = \left(\frac{\lambda}{\mu}\right)^n P_0$$

The use of these equations can now be illustrated with the gas station problem. The original station had one gas pump and two waiting spaces. It had an arrival rate

TABLE 14.3   Values for
μ_n and λ_n

n	λ_n	μ_n
0	20	0
1	20	40
2	20	80
3	0	80

of $\lambda = 20$ and a service rate of $\mu = 40$, and it generated an average profit rate of $28/hour, based upon an average profit of $1.50/car. Now consider adding a new pump in place of one waiting space. The objective of the analysis is to determine the additional profit per unit time of the new pump as if its cost were zero. The analysis begins with the construction of a table of values for μ_n and λ_n, Table 14.3.

The reasoning behind Table 14.3 is that whenever there are two or more customers in the station there are two pumps giving service simultaneously and, therefore, the effective service rate is exactly twice that of one server. (This could be wrong if there were not two attendants to operate both pumps simultaneously.) The effective arrival rate is 20 unless the station is full. The equations are

$$P_1 = \frac{20}{40} P_0 = \frac{1}{2} P_0$$

$$P_2 = \frac{20}{80} P_1 = \frac{1}{4}\frac{1}{2} P_0$$

$$P_3 = \frac{20}{80} P_2 = \frac{1}{4}\frac{1}{4}\frac{1}{2} P_0$$

The normalization equation is

$$P_0 = \left(1 + \frac{1}{2} + \frac{1}{8} + \frac{1}{32}\right)^{-1} = \frac{32}{32 + 16 + 4 + 1} = \frac{32}{53}$$

Finally

$$P_1 = \frac{16}{53} \qquad P_2 = \frac{4}{53} \qquad P_3 = \frac{1}{53}$$

The average profit rate can now be expressed as $1 per service, times the number of services in progress, times the probability of that number:

$$\text{Average profit rate} = 0P_0 + 1P_1 + 2P_2 + 2P_3$$

$$= \frac{26}{53} = \$0.4905/\text{minute}$$

$$= \$29.43/\text{hour}$$

Another way to obtain this result is to find the rate of lost profit from customers unable to get into the system. This is the arrival rate times P_3 times profit per service:

$$(1.50)(20)\left(\frac{1}{53}\right) = \$0.57/hour$$

The actual profit rate is then $30 - .57 = 29.43$, as already found. The gain of replacing one waiting space by one extra service pump is $29.43 - 28.00 = \$1.43/hour$. If the cost of the extra pump were expressed on a per unit time basis, the decision of whether to install it could be made on the basis of its net contribution to profit.

A final question of interest that can be answered using this more powerful model regards the value of additional waiting spaces under the more realistic conditions that potential customers tend to bypass a crowded station to avoid waiting. Consider a possible expansion of the one-pump station from two waiting spaces to nine waiting spaces.

Suppose that a study has shown that, for stations of this type, the fraction of potential customers who will bypass the station, as a function of the number of cars already in the station, is given by Table 14.4.

TABLE 14.4   Lost Customers as a Function of Cars Present

Number of Cars Present (n)	Potential Customers Who Pass By (%)
0	0
1	0
2	10
3	30
4	50
5	80
6	100

This implies immediately that there will never be more than six cars in the station because no cars will enter when six are already present. Therefore $N = 6$ and the effective arrival and service rates are as shown in Table 14.5.

TABLE 14.5   Arrival and Service Rates

n	λ_n	μ_n
0	20	0
1	20	40
2	18	40
3	14	40
4	10	40
5	4	40
6	0	40

The steady-state probabilities are found by

$$P_1 = \frac{20}{40} P_0 = .5 P_0$$

$$P_2 = \frac{20}{40} P_1 = .25 P_0$$

$$P_3 = \frac{18}{40} P_2 = .1125 P_0$$

$$P_4 = \frac{14}{40} P_3 = .0394 P_0$$

$$P_5 = \frac{10}{40} P_4 = .00984 P_0$$

$$P_6 = \frac{4}{40} P_5 = .00098 P_0$$

The normalization is

$$P_0(1 + .50 + .25 + .1125 + .0394 + .00984 + .00098) = 1$$

$$P_0 = .5228$$
$$P_1 = .2614$$
$$P_2 = .1307$$
$$P_3 = .0588$$
$$P_4 = .0206$$
$$P_5 = .0052$$
$$P_6 = .0005$$

The average profit rate of this system is

$$\$1(1 - P_0) = \$0.4772/\text{minute}$$
$$= \$28.63/\text{hour}$$

Therefore if the reluctance of potential customers to wait is adequately reflected by the percentages given, the value of the additional nine waiting spaces is quite small, only $0.63/hour.

14.6   EXAMPLE OF STATE-DEPENDENT ARRIVAL RATES

An amusement park is designing a new Alice in Wonderland house that can service customers at the rate $\mu = 50$ customers per hour. The demand for this new feature is expected to be 100 customers per hour. All that remains to be decided is the design of the waiting line. The architect proposes a design that prevents the arriving customer from knowing the number ahead of him in line, up until there are four waiting. He presents evidence that the percentage of potential customers who are discouraged from entering the line is given by Table 14.6. The feature, considered as a single server, makes a profit of $0.50 per customer while not idle.

TABLE 14.6   Potential Customers Discouraged from Entering Line

Number in System	Discouraged with Hidden Line (%)	Discouraged with Visible Line (%)
0	0	0
1	0	20
2	0	40
3	0	60
4	0	80
5 or more	100	100

The first approach in the analysis of this choice between the alternative designs is to compare their profit rates. Since both are single-server systems, the average profit rate is

($0.50/customer)(50 customers/hour while busy)$(1 - P_0) = 25(1 - P_0)$

The two alternative designs have different P_0 values. Because of the fast service rate the design with the smaller waiting line can empty momentarily due to random fluctuations and therefore have a lower utilization rate. The analysis begins with the table of μ_n as a function of n, the number in the system (Table 14.7).

TABLE 14.7 μ_n as a Function of n

n	Hidden Line (λ_n)	Visible Line (λ_n)	μ_n
0	100	100	0
1	100	80	50
2	100	60	50
3	100	40	50
4	100	20	50
5	0	0	50

The steady-state probability must be determined separately for each case.

CASE 1: HIDDEN LINE

$$P_1 = \frac{100}{50} P_0 = 2P_0$$

$$P_2 = \frac{100}{50} P_1 = 4P_0$$

$$P_3 = \frac{100}{50} P_2 = 8P_0$$

$$P_4 = \frac{100}{50} P_3 = 16P_0$$

$$P_5 = \frac{100}{50} P_4 = 32P_0$$

$$P_0(1 + 2 + 4 + 8 + 16 + 32) = 1$$

$$P_0 = \frac{1}{63} = .01587$$

Therefore the average profit rate is $(25)(.98413) = \$24.60/$hour.

CASE 2: VISIBLE LINE

$$P_1 = \frac{100}{50} P_0 = 2P_0$$

$$P_2 = \frac{80}{50} P_1 = 3.2P_0$$

$$P_3 = \frac{60}{50} P_2 = 1.92P_0$$

$$P_4 = \frac{40}{50} P_3 = 1.536P_0$$

$$P_5 = \frac{20}{50} P_4 = .6144P_0$$

$$P_0(1.0 + 2.0 + 3.2 + 1.92 + 1.536 + .6144) = 1$$

$$P_0 = .0974$$

Therefore the average profit rate is $(25)(.9026) = \$22.55/$hour. The difference, $24.60 - 22.55 = \$2.05/$hour, is because the hidden waiting line provides a more steady stream of customers to the system.

The analysis so far shows that the hidden waiting line is superior. However, that is from the viewpoint of just one of many amusements in the park. From the viewpoint of the whole amusement park there is some disadvantage associated with having customers waiting in line when they could be utilizing the other amusement features in the park. This can be taken into account by assigning to each visitor's time a value which reflects the revenue per unit time that customer would generate if he were not waiting in line. The visitor's time is actually a resource to the amusement park. Suppose that it is estimated to be worth $3/hour per customer. Now the net profit rate of any amusement will be the profit rate less the waiting-time charge per customer times the average number of customers waiting in the amusement ride. This will require the calculation of the average number waiting in the system under each alternative.

CASE 1: HIDDEN LINE

$$L_q = 0P_0 + 0P_1 + 1P_2 + 2P_3 + 3P_4 + 4P_5$$
$$= 4P_0 + 16P_0 + 48P_0 + 128P_0$$
$$= (4 + 16 + 48 + 128)P_0 = \frac{196}{63} = 2.03$$

Waiting-time charge = $3(2.03) = $6.09/hour

CASE 2: VISIBLE LINE

$$L_q = 0P_0 + 0P_1 + 1P_2 + 2P_3 + 3P_4 + 4P_5$$
$$= [3.2 + 2(1.92) + 3(1.536) + 4(.6144)]P_0$$
$$= 1.374$$

Waiting-time charge = $3(1.374) = $4.122/hour

The net profit rates in dollars per hour are

	Hidden	Visible
Profit rate	24.60	22.55
Less waiting cost	6.09	4.12
Net profit rate	18.51	18.43

The comparison shows that the hidden line is still better. However, the two are so close that the cost difference of the two designs should also be considered.

14.7 THE POISSON PROCESS

The process of customers arriving at a stochastic service station has been described so far as a Markov process. This means that there is an arrival rate λ of customers per unit time. The period of the Markov process is chosen to be very small. For example, when λ is expressed in arrivals per hour the period was taken to be 1 second, which is $1/3600$ hour. The notation $m = 3600$ was used. The probability of one arrival in any time period of length $1/m$ is

$$P(\text{one arrival in one period}) = \frac{\lambda}{m}$$

It turned out that the results did not depend upon the size of m so long as it was small enough that the probability of two or more arrivals in one period was small enough to be treated as zero.

This arrival process is known as a *Poisson process*. The description given so far represents the fundamental property of such a process. Another equivalent description of the Poisson process is that the number of arrivals n in any finite time period of length T has the Poisson probability distribution:

$$P(n \mid T) = \frac{(\lambda T)^n e^{-\lambda T}}{n!} \qquad \text{for } n = 0, 1, 2, \ldots$$

The derivation of this second property from the first is instructive in understanding the Poisson process. Suppose that T is expressed in the same time units as λ and $1/m$. Then there are T/m small time periods in the large period T. Consider a Markov process where there are arrivals but no service. The state of this system is the number of arrivals n since the system has started operation. This process will not have a steady state because n will never decrease but only increase with arrivals. The transient probability of being in state n at time T is desired. This process has an infinite Markov matrix with the structure

	s_0	s_1	s_2	s_3	$\cdots$
s_0	$1 - \dfrac{\lambda}{m}$	$\dfrac{\lambda}{m}$	0	0	
s_1	0	$1 - \dfrac{\lambda}{m}$	$\dfrac{\lambda}{m}$	0	
s_2	0	0	$1 - \dfrac{\lambda}{m}$	$\dfrac{\lambda}{m}$	
$\vdots$					

The equation for the transient-state probabilities, denoted by $P(n \mid T)$, all have the following form (except the first equation for $n = 0$, where the term $P[n - 1 \mid T - 1/m]$ is not present):

$$P(n \mid T) = P\left(n - 1 \mid T - \frac{1}{m}\right)\frac{\lambda}{m} + P\left(n \mid T - \frac{1}{m}\right)\left(1 - \frac{\lambda}{m}\right)$$

This can be rearranged to

$$\frac{P(n \mid T) - P(n \mid T - 1/m)}{1/m} = \lambda P\left(n - 1 \mid T - \frac{1}{m}\right) - \lambda P\left(n \mid T - \frac{1}{m}\right)$$

As $1/m$ is allowed to get very small, this left-hand side approaches a derivative. The equation, in the limit as $1/m$ approaches zero, is

$$\frac{dP(n \mid T)}{dT} = \lambda[P(n - 1 \mid T) - P(n \mid T)]$$

The starting condition is $P(0 \mid 0) = 1$, which represents the statement that the state is zero at time zero. For $n = 0$, the equation is

$$\frac{dP(0 \mid T)}{dT} = -\lambda P(0 \mid T)$$

This simple differential equation has the solution

$$P(0 \mid T) = e^{-\lambda T}$$

The equation for $n = 1$ is

$$\frac{dP(1 \mid T)}{dT} = \lambda e^{-\lambda T} - \lambda P(1 \mid T)$$

This has the solution

$$P(1 \mid T) = \lambda T e^{-\lambda T}$$

Successive solutions for $P(n \mid T)$ given $P(n - 1 \mid T)$ can be obtained until finally the general form is recognized:

$$P(n \mid T) = \frac{(\lambda T)^n e^{-\lambda T}}{n!}$$

This demonstrates that the Poisson probability distribution for the number of arrivals in any time period of length T is also a property of the Poisson process.

EXERCISES

1. The arrivals to the gas station obey a Poisson process with rate $\lambda = 20$ cars/hour. The average service time is 1.5 minutes. Compute the probabilities of zero, one, and two arrivals during a time period of 1 second. Use the series expansion for $e^{-\lambda T}$ when λT is small. Compute the probabilities of zero and two arrivals during a time period of length 1.5 minutes.

2. For the Poisson process with rate $\lambda = 20$ cars/hour, find the mean, variance, and ratio of standard deviation to mean for the number of arrivals in an 8-hour period. Instead of 8 hours, how long would the time period have to be so that the ratio of standard deviation to the mean is 1 percent?

3. Suppose that an arrival event occurs at time $t = 0$. What is the probability that the next event has not yet occurred by time t? Consider $\tilde{t}$ to be the random variable representing the time between the first and second arrivals. What is its

probability density function? Use the results of the previous calculation, which is the probability that $\tilde{t}$ exceeds the value t.

4.   Suppose that the exams for each course are scheduled by a Poisson process. Each course has a rate of three exams per 15 weeks or .2 exam per week. A student who takes five courses has a total exam rate of $5 \times .2 = 1$ exam per week. What is the probability of three or more exams in 1 week? What is the probability of no exams in 1 week?

14.8   PROBABILITY DISTRIBUTION OF SERVICE DURATION

The duration of one service is a random variable, described so far as a Markov process. It was assumed that while the server is busy the probability of a service completion within a very small interval of time $1/m$ is

$$P(\text{one service completion in one period}) = 1 - \frac{\mu}{m}$$

where μ is the service rate of the server while continuously busy. To explore the implications of this assumption, consider a system that starts with one arrival at time zero. The service begins at time zero. Then the arrival rate drops to zero for all future time. Thus the system will be empty when the first service is complete. The steady-state probabilities are not of interest. The transient probability $P_1(t)$ is the probability that the first service is not yet complete at time t. The Markov matrix is

	s_0	s_1
s_0	1	0
s_1	$\dfrac{\mu}{m}$	$1 - \dfrac{\mu}{m}$

The equations for the transient probability are

$$P_0(t) = P_0\left(t - \frac{1}{m}\right) + \frac{\mu}{m} P_1\left(t - \frac{1}{m}\right)$$

and

$$P_1(t) = \left(1 - \frac{\mu}{m}\right) P_1\left(t - \frac{1}{m}\right)$$

These are rearranged to

$$\frac{P_0(t) - P_0(t - 1/m)}{1/m} = \mu P_1\left(t - \frac{1}{m}\right)$$

$$\frac{P_1(t) - P_1(t - 1/m)}{1/m} = -\mu P_1\left(t - \frac{1}{m}\right)$$

In the limit, as $1/m \to 0$ the second equation becomes

$$\frac{dP_1(t)}{dt} = -\mu P_1(t)$$

The first equation adds no further information because

$$P_1(t) + P_0(t) = 1 \qquad \text{for all } t$$

The initial condition for the transient solution is $P_1(0) = 1$. The simple differential equation can be solved to give

$$P_1(t) = e^{-\mu t}$$

This is the probability that the random variable $\tilde{t}$, the duration of the service, exceeds t. Let $f(t)$ be the probability density function of $\tilde{t}$. Then $F(t)$ is the probability that $\tilde{t}$ is less than the value t. Therefore

$$F(t) = 1 - P_1(t) = 1 - e^{-\mu t}$$

The density function can always be found as the derivative of $F(t)$. Therefore

$$f(t) = \mu e^{-\mu t}$$

This result is the exponential density function. Therefore all the methods of this chapter have assumed that the service duration is a random variable having this probability density function. The mean service time is $1/\mu$ (see Fig. 14.2). This assumption about the probability distribution of service duration is not always realistic. However, it is a conservative assumption because it represents the most uncertainty possible given only the average rate of service. It may lead to some surplus

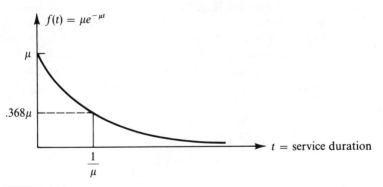

FIGURE 14.2

capacity if service capacity is determined on the assumption of exponential service density when in fact there is more regularity to the service process.

EXERCISES

1.   A service process with variable duration has service rate μ = 20 services per hour. The service duration is a random variable with exponential density function with mean $1/\mu$ = .05 hour = 3 minutes. Suppose that a particular service began 9 minutes ago but is not yet completed. Show that the probability density of the random variable $\tilde{z}$ = remaining time to service completion has the same exponential density as that of one full service duration. Do this by conditioning upon the event "service duration exceeds 9 minutes." You will need the probability of this event. Is this result true for any number of minutes in place of 9?

2.   There are two barbers in a shop and both serve customers at rate μ with an exponential density of service duration. You enter the shop when both are busy and no one else is waiting. What is the probability that you are the last of the three to leave?

14.9   SINGLE SERVER WITH NONEXPONENTIAL SERVICE DENSITY

The analysis of queuing problems becomes much more difficult when the service process has a probability density function other than the exponential density function. The analysis can no longer be performed according to a single Markov process. The probability of future events would depend not only upon the number of customers already in the system but also upon the current "age" of services now in progress.

Some useful results are available for the single server with no space limit. Suppose that the average service time is $1/\mu$ and that the variance of service time is σ_s^2. The service duration could have any density function; these results will depend only upon its mean and variance. Let the arrival process be the usual Poisson process with rate λ, for $\lambda < \mu$. The results are stated without derivation. The probability that the system is idle is

$$P_0 = 1 - \frac{\lambda}{\mu}$$

The average number in the system is

$$L = \frac{\lambda}{\mu} + \frac{(\lambda/\mu)^2 + \lambda^2 \sigma_s^2}{2(1 - \lambda/\mu)}$$

The average number waiting for service is

$$L_q = \frac{(\lambda/\mu)^2 + \lambda^2\sigma_s^2}{2(1 - \lambda/\mu)}$$

The average waiting time for a customer before his service begins is

$$W_q = \frac{(\lambda/\mu)^2 + \lambda^2\sigma_s^2}{2\lambda(1 - \lambda/\mu)}$$

The average time in the system is

$$W = \frac{1}{\mu} + W_q$$

If service duration is completely regular and predictable with length $1/\mu$, these re-sults apply with $\sigma_s^2 = 0$. The length of the queue and the average waiting time are at their smallest when the variance is zero. Any variance at all contributes to the in-efficiency of the system.

If the service duration has an exponential distribution, as in all examples up to this section, the variance is

$$\sigma_s^2 = \left(\frac{1}{\mu}\right)^2$$

Therefore the average number in the system is

$$L = \frac{\lambda}{\mu} + \frac{2(\lambda/\mu)^2}{2(1 - \lambda/\mu)}$$

$$= \frac{\lambda/\mu}{1 - \lambda/\mu}$$

as previously derived in this chapter.

The expressions are readily applicable. For example, suppose that customers arrive randomly at a telephone booth at the rate of six customers per hour. The aver-age length of a phone call is 3 minutes. The telephone company will install a second booth when the expected waiting time for a customer to use the phone is 3 minutes or more. By how much must the arrival rate be increased to justify a second phone? Suppose first that the phone calls have an exponential probability density function. Then the expected wait as a function of λ is

$$W_q = \frac{1}{\mu}\frac{\lambda/\mu}{1 - \lambda/\mu}$$

Using $\mu = \frac{1}{3}$, this is

$$W_q = 3\frac{3\lambda}{1 - 3\lambda}$$

Equate $W_q = 3$ and solve for λ:

$$\lambda = \frac{1}{6} \text{ customer/minute}$$

$$= 10 \text{ customers/hour}$$

However, if phone calls were all of the same duration their variance would be zero. Then the appropriate expression for W_q is

$$W_q = \frac{1}{2} \frac{1}{\mu} \frac{\lambda/\mu}{1 - \lambda/\mu}$$

The value of μ is still $\frac{1}{3}$. The equation for λ is

$$3 = \frac{1}{2} \, 3 \, \frac{3\lambda}{1 - 3\lambda}$$

The result is $\lambda = 13.33$ customers per hour. Thus the uniformity of phone calls improves the capacity of the system. The system can tolerate a higher arrival rate for the same average waiting time than when calls are of highly irregular duration.

Notice that if the phone company used the criterion that the probability of having to wait at all must be up to $\frac{1}{2}$ before a second booth is installed, the regularity of the calls would have no effect because

$$P_0 = 1 - \frac{\lambda}{\mu}$$

holds true regardless of the variance of the service time distribution.

PROBLEMS

1. A repairman is to be hired to repair machines that break down at an average rate of three per hour. Breakdowns are distributed randomly in time. Nonproductive time on any machine is considered to cost the company $5/hour. The company has narrowed the choice to two repairmen: one slow but cheap, the other fast but expensive. The slow but cheap repairman asks $3/hour; in return he will service broken-down machines at an average rate of four per hour. The fast but expensive repairman demands $5/hour and will repair machines at an average rate of six per hour. Which repairman should be hired?

2. An insurance company has one claims adjuster in its branch office. People with claims against the company are found to arrive in a random fashion at an average rate of six per 8-hour day. The amount of time an adjuster spends with a claimant is found to have a mean service time of 40 minutes. Claimants are processed in the order of their appearance. How much time, on the average,

does a claimant spend in the branch office? What fraction of time is the claims adjuster not busy with claimants?

3. We are designing a single-server queuing system with unlimited waiting space. The server's rate μ is a decision variable that must be specified in the design. The operating cost per unit time of having a server of rate μ is $C_s\mu$, even while the server is idle. The other type of operating cost incurred by the system is proportional to the number of customers in the system; while n are in the system there is a cost per unit time of $C_w n$. There is a tradeoff between these two costs. A fast server costs more but reduces the waiting-time cost. The arrival rate to the system, λ, is not under our control.

   (a) Give an expression for the total operating cost per unit time as a function of the decision variable μ, the parameter λ, and the cost parameters C_s and C_w.

   (b) Find the formula for μ^*, the optimum service rate. If $\lambda = 10$, $C_w = 200$, and $C_s = 20$, what μ is best? What cost per unit time does it give?

   (c) If the service rate is chosen so that the server is idle exactly half the time, what is the average wait in the waiting line? (Use $\lambda = 10$.)

4. Men arrive at a barber shop at an average rate of 16 per hour. The average haircut takes 15 minutes. The shop is staffed by two barbers who are paid \$2/hour and work a 40-hour week. When both barbers are busy but no customers are waiting, one-fourth of the men arriving at the shop do not enter because they wish to avoid waiting. Similarly, when one customer is waiting, three-eighths of the arrivals do not enter the shop. Since there are only two chairs in which customers may wait, there are never more than two men waiting for haircuts. The shop charges \$2 for a haircut.

   (a) Give a table showing the effective arrival and service rates for each of the possible states.

   (b) Find the average weekly profit of the shop.

   (c) Find the average rate of arrivals actually entering the shop.

5. The Acme Piano Company carries an inventory of at most three pianos. The demand for pianos is random in time with rate two pianos per month. One piano is ordered every time a piano is sold, and no sales are made when out of stock. The lead time to receipt of an order is random with mean value 1 month (hence the rate one per month per order outstanding). The business operates in a store that rents for \$100/month. There is a holding cost of \$25 per piano per month based upon the interest on the capital invested in inventory. The profit per sale is \$100 per piano sold. Find the average profit per month of the business.

6. A four-line telephone switchboard services only the calls of four subscribers who never call each other. The rate of call completion of existing calls is μ calls per

hour. The rate of initiation of calls per customer is λ calls per hour while that customer does not have a call in progress and zero while he is calling. Set up a Markov process model and determine the steady-state probabilities for the number of lines in use at any time.

7. Consider a two-stage production process such that units are produced by the first stage at random points in time and flow into the second stage at random points in time as demanded by the second stage. The mean output rate of the first stage is 10 units/hour; the mean consumption rate capacity of the second stage is 12 units/hour. Assume that there is an effectively infinite storage area between the two stages and that the process operates 8 hours per day.

    (a)   Find the average bank size between stages ("bank size" means waiting line).

    (b)   Find the daily time lost by stage 2 while waiting for material from stage 1.

    (c)   The storage costs (based on average bank size) are \$1/piece/day, and the idle time for the second stage costs \$3/hour. Assume now that we can control the mean consumption rate of stage 2 but not that of stage 1. What is the optimum mean consumption rate of stage 2? What further gain could be made if stage 2 could be made to operate in a perfectly regular way (zero variance)?

Chapter 15
SIMULATION

Simulation takes a model of reality and produces a likeness of the behavior which is represented by that model. The results of simulation are summaries of the simulated behavior. Simulation is useful when the model is so complex that analytic methods are difficult to apply. Also, simulation, when implemented on a computer, enables the construction of large, complex models that are closer to reality. It replaces analytic methods of predicting the behavior implied by a model. Therefore it could be called too a modeling technique. Another use of simulation is to *illustrate* models by generating artificial but realistic experience. This can serve a very important training function.

This chapter will concentrate on simulation of probabilistic models, excluding deterministic models; this is often called *Monte Carlo* simulation. The chapter will emphasize also the *concept* of simulation because it is beyond the scope of this text to teach the computer skill and statistical techniques needed to practice simulation. Finally, we shall illustrate models from earlier chapters to deepen the understanding of models that are conceptually difficult but very important. Thus the discussion of simulation serves as a natural concluding chapter.

15.1 GENERATING DISCRETE CHANCE OUTCOMES

Simulation of probabilistic models requires the generation of chance outcomes. A model specifies the probabilities of the possible outcomes. A device is needed that will generate outcomes according to those probabilities.

There are many devices that can serve as standard outcome generating tools, such as a "pointer wheel," as shown in Fig. 15.1. This is a heavy disk, like a roulette wheel, which rotates about its center point. The disk has a pointer marked on it, and a stationary outer ring around the disk is calibrated from 0 to 1.

Suppose that the wheel rotates freely and is perfectly balanced. When it is set

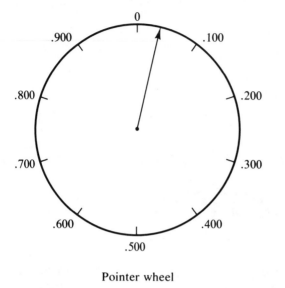

Pointer wheel

FIGURE 15.1

in motion, its stopping point is equally likely to be any point on the circumference. The stopping point will determine a point on the fixed circumference ring. Thus each spin of the pointer wheel will generate an outcome of random variable whose probability is uniformly distributed between zero and 1.

Now the outcome of a spin must be transformed into a chance outcome. Suppose that a chance process has n possible outcomes, with probabilities p_1, p_2, ..., p_n, which sum to unity. These probabilities can be marked on a line of unit length as illustrated in Fig. 15.2. If the pointer wheel produces a number in the interval corresponding to p_i, the ith outcome has occurred. Formally, let x represent the outcome of the spin of the pointer wheel. Then if

$$\sum_{j=0}^{i-1} p_j \leq x < \sum_{j=0}^{i} p_j \qquad \text{where } p_o = 0$$

then the ith outcome has occurred. The general procedure, after the random vari-

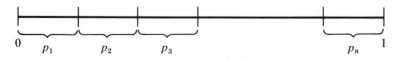

Determination of the outcome

FIGURE 15.2

able x is determined, is to successively add and accumulate the probabilities until the point where one more addition would make the accumulated sum exceed x. For example, the game problem of Sec. 12.5 requires that alternatives A_1 and A_2 be selected, with probability $x_1 = .389$ and $x_2 = .611$, respectively. If the pointer wheel stops on a number less than or equal to .389, then A_1 is selected, as shown in Fig. 15.3. However, if the number exceeds .389, then action A_2 is selected.

The limitation of the pointer wheel device for generating x is the time required to perform the spin. The above example requires just one spin, but simulations require tens of thousands of random numbers, and so time becomes an important consideration. Another limitation is the accuracy of the device. If it is possible to read it to only three-place decimal accuracy, an event whose probability is less than .001 will cause difficulty.

A simpler device with unlimited accuracy is an urn containing 10 balls marked 0, 1, 2, 3, 4, 5, 6, 7, 8, and 9. Drawing a ball is always followed by replacement of the ball drawn. The first ball establishes the first digit of the random number, the second draw establishes the second digit, and so forth. One digit may be enough. In the above example, suppose that the first draw results in the digit 1. This implies that the x value is in the interval $.1 \leq x < .2$. Since $x < .389$, the action A_1 is determined; no greater accuracy is needed. However, if the digit 3 were drawn for the first digit, then at least a second draw would be required to determine whether or not the number exceeds .389. A second draw of 8 or less indicates A_1, whereas a second draw of 9 indicates A_2. Thus any degree of accuracy desired can be met by using a sufficient number of successive draws when they are required.

Many devices for generating random numbers between zero and 1 are possible. The above two procedures are not the most practical; the purpose of their presentation was primarily conceptual. In practice, simulation is almost always done by computer. Therefore it is most efficient to use computer methods of generating random numbers. Computer subroutines are available to generate random numbers having many digits of precision. Because it is beyond the scope of this book to discuss such methods, we shall assume that high-precision random numbers are readily available. Table 15.1, which shows three-digit random numbers, will be used for subsequent examples throughout this chapter.

One interesting fact about computer-generated random numbers is that they are not truly random. In fact, they are generated by a deterministic process as described

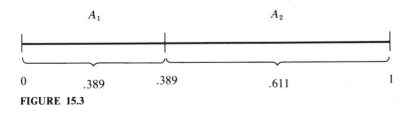

FIGURE 15.3

by the computer program. If this process is repeated at a later time, it will generate the same sequence of random numbers it produced the first time. This repeatability is actually a desirable property in some situations. The term *pseudorandom* is often used for random numbers generated by a deterministic, repeatable process.

TABLE 15.1   Table of
Random Numbers Uni-
    formly Distributed
    between Zero and 1

.699	.441	.819
.283	.215	.209
.122	.570	.926
.170	.040	.899
.153	.194	.634
.656	.009	.479
.121	.105	.441
.656	.814	.665
.077	.721	.053
.557	.840	.323
.071	.379	.150
.863	.844	.450
.135	.058	.990
.642	.179	.047
.432	.294	.638

15.2   SIMULATION OF A DECISION-TREE EXAMPLE

To emphasize the concepts of simulation, it is advantageous to work with problems that have already been studied and solved. It is important for the reader to realize the implications of this pedagogical strategy; simulation is *not* an efficient way to solve the problems used for illustration in this chapter. In fact, it will be obvious that a few calculations have been replaced by a few thousand calculations. This explicit reminder will warn the reader to guard against forming an impression that simulation is an inefficient method for solving all problems. In reality it is not difficult to find important problems so complex that simulation has a real advantage over analytic methods. However, the illustrations in this chapter have not been chosen to illustrate the advantage.

Chapter 9 presented two-stage decision-tree problems. An example of such a problem involves an oil company that must decide whether or not to drill an exploratory oil well on a given site. The company believes that the probability of oil being present is .2 and that the revenue, if oil is present, will be $450,000. The probability of a dry well is .8, and it costs $100,000 to drill regardless of the outcome. Before making this decision, the company can obtain more evidence by an expensive experiment ($10,000) called seismographic recording; this will determine something about the underlying geological structure.

Previous calculations using Bayes' rule have shown that for the three possible test outcomes the revised probability of oil is

Event	$P(O/\text{event})$	$P(\text{event})$
R_1: There is no subsurface structure.	.099	.604
R_2: There is an open subsurface structure.	.243	.296
R_3: There is a closed subsurface structure.	.680	.100

The sequence of action is

1. Decision maker decides whether to buy seismic test.

2. Chance decides outcome of test.

3. Decision maker uses outcome to decide whether to drill.

4. Chance decides whether there is oil present.

The complete decision tree and the analysis for maximization of expected profit are given in Chap. 9. The analytic method requires only five expected-value calculations and five comparisons to find optimum decisions. Yet it is a good example to illustrate the concept of simulation, and knowledge of the answers will be an advantage in understanding the simulation results.

The first step is to identify the list of decision rules that are to be evaluated by simulation. There is no need to consider all possible decision rules; it is enough to use intuition in selecting reasonable candidates, as shown in the following table:

Decision Rules
$A1$: Buy the seismic test. Then drill only if the outcome is R_2 or R_3.
$A2$: Buy the seismic test. Drill only if the outcome is R_3.
$A3$: Do not buy the seismic test. Drill without any further information.
$A4$: Do nothing.

Other possible decision rules such as "Buy seismic and drill only if the outcome is R_1" and "Buy seismic and drill under any outcome" are obviously inferior and will not be considered. Furthermore, decision $A4$ obviously has zero value and requires no evaluation. Thus three alternatives, $A1$, $A2$, and $A3$, will be evaluated by simulation to determine which has the highest expected profit.

The three alternatives will be considered one at a time. Once an alternative is selected, the other possible decisions can be removed from the tree to obtain just a two-stage lottery diagram, as shown in Fig. 15.4.

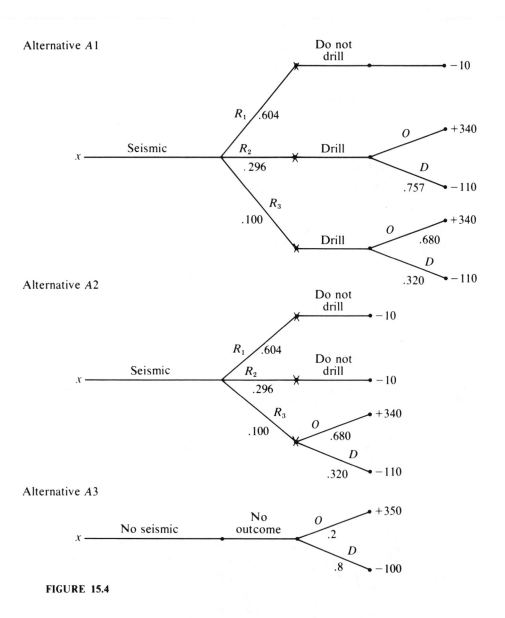

FIGURE 15.4

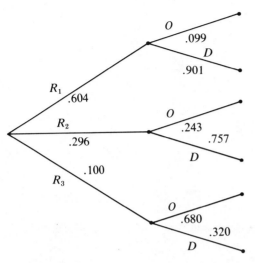

FIGURE 15.5

The chance process that will generate the single actual outcome can be described by the probability tree shown in Fig. 15.5.

The simulation of *one* complete experience can be generated, using two random numbers, as in Fig. 15.6.

Once the complete outcome has been generated, calculations can be done for each alternative, according to Table 15.2.

Draw one random number, x_1.

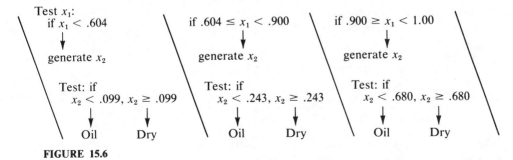

FIGURE 15.6

TABLE 15.2

Outcome	Profit of $A1$	Profit of $A2$	Profit of $A3$
$R_1 \cap O$	-10	-10	$+350$
$R_1 \cap D$	-10	-10	-100
$R_2 \cap O$	$+340$	-10	$+350$
$R_2 \cap D$	-110	-10	-100
$R_3 \cap O$	$+340$	$+340$	$+350$
$R_3 \cap D$	-110	-110	-100

Example of Simulation

The pair of random numbers $x_1 = .699$, $x_2 = .283$ imply outcome R_2 followed by D. The profits are -100 for $A1$, -10 for $A2$, and -100 for $A3$.

Table 15.3 shows 20 simulated outcomes and the profits of the decision rules.

TABLE 15.3 Simulated Outcomes and Profits

	Random Numbers			Profit	Profit	Profit
	x_1	x_2	Outcome	$A1$	$A2$	$A3$
1	.699	.283	$R_2 \cap D$	-110	-10	-100
2	.122	.170	$R_1 \cap D$	-10	-10	-100
3	.153	.656	$R_1 \cap D$	-10	-10	-100
4	.121	.656	$R_1 \cap D$	-10	-10	-100
5	.077	.557	$R_1 \cap D$	-10	-10	-100
6	.071	.863	$R_1 \cap D$	-10	-10	-100
7	.135	.642	$R_1 \cap D$	-10	-10	-100
8	.432	.441	$R_1 \cap D$	-10	-10	-100
9	.215	.570	$R_1 \cap D$	-10	-10	-100
10	.040	.194	$R_1 \cap D$	-10	-10	-100
11	.009	.105	$R_1 \cap D$	-10	-10	-100
12	.814	.721	$R_2 \cap D$	-110	-10	-100
13	.840	.379	$R_2 \cap D$	-110	-10	-100
14	.844	.058	$R_2 \cap O$	$+340$	-10	$+350$
15	.179	.294	$R_1 \cap D$	-10	-10	-100
16	.294	.819	$R_1 \cap D$	-10	-10	-100
17	.209	.926	$R_1 \cap D$	-10	-10	-100
18	.899	.634	$R_2 \cap D$	-110	-10	-100
19	.479	.441	$R_1 \cap D$	-10	-10	-100
20	.665	.053	$R_2 \cap O$	$+340$	-10	$+350$

This set of 20 simulated outcomes can be summarized according to the number of experiences of each possible outcome:

A 1		A 2		A 3	
Possible Outcomes	Number Observed	Possible Outcomes	Number Observed	Possible Outcomes	Number Observed
−110	4	−110	0	−100	18
−10	14	−10	20	+350	2
+340	2	+340	0		

The main result of this simulation is the average profits of each decision rule, which are

$$A1: \quad \text{Av. profit} = \frac{[4(-110) + 14(-10) + 2(340)]}{20} = 5.00$$

$$A2: \quad \text{Av. profit} = \frac{[20(-10)]}{20} = -10.00$$

$$A3: \quad \text{Av. profit} = \frac{[18(-100) + 2(350)]}{20} = -55.00$$

The conclusion of this small simulation would be that $A1$ is the best decision rule, followed by $A2$ and $A3$, in that order. The question arises about the validity of these results. Fortunately the example is simple enough to solve analytically. This would not be possible in a problem large enough to justify the use of simulation on a practical basis. The analysis can be used here to understand the nature of simulation results.

The alternative decision rule $A1$ can be represented as a two-stage lottery by leaving out the decision branches (Fig. 15.7).

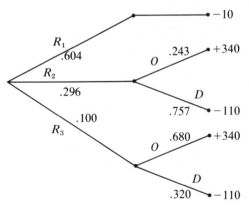

FIGURE 15.7

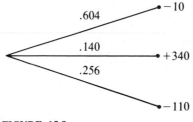

FIGURE 15.8

This can be further compressed into a one-stage lottery by finding the probability of each of the three possible profit outcomes. For example, the probability of a gain of 340 is

$$\text{Pr}\{\text{profit} = 340\} = (.296)(.243) + (.100)(.680)$$
$$= .079 + .068 = .140$$

The single-stage lottery is shown in Fig. 15.8.

This lottery has expected profit

$$E_1 = (-10)(.604) + (340)(.140) + (-110)(.256)$$
$$E_1 = 13.4$$

and its variance of profit is

$$V_1 = (23.4)^2(.604) + (326.6)^2(.140) + (123.4)^2(.256)$$
$$= 5722.33 \quad (\text{SD}_1 = 75.6)$$

Similarly, the alternative $A2$ can be represented by the single-stage lottery shown in Fig. 15.9.

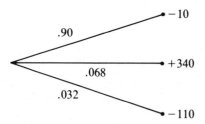

FIGURE 15.9

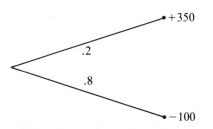

FIGURE 15.10

Its expected profit is

$$E_2 = (-10)(.90) + (340)(.068) + (-110)(.032)$$
$$= 10.60$$

and its variance is

$$V_2 = (20.58)^2(.90) + (329.42)^2(.068) + (120.58)^2(.032)$$
$$= 8225.64 \quad (SD_2 = 90.7)$$

The alternative $A3$ gives the lottery shown in Fig. 15.10. The expected profit is

$$E_3 = (350)(.2) + (-110)(.8) = -10$$

and the variance of profit is

$$V_3 = (360)^2(.2) + (-90)^2(.8)$$
$$= 32,400 \quad (SD_3 = 180)$$

This knowledge of the analytic results can now be used to help understand the validity of the simultion results. The true answer for the expected profit of decision rule $A1$ is \$13.41. The simulation gave 5.00, with 20 simulated trials. Let the difference be denoted $\Delta_1(n)$, when based upon n trials. These errors are summarized in Table 15.4.

TABLE 15.4

True Expected Value	Simulation Estimate	Difference (True Estimate) with 20 Trials
13.41	5.00	$\Delta_1(20) = +8.41$
10.60	-10.00	$\Delta_2(20) = +20.60$
-10.00	-55.00	$\Delta_3(20) = +45.00$

These values of Δ were generated by the actual simulation. Another actual simulation could have given different values. In fact, the simulation results are actually random outcomes. Before the simulation is done they are random variables. Therefore each simulation result has a probability distribution, an expected value, and a variance. These are not known in realistic simulation examples, but they are known in this example; the simulation result is found by averaging the outcomes of n independent simulated trials. The mean and variance of one trial of decision rule A_i are E_i and V_i, for $i = 1, 2$, and 3. The expected value of the average of n independent samples of decision rule A_i is again E_i. The random variable $\tilde{\Delta}_i(n)$ has zero expected value because the expected value E_i has been subtracted. The variance of the average of n independent trials is

$$\frac{1}{n} V_i \qquad \text{for rule } A_i$$

The variance is unchanged by the subtraction; therefore the variance of the difference is

$$V[\tilde{\Delta}_i(n)] = \frac{1}{n} V_i \qquad \text{for } i = 1, 2, 3$$

The standard deviation $SD[\tilde{\Delta}_i(n)] = (1/\sqrt{n})SD_i$ for $i = 1, 2, 3$. The three actual differences and their a priori variances and standard deviations, for the simulation of size $n = 20$ trials, are

$\Delta_i(20)$	$V[\tilde{\Delta}_i(20)]$	$SD[\tilde{\Delta}_i(20)]$
8.41	$\dfrac{5722}{20} = 286$	16.9
20.60	$\dfrac{8225}{20} = 411$	20.2
45.00	$\dfrac{32{,}400}{20} = 1620$	40.2

These standard deviations are comparable to the Δ values. For example, $\Delta_1(20)$ is about one-half the standard deviation of $\tilde{\Delta}_1(20)$. Similarly, $\Delta_2(20)$ and $\Delta_3(20)$ are both about 1 standard deviation in size. One can conclude that these rather large errors in the estimates were quite likely outcomes of a simulation of 20 iterations. The fact that the simulation estimated for rules A_1, A_2, and A_3 were in the same relative order as E_1, E_2, and E_3 was pure luck! The difference between E_1 and E_2 is $13.41 - 10.60 = 2.81$, a very small magnitude compared to the standard deviations of both estimates. Apparently a simulation of size $n = 20$ is completely unreliable for finding the optimum decision rule for this problem.

A sufficient size for the number of samples in the simulation can be found from the standard deviations. The probability distribution of each $\tilde{\Delta}(n)$ can be found by methods beyond the scope of this book.   It is the normal probability distribution for n larger than about 20.   It is known from Chap. 10 that the probability is .9974 that any normally distributed random variable will fall in the interval from minus to plus 3 standard deviations.   Thus an interval of 6 standard deviations is a rather safe interval size for the range of uncertainty.   The 6 standard deviation range of uncertainty for several n values is

n	$SD[\tilde{\Delta}_3(n)]$	6 SD
1	180	1080
100	18.0	108.0
10,000	1.80	10.80
1,000,000	.180	1.08
10^8	.018	.108

Thus even 10,000 samples could fail to show that A_2 is better than A_1 because the difference between E_2 and E_1 is only 2.81, whereas the 6 standard deviation interval for $n = 10^4$ is 10.80, larger than the difference in values.   A sample size of 1 million would be sufficient to distinguish which of the decision rules is optimal.   Thus this section has illustrated the technique of simulation and how the precision of the results depends upon sample size.

15.3   EXAMPLE OF A MARKOV PROCESS

A new state lottery is to be designed with a "tortoise and hare race" theme.   On every day either the tortoise or the hare will be ahead.   If the tortoise was ahead yesterday, then the probability that the hare will be ahead today is .7.   If the hare was ahead yesterday, then the probability that the tortoise will be ahead today is .8.   Every morning at 8:00 A.M. the result is generated by using a computer to simulate the outcome of a Markov process, and the leader is announced.

After the day's results are announced, the sale of tickets begins.   Tickets can be purchased for either the tortoise or the hare, but the prices depend upon which is ahead today.

All tickets will pay $2 if they win.   The tickets specify a resolution date.   For example, a $2 ticket on the hare to be ahead 3 days from the purchase time will pay out $2 if the hare is ahead on that date.   The cost of the ticket is set to be the expected payoff to the holder plus a $0.10 markup for the lottery's profit.

The state lottery commission wants to find the ticket costs which should be charged so that the state has an expected profit of $0.10 on every ticket sold.   The two states of this process are denoted by

H: hare ahead

T: tortoise ahead

The Markov matrix of probabilities is

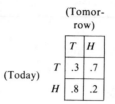

The simulation of this Markov process requires one random number for each day of experience. Suppose that the process starts with the hare ahead on day 1. The probability of the tortoise being ahead on the next day is .8. The random number .699 implies this outcome. Now on day 2, with the tortoise ahead, the probability of the tortoise being ahead on day 3 is .3. The random number .283 results in that outcome. This process continues for as many days as desired, with the probability of the tortoise being ahead next depending upon today's state. Table 15.5 shows the sequence of outcomes for a 25-day simulation.

TABLE 15.5   Outcomes for a 25-day Simulation

Day	State	$P(T$ tomorrow$)$	Random Number	Outcome
1	H	.8	.699	T
2	T	.3	.283	T
3	T	.3	.122	T
4	T	.3	.170	T
5	T	.3	.153	T
6	T	.3	.656	H
7	H	.8	.121	T
8	T	.3	.656	H
9	H	.8	.077	T
10	T	.3	.577	H
11	H	.8	.071	T
12	T	.3	.863	H
13	H	.8	.135	T
14	T	.3	.642	H
15	H	.8	.432	T
16	T	.3	.441	H
17	H	.8	.215	T
18	T	.3	.570	H
19	H	.8	.040	T
20	T	.3	.190	T
21	T	.3	.009	T
22	T	.3	.105	T
23	T	.3	.814	H
24	H	.8	.721	T
25	T	.3	.840	H
26	H			

Given this 25-day experience, the number of wins of each possible bet must be counted. There are two possible states for each day, two possible outcomes to bet on, and four different race lengths from which to select. Thus there are $2 \times 2 \times 4 = 16$ different bets. However, the two possible outcomes are complementary, and so the number of times the hare wins is all that is recorded. Furthermore, each day is either hare ahead (H) or tortoise ahead (T) and thus contributes experience toward only four possible bets. For example, the first five days' experience is $H\ T\ T\ T\ T$. Bets on the hare to be ahead in 1, 2, 3, or 4 days are the four possible bets on day 1. They all result in zero returns according to the experience simulated. All four were on a day when the hare was ahead.

The experience of days 2, 3, 4, 5, and 6 is $T\ T\ T\ T\ T$. Day 2s bets on the hare to be ahead in 1, 2, 3, or 4 days will result in zero returns, and all were on a day

TABLE 15.6 Number of Wins (Hare)

Day	State	Next Four Outcomes				Given H Ahead 1	2	3	4	Given T Ahead 1	2	3	4
1	H	T	T	T	T	0	0	0	0				
2	T	T	T	T	T					0	0	0	0
3	T	T	T	T	H					0	0	0	1
4	T	T	T	H	T					0	0	1	0
5	T	T	H	T	H					0	1	0	1
6	T	H	T	H	T					1	0	1	0
7	H	T	H	T	H	0	1	0	1				
8	T	H	T	H	T					1	0	1	0
9	H	T	H	T	H	0	1	0	1				
10	T	H	T	H	T					1	0	1	0
11	H	T	H	T	H	0	1	0	1				
12	T	H	T	H	T					1	0	1	0
13	H	T	H	T	H	0	1	0	1				
14	T	H	T	H	T					1	0	1	0
15	H	T	H	T	H	0	1	0	1				
16	T	H	T	H	T					1	0	1	0
17	H	T	H	T	T	0	1	0	0				
18	T	H	T	T	T					1	0	0	0
19	H	T	T	T	T	0	0	0	0				
20	T	T	T	T	H					0	0	0	1
21	T	T	T	H	T					0	0	1	0
22	T	T	H	T	H					0	1	0	1
23	T	H	T	H						1	0	1	...
24	H	T	H			0	1	...	...				
25	T	H								1			
26	H												
Total wins						0	7	0	5	9	2	9	4
Total bets						9	9	8	8	16	15	15	14
Fraction							0.777		0.625	.562	.133	.600	.286

when the tortoise was ahead. The number of wins for each bet is counted in Table 15.6.

The results of the simulation are the fraction of wins for each of the eight possible bets. Table 15.7 compares the simulation estimates with the true answers found by the methods of Chap. 13.

TABLE 15.7   Probability of Win on Hare

	Given H Ahead				Given T Ahead			
Days Ahead	1	2	3	4	1	2	3	4
Simulation estimates	0	.777	0	.625	.562	.133	.600	.286
True answers	.2	.6	.4	.5	.7	.35	.525	.4375

As in Sec. 15.2, the number of trials in the simulation is far too small to obtain any accuracy of results. Again it can be shown that about 100,000 trials would give a 6 standard deviation range of uncertainty of about .01, a two-place accuracy of results.

The purpose of the simulation of this problem is to determine the ticket cost of each of the possible bets. The cost is found by multiplying the probability of winning by $2 and then adding .10 for the lottery profit. The results, using the true probabilities found by the methods of Chap. 13, are shown in Tables 15.8 and 15.9.

TABLE 15.8   Ticket Cost when Tortoise Ahead

	Tortoise to Win	Hare to Win
Tomorrow	2(.3) + .10 = .70	2(.7) + .10 = 1.50
2 days away	2(.65) + .10 = 1.40	2(.35) + .10 = .80
3 days away	2(.475) + .10 = 1.05	2(.525) + .10 = 1.15
4 days away	2(.5625) + .10 = 1.225	2(.4875) + .10 = .975

TABLE 15.9   Ticket Cost when Hare Ahead

	Tortoise to Win	Hare to Win
Tomorrow	2(.8) + .10 = 1.70	2(.2) + .10 = .50
2 days away	2(.4) + .10 = .90	2(.6) + .10 = 1.30
3 days away	2(.6) + .10 = 1.30	2(.4) + .10 = .90
4 days away	2(.5) + .10 = 1.10	2(.5) + .10 = 1.10

15.4 OUTCOMES FOR CONTINUOUS RANDOM VARIABLES

Many processes involve *continuous* random variables with known probability distributions. The simulation of such processes requires the generation of outcomes for continuous random variables. Suppose that the random variable $\tilde{x}$ has probability

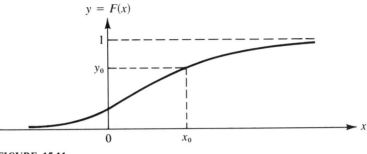

FIGURE 15.11

density function $f(x)$ and cumulative distribution function $F(x)$, as defined in Chap. 10. Suppose that a new random variable y is defined as a function of $\tilde{x}$. As a function of x, the value of y is related by $y = F(x)$.

Since $F(x)$ is an increasing function of x, there is a one-to-one correspondence between x and y values. Since $F(x)$ is a probability, the range of possible y values is zero to 1. The graph of the relationship is shown in Fig. 15.11. For some specific x value, x_0, there is a related y value, y_0, obeying $y_0 = F(x_0)$. The probability that $\tilde{y}$ is less than or equal to y_0 is equal to the probability that $\tilde{x}$ is less than or equal to x_0. Define $G(y)$ as the cumulative distribution function of $\tilde{y}$ and $g(y)$ as the probability density function of $\tilde{y}$. These will be derived from $F(x)$ and $f(x)$ as follows:

$$P(\tilde{y} \leq y_0) = G(y_0) = F(x_0)$$

Now substitute $F(x_0) = y_0$. Therefore $G(y_0) = y_0$, and the density function is

$$g(y) = \frac{d}{dy} G(y) = \frac{d}{dy} y = 1$$

This shows that the random variable defined by $\tilde{y} = F(\tilde{x})$ has a uniform density between the values zero and 1. Every value of y is equally likely between zero and 1. This result is useful in simulation. The y value is determined first, as described in Sec. 15.1. Then the implied x value is determined as the value that satisfies $F(x) = y$. Theoretically it is always possible to invert the function $F(x)$ to solve the equation. Let $F^{-1}(y) = x$ represent the inverse function. Then the value of x is determined in one step by computing $F^{-1}(y)$. This step is not always computationally practical. The following example shows a random variable for which this procedure is easily performed.

An insurance example was given in Sec. 11.6. The size of loss, given that a loss occurs, is a random variable $x > 0$, with exponential probability density function $f(x) = \lambda e^{-\lambda x}$, for $x > 0$, with mean size \$5000. Since the parameter λ is the reciprocal of the mean, its value is $\lambda = 2 \times 10^{-4}$. As shown in Chap. 10, the corresponding cumulative distribution function is

$$F(x) = 1 - e^{-\lambda x}$$

Now the transformation $y = F(x)$ is

$$y = 1 - e^{-\lambda x}$$

This equation can be solved for x as a function of y. The result is

$$x = -\frac{1}{\lambda} \ln (1 - y)$$

One further simplification is possible: if y is uniformly distributed, then so is $1 - y$. It is correct to replace $1 - y$ by y itself and, avoiding one subtraction, use

$$x = -\frac{1}{\lambda} \ln y$$

Notice that since y is between zero and 1 the natural logarithm is always a negative quantity. The negative sign implies that x is always nonnegative. Using $(1/\lambda) = \$5000$, the expression is

$$x = -(5000) \ln y$$

Suppose the random number $y = .699$ is drawn. The corresponding x value is

$$x = -(5000)(-.35810) = \$1791$$

Similarly, the random number $y = .283$ gives

$$x = -(5000) \ln .283 = -(5000)(-1.26231) = \$6311$$

This procedure is not as easy to perform for most other probability density functions. One other easy case of general usefulness is when x has uniform density within an interval $a \leq x \leq b$. Then $F(x)$ is a linear function of x:

$$F(x) = \frac{x - a}{b - a} \qquad \text{for } a \leq x \leq b$$

Then

$$y = \frac{x - a}{b - a}$$

and so

$$x = a + (b - a)y$$

Outcomes from continuous distributions such as the normal, gamma, beta, and others may be more difficult to generate. However, computer subroutines are commonly available to generate outcomes in these cases. A short table of normally distributed random numbers is now presented for use in examples and problems.

TABLE 15.10 Standard Normal Random Numbers, Normally Distributed with Zero Mean and Unit Variance

− 1.329	− 2.015	.791	.639
+ .301	− .623	.890	− 1.168
− 1.772	− .699	.772	− 1.872
+ .905	+ .326	.048	− 1.718
− .481	+ 1.114	− .558	+ .838

15.5 EXAMPLE OF RISK SHARING

This section will illustrate the use of simulation to find the optimal decision when the decision maker is averse to risk. Sections 15.1 to 15.4 involved the criterion of expected-value maximization. The expected-utility criterion presented in Chap. 11 shows how to represent quantitatively the decision maker's attitude toward risk.

Based upon the risk-sharing example in Sec. 11.7, the decision problem is to find the optimum share of a large, risky, capital venture. Problems of this type can be solved by simulation only if risk aversion is taken into account. The criterion of expected-profit maximization will result in the unrealistic answer that either no share or 100 percent share is optimum. Intermediate shares can be optimum only for a risk-aversion decision maker.

Consider a large risky project with an initial cost of $11.5 million. A study of the possible outcomes indicates that the expected return from the project is $14 million and that the probability distribution of profit is normal with a variance of 20. Let $\tilde{z}$ represent the uncertain profit if the project is undertaken. Then $\tilde{z}$ also has a normal probability distribution, with expected value of $2.5 million and a variance of 20.

The firm has an attitude toward risk that is represented by an exponential utility function for wealth x given by

$$U(x) = \frac{1}{r} (1 - e^{-rx})$$

with parameter $r = .50$ when x values are expressed in $1 million units.

The firm can find sharing partners who are willing to accept any fraction of the project. Let α represent the share of the project that will be retained by the firm. This is the decision variable. If the firm retains share α, then they face a profit lottery having a normal probability distribution with expected profit 2.5α and a variance of profit $20\alpha^2$. This problem was solved in Chap. 11 by analytic means. It will now be solved by simulation. However, only a few of the possible α values will be evaluated; the values $\alpha = .25, .50, .75,$ and 1.00 will be used.

This simulation requires generation of outcomes from a normal probability distribution with mean 2.5 and variance 20. Suppose that standard random numbers are available as a starting point. Let $\tilde{y}$ represent such a random variable, with zero mean and unit variance. Then the profit $\tilde{z}$ is found from

$$\tilde{z} = 2.5 + \sqrt{20}\,\tilde{y}$$

For each outcome z it is necessary to compute the utility of the outcome:

$$U(\alpha z) = 2(1 - e^{-1/2\alpha z})$$

This is computed for $\alpha = .25, .50, .75$, and 1.0. For example, if $y = -1.329$, then

$$z = 2.5 + \sqrt{20} \cdot (-1.329)$$
$$= -\$3.443 \text{ million}$$

The utility of share $\alpha = 1$ is

$$U(-3.443) = 2[1 - e^{-1/2(-3.443)}] = -9.186$$

The profit for share $\alpha = .25$ is $.25(-3.443) = -.861$. The utility of share $\alpha = .25$ is

$$U(-.861) = -1.076$$

The utility of share $\alpha = .50$ is

$$U(-1.722) = -2.730$$

The utility of share $\alpha = .75$ is

$$U(-2.582) = -5.274$$

This sample outcome and four others are summarized in Table 15.11.

TABLE 15.11

Outcome y	z = Profit of Whole Project	Utility of Share $\alpha = 1.0$	Utility of Share $\alpha = \frac{3}{4}$	Utility of Share $\alpha = \frac{1}{2}$	Utility of Share $\alpha = \frac{1}{4}$
-1.329	-3.443	-9.186	-5.274	-2.730	-1.076
$+.301$	$+3.846$	$+1.708$	$+1.527$	$+1.235$	$+.763$
-1.772	-5.424	-28.124	-13.289	-5.761	-1.940
$+.905$	$+6.547$	$+1.924$	$+1.828$	$+1.611$	$+1.118$
$-.481$	$+.349$	$+.320$	$+.245$	$+.167$	$+.085$
$-.475$	$+.3750$	-6.672	-2.992	-1.096	$-.210$

The last line shows the average utility of the four alternatives. Comparison of these average utilities reveals that the share $\alpha = .25$ is the best share compared to the alternatives .50, .75, and 1.00. However, the result is not reliable because of the small sample size. It appears that the share $\alpha = 0$ would be optimum because its utility is zero and the best of the other alternatives has smaller (negative) utility. This has happened by chance; the average profit of the five samples is about 1 standard deviation below its expected value. The expected profit of the whole project is 2.5, whereas the sample average is .3750. Thus the actual deviation of the simulation average is 2.125. The variance of one trial is 20. The variance of the average of five trials is $(\frac{1}{5})(20) = 4$. Thus the standard deviation of the sample is $\sqrt{4} = 2$. The actual outcome is about 1 standard deviation low.

This chance distortion may be avoided by taking a much larger sample. Four more separate simulations were performed for this example to show convergence. The results of all five simulation runs are shown in Table 15.12.

TABLE 15.12

Sample Size, n	Average y	Average $U(z)$	Average $U(.75z)$	Average $U(.50z)$	Average $U(.25z)$
5	−.475	−6.672	−2.992	−1.096	−.210
10	−.482	−7.327	−3.126	−1.114	−.214
100	−.304	−8.464	−2.899	− .770	−.025
1000	−.051	−4.272	−1.268	− .104	+.236
10,000	−.015	−4.325	−1.152	− .025	+.272

The last simulation is likely to give the most accurate results because of the large sample size. These results can be compared to the true answers found in Chap. 11. However, rather than comparing the average utility to the true expected utility, it is better to compare the results in terms of the risk-adjusted values. The risk-adjusted value v associated with the expected utility U can be found by solving

$$U = \frac{1}{r}(1 - e^{-rv})$$

for v, to get

$$v = -\frac{1}{r}\ln(1 - rU)$$

For example, the average utility of −4.325 corresponds to

$$v = -2\ln[1 - 2(-4.325)]$$
$$= -2.301$$

The true risk-adjusted value of share α has been found previously to be

$$v(\alpha) = 2.5\alpha - 5\alpha^2$$

The comparison of the simulation with the true values is given in Table 15.13.

TABLE 15.13 Risk-adjusted Values

	Share $\alpha = 1$	Share $\alpha = \frac{3}{4}$	Share $\alpha = \frac{1}{2}$	Share $\alpha = \frac{1}{4}$
Simulation	-2.303	$-.8926$	$-.0248$	$+.2924$
True	-2.500	$-.9375$	0	$+.3125$

It is seen that the simulation results happen to be low by about \$0.02 (million) in all cases but are sufficiently accurate to determine the optimal share.

Simulation has frequently been used in practice to determine the probability distribution of return from large and risky investment projects. Often the probability distribution is found to be significantly different from the normal distribution used in this example.

15.6 A PORTFOLIO EXAMPLE

Section 11.8 presented an example of an investor who has C dollars and is considering two stocks for inclusion in his portfolio. The two stocks are not independent. The investments will be held for a 1-year period. The return per dollar invested in stock i is $1 + \tilde{x}_i$, where $\tilde{x}_i$ is a random variable. The decision variables are c_1 and c_2, the dollar investments in stocks 1 and 2, respectively. The investor can borrow money at interest rate I or lend his idle money at the same riskless interest rate. The total return from the stock investment is

$$c_1(1 + \tilde{x}_1) + c_2(1 + \tilde{x}_2)$$

The net profit, allowing for the options to borrow or lend, is

$$\tilde{z} = CI + c_1(\tilde{x}_1 - I) + c_2(\tilde{x}_2 - I)$$

The random variables $\tilde{x}_1$ and $\tilde{x}_2$ are jointly normally distributed. The meaning of this statement has not been explained in this text. However, it is possible to generate outcomes of this random process by generating just one outcome for the total profit $\tilde{z}$. The single random variable $\tilde{z}$ has a normal distribution with mean $E(\tilde{z}) = CI + c_1(\mu_1 - I) + c_2(\mu_2 - I)$ and variance $V(\tilde{z}) = c_1^2\sigma_1^2 + 2c_1c_2\rho\sigma_1\sigma_2 + c_2^2\sigma_2^2$, where the parameters μ_1, μ_2, σ_1^2, σ_2^2, and ρ are the means and variances of the two random variables $\tilde{x}_1$ and $\tilde{x}_2$, and ρ is the correlation between them, as described in Sec. 11.8.

Suppose that the parameter values are

$$\text{Stock 1:} \quad \mu_1 = .068 \quad \sigma_1^2 = .0009 \quad \sigma_1 = .03$$
$$\text{Stock 2:} \quad \mu_2 = .056 \quad \sigma_2^2 = .0004 \quad \sigma_2 = .02$$

Correlation: $\rho = .2$

Interest rate: $I = .04$

Initial capital: $C = \$5000$

The profit is $\tilde{z} = 200 + c_1(\tilde{x}_1 - .04) + c_2(\tilde{x}_2 - .04)$, a function of the decision variables and the outcomes. The expected profit is

$$E(\tilde{z}) = 200 + c_1(.028) + c_2(.016)$$

The variance of profit is

$$V(\tilde{z}) = 10^{-4}[9c_1^2 + 2.4c_1c_2 + 4c_2^2]$$

These are functions of only the decision variables.

Suppose, as in Sec. 11.8, that the investor's attitude toward risk can be described by an exponential utility function for profit z with parameter $r = .01$.

$$U(z) = 100(1 - e^{-.01z})$$

The optimum portfolio was defined in Chap. 11 in terms of maximization of expected utility, or equivalently, maximization of risk-adjusted value. The optimization problem was solved in Chap. 3; the result obtained was that the optimum investments were $c_1 = \$2685$ and $c_2 = \$3194$ when no constraint on borrowing was imposed. The total investment was $c_1 + c_2 = \$5879$, which was achieved by borrowing \$879 to be repaid at the end of the year. The risk-adjusted profit of this optimum investment was $U(2685,3194) = \$263.16$.

In this chapter the problem will be solved by simulation, considering only a small set of possible decisions. Integer units of \$1000 up to 4 units will be considered for each investment. Thus a total of 25 possible decisions will be evaluated. The decision space is shown in Fig. 15.12.

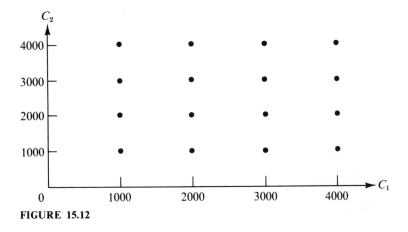

FIGURE 15.12

The first step of one iteration of the simulation process is to generate a random number y from a standard normal probability distribution. For example, $y = -1.329$. Next, transform this into a portfolio profit for each of the 25 possible portfolio decisions, using the mean and variance formulas. For example, for $c_1 = 2000$ and $c_2 = 3000$, the mean and variance are

$$E(\tilde{z}) = 200 + 2000(.028) + 3000(.016)$$
$$= 200 + 56 + 48$$
$$= 304$$

$$V(\tilde{z}) = 10^{-4}[9(2000)^2 + 2.4(2000 \times 3000) + 4(3000)^2]$$
$$= 3600 + 1440 + 3600$$
$$= 8640$$

The standard deviation is $SD(\tilde{z}) = 92.95$. The outcome of portfolio profit, for this portfolio and this random number, is

$$z = E(z) + y \quad SD(\tilde{z})$$
$$= 304 + y(92.95)$$
$$= 304 + (-1.329)(92.95)$$
$$= 180.47$$

Now compute the utility of this profit:

$$U(180.47) = 100[1 - e^{-.01(180.47)}]$$
$$= 83.55$$

This outcome happens to not be a favorable one because the utility of investing the whole $5000 at the riskless rate of return would give a certain profit of $200, whose utility would be $U(200) = 86.46$. Similarly, the utility of all the other 25 possible decisions must be found for this outcome. This whole process must be repeated for many random numbers, and the outcomes must be averaged.

The simulation was done with 10,000 samples. The resulting average utility values are given in Table 15.14.

TABLE 15.14 Average Utilities (Based upon 10,000 Samples)

	$c_2 = 0$	$c_2 = 1000$	$c_2 = 2000$	$c_2 = 3000$	$c_2 = 4000$
$c_1 = 0$	86.467	88.194	89.278	89.867	90.043
$c_1 = 1000$	89.244	90.521	91.295	91.682	91.736
$c_1 = 2000$	90.646	91.662	92.262	92.529	92.506
$c_1 = 3000$	91.119	91.996	92.495	92.685	92.594
$c_1 = 4000$	90.825	91.643	92.087	92.219	92.059

The risk-adjusted values corresponding to these average utilities are found by

$$v = -100 \ln (1 - .01 U)$$

The risk-adjusted values of all 25 decisions are given by Table 15.15.

TABLE 15.15   Risk-adjusted Values Determined by Simulation

	$c_2 = 0$	$c_2 = 1000$	$c_2 = 2000$	$c_2 = 3000$	$c_2 = 4000$
$c_1 = 0$	200.00	213.66	223.29	228.94	230.69
$c_1 = 1000$	222.98	235.60	244.13	248.67	249.33
$c_1 = 2000$	236.94	248.44	255.91	259.43	259.10
$c_1 = 3000$	242.13	252.52	258.96	261.52	260.30
$c_1 = 4000$	238.87	248.21	253.67	255.35	253.32

True values, found by the methods of Chap. 11, are shown in Table 15.16.

TABLE 15.16   True Risk-adjusted Values

	$c_2 = 0$	$c_2 = 1000$	$c_2 = 2000$	$c_2 = 3000$	$c_2 = 4000$
$c_1 = 0$	200.00	214.00	224.00	230.00	232.00
$c_1 = 1000$	223.50	236.30	245.10	249.90	250.70
$c_2 = 2000$	238.00	249.60	257.20	260.80	260.40
$c_3 = 3000$	243.50	253.90	260.30	262.70	261.10
$c_4 = 4000$	240.00	249.20	254.40	255.60	252.80

The simulation has determined that the best of these 25 alternative decisions is $c_1 = \$3000$ and $c_2 = \$3000$. This is verified by the true risk-adjusted values shown.

A further, more refined search could be undertaken around the point $c_1 = 3000$, $c_2 = 3000$ to determine whether a better solution can be found. The results of Chap. 3 indicate that $c_1 = 2500$, $c_2 = 3000$ would be a better solution. However, because the objective function is changing by only a few dollars in the region around the current solution, this additional effort is not worthwhile.

PROBLEMS

1. Refer to the pipeline Prob. 6, Chap. 9. Show how to use simulation to find the valve spacing that minimizes expected total cost. Consider the three alternative decisions $d = 100$, 150, and 200 miles. Generate five samples to illustrate the simulation process.

2. Refer to the bidding problem of Sec. 10.6. The best (lowest) competitor's bid

has uniform probability density between $1.9 and 2.3 million. The firm wishes to find the bid B that maximizes their expected profit.

(a) Give random numbers uniformly distributed between zero and 1 and show how to transform them into observations of the best competitor's bid. Use five samples to illustrate.

(b) Find the actual profit for each of the decisions B = 2.0, 2.1, 2.2, and 2.3 for each of the five outcomes of part (a). Find the average profit of each of the alternative decisions and compare them with the true values found in Chap. 10.

3. The Theatre Corporation leases films for exhibition at its chain of movie theatres. There is considerable uncertainty in the value of any particular film at the time when the decision to enter the lease agreement must be made. Suppose that the lease agreement under consideration requires the Theatre Corporation to pay $1 million in advance payment, for which they will receive 5 percent of gross receipts from the film. Suppose that the probability distribution of gross receipts is normal, with a mean of $60 million and a standard deviation of $20 million.

The Theatre Corporation uses the expected-value decision criterion and wants to find the expected value of perfect information about the future gross receipts of the film.

(a) Let y be a random number from the standard normal distribution. Show how to transform y into z = Theatre Corporation's profit if they enter the lease agreement. Illustrate with five samples.

(b) If the Theatre Corporation has no additional information, their optimum expected-value decision is to enter into the lease agreement. Show how to use simulation to find the expected profit when perfect information is available in time to use in making the lease decision. Illustrate with the five samples of part (a). The savings caused by having perfect information is the expected value of perfect information. Its value, found by analytic methods (not shown in this text) is $0.008491 million = $8491.

(c) Find the actual value of perfect information associated with each outcome of the five samples of part (a).

4. Show how to solve by simulation Prob. 1, Chap. 11. Evaluate the decisions n = 1, 16, 25, and 100, using two samples to illustrate the process.

5. Show how to solve by simulation Prob. 4, Chap. 11. Evaluate the alternative decisions of investing $5000, $10,000, $20,000, and $30,000, using two samples to illustrate the process.

6. The Colorless Cab Corporation (CCC) has a fleet of 100 taxicabs in operation. The total fleet generates accidents at a rate of eight accidents per year. The loss size (severity) of each accident is a random variable. Its probability distribution

is exponential, with an average size of $1000. The CCC has an attitude toward risk that can be represented by the exponential utility function with parameter $r = \frac{1}{2} \times 10^{-3} = .0005$.

(a) Show how to use simulation to find the expected utility of a 1-year insurance policy that would pay all claims fully. (*Hint:* generate first the number of accidents in 1 year, using the Poisson distribution. Then generate the loss size for each accident, using the exponential probability distribution.) The results from analytic analysis show that the expected total loss in 1 year is $8000. The risk-adjusted value of full insurance is $16,000.

(b) The CCC wishes to investigate the alternative of a high deductible level. (A policy having deductible D applied to each accident. For each accident the CCC would pay their whole losses up to size D.) For a loss $x > D$, the insurance company would pay $x - D$ and the CCC would pay D. Show how to find the expected utility of a policy with deductible level $D = \$800$.

SERIES

SUM OF THE FIRST n INTEGERS

$$1 + 2 + 3 + \cdots + n = \sum_{i=1}^{n} i = \frac{n(n + 1)}{2}$$

SUM OF AN ARITHMETIC SERIES

$$a + (a + b) + (a + 2b) + \cdots + [a + (n - 1)b] = \sum_{i=1}^{n} [a + b(i - 1)]$$

Any series whose successive terms all increase by the same constant amount is of this form. Here

$$a = \text{first term}$$

$$b = \text{constant increment}$$

The sum is

$$\sum_{i=1}^{n} [a + b(i - 1)] = \frac{n}{2} [2a + b(n - 1)]$$

This can be derived from the sum of the integers:

$$\sum_{i=1}^{n} [a + b(i - 1)] = an + b \sum_{i=1}^{n} (i - 1) = an + b \frac{n(n - 1)}{2}$$

SUM OF A GEOMETRIC SERIES

$$1 + r + r^2 + \cdots + r^n = \sum_{i=0}^{n} r^i = \frac{1 - r^{n+1}}{1 - r}$$

for any number r, as can be verified by multiplying both sides by $(1 - r)$.

The infinite geometric series

$$1 + r + r^2 + \cdots \qquad \text{to infinity}$$

has a finite sum only if $0 < r < 1$. It is

$$1 + r + r^2 + \cdots = \frac{1}{1 - r}$$

DERIVATIVE GEOMETRIC SERIES

The series

$$1 + 2r + 3r^2 + 4r^3 + \cdots = \sum_{i=0}^{n} i r^{i-1} \qquad \text{for } 0 < r < 1$$

is the derivative of the infinite geometric series with respect to r. The sum is

$$\sum_{i=0}^{n} i r^{i-1} = \frac{1}{(1 - r)^2}$$

This can be verified by differentiation of the sum of the infinite geometric series. It is similarly restricted to $0 < r < 1$.

BINOMIAL SERIES EXPANSION

$$(a + b)^n = \sum_{m=0}^{n} \frac{n!}{m! \, (n - m)!} a^m b^{n-m}$$

For positive integer n, this is a finite series with $n + 1$ terms.

SERIES EXPANSION OF THE EXPONENTIAL FUNCTION

$$e^{ax} = 1 + ax + \frac{(ax)^2}{2!} + \frac{(ax)^3}{3!} + \cdots = \sum_{i=0}^{\infty} \frac{(ax)^i}{i!}$$

SERIES EXPANSION FOR THE NATURAL LOGARITHM FUNCTION

$$\ln(1 + x) = x - \frac{1}{2} x^2 + \frac{1}{3} x^3 - \frac{1}{4} x^4 + \cdots \qquad \text{for } -1 < x < 1$$

Appendix B

DERIVATIVES

The derivative of a function $f(x)$ with respect to its argument x is the slope of the tangent to the curve at x. It is the "instantaneous" rate of change of $f(x)$ with respect to x (see Fig. B.1). The derivative is a function of x. For example, it has different values at x_1 and x_2 in Fig. B.1.

Let a be a constant. Let u and v be functions of x. Let e be the base of the natural logarithm ($e = 2.71828\ldots$). Let $\ln x$ be the natural logarithm. The following derivative formulas are useful:

$$\frac{da}{dx} = 0$$

$$\frac{dx}{dx} = 1$$

$$\frac{dx^n}{dx} = nx^{n-1}$$

$$\frac{de^x}{dx} = e^x$$

$$\frac{d \ln x}{dx} = \frac{1}{x}$$

$$\frac{da^x}{dx} = a^x \ln a$$

The derivative of a function of x:

$$\frac{d}{dx} (au) = a \frac{du}{dx}$$

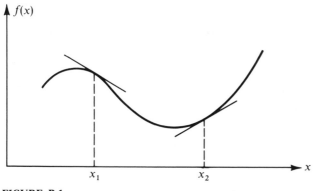

FIGURE B.1

The derivative of a sum of functions:

$$\frac{d}{dx}(u + v) = \frac{du}{dx} + \frac{dv}{dx}$$

The derivative of a product of functions:

$$\frac{d}{dx}(uv) = u\frac{dv}{dx} + v\frac{du}{dx}$$

The derivative of a ratio of functions:

$$\frac{d}{dx}\left(\frac{u}{v}\right) = \frac{v(du/dx) - u(dv/dx)}{v^2}$$

The chain rule for the derivative of a function of a function:

$$\frac{d}{dx}f(u) = \frac{df(u)}{du}\frac{du}{dx}$$

Applications of the chain rule:

$$\frac{d}{dx}e^{ax} = ae^{ax}$$

$$\frac{d}{dx}(\ln u) = \frac{1}{u}\frac{du}{dx}$$

$$\frac{d}{dx}e^u = e^u\frac{du}{dx}$$

$$\frac{d}{dx}a^u = a^u\ln a\frac{du}{dx}$$

FUNCTION OF TWO VARIABLES

The function $f(x,y)$ has two partial derivatives:

$$\frac{\partial f(x,y)}{\partial x}$$

is found by treating y as a constant. Similarly

$$\frac{\partial f(x,y)}{\partial y}$$

is found by treating x as a constant.

The "total derivative" is found from

$$df = \frac{\partial f(x,y)}{\partial x}\, dx + \frac{\partial f(x,y)}{\partial y}\, dy$$

Appendix C

INTEGRALS

The definite integral of the function $f(x)$ with respect to x from $x = a$ to $x = b$ is the area under the $f(x)$ curve between a and b (see Fig. C.1). The notation is

$$\int_a^b f(x)\,dx$$

Let $f'(x)$ represent the derivative of $f(x)$. The following equation shows that the process of integration is opposite to the process of differentiation:

$$\int_a^b f'(x)\,dx = f(x)\bigg|_a^b = f(b) - f(a)$$

It also shows that the vertical bar represents evaluation of the function between two points.

Let a and b continue to represent two specific x values. Let c and d represent constants. Let u and v be functions of x. Then

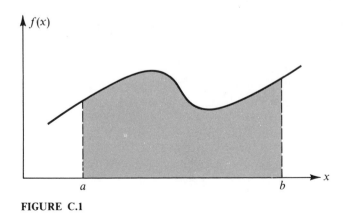

FIGURE C.1

$$\int_a^b c\,dx = cx\,\Big|_a^b = (b-a)c$$

$$\int_a^b cf(x)\,dx = c\int_a^b f(x)\,dx$$

$$\int_a^b (u+v)\,dx = \int_a^b u\,dx + \int_a^b v\,dx$$

$$\int_a^b cx^n\,dx = c\,\frac{x^{n+1}}{n+1}\Big|_a^b \qquad \text{for } n \neq -1$$

$$\int_a^b \frac{1}{x}\,dx = \ln x\,\Big|_a^b = \ln b - \ln a = \ln\frac{b}{a}$$

$$\int_a^b \ln x\,dx = (x\ln x - x)\,\Big|_a^b$$

$$\int_a^b e^{cx}\,dx = \frac{1}{c}\,e^{cx}\,\Big|_a^b$$

$$\int_a^b xe^{cx}\,dx = \left[\frac{1}{c^2}\,e^{cx}(cx-1)\right]\Big|_a^b$$

The definite integral

$$I(x) = \int_{a(x)}^{b(x)} f(x,y)\,dy$$

is a function of x through the limits $a(x)$ and $b(x)$ as well as through $f(x,y)$. Its derivative with respect to x is

$$\frac{d}{dx}I(x) = \int_{a(x)}^{b(x)} \frac{\partial f(x,y)}{\partial x}\,dy + f[x,b(x)]\frac{db}{dx} - f[x,a(x)]\frac{da}{dx}$$

SOME DEFINITE INTEGRALS WITH SPECIFIC LIMITS

$$\int_{-\infty}^{+\infty} e^{-x^2/2}\,dx = \sqrt{2\pi}$$

$$\int_0^\infty x^{n-1}e^{-ax}\,dx = \frac{(n-1)!}{a^n} \qquad \text{for } n > -0, a > 0$$

Appendix D

TABLES

TABLE D.1 Negative Exponential Function —exp(− X), 0.000 to 0.349

	0.000	0.001	0.002	0.003	0.004	0.005	0.006	0.007	0.008	0.009
0.00	1.0000	0.9990	0.9980	0.9970	0.9960	0.9950	0.9940	0.9930	0.9920	0.9910
0.01	0.9900	0.9891	0.9881	0.9871	0.9861	0.9851	0.9841	0.9831	0.9822	0.9812
0.02	0.9802	0.9792	0.9782	0.9773	0.9763	0.9753	0.9743	0.9734	0.9724	0.9714
0.03	0.9704	0.9695	0.9685	0.9675	0.9666	0.9656	0.9646	0.9637	0.9627	0.9618
0.04	0.9608	0.9598	0.9589	0.9579	0.9570	0.9560	0.9550	0.9541	0.9531	0.9522
0.05	0.9512	0.9503	0.9493	0.9484	0.9474	0.9465	0.9455	0.9446	0.9436	0.9427
0.06	0.9418	0.9408	0.9399	0.9389	0.9380	0.9371	0.9361	0.9352	0.9343	0.9333
0.07	0.9324	0.9315	0.9305	0.9296	0.9287	0.9277	0.9268	0.9259	0.9250	0.9240
0.08	0.9231	0.9222	0.9213	0.9204	0.9194	0.9185	0.9176	0.9167	0.9158	0.9148
0.09	0.9139	0.9130	0.9121	0.9112	0.9103	0.9094	0.9085	0.9076	0.9066	0.9057
0.10	0.9048	0.9039	0.9030	0.9021	0.9012	0.9003	0.8994	0.8985	0.8976	0.8967
0.11	0.8958	0.8949	0.8940	0.8932	0.8923	0.8914	0.8905	0.8896	0.8887	0.8878
0.12	0.8869	0.8860	0.8851	0.8843	0.8834	0.8825	0.8816	0.8807	0.8799	0.8790
0.13	0.8781	0.8772	0.8763	0.8755	0.8746	0.8737	0.8728	0.8720	0.8711	0.8702
0.14	0.8694	0.8685	0.8676	0.8668	0.8659	0.8650	0.8642	0.8633	0.8624	0.8616
0.15	0.8607	0.8598	0.8590	0.8581	0.8573	0.8564	0.8556	0.8547	0.8538	0.8530
0.16	0.8521	0.8513	0.8504	0.8496	0.8487	0.8479	0.8470	0.8462	0.8454	0.8445
0.17	0.8437	0.8428	0.8420	0.8411	0.8403	0.8395	0.8386	0.8378	0.8369	0.8361
0.18	0.8353	0.8344	0.8336	0.8328	0.8319	0.8311	0.8303	0.8294	0.8286	0.8278
0.19	0.8270	0.8261	0.8253	0.8245	0.8237	0.8228	0.8220	0.8212	0.8204	0.8195
0.20	0.8187	0.8179	0.8171	0.8163	0.8155	0.8146	0.8138	0.8130	0.8122	0.8114
0.21	0.8106	0.8098	0.8090	0.8082	0.8073	0.8065	0.8057	0.8049	0.8041	0.8033
0.22	0.8025	0.8017	0.8009	0.8001	0.7993	0.7985	0.7977	0.7969	0.7961	0.7953
0.23	0.7945	0.7937	0.7929	0.7922	0.7914	0.7906	0.7898	0.7890	0.7882	0.7874
0.24	0.7866	0.7858	0.7851	0.7843	0.7835	0.7827	0.7819	0.7811	0.7804	0.7796
0.25	0.7788	0.7780	0.7772	0.7765	0.7757	0.7749	0.7741	0.7734	0.7726	0.7718
0.26	0.7711	0.7703	0.7695	0.7687	0.7680	0.7672	0.7664	0.7657	0.7649	0.7641
0.27	0.7634	0.7626	0.7619	0.7611	0.7603	0.7596	0.7588	0.7581	0.7573	0.7565
0.28	0.7558	0.7550	0.7543	0.7535	0.7528	0.7520	0.7513	0.7505	0.7498	0.7490
0.29	0.7483	0.7475	0.7468	0.7460	0.7453	0.7445	0.7438	0.7430	0.7423	0.7416
0.30	0.7408	0.7401	0.7393	0.7386	0.7379	0.7371	0.7364	0.7357	0.7349	0.7342
0.31	0.7334	0.7327	0.7320	0.7312	0.7305	0.7298	0.7291	0.7283	0.7276	0.7269
0.32	0.7261	0.7254	0.7247	0.7240	0.7233	0.7225	0.7218	0.7211	0.7204	0.7196
0.33	0.7189	0.7182	0.7175	0.7168	0.7161	0.7153	0.7146	0.7139	0.7132	0.7125
0.34	0.7118	0.7111	0.7103	0.7096	0.7089	0.7082	0.7075	0.7068	0.7061	0.7054

0.350 to 0.699

	0.000	0.001	0.002	0.003	0.004	0.005	0.006	0.007	0.008	0.009
0.35	0.7047	0.7040	0.7033	0.7026	0.7019	0.7012	0.7005	0.6998	0.6991	0.6984
0.36	0.6977	0.6970	0.6963	0.6956	0.6949	0.6942	0.6935	0.6928	0.6921	0.6914
0.37	0.6907	0.6900	0.6894	0.6887	0.6880	0.6873	0.6866	0.6859	0.6852	0.6845
0.38	0.6839	0.6832	0.6825	0.6818	0.6811	0.6805	0.6798	0.6791	0.6784	0.6777
0.39	0.6771	0.6764	0.6757	0.6750	0.6744	0.6737	0.6730	0.6723	0.6717	0.6710
0.40	0.6703	0.6697	0.6690	0.6683	0.6676	0.6670	0.6663	0.6656	0.6650	0.6643
0.41	0.6637	0.6630	0.6623	0.6617	0.6610	0.6603	0.6597	0.6590	0.6584	0.6577
0.42	0.6570	0.6564	0.6557	0.6551	0.6544	0.6538	0.6531	0.6525	0.6518	0.6512
0.43	0.6505	0.6499	0.6492	0.6486	0.6479	0.6473	0.6466	0.6460	0.6453	0.6447
0.44	0.6440	0.6434	0.6427	0.6421	0.6415	0.6408	0.6402	0.6395	0.6389	0.6383
0.45	0.6376	0.6370	0.6364	0.6357	0.6351	0.6344	0.6338	0.6332	0.6325	0.6319
0.46	0.6313	0.6307	0.6300	0.6294	0.6288	0.6281	0.6275	0.6269	0.6263	0.6256
0.47	0.6250	0.6244	0.6238	0.6231	0.6225	0.6219	0.6213	0.6206	0.6200	0.6194
0.48	0.6188	0.6182	0.6175	0.6169	0.6163	0.6157	0.6151	0.6145	0.6139	0.6132
0.49	0.6126	0.6120	0.6114	0.6108	0.6102	0.6096	0.6090	0.6084	0.6077	0.6071
0.50	0.6065	0.6059	0.6053	0.6047	0.6041	0.6035	0.6029	0.6023	0.6017	0.6011
0.51	0.6005	0.5999	0.5993	0.5987	0.5981	0.5975	0.5969	0.5963	0.5957	0.5951
0.52	0.5945	0.5939	0.5933	0.5927	0.5921	0.5916	0.5910	0.5904	0.5898	0.5892
0.53	0.5886	0.5880	0.5874	0.5868	0.5863	0.5857	0.5851	0.5845	0.5839	0.5833
0.54	0.5827	0.5822	0.5816	0.5810	0.5804	0.5798	0.5793	0.5787	0.5781	0.5775
0.55	0.5769	0.5764	0.5758	0.5752	0.5746	0.5741	0.5735	0.5729	0.5724	0.5718
0.56	0.5712	0.5706	0.5701	0.5695	0.5689	0.5684	0.5678	0.5672	0.5667	0.5661
0.57	0.5655	0.5650	0.5644	0.5638	0.5633	0.5627	0.5621	0.5616	0.5610	0.5605
0.58	0.5599	0.5593	0.5588	0.5582	0.5577	0.5571	0.5565	0.5560	0.5554	0.5549
0.59	0.5543	0.5538	0.5532	0.5527	0.5521	0.5516	0.5510	0.5505	0.5499	0.5494
0.60	0.5488	0.5483	0.5477	0.5472	0.5466	0.5461	0.5455	0.5450	0.5444	0.5439
0.61	0.5434	0.5428	0.5423	0.5417	0.5412	0.5406	0.5401	0.5396	0.5390	0.5385
0.62	0.5379	0.5374	0.5369	0.5363	0.5358	0.5353	0.5347	0.5342	0.5337	0.5331
0.63	0.5326	0.5321	0.5315	0.5310	0.5305	0.5299	0.5294	0.5289	0.5283	0.5278
0.64	0.5273	0.5268	0.5262	0.5257	0.5252	0.5247	0.5241	0.5236	0.5231	0.5226
0.65	0.5220	0.5215	0.5210	0.5205	0.5200	0.5194	0.5189	0.5184	0.5179	0.5174
0.66	0.5169	0.5163	0.5158	0.5153	0.5148	0.5143	0.5138	0.5132	0.5127	0.5122
0.67	0.5117	0.5112	0.5107	0.5102	0.5097	0.5092	0.5086	0.5081	0.5076	0.5071
0.68	0.5066	0.5061	0.5056	0.5051	0.5046	0.5041	0.5036	0.5031	0.5026	0.5021
0.69	0.5016	0.5011	0.5006	0.5001	0.4996	0.4991	0.4986	0.4981	0.4976	0.4971

TABLE D.1 Negative Exponential Function *(Continued)*, 0.700 to 0.999

	0.000	0.001	0.002	0.003	0.004	0.005	0.006	0.007	0.008	0.009
0.70	0.4966	0.4961	0.4956	0.4951	0.4946	0.4941	0.4936	0.4931	0.4926	0.4921
0.71	0.4916	0.4912	0.4907	0.4902	0.4897	0.4892	0.4887	0.4882	0.4877	0.4872
0.72	0.4868	0.4863	0.4858	0.4853	0.4848	0.4843	0.4838	0.4834	0.4829	0.4824
0.73	0.4819	0.4814	0.4809	0.4805	0.4800	0.4795	0.4790	0.4785	0.4781	0.4776
0.74	0.4771	0.4766	0.4762	0.4757	0.4752	0.4747	0.4743	0.4738	0.4733	0.4728
0.75	0.4724	0.4719	0.4714	0.4710	0.4705	0.4700	0.4695	0.4691	0.4686	0.4681
0.76	0.4677	0.4672	0.4667	0.4663	0.4658	0.4653	0.4649	0.4644	0.4639	0.4635
0.77	0.4630	0.4626	0.4621	0.4616	0.4612	0.4607	0.4602	0.4598	0.4593	0.4589
0.78	0.4584	0.4579	0.4575	0.4570	0.4566	0.4561	0.4557	0.4552	0.4548	0.4543
0.79	0.4538	0.4534	0.4529	0.4525	0.4520	0.4516	0.4511	0.4507	0.4502	0.4498
0.80	0.4493	0.4489	0.4484	0.4480	0.4475	0.4471	0.4466	0.4462	0.4457	0.4453
0.81	0.4449	0.4444	0.4440	0.4435	0.4431	0.4426	0.4422	0.4418	0.4413	0.4409
0.82	0.4404	0.4400	0.4396	0.4391	0.4387	0.4382	0.4378	0.4374	0.4369	0.4365
0.83	0.4360	0.4356	0.4352	0.4347	0.4343	0.4339	0.4334	0.4330	0.4326	0.4321
0.84	0.4317	0.4313	0.4308	0.4304	0.4300	0.4296	0.4291	0.4287	0.4283	0.4278
0.85	0.4274	0.4270	0.4266	0.4261	0.4257	0.4253	0.4249	0.4244	0.4240	0.4236
0.86	0.4232	0.4227	0.4223	0.4219	0.4215	0.4211	0.4206	0.4202	0.4198	0.4194
0.87	0.4190	0.4185	0.4181	0.4177	0.4173	0.4169	0.4164	0.4160	0.4156	0.4152
0.88	0.4148	0.4144	0.4140	0.4135	0.4131	0.4127	0.4123	0.4119	0.4115	0.4111
0.89	0.4107	0.4102	0.4098	0.4094	0.4090	0.4086	0.4082	0.4078	0.4074	0.4070
0.90	0.4066	0.4062	0.4058	0.4054	0.4049	0.4045	0.4041	0.4037	0.4033	0.4029
0.91	0.4025	0.4021	0.4017	0.4013	0.4009	0.4005	0.4001	0.3997	0.3993	0.3989
0.92	0.3985	0.3981	0.3977	0.3973	0.3969	0.3965	0.3961	0.3957	0.3953	0.3949
0.93	0.3946	0.3942	0.3938	0.3934	0.3930	0.3926	0.3922	0.3918	0.3914	0.3910
0.94	0.3906	0.3902	0.3898	0.3895	0.3891	0.3887	0.3883	0.3879	0.3875	0.3871
0.95	0.3867	0.3864	0.3860	0.3856	0.3852	0.3848	0.3844	0.3840	0.3837	0.3833
0.96	0.3829	0.3825	0.3821	0.3817	0.3814	0.3810	0.3806	0.3802	0.3798	0.3795
0.97	0.3791	0.3787	0.3783	0.3779	0.3776	0.3772	0.3768	0.3764	0.3761	0.3757
0.98	0.3753	0.3749	0.3746	0.3742	0.3738	0.3734	0.3731	0.3727	0.3723	0.3719
0.99	0.3716	0.3712	0.3708	0.3705	0.3701	0.3697	0.3694	0.3690	0.3686	0.3682

1.00 to 3.99

	0.00	0.01	0.02	0.03	0.04	0.05	0.06	0.07	0.08	0.09
1.0	0.36788	0.36422	0.36059	0.35701	0.35345	0.34994	0.34646	0.34301	0.33960	0.33622
1.1	0.33287	0.32956	0.32628	0.32303	0.31982	0.31664	0.31349	0.31037	0.30728	0.30422
1.2	0.30119	0.29820	0.29523	0.29229	0.28938	0.28650	0.28365	0.28083	0.27804	0.27527
1.3	0.27253	0.26982	0.26714	0.26448	0.26185	0.25924	0.25666	0.25411	0.25158	0.24908
1.4	0.24660	0.24414	0.24171	0.23931	0.23693	0.23457	0.23224	0.22993	0.22764	0.22537
1.5	0.22313	0.22091	0.21871	0.21654	0.21438	0.21225	0.21014	0.20805	0.20598	0.20393
1.6	0.20190	0.19989	0.19790	0.19593	0.19398	0.19205	0.19014	0.18825	0.18637	0.18452
1.7	0.18268	0.18087	0.17907	0.17728	0.17552	0.17377	0.17204	0.17033	0.16864	0.16696
1.8	0.16530	0.16365	0.16203	0.16041	0.15882	0.15724	0.15567	0.15412	0.15259	0.15107
1.9	0.14957	0.14808	0.14661	0.14515	0.14370	0.14227	0.14086	0.13946	0.13807	0.13670
2.0	0.13534	0.13399	0.13266	0.13134	0.13003	0.12873	0.12745	0.12619	0.12493	0.12369
2.1	0.12246	0.12124	0.12003	0.11884	0.11765	0.11648	0.11533	0.11418	0.11304	0.11192
2.2	0.11080	0.10970	0.10861	0.10753	0.10646	0.10540	0.10435	0.10331	0.10228	0.10127
2.3	0.10026	0.09926	0.09827	0.09730	0.09633	0.09537	0.09442	0.09348	0.09255	0.09163
2.4	0.09072	0.08982	0.08892	0.08804	0.08716	0.08629	0.08543	0.08458	0.08374	0.08291
2.5	0.08208	0.08127	0.08046	0.07966	0.07887	0.07808	0.07730	0.07654	0.07577	0.07502
2.6	0.07427	0.07353	0.07280	0.07208	0.07136	0.07065	0.06995	0.06925	0.06856	0.06788
2.7	0.06721	0.06654	0.06587	0.06522	0.06457	0.06393	0.06329	0.06266	0.06204	0.06142
2.8	0.06081	0.06020	0.05961	0.05901	0.05843	0.05784	0.05727	0.05670	0.05613	0.05558
2.9	0.05502	0.05448	0.05393	0.05340	0.05287	0.05234	0.05182	0.05130	0.05079	0.05029
3.0	0.04979	0.04929	0.04880	0.04832	0.04783	0.04736	0.04689	0.04642	0.04596	0.04550
3.1	0.04505	0.04460	0.04416	0.04372	0.04328	0.04285	0.04243	0.04200	0.04159	0.04117
3.2	0.04076	0.04036	0.03996	0.03956	0.03916	0.03877	0.03839	0.03801	0.03763	0.03725
3.3	0.03688	0.03652	0.03615	0.03579	0.03544	0.03508	0.03474	0.03439	0.03405	0.03371
3.4	0.03337	0.03304	0.03271	0.03239	0.03206	0.03175	0.03143	0.03112	0.03081	0.03050
3.5	0.03020	0.02990	0.02960	0.02930	0.02901	0.02872	0.02844	0.02816	0.02788	0.02760
3.6	0.02732	0.02705	0.02678	0.02652	0.02625	0.02599	0.02573	0.02548	0.02522	0.02497
3.7	0.02472	0.02448	0.02423	0.02399	0.02375	0.02352	0.02328	0.02305	0.02282	0.02260
3.8	0.02237	0.02215	0.02193	0.02171	0.02149	0.02128	0.02107	0.02086	0.02065	0.02045
3.9	0.02024	0.02004	0.01984	0.01964	0.01945	0.01925	0.01906	0.01887	0.01869	0.01850

TABLE D.1 Negative Exponential Function *(Continued)*, 4.00 to 6.99

	0.00	0.01	0.02	0.03	0.04	0.05	0.06	0.07	0.08	0.09
4.0	0.01832	0.01813	0.01795	0.01777	0.01760	0.01742	0.01725	0.01708	0.01691	0.01674
4.1	0.01657	0.01641	0.01624	0.01608	0.01592	0.01576	0.01561	0.01545	0.01530	0.01515
4.2	0.01500	0.01485	0.01470	0.01455	0.01441	0.01426	0.01412	0.01398	0.01384	0.01370
4.3	0.01357	0.01343	0.01330	0.01317	0.01304	0.01291	0.01278	0.01265	0.01253	0.01240
4.4	0.01228	0.01216	0.01203	0.01191	0.01180	0.01168	0.01156	0.01145	0.01133	0.01122
4.5	0.01111	0.01106	0.01089	0.01078	0.01067	0.01057	0.01046	0.01036	0.01025	0.01015
4.6	0.01005	0.00995	0.00985	0.00975	0.00966	0.00956	0.00947	0.00937	0.00928	0.00919
4.7	0.00910	0.00900	0.00892	0.00883	0.00874	0.00865	0.00857	0.00848	0.00840	0.00831
4.8	0.00823	0.00815	0.00807	0.00799	0.00791	0.00783	0.00775	0.00767	0.00760	0.00752
4.9	0.00745	0.00737	0.00730	0.00723	0.00715	0.00708	0.00701	0.00694	0.00687	0.00681
5.0	0.00674	0.00667	0.00660	0.00654	0.00647	0.00641	0.00635	0.00628	0.00622	0.00616
5.1	0.00610	0.00604	0.00598	0.00592	0.00586	0.00580	0.00574	0.00568	0.00563	0.00557
5.2	0.00552	0.00546	0.00541	0.00535	0.00530	0.00525	0.00520	0.00514	0.00509	0.00504
5.3	0.00499	0.00494	0.00489	0.00484	0.00480	0.00475	0.00470	0.00465	0.00461	0.00456
5.4	0.00452	0.00447	0.00443	0.00438	0.00434	0.00430	0.00425	0.00421	0.00417	0.00413
5.5	0.00409	0.00405	0.00401	0.00397	0.00393	0.00389	0.00385	0.00381	0.00377	0.00374
5.6	0.00370	0.00366	0.00362	0.00359	0.00355	0.00352	0.00348	0.00345	0.00341	0.00338
5.7	0.00335	0.00331	0.00328	0.00325	0.00321	0.00318	0.00315	0.00312	0.00309	0.00306
5.8	0.00303	0.00300	0.00297	0.00294	0.00291	0.00288	0.00285	0.00282	0.00279	0.00277
5.9	0.00274	0.00271	0.00269	0.00266	0.00263	0.00261	0.00258	0.00255	0.00253	0.00250
6.0	0.00248	0.00245	0.00243	0.00241	0.00238	0.00236	0.00233	0.00231	0.00229	0.00227
6.1	0.00224	0.00222	0.00220	0.00218	0.00215	0.00213	0.00211	0.00209	0.00207	0.00205
6.2	0.00203	0.00201	0.00199	0.00197	0.00195	0.00193	0.00191	0.00189	0.00187	0.00185
6.3	0.00184	0.00182	0.00180	0.00178	0.00176	0.00175	0.00173	0.00171	0.00170	0.00168
6.4	0.00166	0.00165	0.00163	0.00161	0.00160	0.00158	0.00156	0.00155	0.00153	0.00152
6.5	0.00150	0.00149	0.00147	0.00146	0.00144	0.00143	0.00142	0.00140	0.00139	0.00137
6.6	0.00136	0.00135	0.00133	0.00132	0.00131	0.00129	0.00128	0.00127	0.00126	0.00124
6.7	0.00123	0.00122	0.00121	0.00119	0.00118	0.00117	0.00116	0.00115	0.00114	0.00112
6.8	0.00111	0.00110	0.00109	0.00108	0.00107	0.00106	0.00105	0.00104	0.00103	0.00102
6.9	0.00101	0.00100	0.00099	0.00098	0.00097	0.00096	0.00095	0.00094	0.00093	0.00092

7.00 to 9.99

	0.00	0.01	0.02	0.03	0.04	0.05	0.06	0.07	0.08	0.09
7.0	0.00091	0.00090	0.00089	0.00088	0.00088	0.00087	0.00086	0.00085	0.00084	0.00083
7.1	0.00083	0.00082	0.00081	0.00080	0.00079	0.00078	0.00078	0.00077	0.00076	0.00075
7.2	0.00075	0.00074	0.00073	0.00072	0.00072	0.00071	0.00070	0.00070	0.00069	0.00068
7.3	0.00068	0.00067	0.00066	0.00066	0.00065	0.00064	0.00064	0.00063	0.00062	0.00062
7.4	0.00061	0.00061	0.00060	0.00059	0.00059	0.00058	0.00058	0.00057	0.00056	0.00056
7.5	0.00055	0.00055	0.00054	0.00054	0.00053	0.00053	0.00052	0.00052	0.00051	0.00051
7.6	0.00050	0.00050	0.00049	0.00049	0.00048	0.00048	0.00047	0.00047	0.00046	0.00046
7.7	0.00045	0.00045	0.00044	0.00044	0.00044	0.00043	0.00043	0.00042	0.00042	0.00041
7.8	0.00041	0.00041	0.00040	0.00040	0.00039	0.00039	0.00039	0.00038	0.00038	0.00037
7.9	0.00037	0.00037	0.00036	0.00036	0.00036	0.00035	0.00035	0.00035	0.00034	0.00034
8.0	0.00034	0.00033	0.00033	0.00033	0.00032	0.00032	0.00032	0.00031	0.00031	0.00031
8.1	0.00030	0.00030	0.00030	0.00029	0.00029	0.00029	0.00029	0.00028	0.00028	0.00028
8.2	0.00027	0.00027	0.00027	0.00027	0.00026	0.00026	0.00026	0.00026	0.00025	0.00025
8.3	0.00025	0.00025	0.00024	0.00024	0.00024	0.00024	0.00023	0.00023	0.00023	0.00023
8.4	0.00022	0.00022	0.00022	0.00022	0.00022	0.00021	0.00021	0.00021	0.00021	0.00021
8.5	0.00020	0.00020	0.00020	0.00020	0.00020	0.00019	0.00019	0.00019	0.00019	0.00019
8.6	0.00018	0.00018	0.00018	0.00018	0.00018	0.00018	0.00017	0.00017	0.00017	0.00017
8.7	0.00017	0.00016	0.00016	0.00016	0.00016	0.00016	0.00016	0.00016	0.00015	0.00015
8.8	0.00015	0.00015	0.00015	0.00015	0.00014	0.00014	0.00014	0.00014	0.00014	0.00014
8.9	0.00014	0.00014	0.00013	0.00013	0.00013	0.00013	0.00013	0.00013	0.00013	0.00012
9.0	0.00012	0.00012	0.00012	0.00012	0.00012	0.00012	0.00012	0.00012	0.00011	0.00011
9.1	0.00011	0.00011	0.00011	0.00011	0.00011	0.00011	0.00011	0.00010	0.00010	0.00010
9.2	0.00010	0.00010	0.00010	0.00010	0.00010	0.00010	0.00010	0.00009	0.00009	0.00009
9.3	0.00009	0.00009	0.00009	0.00009	0.00009	0.00009	0.00009	0.00009	0.00008	0.00008
9.4	0.00008	0.00008	0.00008	0.00008	0.00008	0.00008	0.00008	0.00008	0.00008	0.00008
9.5	0.00007	0.00007	0.00007	0.00007	0.00007	0.00007	0.00007	0.00007	0.00007	0.00007
9.6	0.00006	0.00006	0.00006	0.00006	0.00006	0.00006	0.00006	0.00006	0.00006	0.00006
9.7	0.00006	0.00006	0.00006	0.00006	0.00006	0.00006	0.00006	0.00006	0.00006	0.00006
9.8	0.00006	0.00005	0.00005	0.00005	0.00005	0.00005	0.00005	0.00005	0.00005	0.00005
9.9	0.00005	0.00005	0.00005	0.00005	0.00005	0.00005	0.00005	0.00005	0.00005	0.00005

TABLE D.1 Exponential Function—exp(X), 0.000 to 0.349

	0.000	0.001	0.002	0.003	0.004	0.005	0.006	0.007	0.008	0.009
0.00	1.0000	1.0010	1.0020	1.0030	1.0040	1.0050	1.0060	1.0070	1.0080	1.0090
0.01	1.0101	1.0111	1.0121	1.0131	1.0141	1.0151	1.0161	1.0171	1.0182	1.0192
0.02	1.0202	1.0212	1.0222	1.0233	1.0243	1.0253	1.0263	1.0274	1.0284	1.0294
0.03	1.0305	1.0315	1.0325	1.0336	1.0346	1.0356	1.0367	1.0377	1.0387	1.0398
0.04	1.0408	1.0419	1.0429	1.0439	1.0450	1.0460	1.0471	1.0481	1.0492	1.0502
0.05	1.0513	1.0523	1.0534	1.0544	1.0555	1.0565	1.0576	1.0587	1.0597	1.0608
0.06	1.0618	1.0629	1.0640	1.0650	1.0661	1.0672	1.0682	1.0693	1.0704	1.0714
0.07	1.0725	1.0736	1.0747	1.0757	1.0768	1.0779	1.0790	1.0800	1.0811	1.0822
0.08	1.0833	1.0844	1.0855	1.0865	1.0876	1.0887	1.0898	1.0909	1.0920	1.0931
0.09	1.0942	1.0953	1.0964	1.0975	1.0986	1.0997	1.1008	1.1019	1.1030	1.1041
0.10	1.1052	1.1063	1.1074	1.1085	1.1096	1.1107	1.1118	1.1129	1.1140	1.1152
0.11	1.1163	1.1174	1.1185	1.1196	1.1208	1.1219	1.1230	1.1241	1.1252	1.1264
0.12	1.1275	1.1286	1.1298	1.1309	1.1320	1.1331	1.1343	1.1354	1.1366	1.1377
0.13	1.1388	1.1400	1.1411	1.1422	1.1434	1.1445	1.1457	1.1468	1.1480	1.1491
0.14	1.1503	1.1514	1.1526	1.1537	1.1549	1.1560	1.1572	1.1584	1.1595	1.1607
0.15	1.1618	1.1630	1.1642	1.1653	1.1665	1.1677	1.1688	1.1700	1.1712	1.1723
0.16	1.1735	1.1747	1.1759	1.1770	1.1782	1.1794	1.1806	1.1818	1.1829	1.1841
0.17	1.1853	1.1865	1.1877	1.1889	1.1901	1.1912	1.1924	1.1936	1.1948	1.1960
0.18	1.1972	1.1984	1.1996	1.2008	1.2020	1.2032	1.2044	1.2056	1.2068	1.2080
0.19	1.2092	1.2105	1.2117	1.2129	1.2141	1.2153	1.2165	1.2177	1.2190	1.2202
0.20	1.2214	1.2226	1.2238	1.2251	1.2263	1.2275	1.2288	1.2300	1.2312	1.2324
0.21	1.2337	1.2349	1.2361	1.2374	1.2386	1.2399	1.2411	1.2423	1.2436	1.2448
0.22	1.2461	1.2473	1.2486	1.2498	1.2511	1.2523	1.2536	1.2548	1.2561	1.2573
0.23	1.2586	1.2599	1.2611	1.2624	1.2636	1.2649	1.2662	1.2674	1.2687	1.2700
0.24	1.2712	1.2725	1.2738	1.2751	1.2763	1.2776	1.2789	1.2802	1.2815	1.2827
0.25	1.2840	1.2853	1.2866	1.2879	1.2892	1.2905	1.2918	1.2930	1.2943	1.2956
0.26	1.2969	1.2982	1.2995	1.3008	1.3021	1.3034	1.3047	1.3060	1.3073	1.3087
0.27	1.3100	1.3113	1.3126	1.3139	1.3152	1.3165	1.3178	1.3192	1.3205	1.3218
0.28	1.3231	1.3245	1.3258	1.3271	1.3284	1.3298	1.3311	1.3324	1.3338	1.3351
0.29	1.3364	1.3378	1.3391	1.3404	1.3418	1.3431	1.3445	1.3458	1.3472	1.3485
0.30	1.3499	1.3512	1.3526	1.3539	1.3553	1.3566	1.3580	1.3593	1.3607	1.3621
0.31	1.3634	1.3648	1.3662	1.3675	1.3689	1.3703	1.3716	1.3730	1.3744	1.3758
0.32	1.3771	1.3785	1.3799	1.3813	1.3826	1.3840	1.3854	1.3868	1.3882	1.3896
0.33	1.3910	1.3924	1.3938	1.3951	1.3965	1.3979	1.3993	1.4007	1.4021	1.4035
0.34	1.4049	1.4064	1.4078	1.4092	1.4106	1.4120	1.4134	1.4148	1.4162	1.4176

0.350 to 0.699

	0.000	0.001	0.002	0.003	0.004	0.005	0.006	0.007	0.008	0.009
0.35	1.4191	1.4205	1.4219	1.4233	1.4248	1.4262	1.4276	1.4290	1.4305	1.4319
0.36	1.4333	1.4348	1.4362	1.4376	1.4391	1.4405	1.4420	1.4434	1.4448	1.4463
0.37	1.4477	1.4492	1.4506	1.4521	1.4535	1.4550	1.4564	1.4579	1.4594	1.4608
0.38	1.4623	1.4637	1.4652	1.4667	1.4681	1.4696	1.4711	1.4726	1.4740	1.4755
0.39	1.4770	1.4785	1.4799	1.4814	1.4829	1.4844	1.4859	1.4874	1.4888	1.4903
0.40	1.4918	1.4933	1.4948	1.4963	1.4978	1.4993	1.5008	1.5023	1.5038	1.5053
0.41	1.5068	1.5083	1.5098	1.5113	1.5129	1.5144	1.5159	1.5174	1.5189	1.5204
0.42	1.5220	1.5235	1.5250	1.5265	1.5281	1.5296	1.5311	1.5327	1.5342	1.5357
0.43	1.5373	1.5388	1.5403	1.5419	1.5434	1.5450	1.5465	1.5481	1.5496	1.5512
0.44	1.5527	1.5543	1.5558	1.5574	1.5589	1.5605	1.5621	1.5636	1.5652	1.5667
0.45	1.5683	1.5699	1.5715	1.5730	1.5746	1.5762	1.5778	1.5793	1.5809	1.5825
0.46	1.5841	1.5857	1.5872	1.5888	1.5904	1.5920	1.5936	1.5952	1.5968	1.5984
0.47	1.6000	1.6016	1.6032	1.6048	1.6064	1.6080	1.6096	1.6112	1.6128	1.6145
0.48	1.6161	1.6177	1.6193	1.6209	1.6226	1.6242	1.6258	1.6274	1.6291	1.6307
0.49	1.6323	1.6339	1.6356	1.6372	1.6389	1.6405	1.6421	1.6438	1.6454	1.6471
0.50	1.6487	1.6504	1.6520	1.6537	1.6553	1.6570	1.6586	1.6603	1.6620	1.6636
0.51	1.6653	1.6670	1.6686	1.6703	1.6720	1.6736	1.6753	1.6770	1.6787	1.6803
0.52	1.6820	1.6837	1.6854	1.6871	1.6888	1.6905	1.6922	1.6938	1.6955	1.6972
0.53	1.6989	1.7006	1.7023	1.7040	1.7057	1.7074	1.7092	1.7109	1.7126	1.7143
0.54	1.7160	1.7177	1.7194	1.7212	1.7229	1.7246	1.7263	1.7281	1.7298	1.7315
0.55	1.7333	1.7350	1.7367	1.7385	1.7402	1.7419	1.7437	1.7454	1.7472	1.7489
0.56	1.7507	1.7524	1.7542	1.7559	1.7577	1.7594	1.7612	1.7630	1.7647	1.7665
0.57	1.7683	1.7700	1.7718	1.7736	1.7754	1.7771	1.7789	1.7807	1.7825	1.7843
0.58	1.7860	1.7878	1.7896	1.7914	1.7932	1.7950	1.7968	1.7986	1.8004	1.8022
0.59	1.8040	1.8058	1.8076	1.8094	1.8112	1.8130	1.8148	1.8167	1.8185	1.8203
0.60	1.8221	1.8239	1.8258	1.8276	1.8294	1.8313	1.8331	1.8349	1.8368	1.8386
0.61	1.8404	1.8423	1.8441	1.8460	1.8478	1.8497	1.8515	1.8534	1.8552	1.8571
0.62	1.8589	1.8608	1.8626	1.8645	1.8664	1.8682	1.8701	1.8720	1.8739	1.8757
0.63	1.8776	1.8795	1.8814	1.8833	1.8851	1.8870	1.8889	1.8908	1.8927	1.8946
0.64	1.8965	1.8984	1.9003	1.9022	1.9041	1.9060	1.9079	1.9098	1.9117	1.9136
0.65	1.9155	1.9175	1.9194	1.9213	1.9232	1.9251	1.9271	1.9290	1.9309	1.9329
0.66	1.9348	1.9367	1.9387	1.9406	1.9425	1.9445	1.9464	1.9484	1.9503	1.9523
0.67	1.9542	1.9562	1.9581	1.9601	1.9621	1.9640	1.9660	1.9680	1.9699	1.9719
0.68	1.9739	1.9759	1.9778	1.9798	1.9818	1.9838	1.9858	1.9877	1.9897	1.9917
0.69	1.9937	1.9957	1.9977	1.9997	2.0017	2.0037	2.0057	2.0077	2.0097	2.0117

TABLE D.1 Exponential Function (*Continued*), 0.700 to 0.999

	0.000	0.001	0.002	0.003	0.004	0.005	0.006	0.007	0.008	0.009
0.70	2.0138	2.0158	2.0178	2.0198	2.0218	2.0238	2.0259	2.0279	2.0299	2.0320
0.71	2.0340	2.0360	2.0381	2.0401	2.0421	2.0442	2.0462	2.0483	2.0503	2.0524
0.72	2.0544	2.0565	2.0585	2.0606	2.0627	2.0647	2.0668	2.0689	2.0709	2.0730
0.73	2.0751	2.0772	2.0792	2.0813	2.0834	2.0855	2.0876	2.0897	2.0917	2.0938
0.74	2.0959	2.0980	2.1001	2.1022	2.1043	2.1064	2.1085	2.1107	2.1128	2.1149
0.75	2.1170	2.1191	2.1212	2.1234	2.1255	2.1276	2.1297	2.1319	2.1340	2.1361
0.76	2.1383	2.1404	2.1426	2.1447	2.1468	2.1490	2.1511	2.1533	2.1555	2.1576
0.77	2.1598	2.1619	2.1641	2.1663	2.1684	2.1706	2.1728	2.1749	2.1771	2.1793
0.78	2.1815	2.1837	2.1858	2.1880	2.1902	2.1924	2.1946	2.1968	2.1990	2.2012
0.79	2.2034	2.2056	2.2078	2.2100	2.2122	2.2144	2.2167	2.2189	2.2211	2.2233
0.80	2.2255	2.2278	2.2300	2.2322	2.2345	2.2367	2.2389	2.2412	2.2434	2.2457
0.81	2.2479	2.2502	2.2524	2.2547	2.2569	2.2592	2.2614	2.2637	2.2660	2.2682
0.82	2.2705	2.2728	2.2750	2.2773	2.2796	2.2819	2.2842	2.2864	2.2887	2.2910
0.83	2.2933	2.2956	2.2979	2.3002	2.3025	2.3048	2.3071	2.3094	2.3117	2.3141
0.84	2.3164	2.3187	2.3210	2.3233	2.3257	2.3280	2.3303	2.3326	2.3350	2.3373
0.85	2.3396	2.3420	2.3443	2.3467	2.3490	2.3514	2.3537	2.3561	2.3584	2.3608
0.86	2.3632	2.3655	2.3679	2.3703	2.3726	2.3750	2.3774	2.3798	2.3821	2.3845
0.87	2.3869	2.3893	2.3917	2.3941	2.3965	2.3989	2.4013	2.4037	2.4061	2.4085
0.88	2.4109	2.4133	2.4157	2.4181	2.4206	2.4230	2.4254	2.4278	2.4303	2.4327
0.89	2.4351	2.4376	2.4400	2.4424	2.4449	2.4473	2.4498	2.4522	2.4547	2.4571
0.90	2.4596	2.4621	2.4645	2.4670	2.4695	2.4719	2.4744	2.4769	2.4794	2.4818
0.91	2.4843	2.4868	2.4893	2.4918	2.4943	2.4968	2.4993	2.5018	2.5043	2.5068
0.92	2.5093	2.5118	2.5143	2.5168	2.5193	2.5219	2.5244	2.5269	2.5294	2.5320
0.93	2.5345	2.5370	2.5396	2.5421	2.5447	2.5472	2.5498	2.5523	2.5549	2.5574
0.94	2.5600	2.5625	2.5651	2.5677	2.5702	2.5728	2.5754	2.5780	2.5805	2.5831
0.95	2.5857	2.5883	2.5909	2.5935	2.5961	2.5987	2.6013	2.6039	2.6065	2.6091
0.96	2.6117	2.6143	2.6169	2.6195	2.6222	2.6248	2.6274	2.6300	2.6327	2.6353
0.97	2.6379	2.6406	2.6432	2.6459	2.6485	2.6512	2.6538	2.6565	2.6591	2.6618
0.98	2.6645	2.6671	2.6698	2.6725	2.6751	2.6778	2.6805	2.6832	2.6859	2.6885
0.99	2.6912	2.6939	2.6966	2.6993	2.7020	2.7047	2.7074	2.7101	2.7129	2.7156

	0.00	0.01	0.02	0.03	0.04	0.05	0.06	0.07	0.08	0.09
1.0	2.718	2.746	2.773	2.801	2.829	2.858	2.886	2.915	2.945	2.974
1.1	3.004	3.034	3.065	3.096	3.127	3.158	3.190	3.222	3.254	3.287
1.2	3.320	3.353	3.387	3.421	3.456	3.490	3.525	3.561	3.597	3.633
1.3	3.669	3.706	3.743	3.781	3.819	3.857	3.896	3.935	3.975	4.015
1.4	4.055	4.096	4.137	4.179	4.221	4.263	4.306	4.349	4.393	4.437
1.5	4.482	4.527	4.572	4.618	4.665	4.711	4.759	4.807	4.855	4.904
1.6	4.953	5.003	5.053	5.104	5.155	5.207	5.259	5.312	5.366	5.419
1.7	5.472	5.529	5.585	5.641	5.697	5.755	5.812	5.871	5.930	5.989
1.8	6.050	6.110	6.172	6.234	6.297	6.360	6.424	6.488	6.554	6.619
1.9	6.686	6.753	6.821	6.890	6.959	7.029	7.099	7.171	7.243	7.316
2.0	7.389	7.463	7.538	7.614	7.691	7.768	7.846	7.925	8.004	8.085
2.1	8.166	8.248	8.331	8.415	8.499	8.585	8.671	8.758	8.846	8.935
2.2	9.025	9.116	9.207	9.300	9.393	9.488	9.583	9.679	9.777	9.875
2.3	9.974	10.074	10.176	10.278	10.381	10.486	10.591	10.697	10.805	10.913
2.4	11.023	11.134	11.246	11.359	11.473	11.588	11.705	11.822	11.941	12.061
2.5	12.182	12.305	12.429	12.554	12.680	12.807	12.936	13.066	13.197	13.330
2.6	13.464	13.599	13.736	13.874	14.013	14.154	14.296	14.440	14.585	14.732
2.7	14.880	15.029	15.180	15.333	15.487	15.643	15.800	15.959	16.119	16.281
2.8	16.445	16.610	16.777	16.945	17.116	17.288	17.462	17.637	17.814	17.993
2.9	18.174	18.357	18.541	18.728	18.916	19.106	19.298	19.492	19.688	19.886
3.0	20.086	20.287	20.491	20.697	20.905	21.115	21.328	21.542	21.758	21.977
3.1	22.198	22.421	22.646	22.874	23.104	23.336	23.571	23.807	24.047	24.288
3.2	24.533	24.779	25.028	25.280	25.534	25.790	26.050	26.311	26.576	26.843
3.3	27.113	27.385	27.660	27.938	28.219	28.503	28.789	29.079	29.371	29.666
3.4	29.964	30.265	30.569	30.877	31.187	31.500	31.817	32.137	32.460	32.786
3.5	33.115	33.448	33.784	34.124	34.467	34.813	35.163	35.517	35.874	36.234
3.6	36.598	36.966	37.338	37.713	38.092	38.475	38.861	39.252	39.646	40.045
3.7	40.447	40.854	41.264	41.679	42.098	42.521	42.948	43.380	43.816	44.256
3.8	44.701	45.150	45.604	46.063	46.525	46.993	47.465	47.942	48.424	48.911
3.9	49.402	49.899	50.400	50.907	51.419	51.935	52.457	52.985	53.517	54.055

TABLE D.1 Exponential Function (Continued), 4.00 to 6.99

	0.00	0.01	0.02	0.03	0.04	0.05	0.06	0.07	0.08	0.09
4.0	54.598	55.147	55.701	56.261	56.826	57.397	57.974	58.557	59.145	59.740
4.1	60.340	60.947	61.559	62.178	62.803	63.434	64.072	64.715	65.366	66.023
4.2	66.686	67.357	68.033	68.717	69.408	70.105	70.810	71.522	72.240	72.966
4.3	73.700	74.440	75.189	75.944	76.708	77.478	78.257	79.044	79.838	80.640
4.4	81.451	82.269	83.096	83.931	84.775	85.627	86.488	87.357	88.235	89.121
4.5	90.017	90.922	91.836	92.759	93.691	94.632	95.583	96.544	97.514	98.494
4.6	99.484	100.484	101.494	102.514	103.544	104.585	105.636	106.698	107.770	108.853
4.7	109.947	111.052	112.168	113.296	114.434	115.584	116.746	117.919	119.104	120.301
4.8	121.510	122.732	123.965	125.211	126.469	127.740	129.024	130.321	131.631	132.954
4.9	134.290	135.639	137.003	138.380	139.770	141.175	142.594	144.027	145.474	146.936
5.0	148.413	149.905	151.411	152.933	154.470	156.022	157.591	159.174	160.774	162.390
5.1	164.022	165.670	167.335	169.017	170.716	172.431	174.164	175.915	177.683	179.469
5.2	181.272	183.094	184.934	186.793	188.670	190.566	192.481	194.416	196.370	198.343
5.3	200.337	202.350	204.384	206.438	208.513	210.608	212.725	214.863	217.022	219.203
5.4	221.406	223.632	225.879	228.149	230.442	232.758	235.097	237.460	239.847	242.257
5.5	244.692	247.151	249.635	252.144	254.678	257.238	259.823	262.434	265.072	267.736
5.6	270.426	273.144	275.889	278.662	281.463	284.291	287.149	290.035	292.949	295.894
5.7	298.867	301.871	304.905	307.969	311.064	314.191	317.348	320.538	323.759	327.013
5.8	330.300	333.619	336.972	340.359	343.779	347.234	350.724	354.249	357.809	361.405
5.9	365.037	368.706	372.412	376.155	379.935	383.753	387.610	391.506	395.440	399.415
6.0	403.429	407.483	411.579	415.715	419.893	424.113	428.375	432.681	437.029	441.421
6.1	445.858	450.339	454.865	459.436	464.054	468.717	473.428	478.186	482.992	487.846
6.2	492.749	497.701	502.703	507.755	512.859	518.013	523.219	528.477	533.789	539.153
6.3	544.572	550.045	555.573	561.157	566.796	572.493	578.246	584.058	589.928	595.857
6.4	601.845	607.894	614.003	620.174	626.407	632.702	639.061	645.484	651.971	658.523
6.5	665.142	671.826	678.578	685.398	692.287	699.244	706.272	713.370	720.539	727.781
6.6	735.095	742.483	749.945	757.482	765.095	772.784	780.551	788.396	796.319	804.322
6.7	812.406	820.571	828.818	837.147	845.561	854.059	862.642	871.312	880.069	888.914
6.8	897.847	906.871	915.985	925.191	934.489	943.881	953.367	962.949	972.626	982.401
6.9	992.275	1002.247	1012.320	1022.494	1032.770	1043.150	1053.634	1064.223	1074.918	1085.721

7.00 to 9.99

	0.00	0.01	0.02	0.03	0.04	0.05	0.06	0.07	0.08	0.09
7.0	1096.633	1107.655	1118.787	1130.031	1141.388	1152.859	1164.445	1176.148	1187.969	1199.908
7.1	1211.967	1224.148	1236.450	1248.877	1261.428	1274.106	1286.911	1299.845	1312.908	1326.103
7.2	1339.431	1352.892	1366.489	1380.223	1394.094	1408.105	1422.257	1436.550	1450.988	1465.571
7.3	1480.300	1495.177	1510.204	1525.382	1540.712	1556.197	1571.837	1587.634	1603.590	1619.706
7.4	1635.984	1652.426	1669.034	1685.808	1702.750	1719.863	1737.148	1754.607	1772.241	1790.052
7.5	1808.042	1826.214	1844.567	1863.106	1881.830	1900.743	1919.846	1939.140	1958.629	1978.314
7.6	1998.196	2018.278	2038.562	2059.050	2079.744	2100.646	2121.757	2143.081	2164.620	2186.375
7.7	2208.348	2230.542	2252.960	2275.602	2298.472	2321.572	2344.905	2368.471	2392.275	2416.318
7.8	2440.602	2465.130	2489.905	2514.929	2540.205	2565.734	2591.520	2617.566	2643.873	2670.444
7.9	2697.282	2724.390	2751.771	2779.427	2807.361	2835.575	2864.073	2892.857	2921.931	2951.297
8.0	2980.958	3010.917	3041.177	3071.742	3102.613	3133.795	3165.290	3197.102	3229.233	3261.688
8.1	3294.468	3327.578	3361.021	3394.800	3428.918	3463.379	3498.187	3533.344	3568.855	3604.722
8.2	3640.950	3677.542	3714.502	3751.834	3789.540	3827.626	3866.094	3904.949	3944.194	3983.834
8.3	4023.872	4064.313	4105.160	4146.418	4188.090	4230.181	4272.695	4315.636	4359.009	4402.818
8.4	4447.067	4491.761	4536.903	4582.500	4628.555	4675.073	4722.058	4769.515	4817.450	4865.866
8.5	4914.769	4964.163	5014.054	5064.446	5115.344	5166.754	5218.681	5271.130	5324.106	5377.614
8.6	5431.660	5486.249	5541.386	5597.078	5653.330	5710.147	5767.535	5825.499	5884.047	5943.182
8.7	6002.912	6063.242	6124.179	6185.728	6247.896	6310.688	6374.112	6438.172	6502.877	6568.232
8.8	6634.244	6700.919	6768.265	6836.287	6904.993	6974.389	7044.483	7115.281	7186.791	7259.019
8.9	7331.974	7405.661	7480.089	7555.265	7631.197	7707.892	7785.357	7863.602	7942.632	8022.457
9.0	8103.084	8184.521	8266.777	8349.860	8433.777	8518.538	8604.151	8690.624	8777.966	8866.186
9.1	8955.293	9045.295	9136.202	9228.022	9320.765	9414.440	9509.057	9604.625	9701.153	9798.651
9.2	9897.129	9996.597	10097.064	10198.542	10301.039	10404.566	10509.133	10614.752	10721.432	10829.184
9.3	10938.019	11047.948	11158.982	11271.131	11384.408	11498.823	11614.389	11731.115	11849.015	11968.099
9.4	12088.381	12209.871	12332.582	12456.527	12581.717	12708.165	12835.884	12964.887	13095.187	13226.795
9.5	13359.727	13493.994	13629.611	13766.591	13904.948	14044.695	14185.846	14328.416	14472.419	14617.870
9.6	14764.782	14913.170	15063.050	15214.436	15367.344	15521.788	15677.785	15835.349	15994.497	16155.244
9.7	16317.607	16481.602	16647.245	16814.552	16983.541	17154.229	17326.632	17500.767	17676.653	17854.306
9.8	18033.745	18214.987	18398.051	18582.954	18769.716	18958.355	19148.889	19341.339	19535.723	19732.060
9.9	19930.370	20130.674	20332.991	20537.341	20743.744	20952.222	21162.796	21375.485	21590.313	21807.299

TABLE D.2   Natural Logarithm—ln(x), 10 to 10,000,000,000

x	ln(x)
10	2.3026
100	4.6052
1000	6.9078
10,000	9.2103
100,000	11.5129
1,000,000	13.8155
10,000,000	16.1181
100,000,000	18.4207
1,000,000,000	20.7233
10,000,000,000	23.0259

The following tables give the natural logarithm ln(x) for values of x between .001 and 9.99. Values of x outside of this range can be expressed as numbers inside this range times powers of 10. For example, for $x = 125$, the ln (x) can be found as follows:

$$\ln 125 = \ln[1.25 \times 10^2] = \ln 1.25 + \ln 10^2$$
$$= .2231 + 4.6052$$
$$= 4.8283$$

TABLE D.2 Natural Logarithm (*Continued*)—ln(x), 0 to 0.349

	0.000	0.001	0.002	0.003	0.004	0.005	0.006	0.007	0.008	0.009
0.00	......	-6.9078	-6.2146	-5.8091	-5.5215	-5.2983	-5.1160	-4.9618	-4.8283	-4.7105
0.01	-4.6052	-4.5099	-4.4228	-4.3428	-4.2687	-4.1997	-4.1352	-4.0745	-4.0174	-3.9633
0.02	-3.9120	-3.8632	-3.8167	-3.7723	-3.7297	-3.6889	-3.6497	-3.6119	-3.5756	-3.5405
0.03	-3.5066	-3.4738	-3.4420	-3.4112	-3.3814	-3.3524	-3.3242	-3.2968	-3.2702	-3.2442
0.04	-3.2189	-3.1942	-3.1701	-3.1466	-3.1236	-3.1011	-3.0791	-3.0576	-3.0366	-3.0159
0.05	-2.9957	-2.9759	-2.9565	-2.9375	-2.9188	-2.9004	-2.8824	-2.8647	-2.8473	-2.8302
0.06	-2.8134	-2.7969	-2.7806	-2.7646	-2.7489	-2.7334	-2.7181	-2.7031	-2.6882	-2.6736
0.07	-2.6593	-2.6451	-2.6311	-2.6173	-2.6037	-2.5903	-2.5770	-2.5639	-2.5510	-2.5383
0.08	-2.5257	-2.5133	-2.5010	-2.4889	-2.4769	-2.4651	-2.4534	-2.4418	-2.4304	-2.4191
0.09	-2.4079	-2.3969	-2.3860	-2.3752	-2.3645	-2.3539	-2.3434	-2.3330	-2.3228	-2.3126
0.10	-2.3026	-2.2926	-2.2828	-2.2730	-2.2634	-2.2538	-2.2443	-2.2349	-2.2256	-2.2164
0.11	-2.2073	-2.1982	-2.1893	-2.1804	-2.1716	-2.1628	-2.1542	-2.1456	-2.1371	-2.1286
0.12	-2.1203	-2.1120	-2.1037	-2.0956	-2.0875	-2.0794	-2.0715	-2.0636	-2.0557	-2.0479
0.13	-2.0402	-2.0326	-2.0250	-2.0174	-2.0099	-2.0025	-1.9951	-1.9878	-1.9805	-1.9733
0.14	-1.9661	-1.9590	-1.9519	-1.9449	-1.9379	-1.9310	-1.9241	-1.9173	-1.9105	-1.9038
0.15	-1.8971	-1.8905	-1.8839	-1.8773	-1.8708	-1.8643	-1.8579	-1.8515	-1.8452	-1.8389
0.16	-1.8326	-1.8264	-1.8202	-1.8140	-1.8079	-1.8018	-1.7958	-1.7898	-1.7838	-1.7779
0.17	-1.7720	-1.7661	-1.7603	-1.7545	-1.7487	-1.7430	-1.7373	-1.7316	-1.7260	-1.7204
0.18	-1.7148	-1.7093	-1.7037	-1.6983	-1.6928	-1.6874	-1.6820	-1.6766	-1.6713	-1.6660
0.19	-1.6607	-1.6555	-1.6503	-1.6451	-1.6399	-1.6348	-1.6296	-1.6246	-1.6195	-1.6145
0.20	-1.6094	-1.6045	-1.5995	-1.5945	-1.5896	-1.5847	-1.5799	-1.5750	-1.5702	-1.5654
0.21	-1.5606	-1.5559	-1.5512	-1.5465	-1.5418	-1.5371	-1.5325	-1.5279	-1.5233	-1.5187
0.22	-1.5141	-1.5096	-1.5051	-1.5006	-1.4961	-1.4917	-1.4872	-1.4828	-1.4784	-1.4740
0.23	-1.4697	-1.4653	-1.4610	-1.4567	-1.4524	-1.4482	-1.4439	-1.4397	-1.4355	-1.4313
0.24	-1.4271	-1.4230	-1.4188	-1.4147	-1.4106	-1.4065	-1.4024	-1.3984	-1.3943	-1.3903
0.25	-1.3863	-1.3823	-1.3783	-1.3744	-1.3704	-1.3665	-1.3626	-1.3587	-1.3548	-1.3509
0.26	-1.3471	-1.3432	-1.3394	-1.3356	-1.3318	-1.3280	-1.3243	-1.3205	-1.3168	-1.3130
0.27	-1.3093	-1.3056	-1.3020	-1.2983	-1.2946	-1.2910	-1.2874	-1.2837	-1.2801	-1.2765
0.28	-1.2730	-1.2694	-1.2658	-1.2623	-1.2588	-1.2553	-1.2518	-1.2483	-1.2448	-1.2413
0.29	-1.2379	-1.2344	-1.2310	-1.2276	-1.2242	-1.2208	-1.2174	-1.2140	-1.2107	-1.2073
0.30	-1.2040	-1.2006	-1.1973	-1.1940	-1.1907	-1.1874	-1.1842	-1.1809	-1.1777	-1.1744
0.31	-1.1712	-1.1680	-1.1648	-1.1616	-1.1584	-1.1552	-1.1520	-1.1489	-1.1457	-1.1426
0.32	-1.1394	-1.1363	-1.1332	-1.1301	-1.1270	-1.1239	-1.1209	-1.1178	-1.1147	-1.1117
0.33	-1.1087	-1.1056	-1.1026	-1.0996	-1.0966	-1.0936	-1.0906	-1.0877	-1.0847	-1.0818
0.34	-1.0788	-1.0759	-1.0729	-1.0700	-1.0671	-1.0642	-1.0613	-1.0584	-1.0556	-1.0527

TABLE D.2 Natural Logarithm (*Continued*), 0.350 to 0.699

	0.000	0.001	0.002	0.003	0.004	0.005	0.006	0.007	0.008	0.009
0.35	-1.0498	-1.0470	-1.0441	-1.0413	-1.0385	-1.0356	-1.0328	-1.0300	-1.0272	-1.0244
0.36	-1.0217	-1.0189	-1.0161	-1.0134	-1.0106	-1.0079	-1.0051	-1.0024	-0.9997	-0.9970
0.37	-0.9943	-0.9916	-0.9889	-0.9862	-0.9835	-0.9808	-0.9782	-0.9755	-0.9729	-0.9702
0.38	-0.9676	-0.9650	-0.9623	-0.9597	-0.9571	-0.9545	-0.9519	-0.9493	-0.9467	-0.9442
0.39	-0.9416	-0.9390	-0.9365	-0.9339	-0.9314	-0.9289	-0.9263	-0.9238	-0.9213	-0.9188
0.40	-0.9163	-0.9138	-0.9113	-0.9088	-0.9063	-0.9039	-0.9014	-0.8989	-0.8965	-0.8940
0.41	-0.8916	-0.8892	-0.8867	-0.8843	-0.8819	-0.8795	-0.8771	-0.8747	-0.8723	-0.8699
0.42	-0.8675	-0.8651	-0.8627	-0.8604	-0.8580	-0.8557	-0.8533	-0.8510	-0.8486	-0.8463
0.43	-0.8440	-0.8416	-0.8393	-0.8370	-0.8347	-0.8324	-0.8301	-0.8278	-0.8255	-0.8233
0.44	-0.8210	-0.8187	-0.8164	-0.8142	-0.8119	-0.8097	-0.8074	-0.8052	-0.8030	-0.8007
0.45	-0.7985	-0.7963	-0.7941	-0.7919	-0.7897	-0.7875	-0.7853	-0.7831	-0.7809	-0.7787
0.46	-0.7765	-0.7744	-0.7722	-0.7700	-0.7679	-0.7657	-0.7636	-0.7614	-0.7593	-0.7572
0.47	-0.7550	-0.7529	-0.7508	-0.7487	-0.7465	-0.7444	-0.7423	-0.7402	-0.7381	-0.7361
0.48	-0.7340	-0.7319	-0.7298	-0.7277	-0.7257	-0.7236	-0.7215	-0.7195	-0.7174	-0.7154
0.49	-0.7133	-0.7113	-0.7093	-0.7072	-0.7052	-0.7032	-0.7012	-0.6992	-0.6972	-0.6951
0.50	-0.6931	-0.6911	-0.6892	-0.6872	-0.6852	-0.6832	-0.6812	-0.6792	-0.6773	-0.6753
0.51	-0.6733	-0.6714	-0.6694	-0.6675	-0.6655	-0.6636	-0.6616	-0.6597	-0.6578	-0.6559
0.52	-0.6539	-0.6520	-0.6501	-0.6482	-0.6463	-0.6444	-0.6425	-0.6406	-0.6387	-0.6368
0.53	-0.6349	-0.6330	-0.6311	-0.6292	-0.6274	-0.6255	-0.6236	-0.6218	-0.6199	-0.6180
0.54	-0.6162	-0.6143	-0.6125	-0.6106	-0.6088	-0.6070	-0.6051	-0.6033	-0.6015	-0.5997
0.55	-0.5978	-0.5960	-0.5942	-0.5924	-0.5906	-0.5888	-0.5870	-0.5852	-0.5834	-0.5816
0.56	-0.5798	-0.5780	-0.5763	-0.5745	-0.5727	-0.5709	-0.5692	-0.5674	-0.5656	-0.5639
0.57	-0.5621	-0.5604	-0.5586	-0.5569	-0.5551	-0.5534	-0.5516	-0.5499	-0.5482	-0.5465
0.58	-0.5447	-0.5430	-0.5413	-0.5396	-0.5379	-0.5361	-0.5344	-0.5327	-0.5310	-0.5293
0.59	-0.5276	-0.5259	-0.5242	-0.5226	-0.5209	-0.5192	-0.5175	-0.5158	-0.5142	-0.5125
0.60	-0.5108	-0.5092	-0.5075	-0.5058	-0.5042	-0.5025	-0.5009	-0.4992	-0.4976	-0.4959
0.61	-0.4943	-0.4927	-0.4910	-0.4894	-0.4878	-0.4861	-0.4845	-0.4829	-0.4813	-0.4797
0.62	-0.4780	-0.4764	-0.4748	-0.4732	-0.4716	-0.4700	-0.4684	-0.4668	-0.4652	-0.4636
0.63	-0.4620	-0.4604	-0.4589	-0.4573	-0.4557	-0.4541	-0.4526	-0.4510	-0.4494	-0.4479
0.64	-0.4463	-0.4447	-0.4432	-0.4416	-0.4401	-0.4385	-0.4370	-0.4354	-0.4339	-0.4323
0.65	-0.4308	-0.4292	-0.4277	-0.4262	-0.4246	-0.4231	-0.4216	-0.4201	-0.4186	-0.4170
0.66	-0.4155	-0.4140	-0.4125	-0.4110	-0.4095	-0.4080	-0.4065	-0.4050	-0.4035	-0.4020
0.67	-0.4005	-0.3990	-0.3975	-0.3960	-0.3945	-0.3930	-0.3916	-0.3901	-0.3886	-0.3871
0.68	-0.3857	-0.3842	-0.3827	-0.3813	-0.3798	-0.3783	-0.3769	-0.3754	-0.3740	-0.3725
0.69	-0.3711	-0.3696	-0.3682	-0.3667	-0.3653	-0.3638	-0.3624	-0.3610	-0.3595	-0.3581

0.700 to 0.999

	0.000	0.001	0.002	0.003	0.004	0.005	0.006	0.007	0.008	0.009
0.70	-0.3567	-0.3552	-0.3538	-0.3524	-0.3510	-0.3496	-0.3481	-0.3467	-0.3453	-0.3439
0.71	-0.3425	-0.3411	-0.3397	-0.3383	-0.3369	-0.3355	-0.3341	-0.3327	-0.3313	-0.3299
0.72	-0.3285	-0.3271	-0.3257	-0.3243	-0.3230	-0.3216	-0.3202	-0.3188	-0.3175	-0.3161
0.73	-0.3147	-0.3133	-0.3120	-0.3106	-0.3092	-0.3079	-0.3065	-0.3052	-0.3038	-0.3025
0.74	-0.3011	-0.2998	-0.2984	-0.2971	-0.2957	-0.2944	-0.2930	-0.2917	-0.2904	-0.2890
0.75	-0.2877	-0.2863	-0.2850	-0.2837	-0.2824	-0.2810	-0.2797	-0.2784	-0.2771	-0.2758
0.76	-0.2744	-0.2731	-0.2718	-0.2705	-0.2692	-0.2679	-0.2666	-0.2653	-0.2640	-0.2627
0.77	-0.2614	-0.2601	-0.2588	-0.2575	-0.2562	-0.2549	-0.2536	-0.2523	-0.2510	-0.2497
0.78	-0.2485	-0.2472	-0.2459	-0.2446	-0.2433	-0.2421	-0.2408	-0.2395	-0.2383	-0.2370
0.79	-0.2357	-0.2345	-0.2332	-0.2319	-0.2307	-0.2294	-0.2282	-0.2269	-0.2256	-0.2244
0.80	-0.2231	-0.2219	-0.2206	-0.2194	-0.2182	-0.2169	-0.2157	-0.2144	-0.2132	-0.2120
0.81	-0.2107	-0.2095	-0.2083	-0.2070	-0.2058	-0.2046	-0.2033	-0.2021	-0.2009	-0.1997
0.82	-0.1985	-0.1972	-0.1960	-0.1948	-0.1936	-0.1924	-0.1912	-0.1900	-0.1887	-0.1875
0.83	-0.1863	-0.1851	-0.1839	-0.1827	-0.1815	-0.1803	-0.1791	-0.1779	-0.1767	-0.1755
0.84	-0.1744	-0.1732	-0.1720	-0.1708	-0.1696	-0.1684	-0.1672	-0.1661	-0.1649	-0.1637
0.85	-0.1625	-0.1613	-0.1602	-0.1590	-0.1578	-0.1567	-0.1555	-0.1543	-0.1532	-0.1520
0.86	-0.1508	-0.1497	-0.1485	-0.1473	-0.1462	-0.1450	-0.1439	-0.1427	-0.1416	-0.1404
0.87	-0.1393	-0.1381	-0.1370	-0.1358	-0.1347	-0.1335	-0.1324	-0.1312	-0.1301	-0.1290
0.88	-0.1278	-0.1267	-0.1256	-0.1244	-0.1233	-0.1222	-0.1210	-0.1199	-0.1188	-0.1177
0.89	-0.1165	-0.1154	-0.1143	-0.1132	-0.1120	-0.1109	-0.1098	-0.1087	-0.1076	-0.1065
0.90	-0.1054	-0.1043	-0.1031	-0.1020	-0.1009	-0.0998	-0.0987	-0.0976	-0.0965	-0.0954
0.91	-0.0943	-0.0932	-0.0921	-0.0910	-0.0899	-0.0888	-0.0877	-0.0866	-0.0856	-0.0845
0.92	-0.0834	-0.0823	-0.0812	-0.0801	-0.0790	-0.0780	-0.0769	-0.0758	-0.0747	-0.0736
0.93	-0.0726	-0.0715	-0.0704	-0.0694	-0.0683	-0.0672	-0.0661	-0.0651	-0.0640	-0.0629
0.94	-0.0619	-0.0608	-0.0598	-0.0587	-0.0576	-0.0566	-0.0555	-0.0545	-0.0534	-0.0523
0.95	-0.0513	-0.0502	-0.0492	-0.0481	-0.0471	-0.0460	-0.0450	-0.0440	-0.0429	-0.0419
0.96	-0.0408	-0.0398	-0.0387	-0.0377	-0.0367	-0.0356	-0.0346	-0.0336	-0.0325	-0.0315
0.97	-0.0305	-0.0294	-0.0284	-0.0274	-0.0263	-0.0253	-0.0243	-0.0233	-0.0222	-0.0212
0.98	-0.0202	-0.0192	-0.0182	-0.0171	-0.0161	-0.0151	-0.0141	-0.0131	-0.0121	-0.0111
0.99	-0.0101	-0.0090	-0.0080	-0.0070	-0.0060	-0.0050	-0.0040	-0.0030	-0.0020	-0.0010

TABLE D.2 Natural Logarithm (Continued), 1 to 3.99

	0.00	0.01	0.02	0.03	0.04	0.05	0.06	0.07	0.08	0.09
1.0	0.0000	0.0100	0.0198	0.0296	0.0392	0.0488	0.0583	0.0677	0.0770	0.0862
1.1	0.0953	0.1044	0.1133	0.1222	0.1310	0.1398	0.1484	0.1570	0.1655	0.1740
1.2	0.1823	0.1906	0.1989	0.2070	0.2151	0.2231	0.2311	0.2390	0.2469	0.2546
1.3	0.2624	0.2700	0.2776	0.2852	0.2927	0.3001	0.3075	0.3148	0.3221	0.3293
1.4	0.3365	0.3436	0.3507	0.3577	0.3646	0.3716	0.3784	0.3853	0.3920	0.3988
1.5	0.4055	0.4121	0.4187	0.4253	0.4318	0.4383	0.4447	0.4511	0.4574	0.4637
1.6	0.4700	0.4762	0.4824	0.4886	0.4947	0.5008	0.5068	0.5128	0.5188	0.5247
1.7	0.5306	0.5365	0.5423	0.5481	0.5539	0.5596	0.5653	0.5710	0.5766	0.5822
1.8	0.5878	0.5933	0.5988	0.6043	0.6098	0.6152	0.6206	0.6259	0.6313	0.6366
1.9	0.6419	0.6471	0.6523	0.6575	0.6627	0.6678	0.6729	0.6780	0.6831	0.6881
2.0	0.6931	0.6981	0.7031	0.7080	0.7129	0.7178	0.7227	0.7275	0.7324	0.7372
2.1	0.7419	0.7467	0.7514	0.7561	0.7608	0.7655	0.7701	0.7747	0.7793	0.7839
2.2	0.7885	0.7930	0.7975	0.8020	0.8065	0.8109	0.8154	0.8198	0.8242	0.8286
2.3	0.8329	0.8372	0.8416	0.8459	0.8502	0.8544	0.8587	0.8629	0.8671	0.8713
2.4	0.8755	0.8796	0.8838	0.8879	0.8920	0.8961	0.9002	0.9042	0.9083	0.9123
2.5	0.9163	0.9203	0.9243	0.9282	0.9322	0.9361	0.9400	0.9439	0.9478	0.9517
2.6	0.9555	0.9594	0.9632	0.9670	0.9708	0.9746	0.9783	0.9821	0.9858	0.9895
2.7	0.9933	0.9969	1.0006	1.0043	1.0080	1.0116	1.0152	1.0188	1.0225	1.0260
2.8	1.0296	1.0332	1.0367	1.0403	1.0438	1.0473	1.0508	1.0543	1.0578	1.0613
2.9	1.0647	1.0682	1.0716	1.0750	1.0784	1.0818	1.0852	1.0886	1.0919	1.0953
3.0	1.0986	1.1019	1.1053	1.1086	1.1119	1.1151	1.1184	1.1217	1.1249	1.1282
3.1	1.1314	1.1346	1.1378	1.1410	1.1442	1.1474	1.1506	1.1537	1.1569	1.1600
3.2	1.1632	1.1663	1.1694	1.1725	1.1756	1.1787	1.1817	1.1848	1.1878	1.1909
3.3	1.1939	1.1969	1.2000	1.2030	1.2060	1.2090	1.2119	1.2149	1.2179	1.2208
3.4	1.2238	1.2267	1.2296	1.2326	1.2355	1.2384	1.2413	1.2442	1.2470	1.2499
3.5	1.2528	1.2556	1.2585	1.2613	1.2641	1.2669	1.2698	1.2726	1.2754	1.2782
3.6	1.2809	1.2837	1.2865	1.2892	1.2920	1.2947	1.2975	1.3002	1.3029	1.3056
3.7	1.3083	1.3110	1.3137	1.3164	1.3191	1.3218	1.3244	1.3271	1.3297	1.3324
3.8	1.3350	1.3376	1.3403	1.3429	1.3455	1.3481	1.3507	1.3533	1.3558	1.3584
3.9	1.3610	1.3635	1.3661	1.3686	1.3712	1.3737	1.3762	1.3788	1.3813	1.3838

	0.00	0.01	0.02	0.03	0.04	0.05	0.06	0.07	0.08	0.09
4.0	1.3863	1.3888	1.3913	1.3938	1.3962	1.3987	1.4012	1.4036	1.4061	1.4085
4.1	1.4110	1.4134	1.4159	1.4183	1.4207	1.4231	1.4255	1.4279	1.4303	1.4327
4.2	1.4351	1.4375	1.4398	1.4422	1.4446	1.4469	1.4493	1.4516	1.4540	1.4563
4.3	1.4586	1.4609	1.4633	1.4656	1.4679	1.4702	1.4725	1.4748	1.4770	1.4793
4.4	1.4816	1.4839	1.4861	1.4884	1.4907	1.4929	1.4951	1.4974	1.4996	1.5019
4.5	1.5041	1.5063	1.5085	1.5107	1.5129	1.5151	1.5173	1.5195	1.5217	1.5239
4.6	1.5261	1.5282	1.5304	1.5326	1.5347	1.5369	1.5390	1.5412	1.5433	1.5454
4.7	1.5476	1.5497	1.5518	1.5539	1.5560	1.5581	1.5602	1.5623	1.5644	1.5665
4.8	1.5686	1.5707	1.5728	1.5748	1.5769	1.5790	1.5810	1.5831	1.5851	1.5872
4.9	1.5892	1.5913	1.5933	1.5953	1.5974	1.5994	1.6014	1.6034	1.6054	1.6074
5.0	1.6094	1.6114	1.6134	1.6154	1.6174	1.6194	1.6214	1.6233	1.6253	1.6273
5.1	1.6292	1.6312	1.6332	1.6351	1.6371	1.6390	1.6409	1.6429	1.6448	1.6467
5.2	1.6487	1.6506	1.6525	1.6544	1.6563	1.6582	1.6601	1.6620	1.6639	1.6658
5.3	1.6677	1.6696	1.6715	1.6734	1.6752	1.6771	1.6790	1.6808	1.6827	1.6845
5.4	1.6864	1.6882	1.6901	1.6919	1.6938	1.6956	1.6974	1.6993	1.7011	1.7029
5.5	1.7047	1.7066	1.7084	1.7102	1.7120	1.7138	1.7156	1.7174	1.7192	1.7210
5.6	1.7228	1.7246	1.7263	1.7281	1.7299	1.7317	1.7334	1.7352	1.7370	1.7387
5.7	1.7405	1.7422	1.7440	1.7457	1.7475	1.7492	1.7509	1.7527	1.7544	1.7561
5.8	1.7579	1.7596	1.7613	1.7630	1.7647	1.7664	1.7681	1.7699	1.7716	1.7733
5.9	1.7750	1.7766	1.7783	1.7800	1.7817	1.7834	1.7851	1.7867	1.7884	1.7901
6.0	1.7918	1.7934	1.7951	1.7967	1.7984	1.8001	1.8017	1.8034	1.8050	1.8066
6.1	1.8083	1.8099	1.8116	1.8132	1.8148	1.8165	1.8181	1.8197	1.8213	1.8229
6.2	1.8245	1.8262	1.8278	1.8294	1.8310	1.8326	1.8342	1.8358	1.8374	1.8390
6.3	1.8405	1.8421	1.8437	1.8453	1.8469	1.8485	1.8500	1.8516	1.8532	1.8547
6.4	1.8563	1.8579	1.8594	1.8610	1.8625	1.8641	1.8656	1.8672	1.8687	1.8703
6.5	1.8718	1.8733	1.8749	1.8764	1.8779	1.8795	1.8810	1.8825	1.8840	1.8856
6.6	1.8871	1.8886	1.8901	1.8916	1.8931	1.8946	1.8961	1.8976	1.8991	1.9006
6.7	1.9021	1.9036	1.9051	1.9066	1.9081	1.9095	1.9110	1.9125	1.9140	1.9155
6.8	1.9169	1.9184	1.9199	1.9213	1.9228	1.9242	1.9257	1.9272	1.9286	1.9301
6.9	1.9315	1.9330	1.9344	1.9359	1.9373	1.9387	1.9402	1.9416	1.9430	1.9445

TABLE D.2 Natural Logarithm *(Continued).* 7 to 9.99

	0.00	0.01	0.02	0.03	0.04	0.05	0.06	0.07	0.08	0.09
7.0	1.9459	1.9473	1.9488	1.9502	1.9516	1.9530	1.9544	1.9559	1.9573	1.9587
7.1	1.9601	1.9615	1.9629	1.9643	1.9657	1.9671	1.9685	1.9699	1.9713	1.9727
7.2	1.9741	1.9755	1.9769	1.9782	1.9796	1.9810	1.9824	1.9838	1.9851	1.9865
7.3	1.9879	1.9892	1.9906	1.9920	1.9933	1.9947	1.9961	1.9974	1.9988	2.0001
7.4	2.0015	2.0028	2.0042	2.0055	2.0069	2.0082	2.0096	2.0109	2.0122	2.0136
7.5	2.0149	2.0162	2.0176	2.0189	2.0202	2.0215	2.0229	2.0242	2.0255	2.0268
7.6	2.0281	2.0295	2.0308	2.0321	2.0334	2.0347	2.0360	2.0373	2.0386	2.0399
7.7	2.0412	2.0425	2.0438	2.0451	2.0464	2.0477	2.0490	2.0503	2.0516	2.0528
7.8	2.0541	2.0554	2.0567	2.0580	2.0592	2.0605	2.0618	2.0631	2.0643	2.0656
7.9	2.0669	2.0681	2.0694	2.0707	2.0719	2.0732	2.0744	2.0757	2.0769	2.0782
8.0	2.0794	2.0807	2.0819	2.0832	2.0844	2.0857	2.0869	2.0882	2.0894	2.0906
8.1	2.0919	2.0931	2.0943	2.0956	2.0968	2.0980	2.0992	2.1005	2.1017	2.1029
8.2	2.1041	2.1054	2.1066	2.1078	2.1090	2.1102	2.1114	2.1126	2.1138	2.1150
8.3	2.1163	2.1175	2.1187	2.1199	2.1211	2.1223	2.1235	2.1247	2.1258	2.1270
8.4	2.1282	2.1294	2.1306	2.1318	2.1330	2.1342	2.1353	2.1365	2.1377	2.1389
8.5	2.1401	2.1412	2.1424	2.1436	2.1448	2.1459	2.1471	2.1483	2.1494	2.1506
8.6	2.1518	2.1529	2.1541	2.1552	2.1564	2.1576	2.1587	2.1599	2.1610	2.1622
8.7	2.1633	2.1645	2.1656	2.1668	2.1679	2.1691	2.1702	2.1713	2.1725	2.1736
8.8	2.1748	2.1759	2.1770	2.1782	2.1793	2.1804	2.1815	2.1827	2.1838	2.1849
8.9	2.1861	2.1872	2.1883	2.1894	2.1905	2.1917	2.1928	2.1939	2.1950	2.1961
9.0	2.1972	2.1983	2.1994	2.2006	2.2017	2.2028	2.2039	2.2050	2.2061	2.2072
9.1	2.2083	2.2094	2.2105	2.2116	2.2127	2.2138	2.2148	2.2159	2.2170	2.2181
9.2	2.2192	2.2203	2.2214	2.2225	2.2235	2.2246	2.2257	2.2268	2.2279	2.2289
9.3	2.2300	2.2311	2.2322	2.2332	2.2343	2.2354	2.2364	2.2375	2.2386	2.2396
9.4	2.2407	2.2418	2.2428	2.2439	2.2450	2.2460	2.2471	2.2481	2.2492	2.2502
9.5	2.2513	2.2523	2.2534	2.2544	2.2555	2.2565	2.2576	2.2586	2.2597	2.2607
9.6	2.2618	2.2628	2.2638	2.2649	2.2659	2.2670	2.2680	2.2690	2.2701	2.2711
9.7	2.2721	2.2732	2.2742	2.2752	2.2762	2.2773	2.2783	2.2793	2.2803	2.2814
9.8	2.2824	2.2834	2.2844	2.2854	2.2865	2.2875	2.2885	2.2895	2.2905	2.2915
9.9	2.2925	2.2935	2.2946	2.2956	2.2966	2.2976	2.2986	2.2996	2.3006	2.3016

The normal density with parameters μ and σ^2 is

$$f(z) = (2\pi\sigma^2)^{-1/2} \exp\left\{-\frac{(z-\mu)^2}{2\sigma^2}\right\}$$

The standard normal distribution has density function

$$f(y) = (2\pi)^{-1/2} \exp\left\{-\frac{1}{2}y^2\right\}$$

It has zero mean and unit variance. The relationship between these two random variables is

$$y = \left(\frac{z-\mu}{\sigma}\right)$$

Table D.3 gives the standard normal cumulative distribution function:

$$F(y) = \int_{-\infty}^{y} (2\pi)^{-1/2} \exp\left\{-\frac{1}{2}t^2\right\} dt$$

for y values from 0 to 3.9. This is the area under the density curve up to the point y.

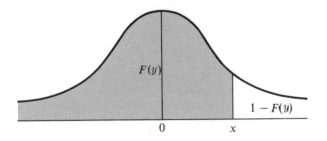

For negative values of y the relationship

$$F(-y) = 1 - F(y)$$

can be used because the density function is symmetric about the origin.

TABLE D.3   Cumulative Normal Distribution, 0.0 to 3.9

	0.0	0.1	0.2	0.3	0.4	0.5	0.6	0.7	0.8	0.9
0.0	0.5000	0.5398	0.5793	0.6179	0.6554	0.6915	0.7257	0.7580	0.7881	0.8159
1.0	0.8413	0.8643	0.8849	0.9032	0.9192	0.9332	0.9452	0.9554	0.9641	0.9713
2.0	0.9772	0.9821	0.9861	0.9893	0.9918	0.9938	0.9953	0.9965	0.9974	0.9981
3.0	0.9987	0.9990	0.9993	0.9995	0.9997	0.9998	0.9998	0.9999	0.9999	0.9999

TABLE D.4   Normal Density Function—Ordinate Values, 0.0 to 3.9

	0.0	0.1	0.2	0.3	0.4	0.5	0.6	0.7	0.8	0.9
0.0	0.3989	0.3970	0.3910	0.3814	0.3683	0.3521	0.3332	0.3123	0.2897	0.2661
1.0	0.2420	0.2179	0.1942	0.1714	0.1497	0.1295	0.1109	0.0940	0.0790	0.0656
2.0	0.0540	0.0440	0.0355	0.0283	0.0224	0.0175	0.0136	0.0104	0.0079	0.0060
3.0	0.0044	0.0033	0.0024	0.0017	0.0012	0.0009	0.0006	0.0004	0.0003	0.0002

TABLE D.5   The Poisson Probability Function (The Poisson probability function is $f(z) \doteq \lambda^z e^{-\lambda}/z!$ for $z = 0, 1, 2, \ldots$ for any positive λ. The table gives the function for integer values of λ from 1 to 20.)

Poisson Distribution with Mean $\lambda, Z = 0$ to 9									

λ/Z	0	1	2	3	4	5	6	7	8	9
1	0.36788	0.36788	0.18394	0.06131	0.01533	0.00307	0.00051	0.00007	0.00001	0.00000
2	0.13534	0.27067	0.27067	0.18045	0.09022	0.03609	0.01203	0.00344	0.00086	0.00019
3	0.04979	0.14936	0.22404	0.22404	0.16803	0.10082	0.05041	0.02160	0.00810	0.00270
4	0.01832	0.07326	0.14653	0.19537	0.19537	0.15629	0.10420	0.05954	0.02977	0.01323
5	0.00674	0.03369	0.08422	0.14037	0.17547	0.17547	0.14622	0.10444	0.06528	0.03627
6	0.00248	0.01487	0.04462	0.08924	0.13385	0.16062	0.16062	0.13768	0.10326	0.06884
7	0.00091	0.00638	0.02234	0.05213	0.09123	0.12772	0.14900	0.14900	0.13038	0.10140
8	0.00034	0.00268	0.01073	0.02863	0.05725	0.09160	0.12214	0.13959	0.13959	0.12408
9	0.00012	0.00111	0.00500	0.01499	0.03374	0.06073	0.09109	0.11712	0.13176	0.13176
10	0.00005	0.00045	0.00227	0.00757	0.01892	0.03783	0.06306	0.09008	0.11260	0.12511
11	0.00002	0.00018	0.00101	0.00370	0.01019	0.02242	0.04109	0.06458	0.08879	0.10853
12	0.00001	0.00007	0.00044	0.00177	0.00531	0.01274	0.02548	0.04368	0.06552	0.08736
13	0.00000	0.00003	0.00019	0.00083	0.00269	0.00699	0.01515	0.02814	0.04573	0.06605
14	0.00000	0.00001	0.00008	0.00038	0.00133	0.00373	0.00870	0.01739	0.03044	0.04734
15	0.00000	0.00000	0.00003	0.00017	0.00065	0.00194	0.00484	0.01037	0.01944	0.03241
16	0.00000	0.00000	0.00001	0.00008	0.00031	0.00098	0.00262	0.00599	0.01199	0.02131
17	0.00000	0.00000	0.00001	0.00003	0.00014	0.00049	0.00139	0.00337	0.00716	0.01353
18	0.00000	0.00000	0.00000	0.00001	0.00007	0.00024	0.00072	0.00185	0.00416	0.00833
19	0.00000	0.00000	0.00000	0.00001	0.00003	0.00012	0.00037	0.00099	0.00236	0.00498
20	0.00000	0.00000	0.00000	0.00000	0.00001	0.00005	0.00018	0.00052	0.00131	0.00291

TABLE D.5 **Poisson Distribution with Mean** λ *(Continued)*, *Z* = **10 to 19**

λ/Z	10	11	12	13	14	15	16	17	18	19
1	0.00000	0.00000	0.00000	0.00000	0.00000	0.00000	0.00000	0.00000	0.00000	0.00000
2	0.00004	0.00001	0.00000	0.00000	0.00000	0.00000	0.00000	0.00000	0.00000	0.00000
3	0.00081	0.00022	0.00006	0.00001	0.00000	0.00000	0.00000	0.00000	0.00000	0.00000
4	0.00529	0.00192	0.00064	0.00020	0.00006	0.00002	0.00000	0.00000	0.00000	0.00000
5	0.01813	0.00824	0.00343	0.00132	0.00047	0.00016	0.00005	0.00001	0.00000	0.00000
6	0.04130	0.02253	0.01126	0.00520	0.00223	0.00089	0.00033	0.00012	0.00004	0.00001
7	0.07098	0.04517	0.02635	0.01419	0.00709	0.00331	0.00145	0.00060	0.00023	0.00009
8	0.09926	0.07219	0.04813	0.02962	0.01692	0.00903	0.00451	0.00212	0.00094	0.00040
9	0.11858	0.09702	0.07277	0.05038	0.03238	0.01943	0.01093	0.00579	0.00289	0.00137
10	0.12511	0.11374	0.09478	0.07291	0.05208	0.03472	0.02170	0.01276	0.00709	0.00373
11	0.11938	0.11938	0.10943	0.09259	0.07275	0.05335	0.03668	0.02373	0.01450	0.00840
12	0.10484	0.11437	0.11437	0.10557	0.09049	0.07239	0.05429	0.03832	0.02555	0.01614
13	0.08587	0.10148	0.10994	0.10994	0.10209	0.08848	0.07189	0.05497	0.03970	0.02716
14	0.06628	0.08436	0.09842	0.10599	0.10599	0.09892	0.08656	0.07128	0.05544	0.04085
15	0.04861	0.06629	0.08286	0.09561	0.10244	0.10244	0.09603	0.08474	0.07061	0.05575
16	0.03410	0.04960	0.06613	0.08139	0.09302	0.09922	0.09922	0.09338	0.08301	0.06990
17	0.02300	0.03554	0.05036	0.06585	0.07996	0.09062	0.09628	0.09628	0.09094	0.08136
18	0.01499	0.02452	0.03678	0.05093	0.06548	0.07858	0.08840	0.09360	0.09360	0.08867
19	0.00947	0.01635	0.02589	0.03784	0.05135	0.06504	0.07724	0.08633	0.09112	0.09112
20	0.00582	0.01058	0.01763	0.02712	0.03874	0.05165	0.06456	0.07595	0.08439	0.08884

Z = **20 to 29**

λ/Z	20	21	22	23	24	25	26	27	28	29
1	0.00000	0.00000	0.00000	0.00000	0.00000	0.00000	0.00000	0.00000	0.00000	0.00000
2	0.00000	0.00000	0.00000	0.00000	0.00000	0.00000	0.00000	0.00000	0.00000	0.00000
3	0.00000	0.00000	0.00000	0.00000	0.00000	0.00000	0.00000	0.00000	0.00000	0.00000
4	0.00000	0.00000	0.00000	0.00000	0.00000	0.00000	0.00000	0.00000	0.00000	0.00000
5	0.00000	0.00000	0.00000	0.00000	0.00000	0.00000	0.00000	0.00000	0.00000	0.00000
6	0.00000	0.00000	0.00000	0.00000	0.00000	0.00000	0.00000	0.00000	0.00000	0.00000
7	0.00003	0.00001	0.00000	0.00000	0.00000	0.00000	0.00000	0.00000	0.00000	0.00000
8	0.00016	0.00006	0.00002	0.00001	0.00000	0.00000	0.00000	0.00000	0.00000	0.00000
9	0.00062	0.00026	0.00011	0.00004	0.00002	0.00001	0.00000	0.00000	0.00000	0.00000
10	0.00187	0.00089	0.00040	0.00018	0.00007	0.00003	0.00001	0.00000	0.00000	0.00000
11	0.00462	0.00242	0.00121	0.00058	0.00027	0.00012	0.00005	0.00002	0.00001	0.00000
12	0.00968	0.00553	0.00302	0.00157	0.00079	0.00038	0.00017	0.00008	0.00003	0.00001
13	0.01766	0.01093	0.00646	0.00365	0.00198	0.00103	0.00051	0.00025	0.00011	0.00005
14	0.02860	0.01906	0.01213	0.00738	0.00431	0.00241	0.00130	0.00067	0.00034	0.00016
15	0.04181	0.02986	0.02036	0.01328	0.00830	0.00498	0.00287	0.00160	0.00086	0.00044
16	0.05592	0.04261	0.03099	0.02156	0.01437	0.00920	0.00566	0.00335	0.00192	0.00106
17	0.06916	0.05599	0.04326	0.03198	0.02265	0.01540	0.01007	0.00634	0.00385	0.00226
18	0.07980	0.06840	0.05597	0.04380	0.03285	0.02365	0.01637	0.01092	0.00702	0.00436
19	0.08657	0.07832	0.06764	0.05588	0.04424	0.03362	0.02457	0.01729	0.01173	0.00769
20	0.08884	0.08461	0.07691	0.06688	0.05573	0.04459	0.03430	0.02541	0.01815	0.01252

TABLE D.5   Poisson Distribution with Mean λ *(Continued)*, **Z = 30 to 39**

λ/Z	30	31	32	33	34	35	36	37	38	39
1	0.00000	0.00000	0.00000	0.00000						
2	0.00000	0.00000	0.00000	0.00000	0.00000	0.00000	0.00000	0.00000	0.00000	0.00000
3	0.00000	0.00000	0.00000	0.00000	0.00000	0.00000	0.00000	0.00000	0.00000	0.00000
4	0.00000	0.00000	0.00000	0.00000	0.00000	0.00000	0.00000	0.00000	0.00000	0.00000
5	0.00000	0.00000	0.00000	0.00000	0.00000	0.00000	0.00000	0.00000	0.00000	0.00000
6	0.00000	0.00000	0.00000	0.00000	0.00000	0.00000	0.00000	0.00000	0.00000	0.00000
7	0.00000	0.00000	0.00000	0.00000	0.00000	0.00000	0.00000	0.00000	0.00000	0.00000
8	0.00000	0.00000	0.00000	0.00000	0.00000	0.00000	0.00000	0.00000	0.00000	0.00000
9	0.00000	0.00000	0.00000	0.00000	0.00000	0.00000	0.00000	0.00000	0.00000	0.00000
10	0.00000	0.00000	0.00000	0.00000	0.00000	0.00000	0.00000	0.00000	0.00000	0.00000
11	0.00000	0.00000	0.00000	0.00000	0.00000	0.00000	0.00000	0.00000	0.00000	0.00000
12	0.00001	0.00000	0.00000	0.00000	0.00000	0.00000	0.00000	0.00000	0.00000	0.00000
13	0.00002	0.00001	0.00000	0.00000	0.00000	0.00000	0.00000	0.00000	0.00000	0.00000
14	0.00008	0.00003	0.00001	0.00001	0.00000	0.00000	0.00000	0.00000	0.00000	0.00000
15	0.00022	0.00011	0.00005	0.00002	0.00001	0.00000	0.00000	0.00000	0.00000	0.00000
16	0.00056	0.00029	0.00015	0.00007	0.00003	0.00002	0.00001	0.00000	0.00000	0.00000
17	0.00128	0.00070	0.00037	0.00019	0.00010	0.00005	0.00002	0.00001	0.00000	0.00000
18	0.00261	0.00152	0.00085	0.00047	0.00025	0.00013	0.00006	0.00003	0.00001	0.00001
19	0.00487	0.00298	0.00177	0.00102	0.00057	0.00031	0.00016	0.00008	0.00004	0.00002
20	0.00834	0.00538	0.00336	0.00204	0.00120	0.00069	0.00038	0.00021	0.00011	0.00006

INDEX